D0931433

The
Immortality
Factor

Also by Osborn Segerberg, Jr.

*Where Have All the Flowers Fishes Birds Trees Water
and Air Gone? What Ecology Is All About*

THE
IMMORTALITY
FACTOR

Osborn Segerberg, Jr.

E. P. Dutton & Co., Inc. | New York | 1974

Library of Congress Cataloging in Publication Data

Segerberg, Osborn.
The immortality factor.

Includes bibliographical references.
1. Aging.　2. Death.　3. Immortality.　4. Biology
—Philosophy.　I. Title.
QP84.S43　612.6'7　73-79538
ISBN 0-525-13190-6

Published simultaneously in Canada by
Clarke, Irwin & Company Limited, Toronto and Vancouver

Grateful acknowledgment is made to the following for permission to quote at length:

From *The Travels of Marco Polo* by Manuel Komroff. Copyright © 1953 by Manuel Komroff. Reprinted by permission of Liveright Publishers, New York.

From "To an Athlete Dying Young" from "A Shropshire Lad"—Authorized Edition —from *The Collected Poems of A.E. Housman.* Copyright © 1939, 1940, by Holt, Rinehart and Winston, Inc. Copyright © 1967, 1968 by Robert E. Symons. Reprinted by permission of Holt, Rinehart and Winston, Inc. And by permission of The Society of Authors as the literary representative of the estate of A.E. Housman; and Jonathan Cape Ltd., publishers of A.E. Housman's *Collected Poems.*

From *Of The Nature of Things* by Lucretius translated by William E. Leonard. Everyman's Library Series. Published by E. P. Dutton & Co., Inc., and used with its permission and with the permission of J. M. Dent & Sons Ltd.

From *The Dying Patient* edited by Orville G. Brim, Jr., Howard E. Freeman, Sol Levine and Norman A. Scotch © 1970 Russell Sage Foundation.

From *On Death and Dying* by Elisabeth Kubler-Ross (Copyright © 1969 by Elisabeth Kubler Ross) and published by Macmillan Co., Inc.

From *The Golden Bough* by Sir James G. Frazer (Copyright © 1922 by Macmillan Publishing Co., Inc., renewed 1950 by Barclays Bank Ltd.) and with permission from the estate of Sir James Frazer.

From *Magic, Science and Religion* by Bronislaw Malinowski from *Science, Religion and Reality* edited by Joseph Needham, copyright 1925, published by The Society for Promoting Christian Knowledge.

From *Life Against Death* by Norman O. Brown, copyright © 1959 by Wesleyan University, reprinted by permission of Wesleyan University Press.

To
my father, Osborn,
and the memory of my mother,
Elsie

Acknowledgments

I wish to give thanks to William Reichel of Franklin Square Hospital, Baltimore, for his help in threading through important developments in molecular biology pertinent to the aging process and for reading this manuscript and commenting upon it; to Director Walter Beattie, Jr., of the All-University Gerontology Center at Syracuse University for permission to attend a Seminar on Gerontology and Higher Education in New York City in December, 1971; to Ruth Bennett of Columbia University and New York State Department of Mental Hygiene for her discussion with me of social gerontology; to Bernard L. Strehler and members of his staff, particularly Gerald Hirsch, for their help while visiting their molecular biology laboratory at the Gerontology Center of the University of Southern California and to Dr. Strehler for an interview; to Marvin Schreiber of the Gerontological Society for his help; to Frank Kelly of The Center for the Study of Democratic Institutions at Santa Barbara, California, for sending me a complete set of papers presented at the Center's Conference on Extension of Human Life-Span; to Daniel Rogers, information officer at the Gerontology Research Center in Baltimore and several staff scientists including Dorothy Travis, Charles Barrows, Clyde Martin, and David Arenberg; to Charles Taylor of The Pennsylvania State University, who during a chance meeting kindly provided me with a number of leads and evaluations; and to the following scientists for taking time to give interviews: Denham Harman of the University of Nebraska, Paul Knopf at the Salk Institute, Carl Eisdorfer, then director of the Gerontology Center at Duke University; Lissy Jarvik at the Department of Genetics, New York State Psychiatric Institute; Johan Bjorksten of the Bjorksten Research Foundation at Madison, Wisconsin; Carlis Osis of the American Society for Psychical Research; James Carse, chairman of the Department of History of Religion, New York University; Gerald Feinberg of Columbia University; Benjamin Schloss of the Foundation for Aging Research in Brooklyn, New York; and to Chairman Robert Sinsheimer of the Division of Biology, California Institute of Technology, for a lengthy and thoughtful response to written inquiries; to Bernard

Davis of Harvard Medical School for a helpful letter setting forth his estimate on genetic manipulation; to Lt. Col. Donald Carpenter of the U.S. Air Force for correspondence on the gerontological outlook; and to Edwin Marston, School of Science, Ramapo College of New Jersey, for reading and commenting upon manuscript chapters related to science.

I must also acknowledge my indebtedness to *The Story of Philosophy* and its author, Will Durant, who has been able to make philosophy for me the exciting, vital stuff of life.

Finally, to my wife, Nancy, for helping with the onerous job of typing and without whom this book would not have come into being.

Osborn Segerberg, Jr.
September, 1973

Contents

Preface

I am not a scientist, historian, educator, philosopher, or theologian, nor have I held government office allowing me to be privy to special information. Therefore I can state that I am beholden to no particular institution or cause or school of thought or field of study or discipline except journalism.

This is not to contend that the book is a confetti shower of indiscriminate information. First, I am a product of my time, place, and culture, and I do hold certain values. Second, my aim has been to give the general reader a better understanding of the implications of certain scientific advances. In order to do that properly, it has been necessary to cast the present within the context of the past in an attempt to draw a more accurate perspective on where we are going. In the light of these influences, values, and intentions, I have evaluated—that is, selected from and judged—the material within my knowledge.

Although every book is the end-result of such a process of editing, this one invades areas of deeply held convictions, long-held beliefs, and considerable expertise—the provinces of specialists. For this reason, the reader is entitled to know my qualifications for undertaking such an exploration. For a quarter of a century I have earned my living in a variety of roles and media of journalism. I have worked as writer, reporter, editor, also as television news producer; at different times, I have worked with a newspaper, a wire service, radio stations, television stations, television film syndication services, documentary films, theater newsreel, magazines, books. These assignments have required dealing with the full spectrum of human activities and making editorial evaluations in a professional and publicly accountable way. The majority of these working years were spent either with a wire service or with television and radio stations. A wire-service journalist learns that he serves a wide array of clients, and any suppression or distortion of information is likely to be detected by the offended customer and therefore is intolerable to the wire-service employer. The broadcast journalist becomes even more sensitized to the "fairness doctrine" of the Federal Communications Commission and is constantly alert to protect his employer and himself in controversial issues.

Beyond this, the journalist who is to survive for any length of time at his profession is forced to let life tell him.

For the interested reader, I have included in the Notes a complete documentation, as well as buttressing data, for the factual information and quotations used in the book. This source material details the extent, and limits, of my research. The references have not been numbered in the text because the book is written for the general reader and I wished to keep him free of encumbrances.

My purpose in writing the book is to bring to general attention a subject sequestered from public discussion by specialized knowledge, scientific jargon, and lack of exploration. The book is written with the conviction that everyone should be aware of a contingency important to his welfare and/or that of posterity so that he can exert his rightful influence in the issue. It is my hope that the book will be a vehicle of enfranchisement.

Introduction

Life, said Dr. Walter Kring of All Souls Unitarian Church in New York City, is "a transaction with reality." Life courses through us, reality surrounds us. Despite this intimacy, however, life is not easily defined and reality is as opaque and impenetrable and unyielding as ever at the frontiers of ignorance.

Yet our species has extended the perimeter of understanding remarkably. The corporate quest for understanding is a distinguishing human trait. "What is truth?" asked Pontius Pilate and innumerable scholars, scientists, seers—and every other human being forced to deal with the puzzle of existence. Again and again, that question has been posed, in uncountable contexts, and answered. And the answers acted upon, because existence is not an ivory tower but a pragmatic transaction with reality.

Often enough, answers were incorrect . . . and consequent actions disastrous. The primitive who ate the wrong mushroom paid with his life, as does the modern who gets his high from methyl rather than ethyl alcohol. Too often, answers are ambiguous. Fools rush in, but stand-patters atrophy. Some questions had to be asked over and over, receiving different answers according to the level of enlightenment. Some questions we ask still—how to cure or prevent cancer, for instance —and still solutions elude us. Today, however, we have powerful intellectual and technological instruments to probe the ring of darkness. We have science.

If we think of science as a front of locomotives advancing into the black unknown along tracks we call biology, chemistry, and so on, with spurs branching out and sometimes interconnecting, as in biochemistry or ecology, we might imagine the locomotives' headlights continually illuminating new information. Since no one knows precisely what the new information will be, no one can be sure what it portends. The raw information must be processed—disseminated, codified, evaluated, integrated—before it can be fully understood and exploited, if at all. One takes the benefits of basic science as one finds them and puts them to use where feasible. From time to time, we strike a bonanza.

This method can be maddeningly crude, it must be pointed out, when one seeks a specific answer to a particular problem, such as a cancer cure or prevention. That infinitely more difficult problem means an investigator must find a path through a forest of known and unknown facts from here to there or from there to here. (Science already knew that Neil Armstrong could go from here to there and from there to here before his Apollo voyage—only engineering technology, skill, and courage were necessary to ratify the basic knowledge.) For all its dazzling success, science knows only one sure—and inefficient—way to solve this kind of problem. That is, to substitute metaphors, to pick up each straw in the haystack until the needle is uncovered, presuming there is a needle. In the case of cancer (presuming there is a cure or prevention), this process of elimination might not discover a payoff until the sun begins to cool . . . although it is possible that the correct straw could be picked up early in the game or, what is more likely, that a solution could appear tomorrow as the serendipity of basic science.

There are shortcuts to arriving at a desired answer. Elimination of one potential solution may reasonably obviate a whole family of possibilities, steering researchers toward more fruitful areas. An investigator may guess at an answer, then test to see whether his intuition is correct. Such guesses, of course, are educated suppositions. By speculating and testing, observing and adducing knowledge, the scientific detective gets to know more and more about what his objective is and is not; preconceptions come into sharper focus until one researcher is enabled to take a decisive step: he *asks the right question.*

The direct route to a solution is the one least accessible to scientific inevitability: inspiration. Through the mysterious linkages of ten billion neurons in one human brain, mastered data is coalesced with gaps of ignorance to construct an hypothesis: an imagined representation of reality. It is somewhat like imagining a model lock and then honing an actual key. If the lock approximates what exists and the key fits: breakthrough! Dr. Ehrlich's magic bullet to cure syphilis, Dr. Salk's polio vaccine, Dr. Einstein's atomic bomb. Man turns the key and nature opens obediently.

From time to time, enough light of knowledge is cast upon the strange landscape of the unknown for a master intelligence to formulate a broad interpretation of reality that is known scientifically as a paradigm. Postulation of this framework offers the promise of greater success in solving one or a number of current problems, the promise attracts scientists to try the new intellectual tool, and successes in puzzle-solving both validate and flesh out the paradigm. Most scientists are occupied in elaborating the models and theories and relationships flowing from and explicating a paradigm. The data and theories inconsistent with the overview are rejected, discarded, or never thought about in the first place. This intellectual loyalty continues unless or until the amount of unexplainable evidence becomes significant enough to undermine the reigning paradigm and to prepare the stage for some refinement or alternative. Thus Einstein wins followers of Newton and Darwin explains the workings of nature better than Aristotle.

Essentially, then, a paradigm is *a new way of looking at things*. The great paradigms of Copernicus, Galileo, Newton, Darwin, Mendel, Pasteur, Einstein, Freud, Watson and Crick have given us important methods of piercing the translucent complexity of existence. The ideal, the absolute correspondence of hypothesis with reality, is what we call truth.

On this level, we find that there is nothing exclusively scientific about the hypothetical method nor the search for truth. In such endeavors, science joins such other human pursuits as philosophy, religion, theology, art, literature, law, history. A religion or coherent philosophy is a paradigm for ultimate reality—all the reality we can see, hear, touch, smell, taste plus the unseen phenomena that we intuit or divine or "know." By accepting the unseen parts on faith or the logic of the explanatory argument, the believer gains a rationale to deal with all aspects of life. Abstemious science sacrifices this all-inclusiveness. It confines its competence to anything accessible to the senses, amenable to proof, and open to public verification.

Science includes physics but leaves metaphysics to philosophy, adheres to the natural and leaves the supernatural to religion. While science uses logic and intuition, it is not based on them; while it relies on faith (in an orderly universe, for example), it does not use faith. Science avowedly avoids value judgments since they elude proof and thus eschews questions of sentiment, esthetics, ethics—right and wrong —and morality—good and evil. Science exalts exactitude but will not insist upon immutable certitude. All paradigms finally are tentative. Whoever builds a better paradigm wins (or deserves to win) the loyalty of all scientists. If such inconstancy in other human affairs is called infidelity, opportunism or cynicism, in science it is esteemed an open mind. For science professes a single allegiance—to truth.

The search for truth—or understanding—is not simply an indulgence of curiosity nor merely an intellectual exercise. It is a sophisticated means to survive. For instance, we know that when a spermatozoon unites with the ovum the female is fertilized and in our species under favorable circumstances she will deliver a child in approximately nine months. We know how the fertilized egg-embryo-fetus will develop almost hour by hour in the uterus. This knowledge improves the prospects of reproductive success. We control and manipulate our environment in countless ways. Our species prospers. The prospects for survival of our closest animal relatives—the other primates—are far less sanguine.

Survival (which often requires domination) is the ultimate test we have for efficacy, or congruence with reality, whether applied to a belief, an idea, a system of thought, a way of doing things, or an individual and his descendants, his group, his species.

The problem of survival has been a central preoccupation of human intelligence no less than the intelligence of other organisms. For all creatures, the matter of survival has meant dealing with and overcoming a succession of immediate problems. For other species, however, solutions could be preserved only as they were incorporated biologically. With speech, writing, and other methods of recording and transmitting information, the human species has accumulated various and detailed strategies for dealing with reality, for surviving. The prodigies of human knowledge and intelligence, however, have been unavailing in one central aspect of survival. The individual suffers the same fate as other living creatures despite the unique ability to conceive another destiny.

Death and immortality, like binary suns, have held us in their thrall. Hostages to the former, agents of the latter, we orbit through fixed and finite spans relaying the spark of sentience in the ancient pattern of birth, death, and endless life. But the old, seemingly immutable order may be changing. We have learned enough about the nature of life to cause certain scientists to ask whether the human lifespan is, indeed, fixed. Or, is the lifespan potentially mutable? If mutable, is it, indeed, finite? Or, is it possibly open-ended?

It is time to take note of the continuity and tenacity of the human campaign to deal with an unpalatable reality, and the campaign's evolution with the accretion of knowledge: the strategy shifting from mythical to magical to metaphysical to medical to biomedical; the targets shifting from the constellation of infectious ills to the core degenerative diseases to, finally, the aging process.

There is a story from World War I of an American sergeant who exhorted his men to charge during the murderous battle of Belleau Wood. "Come on," the sergeant cried, "do you want to live forever?" Under the circumstances, the question was rhetorical.

But has anyone asked a question closer to our hearts?

Part One

QUEST

I. A Loss of Paradise

In the beginning, the dark heavens were seeded with hydrogen atoms. Hydrogen is the elemental element: one negatively charged electron circling one positively charged proton nucleus in the courtship ordained by the electromagnetic force. Attracted by another, weaker force, that of gravity, the atoms drifted into loose associations, swirled apart, clustered into more dense pockets of gas. With accumulation, gravity gathered strength and began pulling the atoms toward a common center, collapsing a vast hydrogen cloud. The falling atoms picked up speed and energy, warming the gas. If the cloud were big enough so that the implosion lasted long enough, the heat reached a threshold temperature of 20 million degrees Fahrenheit.

And God said, Let there be light . . .
The protons now moved with a violence sufficient to overcome their electromagnetic repulsion and enter the embrace of the all-powerful nuclear force. Protons rushed together, collided, fused, releasing tremendous light-and-heat energy: the thermonuclear process begins, a star is born.

Still heeding the commands of gravity, the stars assembled in majestic pinwheeling galaxies. All the other heavier elements were fused in the thermonuclear furnaces without walls and then broadcast into space with the stellar death convulsions known as supernovas.

The solar system was formed out of such materials 4.5 billion years ago. On sterile earth, the evolving chemical preparations for life took upward of 1.5 billion years. The oceans were a hospitable medium for organic molecules of increasing complexity until the synthesis of amino acids (building blocks for protein), and the formation of nucleic acids (building blocks for DNA).

And God said, Let the waters bring forth abundantly the moving creature that hath life . . .
The first creatures must have been modest, minimal structures of life,

3

microscopically small. But with evolution the advantages are retained, the failures discarded. The living molecules achieved the advantages of a cell with walls to defend the nucleus and to corral ingredients necessary for growth and reproduction. Some one-celled organisms united and subordinated themselves to the welfare of the whole. Life needs energy and the primeval organisms fed on the prefabricated organic matter. With photosynthesis, living creatures were able to tap the sun's energy directly. Different types of organisms evolved as they were able to exploit new niches in the ecosystem, but all the diversity rested on an underlying unity: all living matter was made up of combinations of the same 20 subprotein amino acids. The originally captured solar energy began to pass through a food chain and a food web.

Mountains were violently thrust upward and then eroded smooth; huge surface plates shifted and drifted; glaciers advanced and retreated. Experimental life proliferated with newer forms and with newer ways of doing things, elaborating nervous systems to monitor external and internal environments and to signal the approach of food or danger. After 2.5 billion years of life, the land areas still were barren, life was confined to the seas, and this life still was carried in small, soft-bodied organisms. It had taken all this time to reach another threshold.

And God said, Let the earth bring forth the living creature after his kind, cattle, and creeping thing, and beast of the earth after his kind . . .

Beginning with the Cambrian period about 600 millions years ago, life began to appear in forms familiar to us today—horseshoe crabs, snails, starfish, corals—hard-bodied animals followed by the first vertebrates, an organism with a spine and internal skeleton. Plants began to invade the land areas. The oxygen given off by sea and then proliferating land plants had helped to create an atmosphere and a sheltering sky against the sun's lethal ultra-violet light. Conditions were propitious about 350 million years ago for air-breathing amphibians to venture out of the amniotic ocean to explore and exploit the new resources on land, and to flourish. Fifty million years later, reptiles cut the umbilical to the sea. Reptiles evolved into snakes, turtles, birds, dinosaurs, and mammals.

Amphibians reached their zenith about 250 million years ago, then began to disappear, leaving such survivors as the frog and the salamander. By that time, the magnificent forest ecosystems we see today were beginning to form. Dominance among animals passed to the dinosaurs, and with them the limits to growth in land animals were realized. The archetypal dragon *Tyrannosaurus rex*, rising 20 feet or more from its powerful hind legs and tail, was the most fearsome predator ever to walk the earth. Colossal *Brontosaurus* weighed 30 tons. The dinosaurs ruled for 100 million years and then departed from life's stage, perhaps because of climatic changes to which they could not adapt.

Whatever the cause, the result was that mammals, less powerful life forms that had maintained a low profile while dinosaurs thundered about, came into their inheritance. Mammals had certain advantages for survival: furry coats, for one thing; internal thermostats to maintain the even body temperature of warm-blooded animals that permits steady metabolism and activity despite external conditions; and a new way of reproduction—nurturing the fertilized egg within the mother's body and then providing the newborn with care and supervision.

And God said, Let us make man . . .

The final sculpting took perhaps 100 million years. The candidate models were small, long-tailed, tree-living, rodentlike, the size of squirrels. These animals relied on their eyes more than their noses in order to find food: insects, grubs, fruit, birds' eggs. In order to make accurate leaps among branches, their vision was binocular. And they had a tendency to hold objects in their claws, much as a raccoon or a squirrel does. Over tens of millions of years some of these organisms grew larger, their forelegs veered toward arms and the front paws toward hands; from tree shrews and tarsiers to lemurs and lorises to monkeys and, perhaps 37 million years ago, the division of the tailless anthropoid stocks of gibbons and orangutans, gorillas, chimpanzees to the splitting off some 14 million years ago of the ape ancestors of human beings.

The last part of the pilgrimage began some 2.5 to 5 million years ago with the appearance of the first hominids, proto humans. By this time, it is evident, nature was emphasizing a new strategy to deal with the realities of existence. In place of monstrous size and brute strength were cooperation and intelligence. Like other anthropoids, hominids lived and, after the discovery of tools and weapons, hunted in groups. Using tools invites skill, acting in concert demands rules and communication. Communication involves speech, language, auditory monitoring.

Mammals possessed one other distinguishing feature: the capacity to develop a cerebral cortex. In fish and lower vertebrates, four tiny humps above the spinal cord, the optic and auditory lobes, were the most prominent part of the brain. These colliculi were perfectly adequate for processing information most necessary for the survival of those organisms. These vestigial and low-echelon parts of the human brain still control such automatic functions as blinking or starting at a loud noise, but long ago relinquished most other perceptual decisions to the cerebrum. Similarly, the thalamus seems to be the highest center of perception in reptiles; in the human mental organization it is no more than a crude way-station that sorts information and relays it to appropriate areas in the cerebral cortex. In the convoluted gray forebrain is carried out the final, refined analysis of sensory information, speech and language, symbolic thought, abstract reasoning, foresight. In the human brain, the automatic stimuli-response system of ancient glands and organs that rules lower orders (flight-or-fight, lust, terror, hunger) clusters around the brain stem at the top of the spinal cord. Four-fifths of the human brain is cerebral cortex.

Paleoanthropologists are tracing the development of that intellect through enlargement of the cranial cavity, redesign of the skull, and artifacts produced by the intelligence. Early hominids, inhabitants of East Africa 2.5 to 3 million years ago, possessed brains not much larger than apes. However, a skull with a cranial cavity half again as large was discovered recently and dated at 2.6 million years ago. These early ape-men collected stones, used stones, and possibly made tools. Some 1 million years ago there appeared a creature manlike enough to be called *Homo erectus* with an average brain size of nearly 1,000 cubic centimeters, roughly halfway between that of a chimpanzee and *Homo sapiens*. The cortex similarly was about halfway developed. Perhaps 300,000 years ago, perhaps a half million years ago, this primitive Prometheus learned to capture fire and may have deliberately set wild fires in order to stampede animal herds over a cliff or into a bog. Such an organized enterprise implies a rudimentary use of language. *Homo erectus* probably traveled in migratory bands, but we know little more of his habits or social organization.

A 200,000-year-old skull found in a cave in the French Pyrenees was surrounded by bones from rhinoceros, bear, panther, deer, wolf, a form of elephant, birds, and other species—evidence of a potent hunter—and more than 100,000 pieces of worked stone. The intelligence that could stalk and kill physically superior or more elusive animals was reaching a power of comprehension to grasp a great deal about existence. The brain size of Neanderthal man, who lived in Europe 100,000 years ago, had reached that of modern man. Neanderthal man not only was a cave dweller but probably built primitive homes (wood or tusk frames covered by skins) as well. There is the first appearance of esthetic expression with designs scratched on bones.

Researchers believed they had uncovered more advanced artistic artifacts in a field dated 34,000 years ago. The objects were palm-sized stones or bones with a great number of seemingly identical, decorative notches cut into them. Seven years of study, employing the high-magnification photography that enables ballistic experts to decide if a bullet has been fired from a particular pistol, showed that the notches had been carved, not at the same time, but in succession over an extended period and by at least two dozen different tools. It is now widely agreed that those notches were records, probably of different phases of the moon. This was a primitive calendar to help Cro-Magnon man keep track of time. Here was the rudimentary concept of numbers in anticipation of arithmetic. Here was the use of abstract symbols; by the fourth millennium B.C. and perhaps earlier it would become hieroglyphics in Egypt and cuneiform in Mesopotamia. With writing, knowledge could be recorded and accumulated. History could begin.

And so the spark of life had spread from individual to individual over countless generations in ever widening circles until it glowed in 10 million species over the entire planet. The sun rose and set, rose and set, rose and set, a trillion times. Life pulsed to the diurnal metronome while experimenting with variations on the theme, in the process spinning out an exquisite complexity from the basic simplicity. Millions of species of organisms came and died out or evolved into other forms of life, each individual enjoying its moment in the sun, basking in the goodness of life unaware of the finite nature of its experience in an unbroken ignorance. The human cerebral cortex, the crowning jewel of evolution, was the instrument to break the primeval innocence. At some point our ancestors reached a watershed ridge, peered out, and recoiled from what they saw. The courageous hunter, the true king of beasts, was impaled by fear. The instinct is flight, but this discovery once made, there was no going back. The transfiguring knowledge, like Adam touching the finger of God, created that unique animal, the human being.

"The oldest, most numerous, and most imposing relics of our ancestors are funerary," states historian Arnold Toynbee. Writes Lewis Mumford: "Soon after one picks up man's trail in the earliest campfire or chipped stone tool one finds evidence of interests and anxieties that have no animal counterpart; in particular, a ceremonious concern for the dead, manifested in their deliberate burial—with growing evidence of pious apprehension and dread. . . . Mid the uneasy wanderings of paleolithic man, the dead were the first to have a permanent dwelling: a cavern, a mound marked by a cairn, a collective barrow. The city of the dead antedates the city of the living."

After three billion years of evolution, there appeared on the planet the distinctive mark of a new species: a grave, a burial site thoughtfully provided with things for the dead one. "And down the untold centuries," says anthropologist Loren Eiseley, "the message had come without words:

'We too were human, we too suffered, we too believed that the grave is not the end. We too, whose faces affright you now, knew human agony and human love.' "

Was the skull found in the Pyrenees cave from a man deliberately buried 200,000 years ago? We don't know. We do know that Neanderthal people buried their dead. A number of Neanderthal burial sites have been found in western and eastern Europe. The circumstances suggest an awareness of the transitoriness of life and concern over the future. At Le Moustier in southern France, the body of an 18-year-old youth was found in a grave carefully and reverently buried on his side, his legs bent, his head cushioned on a pile of flaked flints and resting on his right arm as he might in sleep. In a cave at La Ferrassie, France—dating back 40,000 years—were discovered the burial sites of two adults and four children. All bodies were carefully lined in an east-west position. One of the six graves contained bones so small they may have belonged to a stillborn infant. The grave was one of nine hillocks, all the same size and height, arranged in rows of three. Another grave, containing the skeleton of a six-year-old child, was covered by a triangular slab that had been hollowed out on its under surface. In several Neanderthal graves, the skeletons were accompanied by carefully carved stone implements—treasures that the living bequeathed to the dead. In some graves, too, were animal bones. It seems clear that the survivors intended to help the dead, wherever they were, wherever they were going, with tools and food.

It is difficult, probably impossible, to know how those first paleolithic minds regarded death, but we get clues from primitive peoples still existing today.

> Nowhere is the duality of natural and supernatural causes divided by a line so thin and intricate, yet, if carefully followed up, so well marked, decisive, and instructive, as in the two most fateful forces of human destiny: health and death, [Bronislaw Malinowski wrote in *Magic, Science, and Religion*, his classic anthropological study of Trobriand Islanders in the southwest Pacific.] Health to the Melanesians is a natural state of affairs and, unless tampered with, the human body will remain in perfect order. But the natives know perfectly well that there are natural means which can affect health and even destroy the body. Poisons, wounds, burns, falls, are known to cause disablement or death in a natural way. And this is not a matter of private opinion of this or that individual, but it is laid down in traditional lore and even in belief, for there are considered to be different ways to the nether world for those who died by sorcery and those who met "natural" death. Again, it is recognized that cold, heat, overstrain, too much sun, overeating, can all cause minor ailments, which are treated by natural remedies such as massage, steaming, warming at a fire and certain potions. Old age is known to lead to

bodily decay and the explanation is given by the natives that very old people grow weak, their oesophagus closes up, and therefore they must die.

But besides these natural causes there is the enormous domain of sorcery and by far the most cases of illness and death are ascribed to this. The line of distinction between sorcery and the other causes is clear in theory and in most cases of practice, but it must be realized that it is subject to what could be called the personal perspective. That is, the more closely a case has to do with the person who considers it, the less will it be "natural," the more "magical."

Anthropologist Sir James Frazer, who carried out unparalleled encyclopedic studies of primitive cultures and beliefs, later commented that the reaction of Trobriand Islanders to death was atypical in one respect. Absent was the almost universal fear of the dead. "The general attitude of primitive man, and by primitive man I mean the savage," Sir James told an audience at Trinity College, Cambridge, in 1932, "towards the spirits of the dead is very different from ours in that, on the whole, it is dominated by fear rather than affection."

Aside from archeological and anthropological research, there is another bridge back to the aboriginal vision—through our own minds, which carry the vestigial heritage that psychological pioneer Carl Jung called the collective unconscious. "[S]ince as far as we know the fear of death is derived from an archetypal pattern whose total extent can never be made visible in this life; the image is present, but the actual experience is forever withheld, and we try to know and yet do not know its full meaning. All the rest is symbol . . ." So wrote psychologist Joseph Henderson in an introduction to a book on myths about death. Through myths, stories from an obscure past, we gain a measure of understanding how our distant ancestors explained newly discovered realities and how they grappled with the traumatic mystery: Where did death come from?

Hans Abrahamson in *The Origin of Death* has painstakingly categorized myths from all over the continent of Africa according to type and geographical locale. One is impressed with the ingenious variety of explanations; one marvels that they are variations on a few recurring themes.

According to a Liberian myth, Sno-Nysoa, the Creator, sent his four sons to earth. After a time, he wanted them to return home to him, but they liked it on earth and wanted to remain. Earth, too, defied Sno-Nysoa and tried to keep them. Thereupon God used his "secret power." One morning, the eldest son could not wake up. God said to Earth: "I have simply called him home. I leave the body with you." Afterward, the same thing happened to the three remaining brothers . . . and all other human beings. Before Sno-Nysoa and Earth quarreled, death did not exist among men, but afterward there was sickness, suffering, and death.

Therefore a meeting was held to decide what should be done. The decision of this human council was to send a cat to a medicine-man to bring a remedy to cure the sick and awaken the dead. On the way back with the panacea, the cat stopped to bathe in a river, putting the medicine on a tree stump. Going on, the cat forgot to take the potion. The cat returned but was unable to find the medicine. The cat then went back to the medicine-man who was angered at the cat's carelessness and pronounced that "although a tree be cut, if the stump remain, the tree will grow again; but when men die, it will be the end."

This is a variation of the most common and widespread myth-theme to account for death found all through the southern two-thirds of Africa: the message that failed. Men pray to God for life. God sends a chameleon with the message that they shall have eternal life, then changes his mind—or in any event subsequently sends a lizard with the message that they must die. The slow-moving chameleon dawdles along the way and the lizard arrives first with the message that then takes effect. As a consequence of this legend, the chameleon is hated in many parts of Africa. The Ngoni people cram snuff into its mouth until it dies as a punishment for inflicting death upon the human race.

The Galla say that God sent the bird Holawaka to tell humans the secret of immortality: when they find themselves growing old and weak, they should slip off their skins and become young again. On the way, the bird meets a serpent which is eating a dead animal. Holawaka asks to share the food, but the snake consents to do so only after the bird promises to reveal God's message. Thus it is that snakes can shed their skins and grow young again, while humans must die.

Among the Gudji, God once wished to know whether man or the snake was worthy of immortality, and so he arranged a race between them. In the course of the race, the man met a woman and stopped to chat with her so long that the snake reached God first and won immortality.

Several of the myths exhibit an ecological awareness which distinguishes primitive men from civilized men. Among the Gogo, it is related that a man once told a hyena that men wished to live forever. But the scavenger replied, "You had better not, as we want to eat your dead bodies." So men must die because of the needs of hyenas.

In the Zambezi River valley, it was said that men did not die originally, but the population increased at such a rate that it was feared that soon there would not be enough food for all. The rulers held a council where it was decided to send a lizard to the world of spirits to request that after a certain time on earth men should be admitted to "membership of the celestial circle." When the people found out what their leaders had done, they were outraged and sent a chameleon with a countermanding message that they wanted no changes. The chameleon arrived, too late, to learn that "the lizard already had been entrusted with full powers to introduce death into the world by natural causes."

Another *leit motif* is that of giving mankind a choice, or testing human beings. God summons into his presence a man, a woman, and a serpent. God holds out his clenched fists. In one he holds death, in the other immortality. The woman and the serpent are designated to choose. The woman picks the wrong hand. In a variation, God gives man a bundle with death in it and instructions not to open it, but curiosity and disobedience become the human undoing. The Lala tell of an old wizard who, before dying, bequeathed to his son his cattle and a little box which he commanded his son not to open. But the man's wife was curious and insisted that the box be opened. When it was, two tsetse flies flew out. The man and woman managed to catch one, but the other killed all their cattle. This was the start of sleeping sickness. The Kumbi said that men were immortal until one day someone cut open a gourd whereby sickness, poverty, misfortune, and death entered the world.

The pygmies tell of a member of the Ewe tribe who lost his way in the forest and came to Tore's fire. The god was away and his mother was asleep. The pygmy stole the fire. Tore's mother awoke from the cold and called her son to tell him what had happened. Tore seized the Ewe and took back the fire. Undaunted, another pygmy outfitted himself with raven's feathers, flew up to heaven, and again stole the fire in an unguarded moment. This time the god chased the thief, but could not catch him. When Tore returned, he found his mother frozen to death. In resentment the god punished men with death.

According to Greek myth, men acquired fire through Prometheus, a son of two Titans, the race of gods who lived before humans and who were overthrown from Mount Olympus by Zeus. Prometheus foresaw the success of Zeus and persuaded his brother Epimetheus to join him in supporting the new ruler. Subsequently, Prometheus and Epimetheus were commissioned to the task of creating man and equipping all the other creatures with the faculties necessary for their survival. Epimetheus endowed the different animals with the various gifts of courage, strength, swiftness, sagacity; wings to one, claws to another, and so on. Epimetheus was so lavish with his resources that when he came to man, who was supposed to be superior to the others, there was nothing left. He confided this problem to Prometheus.

There is a concomitant part to the myth which must be told at this point. In a dispute about which shares of a sacrificial victim should be given to the gods and which to men, Zeus appointed Prometheus as arbiter. Prometheus put all the edible flesh into one bundle concealed beneath the distasteful stomach organ. Into the other bundle, he put the bones with a covering of fat. Zeus was deceived into selecting the bag of bones. In a fit of pique, he decided that men should eat their meat raw and withheld fire from mankind.

In defiance of Zeus, Prometheus stole fire for men by lighting his torch at the chariot of the sun. With the promethean gift, men not only could cook their food but were able to gain independence from the climate, to shape tools with which to cultivate the earth, and to fashion the weapons which made them superior to all the other animals.

Zeus punished Prometheus for this arrogant disobedience by binding him in chains, naked, to a frozen crag in the Caucasus Mountains and setting an eagle or a vulture to feed on his liver. The torture was endless because each night the liver was restored to its original size.

Zeus decided to punish men also for accepting the illicit gift. He created Pandora, the first woman. Each god or goddess contributed to Pandora's perfection. Aphrodite gave voluptuous beauty, Hermes the gift of persuasion, Apollo the art of music. Then Zeus offered his creation to Epimetheus who, even though his brother Prometheus had warned him to beware of Greek gods bearing gifts, understandably accepted Pandora on behalf of man. It so happened that Epimetheus had in his house a jar of noxious leftovers he did not need for the happiness of men and other living things. Out of curiosity, Pandora opened the jar and released a multitude of irretrievable plagues, among them envy, spite, revenge, various sicknesses, old age, and death.

There is another class of African myths of even greater interest to us today. The Ewe in Togo believe that only an old married couple originally lived on earth. At that time, the sky was so close that the man and his wife could touch it with their hands. They tilled the fields and lived happily together. The woman suggested that they throw a stone at the sky, but the man forbade this. He said the sky would collapse and fall upon them. One day when the man was away, however, the woman did throw a stone and in that same instant the sky receded to where it is now. At the same time she heard a voice from the sky pronouncing a death sentence upon humankind.

A Pangwe myth says that Essemnyamoboge (God) had four sons: the gorilla, the chimpanzee, the serpent, and Mode (man). One day God went away with three of his sons, but left Mode behind with a woman.

Before leaving, God gave certain instructions to Mode and warned him not to eat the fruit ebon. This stricture implied he was forbidden to have sexual intercourse. Afterward, God considered that he had not provided for Mode's needs, so he sent back the gorilla with maize, manioc, peanuts, and fire. But the gorilla interrupted his journey and never arrived at his destination. Therefore, God sent the chimpanzee, with the same result. Finally, God sent the serpent. Instead of carrying out the errand, the serpent told Mode to eat the forbidden fruit, which he did. When God discovered this, he drove the serpent away and went to Mode's village. Mode and the woman ran away and hid themselves behind some banana trees. When God asked why they were hiding, Mode answered that they were afraid. In punishment, God brought death into the world, while he himself left and went to heaven.

This myth probably reflects missionary influence, but the themes "begetting and death" and "the forbidden fruit" are told in variations that do not necessarily have biblical connotations. In the Cameroons, the origin of death is commonly associated with the notion of a life-tree.

According to an Efik myth, Abassi, the supreme being, follows the advice of his wife, Atai, and lets a human couple settle upon the earth. Abassi is reluctant to do this because he fears that the humans might become his equals, might even excel him in knowledge, but his wife assures him she will not allow this to come about. Now these people were forbidden to work and procure food for themselves. When the bell rang at mealtimes, they were to go and eat with Abassi in heaven. Nor was the human couple permitted to live together as man and wife and give birth to children. This would cause them to forget God. However, a friend of the woman's comes for a visit and remarks how wrong it is for people not to till the soil for themselves and to get their own food. She urges them to do so and gives them fire and the necessary tools. In the course of time, they till the soil, eat at their own table, and live together as man and wife. When Abassi meets the man and asks after his wife, the man replies that she is ill. He dares not confess that she is pregnant. The wife gives birth to a son and later to a daughter. Abassi points out to his wife, Atai, that his fears were well founded, that the humans have forgotten him, and so she fulfills her pledge. "Then his Atai sends death; death comes and destroys the husband of the woman and the woman. Both die in one day, and leave the children."

These are stories of paradise lost. But what is paradise? Is it a place with benign climate and with food so plenteous that one need never exert oneself, a place with love and other manner of delights? If so, then it existed in historical time. Marco Polo, the thirteenth-century

Venetian traveler to the court of Kublai Khan, learned of it as he crossed northern Persia, the land where the word "paradise" originated. This is Polo's account of the Old Man of the Mountain:

In a beautiful valley enclosed between two lofty mountains, he had formed a luxurious garden, stored with every delicious fruit and every fragrant shrub that could be procured. Palaces of various sizes and forms were erected in different parts of the grounds, ornamented with works in gold, with paintings, and with furniture of rich silks. By means of small conduits contrived in these buildings, streams of wine, milk, honey, and some of pure water, were seen to flow in every direction.

The inhabitants of these palaces were elegant and beautiful damsels, accomplished in the arts of singing, playing upon all sorts of musical instruments, dancing, and especially those of dalliance and amorous allurement. Clothed in rich dresses they were seen continually sporting and amusing themselves in the garden and pavilions, their female guardians being confined within doors and never suffered to appear. The object which the chief had in view in forming a garden of this fascinating kind, was this: that Mahomet having promised to those who should obey his will the enjoyments of Paradise, where every species of sensual gratification should be found, in the society of beautiful nymphs, he was desirous of its being understood by his followers that he also was a prophet and compeer of Mahomet, and had the power of admitting to Paradise such as he should choose to favor.

In order that none without his license might find their way into this delicious valley, he caused a strong and inexpugnable castle to be erected at the opening of it, through which the entry was by a secret passage. At his court, likewise, this chief entertained a number of youths, from the age of 12 to 20 years, selected from the inhabitants of the surrounding mountains, who showed a disposition for martial exercises, and appeared to possess the quality of daring courage. To them he was in the daily practice of discoursing on the subject of the paradise announced by the prophet, and of his own power of granting admission. And at certain times he caused opium to be administered to 10 or a dozen of the youths; and when half dead with sleep he had them conveyed to the several apartments of the palaces in the garden.

Upon awakening from the state of stupor, their senses were struck with all the delightful objects that have been described, and each perceived himself surrounded by lovely damsels, singing, playing, and attracting his regards by the most fascinating caresses, serving him also with delicate foods and exquisite wines; until intoxicated with excess of enjoyment amidst actual rivulets of milk and wine, he believed himself assuredly in Paradise, and felt an unwillingness to relinquish its delights.

When four or five days had thus been passed, they were thrown once more into a drugged state, and carried out of the garden. Upon their being introduced to his presence, and questioned by him as to where they had been, their answer was, "In Paradise, through the favour of your highness": and then before the whole court, who listened to them with eager curiosity and astonishment, they gave a circumstantial account of the scenes to which they had been witnesses.

The chief thereupon addressing them, said: "We have the assurances of our prophet that he who defends his lord shall inherit Paradise, and if you show yourselves devoted to the obedience of my orders, that happy lot awaits you." Animated to enthusiasm by words of this nature, all deemed themselves happy to receive the commands of their master, and went forward to die in his service.

The consequence of this system was, that when any of the neighboring princes, or others, gave offense to this chief, they were put to death by his disciplined assassins; none of whom felt terror at the risk of losing their own lives, which they held in little estimation, provided they could execute their master's will. On this account his tyranny became the subject of dread in all the surrounding countries.[1]

People search still for paradise in the Bahamas or on the Riviera or at the nearest Playboy Club, but isn't it evident that paradise has proved to be so elusive because it was a state of mind, a blissful innocence that once violated never could be restored?

And the Lord God said, Behold, the man is become as one of us, to know good and evil: and now, lest he put forth his hand, and take also of the tree of life, and eat, and live for ever: Therefore the Lord God sent him forth from the garden of Eden . . .

What is probably mankind's earliest epic committed to writing is the story of a superhuman effort to find the road back to Eden. The tale in its most complete form comes from Babylonian clay tablets dating from about 650 B.C., but there are Hittite, Assyrian, and Sumerian fragments and versions. It is evident that the story goes back at least to the original Sumerian civilization of 5,000 years ago, and no one knows how far back into oral history the various elements reach.

The *Epic of Gilgamesh* tells the story of a hero, the child of a goddess and a high priest in the Sumerian city of Uruk on the Euphrates River. Gilgamesh builds the strong walls that protect Uruk and the temple where the people worship the goddess Inanna. In his reign as king, Gilgamesh becomes oppressive and the people pray to the gods to divert Gilgamesh from his tyrannical ways of ravishing the maidens and over-burdening the young men with forced labor on the city's walls. The

---

[1] Thus was inaugurated the sect of Assassins and terrorism as a political instrument. The word "assassin" comes from "hashish," the drug used to intoxicate the young men. The first Old Man of the Mountain was one Hassan, an Egyptian who gained control of the fortress of Alamut in Persia in 1090. This territory came under the control of the Mongols with the conquests of Genghis Khan early in the thirteenth century. Determined to stop the atrocious practice of assassination as well as put an end to the harassment and robbery of travelers, a Mongol force laid siege to the fortress in 1252. The castle held out for three years until the last Old Man of the Mountain was slain and 1,200 Assassins massacred. The castle was dismantled and "paradise" destroyed.

gods respond by creating Enkidu, a wild-looking man with tremendous strength. Enkidu tries to stop Gilgamesh from going to an orgy, and a titantic struggle ensues in the city square. The two men fight like infuriated bulls until Gilgamesh finally subdues Enkidu. Whereupon they become great friends.

Gilgamesh now sets off with his new friend in search of adventure and everlasting fame. The heroes slay an ogre in the sacred cedar forest and later kill a divine bull sent against Uruk at the request of Ishtar (the Babylonian name for the Sumerian Inanna), the goddess of love, because Gilgamesh spurned her proposal of marriage. After the bull is slain, Enkidu insults Ishtar. Gilgamesh exults in this victorious salvation of the city, and his people acclaim him "the most glorious among heroes!"

But that night Enkidu dreams of a meeting of the gods and their decision to punish one of the two heroes for their arrogant acts. The lot falls to Enkidu. He soon takes ill and dies.

The death has an overpowering effect upon Gilgamesh. He cries "bitterly like unto a wailing woman." He refuses to give up the body of his friend for burial, hoping that Enkidu will revive after prodigious lamentations. But after seven days and nights, Gilgamesh acknowledges that it is hopeless. Enkidu is buried with honors. Gilgamesh leaves Uruk and roams the desert. He is inconsolable—now, however, no longer for Enkidu who is beyond recall, but for himself. "When I die," he asks, "shall I not be like unto Enkidu?" He becomes obsessed with fear of death; his past accomplishments are no comfort in the shadow of this dreadful fate. He escapes from this depression only through a resolve to escape the fate of mankind and gain immortal life.

Gilgamesh sets out to see Utnapishtim, who was rewarded with immortality for saving humanity from destruction in the great flood. Gilgamesh crosses several mountain ranges and finally arrives at a sea (presumably the Mediterranean on the Phoenician coast). Gilgamesh goes to a divine barmaid, Siduri, explains his mission, and inquires how he can cross the sea in order to visit Utnapishtim. She tries to dissuade him from his quest, explaining that there is no escape from death. Siduri advises him to return home and enjoy life; forget about this hopeless undertaking. But Gilgamesh is not to be turned aside and finally the barmaid informs him that Utnapishtim's boatman is presently at their shores. Gilgamesh leaves the goddess and persuades the boatman to take him to his master.

Utnapishtim explains to his petitioner that he was rewarded with immortality for performing a superhuman service to mankind. What is Gilgamesh to do to merit a similar reward? This seems to be a crushing argument without an answer, but on second thought Utnapishtim suggests that Gilgamesh stay awake for six days and seven nights. If Gilgamesh can master sleep, his tutor implies, he may also be able to overcome death. However, the hero, exhausted from his labors and travels, soon falls asleep and sleeps for six days.

Having failed, Gilgamesh starts back in the boat, but just as he is leaving, Utnapishtim tells him of a wondrous, thorny plant that can rejuvenate a person when he gets old. However, the plant is inaccessible, at the bottom of the sea. Gilgamesh successfully undergoes one more trial, descends to the sea's depths and retrieves the plant. Now, with unbounded joy, he sets out for Uruk. But on the way he stops by a clear pool to swim, and while he is absent a snake spies the plant and eats it, thus winning the power to shed its old skin and thereby renew its life. Gilgamesh weeps bitterly when he discovers that this final chance to gain perpetual life is lost.

Professor Alexander Heidel, who translated the Gilgamesh epic, sums up the hero's final reaction: "But since there is nothing he can do about it, he returns to Uruk; and since he cannot change the course of destiny, he decides to be content with his lot and to rejoice in the work of his hands, the great city which he had built."

There is no road back. Death is inevitable for every man. In the end, Gilgamesh follows the advice of the divine barmaid, Siduri:

> Gilgamesh, whither runnest thou?
> The life which thou seekest thou wilt not find;
> (For) when the gods created mankind,
> They allotted death to mankind,
> (But) life they retained in their keeping.
> Thou, O Gilgamesh, let thy belly be full;
> Day and night be thou merry;
> Make every day (a day of) rejoicing.
> Day and night do thou dance and play.
> Let thy raiment be clean,
> Thy head be washed, (and) thyself be bathed in water.
> Cherish the little one holding thy hand,
> (And) let the wife rejoice in thy bosom.
> This is the lot of (mankind . . .).

The sentiments, even the words, are remarkably similar to those in the biblical book of Ecclesiastes:

> Go thy way, eat thy bread with joy, and drink thy wine with a merry heart; for God now accepteth thy works.
> Let thy garments be always white; and let thy head lack no ointment.
> Live joyfully with the wife whom thou lovest all the days of the life of thy vanity, which he hath given thee under the sun, all the days of thy vanity: for that is thy portion in this life, and in thy labor which thou takest under the sun.

Whatsoever thy hand findeth to do, do it with thy might; for there is
no work, no device, nor wisdom, in the grave whither thou goest.

Already visible in the Gilgamesh epic and Ecclesiastes are seedlings
of "philosophy," that brave attempt to conduct a reasonable life before
an unreasonable death: hedonism—"eat, drink and be merry, for tomorrow we die"—pessimism, stoicism. In fifth-century B.C. Greece, the
philosopher Socrates advised the use of reason as the means to pierce
the opaque curtain to meaningful existence. Men achieved happiness by
seeking the highest excellence. And this highest excellence, or virtue, is
knowledge. The world's evils are caused through ignorance of the truth.

But the evil of inevitable death contradicted the inner truth nourished
by 3 billion years of evolution: one's craving to live. Socrates and Plato
chose to dissolve the indigestible fact of death by denying it was a
termination. The soul—nurtured and perfected through the practice of
philosophy—could continue an immaterial existence of thought. Of course,
the Greeks already had a tradition of afterlife—a dismal Hades for the
departed shades of living persons—which corresponded to the underworld of the ancient Sumerians, their Babylonian and postexilic Hebrew
successors. The privileged Greek hero was entitled to a blissful afterlife
in Elysium, as was the Scandinavian hero in Valhalla, and the aristocratic
Egyptian in the Kingdom of the West. With Zoroastrianism and Christianity, eternal heaven or hell existed after the final judgment of conduct
in this world.

Afterlife depended on faith, however, while life and death in this
world were certainties that still had to be dealt with one way or another. Some people surrendered unconditionally to pessimism. Said
Sophocles in *Oedipus Coloneus:* "Never to have been born is much the
best; and the next best, by far, to return thence, by the way speediest,
where our beginnings are." "Whom the gods love, die young," said Lord
Byron. And the twentieth-century poet A. E. Housman wrote in "To
an Athlete Dying Young":

> Smart lad, to slip betimes away
> From fields where glory does not stay
> And early though the laurel grows
> It withers quicker than the rose.
>
> * * *
>
> Now you will not swell the rout
> Of lads that wore their honors out,
> Runners whom renown outran
> And the name died before the man.

In May 1972 nineteen-year-old Roman Kalanta sat down in a park in
Kaunas, the second largest city in Lithuania, poured a gallon of gasoline

over himself, and ignited it. The suicide torched long-smoldering Lithuanian resistance to Russian domination; it flared into riots, a sitdown strike, three more fire-suicides, and more insistent demands for freedom. It is but a step from the martyr to the youth who risks his life in battle for a cause. "I only regret that I have but one life to lose for my country," said Nathan Hale as he was about to be executed by the British as a spy in the War for Independence. And from there but an imperceptible gradation to the self-sacrifices held up as the human being's most noble act. "It is a far, far better thing that I do, than I have ever done," said Sydney Carton as he was about to substitute his neck on the guillotine for that of a more worthy character in Dickens' *A Tale of Two Cities*. "Greater love hath no man than this," said Christ, "that a man lay down his life for his friends."

The martyr does what he does, said the Hedonists, because it gives him greater pleasure than denying himself such a pleasurable death. The chief good is not knowledge, the Hedonists said, but happiness. Hedonism held that not only does a person strive for enjoyment in his every act, but it is his duty to do so. Virtue is happiness and vice versa.

Epicurus, with the Greek penchant for intellectualization, turned this pleasure-principle inside out. Sure, pleasure is the only good and pain the only evil, he agreed, but mental pleasure and pain outweigh physical pleasure and pain; similarly, enduring pleasure is superior to the momentary kind, while one seeks to avoid long-term pain more than the transient variety. Therefore, the fastidious sage will forgo temporary pleasures that lead to chronic pain and will seek, in fact, the absence of pain that is serenity and freedom from fear, particularly the fear of death. Virtue is equanimity.

Epicurus believed in the teaching of Socrates' contemporary, Democritus, that the world is composed of atoms and after death there is only dissolution. Lucretius, a Roman poet and exponent of Epicureanism who lived in the first half of the first century B.C., made it his goal to rid the human mind once and for all of the fear of death. Lucretius subtitled one section of his masterpiece, *De rerum natura* ("Of the Nature of Things") "Folly of the Fear of Death." The soul is mortal and death is annihilation, said Lucretius. Therefore, why fear death? It is an end to misery, said the sickly philosopher, the person is beyond the reach of revenge and punishment. It is a benign fate; really, considering the alternatives, a blessing. People make life a hell in this world through their own stupidity. The third book of *De rerum* concludes:

> Therefore, O man, by living on, fulfil
> As many generations as thou may:
> Eternal death shall be waiting still;

And he who died with the light of yesterday
Shall be no briefer time in death's No-more
Than he who perished months or years before.

Faithful to his own philosophy, the critic who excoriated contemporary Roman society departed from it by his own hand at the age of forty-four.

From the prism of the ancient Greek mind also came the Cynics. They believed that virtue was simply right action, and right action was complete indifference to external circumstances, rigid self-control of desires, and ascetic simplicity in life. Cynicism degenerated into a sect of sneering professional beggars from which the word gets its modern connotation; but out of it evolved Stoicism through which the philosophy of acceptance was given its most eloquent expression. The world is ordered for the best by divine reason through nature; the virtuous person—the wise person—will fulfill his role, whatever it is, realizing that it is neither good nor bad but part of the scheme entire. He will carry out his social responsibilities yet preserve his personal integrity. Through this divine reason, *logos,* all men share a common brotherhood which transcends their particular station in life. True to this belief, Stoicism reached its finest flower in a slave and an emperor.

Epictetus, the first-century Phrygian slave who studied philosophy in Rome, displayed the fortitude now associated with the word "stoicism." He became lame early in life. His master twisted his leg and Epictetus is said to have smiled through his pain and cautioned, "You will break it." When the master, undeterred, kept twisting, the leg was broken. Epictetus then said evenly, "I told you so." That slave's unbreakable mind was to be master to the most powerful man in the world.

Marcus Aurelius Antoninus was the preeminent, if not only, flesh-and-blood realization of the platonic ideal, the philosopher-king. The first forty years of his life were a preparation both to be a philosopher (when he studied Epictetus) and an emperor. Marcus ruled the Roman Empire for two decades. While he led the Roman legions along the rude frontiers of barbarism, he recorded elegant thoughts about life and death in *The Meditations:*

> Of human life the time is a point, and the substance is in a flux, and the perception dull, and the composition of the whole body subject to putrefaction, and the soul a whirl, and fortune hard to divine, and fame a thing devoid of judgment. And, to say all in a word, everything which belongs to the body is a stream, and what belongs to the soul is a dream and vapor, and life is a warfare and a stranger's sojourn, and after-fame is oblivion. What, then, is that which is able to conduct a man? One thing, and only one—philosophy. But this consists in . . . finally, waiting for death with a cheerful mind, as being nothing else than a dissolution of the elements of which every living being is compounded. But if there

is no harm to the elements themselves in each continually changing into another, why should a man have any apprehension about the change and dissolution of all the elements. For it is according to nature, and nothing is evil which is according to nature. . . .

Though thou shouldest be going to live three thousand years, and as many times ten thousand years, still remember that no man loses any other life than this which he now lives, nor lives any other than this which he now loses. The longest and shortest are thus brought to the same. For the present is the same to all. . . .

Alexander the Macedonian and his groom by death were brought to the same state; for either they were received among the same seminal principles of the universe, or they were alike dispersed among the atoms. . . .

Nature which governs the whole will soon change all things which thou seest, and out of their substance will make other things, and again other things from the substance of them, in order that the world may be ever new. . . .

He who fears death either fears the loss of sensation or a different kind of sensation. But if thou shalt have no sensation, neither wilt thou feel any harm; and if thou shalt acquire another kind of sensation, thou wilt be a different kind of living being, and thou wilt not cease to live. . . .

If then, whatever the time may be when thou shalt be near to thy departure, neglecting everything else thou shalt respect only thy ruling faculty and the divinity within thee, and if thou shalt be afraid not because thou must some time cease to live, but if thou shalt fear never to have begun to live according to nature, then thou wilt be a man worthy of the universe which has produced thee, and thou wilt cease to be a stranger in thy native land. . . .

The author of that philosophy as emperor founded schools for poor children, endowed orphanages and hospitals, reformed taxation, abolished cruelty in criminal laws, stopped the use of informers, diminished the absolute power of masters over slaves and fathers over their children, gave women equal rights to property left by their children, and based promotion in public service on merit rather than birth, rank, or friendship. In foreign affairs, he preserved the empire he inherited.

Edward Gibbon says of Marcus Aurelius in *The Decline and Fall of the Roman Empire:* "He was severe to himself, indulgent to the imperfections of others, just and beneficent to all mankind. . . . War he detested, as the disgrace and calamity of human nature; but when the necessity of a just defense called upon him to take up arms, he readily exposed his person to eight winter campaigns on the frozen banks of the Danube, the severity of which was at last fatal to the weakness of his constitution."

But even a philosopher-king, alas for Plato, is human and imperfect. The memory of Marcus Aurelius is forever stained in Christendom for his persecution of Christians, whom he regarded as fanatics. In his own household, the empress Faustina cuckolded him with a series of lovers. And his son Commodus, whom he chose for a successor, was a throwback to the despots who weakened the Roman foundations during the first century A.D.

It is with the death of Marcus Aurelius in A.D. 180 that Gibbon marks the beginning of the long descent of Western civilization into the medieval darkness.

In 1968 a Gallup survey showed that 73 percent of Americans believed in life after death, 19 percent believed there is no life after death, 8 percent had no opinion. Both the believers and the nonbelievers in an afterlife had increased 5 to 6 percent over the figures 20 years earlier, at the expense of the no-opinions. In France, where the philosophy of Existentialism was an important influence during the 20-year period 1948–1968, there was a violent swing of the pendulum. The percentage of believers in life after death dropped from 58 to 35 percent, while those who believed there is no life after death more than doubled, from 22 to 53 percent. In Britain the swings were more moderate; the decline in afterlife believers and the increase in nonbelievers brought the two camps close to equilibrium with more than a quarter of those Britons polled expressing no opinion.

In August 1970 the magazine *Psychology Today* polled its readership on attitudes toward death. More than 30,000 questionnaires were returned by readers (compared to about 20,000 returns in an earlier survey on sex). Five of eight respondents were women, one in three students. A typical respondent would have been a Caucasian Protestant college-graduate woman twenty to twenty-four years old, earning between $10,000 and $15,000 a year.

The respondents were about evenly divided in beliefs in life after death, and death as a complete termination. The belief in an afterlife and particularly in a heaven and hell is strong in childhood but dwindles with age; the older one becomes, the more likely to believe that death is the end. About two-thirds of the Jews questioned tended to doubt or not believe in an afterlife, whereas only 18 percent believed there is. Forty-two percent of the Protestants and 55 percent of the Roman Catholics believed or tended to believe in a hereafter, with 38 percent of the Protestants and 25 percent of the Roman Catholics disbelieving. Whatever the beliefs, a significantly large group—55 percent—hoped that there is a life after death. The most distasteful part of death for the largest bloc (36 percent) was "I could no longer have any experiences." If the 11 percent who selected "All my plans and projects would come to an end" are added, it can be seen that loss of self accounts for nearly half the objections to death. Dying might be painful (15 percent) and uncertainty about what might happen to the person if there is an afterlife (12 percent) are other considerations.

Another part of the survey reflected one of the most remarkable features of contemporary American culture: isolation from death, both physically and mentally. Until the last two generations, by the time a person had reached adolescence he usually had a close experience with death, probably seeing it in his home with the dying of a parent or a baby brother or sister. The first contemporary involvement came with the death of a grandparent (43 percent) or an animal (18 percent). Furthermore, as many commentators have noted, death no longer takes place in the home but in the remote, aseptic isolation of the hospital. The topic of dying has been banished along with the event. One-third of the respondents could recall not a single instance in childhood when death was discussed within the family; more than another third said the subject was brought up only with discomfort; in only a minority 30 percent of the families was death discussed openly.

Recently a number of books began appearing with the purpose of explaining death to children; some were "approved" by a panel of psychologists. Sheila R. Cole, a reviewer for the *New York Times Book Review*, wrote:

> All of these stories were written with a didactic purpose: to give a child a way of looking at death and living with the knowledge of it. All of them try to diffuse the finality and fearfulness by presenting death as just another natural process. But to most adults in our culture, death is more than just another natural process. It is an occasion surrounded with mystery and deep emotions. Presenting it to a child as just another change we go through is less than candid. Adults often present a prettier reality to children than actually exists. But to give easy answers to a child's questions about death is to deny reality and to diminish both life and death and ultimately to turn our children from our counsel.

It is difficult to avoid the realization that Americans have embarked on a thorough, dedicated, altogether amazing conspiracy to ignore—deny—the existence of death. The very word is avoided. Socially, death is as taboo as Victorian sex. People don't die, they just pass away. It has been *de rigeur* for popular entertainment to have a "happy" ending. The culture has dwelled to obsession on death's antithesis: youth. The opposite end from a death's head is an undulating rump. Jessica Mitford called attention to one facet of the organized program to disguise death in 1963 with *The American Way of Death*. From the sanitized hospital the cadaver is whisked to the cosmetized mortuary for the obligatory layover before being booked into the resort cemetery for "perpetual care." Evelyn Waugh's acidulous novel *The Loved One* satirized the exercise in mass deception.

So complete was this national blindness that during the 1960s medical science—so advanced in other areas—discovered it had no prescribed methods to cope with the desolation of the dying patient and those who loved him. Dying patient, bereaved survivors, and medical practitioner, one and all, were totally unprepared for death. In *Awareness of Dying*, written in 1965, two sociologists found that the terminal patient gets a clue to the seriousness of his illness only from the strange behavior of doctors, hospital staff, and family, none of whom would discuss the nature of his ailment. Barney Glaser and Anselm Strauss wrote that awareness of the truth grew through indirection—doctors who dash in and out of the room barely stopping at bedside, visitors who "distance" themselves, and so on. One hospital study showed—another clue—that nurses did not respond as quickly to calls of terminal patients. Another survey among dying patients revealed that 80 percent of them believed that they should be told their prognosis while 80 percent of their physicians believed that the truth should be withheld because it would be too upsetting to their patients.

Dr. Herman Feifel, a psychiatry professor at the University of Southern California and editor of *The Meaning of Death*, believes that physicians have "significantly stronger death fears than do most other persons." "There is no justification for the abandonment of the bereaved immediately following the death of a loved one in a hospital," declares Dr. Austin Kutscher. "Abandonment should be recognized for what it is: a retreat from the doctor's own unresolved conflicts concerning death." Dr. Kutscher believes that subconsciously a physician feels guilty when his patient dies, regarding the death as an instance of professional failure.

Dr. Kutscher, a professor of dentistry at Columbia University, is one of the formulators of the new discipline of thanatology, the medical study of the problems of death, bereavement, and grief. In 1967 Dr. Kutscher's wife died after a long struggle with cancer. Two months after her death, Kutscher himself was admitted to a hospital for ailments of his own. While there, doctors wishing to understand his grief and console him searched the medical literature for guidance—and found virtually nothing. A British study leaves no doubt that the management of bereavement and grief is a medical problem as well as a personal, religious, and philosophical one. In the British survey, first-year widows and widowers died at a rate ten times higher than that for contemporaries not recently bereaved. Out of his personal curiosity about the subject, Dr. Kutscher published along with psychiatrists Bernard Schoenberg and David Peretz and psychologist Arthur Carr what they called the first textbook in thanatology, *Loss and Grief: Psychological Management in Medical Practice*, designed to aid medical doctors in handling the severe emotional problems attendant with dying.

Other observers began to remark that segregating the dying person in the alien confines of a hospital often could be a cruel or heartless way to dispose of an individual. He was forced to die alone, away from the bosom of his family, deprived of the emotional warmth that could ease the wrenching away from life in the person's final crisis. Moreover, the very proficiency of medical science in prolonging life in some instances had the grotesque consequence of degrading this final experience. With artificial extension went loss of naturalness, descent into mental and physical incompetence all the way down to the vegetative level. Beyond some point, physical extension of life became pointless. An entirely new issue was propelled into public attention as other values vied with medical utility: a person's right to die with dignity. Euthanasia groups began to militate for this new civic and personal right.

In January 1973 the New York State Medical Society announced a new policy: "The use of euthanasia is not in the province of the physician. The right to die with dignity, or the cessation of the employment of extraordinary means to prolong the life of the body when there is irrefutable evidence that biological death is inevitable, is the decision of the patient and-or the immediate family with the approval of the family physician." At almost the same time, the American Hospital Association proclaimed a "Bill of Rights for Patients" which included both the right "to refuse treatment to the extent permitted by law" and the right "to obtain from his physician complete current information concerning his diagnosis, treatment, and prognosis in terms the patient can reasonably be expected to understand."

The University of Chicago's Billings Memorial Hospital began a course in 1964 to instruct chaplains-in-training, medical internes, nurses, and social workers on the psychological needs of the terminally ill. Since then, more than 400 dying patients have been persuaded to "teach" the weekly seminars. The first seminars were set up by Dr. Elizabeth Kubler-Ross, a Swiss-born psychiatrist who came to the United States in 1958. Dr. Ross found that the dying person needs to share this private fact of impending death. Deprived of this balm, the loneliness is like the aloneness of the person who wants but is unable to share his life, except that this time the deprivation is final. The dying person desperately needs to come to terms with himself and his coming death, Dr. Ross says, and it is the job of the doctor, chaplain, and family to help him do it.

Dr. Ross tells of a young black woman in her thirties, single and self-supporting. She lost a hand in an accident, but had done a masterful job of overcoming this handicap. Then she became a victim of kidney failure. She required regular renal dialysis—treatment with a blood-cleaning machine—in order to live. The woman could not afford to pay for such treatment and the two local hospitals with free programs turned her down. Staff members and workers at Billings Hospital, where Miss T. finally came, felt both guilty and angry that this kind, soft-spoken person should be, as they felt, "condemned to death." And so Dr. Ross went to see her.

During the early part of her illness, the patient told Dr. Ross, she felt rejected and found herself slipping into a mental confusion, having difficulty distinguishing between reality and dreams that she would undergo an operation and be cured. As her disease progressed, her eyes began to fail; she could not crochet, knit, or read the Bible. Friends and her nephews visited her, but her mother and sisters lived too far away to be with her.

She had been a generous person who had helped people in greater need than herself, but still felt a troubled relationship with God. Why didn't God take her from her misery or else help her to be cured? "I have a set-up in my mind like there are two gardens," she told Dr. Ross, "a garden here on earth and a garden in heaven; and I'm just waiting on God to say which of the gardens he wants me to work in."

The patient tired at this point and the first interview ended. At the end of the following week, Dr. Ross was possessed by a sense of urgency to see Miss T. The patient admitted that she, too, felt urgency. "She too felt that there was a big and important question which she wanted to ask and which needed an answer. And so we sat—almost like two children—digging in the dark and searching for something lost, not quite knowing what we had lost." Miss T. kept saying she knew she was bad and Dr. Ross could not discover what she meant by that. Finally, the dying woman admitted that for the past few days she had been calling on God for help. "And I hear Him say in the back of my mind: 'Why are you calling for help now and have never called when things were well?' What do you say to that, Doctor Ross?"

The psychiatrist did not have a ready answer and was pressed again by the woman.

It suddenly seemed to be a very simple question. I asked her to share with me a picture of children playing in the playground. Mother is in the house minding her own work. Suddenly a little boy falls and hurts his knees. What do you think happens?

She looked at me surprised and answered: "The little boy cries and calls for his mother."

"What happens next?" I said.

The same surprised look came over her face, as if she wondered why I would ask such a simple, almost silly question. "The boys go back to play and Mother continues her housework."

"The children have no use for her right now, isn't that right?"

She confirmed it and I continued: "Do you think mother resents that?"

"A mother," she said almost angrily, "wouldn't resent that!"

I looked at her very seriously and replied, "A mother wouldn't resent it, and Father would?" pointing up into the sky. . . .

She looked with the happiest face I had seen in a long time, holding my hand lightly and smiled. She repeated almost inaudibly: "If a mother can accept that, Father will, too. How could I ever doubt that?" After a few moments of the most peaceful silence, she continued, "My time comes very close now, but everything is all right. I shared with you my concept of death, passing from this garden into the next. What is your concept?"

I thought for a while, and still looking at her face, I said, "Peace." Her last words were: "I will pass into my garden very peacefully now."

Miss T. died a few hours later in her sleep.

In her book *On Death and Dying,* Dr. Ross states that the dying person passes through five psychological stages—if he can make it all the way through. The first is denial and isolation. "Among the over two hundred dying patients we have interviewed, most reacted to the awareness of a terminal illness at first with the statement, 'No, not me, it cannot be true.'" The initial reaction was the same whether the person was given the diagnosis outright or came to this conclusion gradually on his own. After a period of time, the person no longer is able to maintain the fantasy of denial and admits the reality.

The statement "No, not me" turns into the question, "Why me?" Now he becomes angry, enraged, embittered, resentful. Why has he been singled out? This psychological cast of mind finally yields to a bargaining attitude. If God has not heeded my angry demands, perhaps he will be more disposed to my request if I ask nicely, and Dr. Ross likens this attitude to a child's reaction when his parent says no to a request.

Next, the patient passes into a state of profound depression which is really a mourning for the loss of himself and all the important people and things in his life. "If a patient has had enough time (i.e., not a sudden, unexpected death) and has been given some help in working through the previously described stages, he will reach a stage during which he is neither depressed nor angry about his 'fate.' He will have

been able to express his previous feelings, his envy for the living and
the healthy, his anger at those who do not have to face their end so
soon. He will have mourned the impending loss of so many meaningful
people and places and he will contemplate his coming end with a certain degree of quiet expectation. He will be tired and, in most cases,
quite weak. He will also have a need to doze off to sleep often and in
brief intervals, which is different from the need to sleep during the
times of depression. This is not a sleep of avoidance or a period of rest
to get relief from pain, discomfort, or itching. It is a gradually increasing need to extend the hours of sleep very similar to that of a newborn child but in reverse order. It is not a resigned and hopeless 'giving
up,' a sense of 'what's the use' or 'I just cannot fight it any longer,'
though we hear such statements too."

Dr. Ross calls this stage, 18 centuries after Marcus Aurelius, acceptance.

The foregoing chronicle of the human association with death might
be likened to an official "approved" version which would be acceded
to by most reasonable people. But there is a dark subterranean relationship to which no one wishes to put his imprimatur. If, as La Rochefoucauld put it, "One can no more look steadily at death than at the
sun," still mankind has been hypnotized by its fascination. If Americans
could see no death, hear no death, speak no death, still they could
commit more murders than any other citizens in Western civilization—
one criminal homicide every 33 minutes in 1970. We speak today of the
pornography of violence or of the pornography of death as though this
were some fresh, electronically induced phenomenon, when we know
it is simply the latest fillip in the long, incestuous love-hate affair.

Murder is as old as Cain and Abel. Other animals—a notable exception is the social ant—do not kill members of their own species. The
wolf, a predator which humans often link with the adjective ravening,
is incapable of killing his kind. Ethologist Konrad Lorenz in *King
Solomon's Ring* described a battle of two wolves in which one opponent gains superiority and stands over his prostrate rival with bared
fangs an inch away from his rival's neck. "Every second you expect
violence and await with bated breath the moment when the winner's
teeth will rip the jugular vein of the loser. But your fears are ground-
less, for it will not happen. In this particular situation, the victor will
definitely not close on his less fortunate rival. You can see that he would
like to, but he just cannot! A dog or wolf that offers its neck to its adversary in this way will never be bitten seriously."

In a comparable situation, the human animal knows that this is the opportunity to plunge home the knife, for he can never be sure that his antagonist will respond with similar forebearance if he is spared and later gains the advantage.

Murder is spontaneous, random, individualized; human sacrifice is ritualized. Undoubtedly, the primitive mind had its good logical reasons for sacrificing a fellow human—to propitiate demanding gods, to bring about desired earthly benefits. But ritualized murder evoked the wild excitement—experienced nowhere else in nature—produced by general foreknowledge.

It is customary to think of human sacrifice as the primitive acts of appeasing Moloch and other savage gods. Indeed, Abraham's substituting an animal sacrifice for his firstborn child is a symbolic step toward civilization. But the barbaric practice carried late into Roman civilization.[2] The Saturnalia, conducted for seven days from the 17th to 23rd of December, commemorated the merry reign of Saturn, the god of sowing and husbandry who lived on earth long ago as a beneficent king of Italy. It was a time for feasting, drinking, and orgiastic revelry—a period of release after the harvest. As part of the festival, someone would assume a mock kingship which gave him the authority to issue fanciful, ludicrous commands to his temporary subjects. That was the way it was celebrated in Rome. But further away from the restraints of civilization, its dark and barbarous origins persisted. Sir James Frazer in *The Golden Bough* describes the Saturnalia of Roman soldiers at Durostorum on the Danube during the reigns of emperors Maximus and Diocletian:

> Thirty days before the festival they chose by lot from amongst themselves a young and handsome man, who was then clothed in royal attire to resemble Saturn. Thus arrayed and attended by a multitude of soldiers he went about in public with full license to indulge his passions and to taste of every pleasure, however base and shameful. But if his reign was merry, it was short and ended tragically; for when the thirty days were up and the festival of Saturn had come, he cut his own throat on the altar of the god whom he personated. In the year A.D. 303 the lot fell upon the Christian soldier Dasius, but he refused to play the part of the heathen god and soil his last days by debauchery. The threats and arguments of his commanding officer Bassus failed to shake his constancy, and accordingly he was beheaded.

The martyr St. Dasius lost his life a decade before the emperor Constantine declared Christianity to be the state religion of Rome. But even under the civilizing influence of Christianity, human sacrifice was

[2] It was only June 1972 that the Supreme Court of the United States ruled that most forms of capital punishment, particularly in the capricious way most sentences are meted out, violate the constitutional provisions against cruel or unusual punishment.

not totally abandoned, as Joan of Arc, Savonarola, and the "witches" of Salem and other God-fearing localities attest.

With organized warfare, which could be practiced only after the arrival of civilization, the savage fascination with death and the primordial excitement of the human sacrifice became merged with the obvious utility in purposeful killing. To the victors belonged the spoils, while the losers' beliefs tended to disappear with the believers. The Mongols practiced genocide as an expedient way for a relatively few conquerors to subdue permanently the vast Middle East–Middle Asian territory they seized in the thirteenth century. Mohammed forthrightly spread his religion at the point of a sword. The reason that seminal Zoroastrianism is virtually nonexistent in its native Iran is that it was extirpated by Islam. Nor was Christianity above this method of conversion, especially in dealing with its own dissidents.

Inflicting death has been a major occupation and consuming preoccupation of the human species during the 5,000 years of recorded history.

The discrepancy of this human practice with human preachments came to the attention of the pessimistic philosopher Arthur Schopenhauer at the beginning of the nineteenth century. He had been preceded by the vainglorious Age of Enlightenment with its premise that men guided their behavior through intelligence and thus were continually improving their lot in a never-ending spiral of progress. In the second decade of the nineteenth century, young Schopenhauer looked out upon a Europe devastated from the Napoleonic wars, the prime mover himself ignominiously immobilized on St. Helena, his and the great reforms of the French Revolution threatened by reaction, a Bourbon back in power in France, and misery the tenor of individual lives. If there was a method in all this, it was difficult to discern through the rose-tinted lens of reason.

Hegel, the Establishment philosopher of the day, explained it this way: "To him who looks upon the world rationally, the world in its turn presents a rational aspect. The relation is mutual." And history, Hegel's beloved synthesis of dialectical opposites, is the slaughter bench on which the happiness of individuals is sacrificed to the progress of reason. Schopenhauer, who despised Hegel and his philosophy, presented his own thoughts about what was going on in *The World as Will and Idea*, published in 1818 when he was thirty years old. His contemporaries accorded the offering a profound disinterest; 16 years after publication most of the edition was sold for waste paper. Schopenhauer sought sanctuary in the belief that he was ahead of his times.

The "Idea" part of the title was an acknowledgment of the idealism championed by Immanuel Kant. "The world is my idea," Schopenhauer wrote, meaning that the external world is known to us only through sensations and ideas. But after the conventional beginning, Schopenhauer turned iconoclast. The idol he fractured was *Homo sapiens*. Intelligent man is something of a misnomer, he contended, not questioning the caliber of the intelligence but its role. The intellect is not the master, not the director sitting in the control room, but an agent in the employ of the organism. Try convincing a man by logic against his will, Schopenhauer dares his doubters. We do not want a thing because we have found reasons, we find reasons because we want it. We elaborate philosophies and theologies to buttress our desires. He calls man the "metaphysical" animal because other animals desire without metaphysics.

If intellect is not the mainspring of the individual, what is?

Will. If we look at the strivings of people for mates, money, food, and all the rest as expressions of their desires, their imperious wills— and disregard their explanations, their *rationalizations* for their acts— then the strife of life and the anarchy of human affairs begin to make sense.

"Consciousness is the mere surface of our minds," Schopenhauer says, "of which, as of the earth, we do not know the inside but only the crust." Even if the cerebral cortex is four-fifths of the human brain by volume, he could be saying, it has been with us for merely a geological instant whereas the more primitive—and decisive—core goes back, back through the eons. The lower we go among life forms the smaller the role of intellect; but not so with will. "Unconsciousness is the original and natural condition of all things, and therefore also the basis from which, in particular species of beings, consciousness results as their highest efflorescence; wherefore even the unconsciousness always continues to predominate. Accordingly, most existences are without consciousness; but they act according to the laws of their nature—i.e., of their will."

This universal will is the will to live and to live fully. Its eternal enemy is death. The will has been able to defeat death through reproduction. Reproduction is the ultimate purpose of every organism, and this tyrannical instinct coerces even the knowledgeable human organism to immolate himself in marriage, parenthood, and the exhausting efforts to provide for his offspring.

Here was the point to puncture the comforting assurance that had ballooned ever since René Descartes said two centuries before, *Cogito, ergo sum* ("I think, therefore I am").

Wrong, said Arthur Schopenhauer, I desire, therefore I am.

Philosophy, said author-historian Will Durant, "is the front trench in the siege of truth. Science is the captured territory." Forty-one years after *The World as Will and Idea*—the year before Schopenhauer's death—Charles Darwin published *The Origin of Species*. Here was scientific validation of the unceasing competition for existence within and among species (although there were accommodation and cooperation, too) and scientific affirmation that survival was the main business of all creatures. Successful ones got to pass life to their heirs. And through the device of reproduction, the clay of life could be molded subtly through selection and the pressures to survive.

Friedrich Nietzsche was the intellectual descendant of Schopenhauer and Darwin, and the neurasthenic son of a Prussian minister. Nietzsche rejected his father's Christianity, and his philosophy was an apostasy from his intellectual inheritance. Like Schopenhauer, he saw will as the driving force of men, but it was not a will to live. As he watched a troop of cavalry in martial regalia clatter by on the way to the front in the Franco-Prussian War, "I felt for the first time that the strongest and highest Will to Life does not find expression in a miserable struggle for existence, but in a Will to War, a Will to Power, a Will to Overpower!"

Love is the desire for possession, mating is mastery. Instead of seeing marriage and reproduction as the sacrifice of the individual in the interests of the species, Nietzsche hails the triumph of the individual. But not just any individual. This parlor soldier who was unnerved by the sight of blood scorned the weak, the sickly, the mediocre, the democratic. He extolled nature's aristocracy, the strong, the elite who allowed no moral handcuffs to keep him from seizing whatever he could. His endowments entitled him to no less. "I teach you the Superman," spake Zarathustra, unveiling Nietzsche's goal of evolution.

"Man is the cruellest animal," Zarathustra observed. "When gazing at tragedies, bull-fights and crucifixions he hath felt happier than at any other time on earth." Napoleon was not a butcher but a benefactor; he offered—and this is why men flocked to his tricolor—the opportunity to die heroically instead of the slow death from economic predators.

"Too long," said Nietzsche of his efforts to explain the riddle of history, "has the world been a madhouse." He took leave of the world at the age of forty-five, 11 years before his death, overwhelmed by delusions of persecution and of grandeur. Like Schopenhauer, this herald of the death of God believed he was ahead of his contemporaries and forecast he would be "born posthumously."

A half century later the world heard the strident tirades against the decadent democracies, the weak, the mentally incompetent, the physically impure. A physical weakling in the toils of madness preached a distorted Nietzschean master race and conceived the demented "final solution" for an "inferior" race. Drawn into the madhouse, humanity acted out the world as will and idea of Adolf Hitler.

Is Nietzsche's hypothesis, then, the accurate one? If so, what about Schopenhauer's will to live, Darwin's evolutionary drive to survive?

It was not until the end of the nineteenth century and well into the twentieth that Sigmund Freud began scientific occupation of the mental territory explored by Schopenhauer and Nietzsche. Freud started with clinical observations of irrational behavior. Some displays of misery and madness disputed even the existence of sweet reason. These aberrations crippled a person as surely as physical illness, but their pathogenesis was a mystery. To treat such disturbances effectively required, really, a comprehension of the human mental apparatus. The search for that understanding occupied Freud's entire lifetime.

At the end of the long exploration, when the verbiage and most of the jargon were stripped away along with the case histories that titillated as well as instructed and the violated taboos that infuriated as well as instructed and the psychological revelations that appalled as well as instructed—when they were cast aside like the matrix wrappings that they were, there stood in classic simplicity and symmetry the Freudian paradigm.

In his last book, the brief *An Outline of Psychoanalysis*, a distillation of his life's work composed not long before his death in 1939, Freud limpidly portrays a landscape of the invisible mind. All mind is divided into three parts, and two of the three parts are outgrowths of the original totality: the id. The id, Latin for "it," contains everything that is inherited, particularly the instincts. "The power of the id expresses the purpose of the individual's life. This consists in the satisfaction of its innate needs." The mental activities of the id are unconscious—the person is totally unaware of them—and follow rules quite different from those of the conscious mind; logic is not one of those rules, the tensions of pleasure-unpleasure hold despotic sway. The workings of the id can be detected in dreams and, interestingly, "dreams bring to light material which could not originate either from the dreamer's adult life or from his forgotten childhood. We are obliged to regard it as part of the *archaic heritage* which a child brings with him into the world, before any experience of his own, as a result of experiences of his ancestors. We find elements corresponding to this phylogenetic material in the earliest human legends and in surviving customs. Thus dreams offer a course of human prehistory which is not to be despised."

A part of the submerged mind was modified by the insistent pressures—since it was totally cut off from the outside world—of external reality. This internal mind needed an agency to monitor stimuli and mediate between the wants of the id and the perils outside. This agency is the ego, Latin for "I." Its task is self-preservation. It controls voluntary movement. Most of the ego, but not all, is preconscious, that is, its elements and materials can readily be called into consciousness. The ego is our thinking process as we are usually aware of it; those spontaneous acts we make without a moment's thought spring from the unconscious part of the I.

Part of the ego underwent still further development once the species embarked upon the practice of extended childhood, during which the young human being is dependent upon his parents. A portion of the world becomes internalized: the rules and admonitions taught by parents form a new mental agency which supervises the ego by observing it, giving orders, threatening punishment. This agency is the superego, which absorbs not only parental teaching, but family, racial, social, national, and religious influences as well. Since the superego still has roots in the instinctual id, it may enforce its punitive strictures through feelings of guilt so severe that the individual tries to assuage them by adopting attitudes of inferiority or by various forms of self-punishment.

There is a marked correspondence between these mental provinces and what we know of life's evolution (some of Freud's early laboratory investigations were important contributions to evolutionary theory). The primal, central id extends back to inchoate beginnings of life. The ego, with the ascending scale of organisms, learns to assess external stimuli through memory, to avoid hostile stimuli through flight, to cope with less perilous stimuli through adaptation, to change environment through manipulation. The newcomer superego arrives only with the lengthening dependence of plastic childhood. While the id represents the hereditary organic past and the superego the cultural past, the ego represents the power of the present and is determined mainly by the individual's own experience.

This division of the mind accounts for the difficulty each of us has in imagining his own death and for feeling that he is immortal even though he knows rationally that everyone dies. The instinctual unconscious, which has no contact with external reality, believes it is immortal. It is only the ego that is aware of the finite nature of individual existence.

The ego tries to satisfy simultaneously—reconcile—the demands of the id, the superego, and reality. It seeks the pleasurable and avoids the unpleasurable within the bounds of safety. This obviously is a difficult course to steer, as the case load in our mental hospitals and the suicide statistics inform us. The most difficult part of the task is controlling the demands of the id. What frequently happens is that the ego gets caught in a crossfire between the id and the superego or the two gang up on the rational agency. If these assaults become too severe, they can damage the ego and loosen its hold on reality.

The disturbance of the ego's relation to reality—an abnormal response, an ineffective pattern of behavior, an inability to assess certain stimuli correctly—is neurosis. Neuroses shade into normal behavior on the one side and into psychosis on the other. If the ego becomes so impaired that its relation to reality is severed, this is psychosis.

Psychoanalysis seeks to cure neurosis by strengthening the weakened ego and does this through application of the Socratic advice "Know thyself": by increasing the ego's self-knowledge, by bringing to the surface from the unconscious the hidden (and thus uncontrollable) in-stinctual demands as well as past experiences that were repressed. Re-pression means that these unpleasant experiences were banished from the conscious mind to the unconscious where they go on thereafter as unmanageable sources of mental dysfunction. Neuroses are caused in the first six years of life when the young ego is not mature enough to cope with problems that might be handled by the healthy adult. The activating force for both repression and neurosis is anxiety, or vague, unfocused fear.

But what is the current running through the id, the trunk of life? What drives saint and sex fiend, imperial conqueror and impotent masochist, hysterical wife and cruel father, insatiable Romeo and un-sated scientist? Is there a simple explanation, the scientist's ideal, for the bewildering variety in human behavior? Freud's response to this challenge led to the most august part of his formulation.

There are two basic instincts, Freud concluded after "long doubts and vacillations." They are Eros and the destructive instinct. The love instinct aims to bind together, to establish and preserve ever greater unities. The other instinct wants to break connections, to destroy. "We may suppose that the final aim of the destructive instinct is to reduce living things to an inorganic state. For this reason we also call it the *death instinct.*"

The dual instincts either combine in various ways and to various degrees or work against one another. "This interaction . . . gives rise to the whole variegation of the phenomena of life." The act of eating destroys an object but incorporates it; sexual intercourse, an act of aggression, achieves intimate union. Too much aggressiveness turns a lover into a sexual murderer while too little produces shyness or impotence. When the instincts become segregated, we see the violent swings of a love-hate relationship.

"If we suppose that living things appeared later than inanimate ones and rose out of them," Freud writes, "then the death instinct agrees with the formula that we have stated, to the effect that instincts tend toward a return to an earlier state." And that would appear to be Freud's answer to the question posed by our primitive ancestors. Death originates in the inclination to go back to an earlier, lifeless condition. The older death instinct always wins in the contention for the individual, although Eros averts defeat through propagation of the species.

By the same rule of conservatism, Freud admits, the love instinct should imply that living substance once was unified and subsequently sundered, and now is seeking to reunite. He says that scientifically he cannot make the inference. But he points out that Eros is a house divided between the instincts of self-preservation of the individual and preservation of the species (and sacrifice of the individual). This is the conflict between narcissistic, egoistic, self-love and sexual-romantic, altruistic, object-love; the perennial fight between self-interest and the commonwealth; individual happiness versus society's welfare; personal dignity versus social harmony.

Finally, Freud says that the two basic instincts which govern in life are analogous "to the pair of opposing forces—attraction and repulsion —which rule in the inorganic world." And so the model for one human mind encompasses the vast continuum of time and space.

The positing of an always immaterial, unconscious death instinct is a difficult theory to accept for people accustomed to seeing evidence in stained cultures or electron micrographs. Still, the death-instinct theory has proved useful therapeutically. Psychiatrist Karl Menninger asked why some suicide attempts are successful while others fail. He found that the destructive instinct divides into three distinct elements: the wish to kill, the wish to be killed, and the wish to die. If the first wish is overpowering, the person becomes a murderer. If the first two reign, the person may try suicide and often fail—while he is in the thrall of self-directed murderous impulses, he is reluctant to pay the price for their satisfaction. Often such an act is a warning, a cry for help. If the three rays of the death instinct come into focus, suicide is carried out.

"The fateful question of the human species seems to me to be whether and to what extent the cultural process developed in it will succeed in mastering the derangements of communal life caused by the human instinct of aggression and self-destruction," Freud wrote in *Civilization and Its Discontents.* "Men have brought their powers of subduing the forces of nature to such a pitch that by using them they could now very easily exterminate one another to the last man. They know this —hence arises a great part of their current unrest, their dejection, their mood of apprehension. And now it may be expected that the other of the two 'heavenly forces,' eternal Eros, will put forth his strength so as to maintain himself alongside of his equally immortal adversary."

That passage was written in 1930, before Hitler came to power, before Coventry and Antwerp, Hamburg and Dresden, Lidice and Warsaw and Auschwitz, Hiroshima and the Cuban missile crisis, before we bombarded and defoliated forests, before the general realization that the imminent extinction of other mammalian species is but the latest culmination of a relentless extermination that goes far back into the prehistory of men.

One thinks of lovers holding hands, of gurgling, creamy-skinned babes at their mothers' breasts—madonna and child; one thinks of youngsters exulting in play, in growing, in burgeoning acquaintance with wondrous existence; one thinks of the thermonuclear-tipped missiles in their silos— buds of miniature stars waiting to bloom into the holocaust—while the antagonists have feinted and bluffed, boasted, threatened and haggled, scared only of disadvantage. After Freud it took a stubborn intellect still to ask why.

Freud, however, was not simply a mental cartographer or even philosopher, but basically a healer. He revealed the human being's hidden self not to affirm the weakness of human rationality, but to strengthen it . . . and give the intellect a greater role in human behavior and destiny.

The original intelligent animal divined by the anthropologists, the rational animal assumed by the first philosophers, had evolved by the middle of the twentieth century into the neurotic animal. "[I]t begins to be apparent," Norman O. Brown wrote in the introduction to *Life Against Death,* "that mankind, in all its restless striving and progress, has no idea of what it really wants."

Nearly a century and a half after Schopenhauer, Dr. Brown undertook a fresh attempt to understand the broad course of human events. How he meant to do so is indicated by the subtitle of his anthropological-philosophical-psychological study: *The Psychoanalytical Meaning of History.*

Human beings alone among animals, Dr. Brown begins his thesis, have fractured the unity of their minds. They have done this by repression: that is, by banishing an unbearable idea from their consciousness to the unconscious where the detached, unassimilated concept not only continues to exist but engages the mental organization in an undeclared civil war that cannot be consciously understood (without psychoanalytical assistance).

Stated in more general terms, the essence of the repression lies in the refusal of the human being to recognize the realities of his human nature. . . .

[T]he existence of a repressed unconscious necessarily implies . . . the universal neurosis of mankind. . . . Neurosis is not an occasional aberration; it is not just in other people; it is in us, and in us all the time. . . . [T]he doctrine of the universal neurosis of mankind is the psychoanalytical analogue of the theological doctrine of original sin. . . .

The necessity of the psychoanalytical approach to history is pressed upon the historian by one question: Why does man, alone of all animals, have a history? . . . [T]he historical process is sustained by man's desire to become other than what he is. And man's desire to become something different is essentially an unconscious desire. . . . Mankind today is still making history without having any conscious idea of what it really wants or under what conditions it would stop being unhappy; in fact what it is doing seems to be making itself more unhappy and calling that unhappiness progress. . . .

Archaic man conquers death by living the life of his dead ancestors. . . . what we do now is only a repetition of what they did then. This is the pattern of eternal return. Hence archaic society has no real history; and within archaic society there is no individuality. There is no history because there is no individuality; individuality is asserted by breaking with the ancestral archetypes and thus making history. . . . Man, the discontented animal, unconsciously seeking the life proper to his species, is man in history. . . . Repression transforms the timeless instinctual compulsion to repeat into the forward-moving dialectic of neurosis which is history. . . . Hegel was able to develop a philosophy of history only by making a fresh start and identifying man with death. And he develops the paradox that history is what man does with death, along lines almost identical with Freud's. Freud suggests that the aggression in human nature—the drive to master nature as well as the drive to master man—is the result of an extroversion of the death instinct, the desire to die being transformed into the desire to kill, destroy, or dominate. . . .

The death instinct is the core of the human neurosis. . . . The incapacity to accept death turns the death instinct into its distinctively human and distinctively morbid form. The distraction of human life to the war against death, by the same inevitable irony, results in death's dominion over life. The war against death takes the form of preoccupation with the past and the future, and the present tense, the tense of life, is lost.

Take therefore no thought for the morrow, said the teacher, *for the morrow shall take thought for the things of itself. Sufficient unto the day is the evil thereof.*

This is an evil among all things that are done under the sun, said the ancient wisdom, *that there is one event unto all: yea, also the heart of the sons of men is full of evil, and madness is in their heart while they live, and after that they go to the dead.*

II. Regaining Paradise

Myths document that the idea of immortality accompanied death and in some cases—in Genesis, for instance—preceded its discovery. Sir James Frazer, the British explorer òf primitive cultures, found that "belief in immortality has been remarkably widespread and persistent among mankind from the earliest times down to the present. Scepticism on the subject is rare and exceptional; it is hardly found among savages but seems to grow commoner with the advance of civilization and the progress of thought."

However, anthropologist Frazer restricts the primitive belief in immortality to an indefinite persistence of personality after death and makes his point with this illustration:

> [T]he eminent Finnish scholar Professor Karsten, a high authority on the South American Indians, tells us that the Tobas of the Bolivian Gran Chaco "certainly do not believe in immortality of the soul, an expression often abused especially by the Christian missionaries," but he immediately adds: "On the other hand, the conviction of the continued existence of the soul after death is a positive dogma of their religion." What Professor Karsten here affirms of the Toba Indians of Bolivia might probably, if we knew all the facts, be affirmed with truth of all primitive races without distinction: they do not believe in the immortality of the soul in the strict sense of the word, for the simple reason that they lack the conception of eternity which that word implies; but they do most strongly believe in the continued existence of the human spirit after death, and they act on that belief with logical consistency in everyday life by seeking to gain from the spirits of the dead all the benefits, and to avert all the evils, which these ghostly powers are supposed to bestow or to inflict upon mankind.

Certainly belief in the continued existence of spirits is consistent with the placing of artifacts in the earliest known human graves. Indeed, the belief is intimately entwined with what, therefore, is the oldest human custom: burial of the dead. And it explains the unshakable grip that ghosts exerted on the primitive imagination. Frazer and other investigators found that in the primitive mind a person after death still experienced pain,

40

hunger, and disease as he did before. It was simply that he had taken on a new existence and, like the wind, no longer could be seen. But like the humans still alive, these spirits needed such material things as food and drink and, since they were believed to exert important influences over the affairs of the living, a good deal of attention. Even in the most benign circumstances, the personalities of the departed were believed to have undergone changes for the worse—they became more jealous of their prerogatives, more petulant. So they required special handling—coddling. Since a man loved to be praised in life, for instance, he was lavished with flattery after death.

This early primitive belief that the world is pervaded by a living force or spiritual forces is known as animism from the Latin *anima* for "breath of life." Such a belief was ubiquitous in the various primitive cultures and anthropologists have arbitrarily assigned the Melanesian and Polynesian term *mana* to such a force or forces. Characteristics of mana were that it was invisible; powerful—more or less, depending; dynamic in that it could come and go in a thing or place, and a person or group could gain it or lose it; not necessarily conscious, intentional, personal, or moral; and finally, sometimes controllable, sometimes not.

Primitive man tried to control mana through magic. Not knowing the true cause and effect, he did the best he could. If a certain ritual happened to be followed by the rain men wanted, thereafter the ritual was repeated.

> Early man seeks above all to control the course of nature for practical ends [Bronislaw Malinowski writes in *Magic, Science and Religion*] and he does it directly, by rite and spell, compelling wind and weather, animals and crops to obey his will. Only much later, finding the limitations of his magical might, does he in fear or hope, in supplication or defiance, appeal to higher beings; that is, to demons, ancestor-spirits, or gods. It is in this distinction between direct control on the one hand and propitiation of superior powers on the other that Sir James Frazer sees the difference between religion and magic. Magic, based on man's confidence that he can dominate nature directly, if only he knows the laws which govern it magically, is in this akin to science. Religion, the confession of human impotence in certain matters, lifts man above the magical level, and later on maintains its independence side by side with science, to which magic has to succumb.

And in Frazer's words:

> Wherever sympathetic magic occurs in its pure unadulterated form it assumes that in nature one event follows another necessarily and invariably without the intervention of any spiritual or personal agency. Thus its fundamental conception is identical with that of modern science; underlying the whole system is a faith, implicit but real and firm, in the

order and uniformity of nature. . . . The fatal flaw of magic lies not in its general assumption of a sequence of events determined by law, but in its total misconception of the nature of the particular laws which govern that sequence. . . . A mistaken association of similar ideas produces homeopathic or imitative magic: a mistaken association of contiguous ideas produces contagious magic. The principles of association are excellent in themselves, and indeed absolutely essential to the working of the human mind. Legitimately applied they yield science; illegitimately applied they yield magic, the bastard sister of science.

In many primitive beliefs, a shaman served as intermediary with this unpredictable life force or hierarchy of forces. He could be primitive healer, medicine man, magician, priest, initiate into the divine mysteries, teacher, educator, civil magistrate, war chief.

A Dutch missionary, Dr. Albert Krujit, early in this century found that among Indonesians there was great fear of dead people's souls. "They naturally think that the dead person resents leaving this earth, and in his resentment wishes to have his fate shared by others. He therefore tries to carry off the soul-substance of the surviving people into the grave, which will cause them to die."

Frazer felt that here was the core of the fear of the dead. Man fears dead spirits "because he feels instinctively that they are angels and ministers of death hovering about him in the air and ready to bear away his own soul with them to the unknown world beyond the grave."

Sir James discovered certain variations in the belief in immortality (including, of course, the exception that proves the rule: a tribe living on the slopes of Mount Kenya in East Africa that maintained there is no existence after death). The Margi of northern Nigeria believed in immortality through reincarnation of the souls of the dead in human infants, but the privilege was restricted to the souls of good people. The souls of the bad were said to be destroyed by fire. The Binjhwar, a Dravidian tribe in central India, on the other hand, believed that only the wicked survived, becoming malignant ghosts. Good people perished. Opposed to the idea of the democratic survival of all spirits, inhabitants of the Tonga Islands in the Pacific thought that only the souls of noblemen were immortal; the common people died forever.

These could serve as prototypical models for more advanced myths and religions: in one case, the beginning evolution away from the unpredictable, arbitrary, essentially amoral animism toward investing religion with ethical behavior and the concept of a person's moral responsibility; in other cases, an erosion of the belief in universal immortality. From survival of the spirits of noblemen, it is but another step to the myths of immortal gods as opposed to mortal man. Just as the knowledge of inevitable death separated men from beasts, so the experience of death separated men from gods. In the various mythologies, immortality is the dividing line, even as we make the inability to interbreed the rule-of-thumb division between species. Gods and humans might have sexual intercourse, but by definition the humans are the mortals.

Men and women, humans, might achieve different kinds of immortality and in various ways. In this sense the history of mythology and religion might be regarded as the record of humankind's valorous defense against the cerebral insistence of human finitude. Humanity's most beautiful art, noblest qualities, most ingenious reasoning, and remarkable tenacity have gone into the struggle. Even so, it has been a long, forced retreat. Perhaps the growth of our unhappiness simply is an index to how far we have been pushed from the warm inchoate confidence in our everlastingness into the bleak knowledge of our nothingness.

"Whenever we find the theme of death, whether in recurrent myths or modern dreams," Joseph Henderson writes in *The Wisdom of the Serpent*, a study of myths about death, "we find that it is never seen to stand alone as a final act of annihilation. Apart from extreme forms of pathological depression or of infantile sadism [Dr. Henderson is a psychologist and psychotherapist] death is universally found to be part of a cycle of death and rebirth, or to be the condition necessary to imagine transcendence of life in an experience of resurrection." Somewhere between the two, he says, are myths of initiation, harking back to shamanism and the use of special knowledge or spiritual liberation to overcome death. And so we have saints and master yogis and alchemists and Gilgamesh.

One of the most commonly recurring myths is the one told of the Sumerian goddess Inanna, or Ishtar as she was known in the later Babylonian period. Inanna descends to the underworld, the Land of No Return, dies and then returns to life. In a variation of the myth, Inanna goes in quest of herself and comes back as one reborn from a symbolic sacrifice and death. Ishtar, the Babylonian goddess, goes to the Land of No Return to procure the life of her son-lover, Tammuz. The mother goddess succeeds on a conditional basis. That is, Tammuz yearly came to life in the springtime as a vegetation god and subsequently died, to be resurrected in the following year.

In Greek legend, the goddess Persephone is kidnaped by Hades and taken to his kingdom in the underworld. Persephone's mother, Demeter, succeeds in procuring her release. But just as she is leaving, Persephone swallows a pomegranate seed given her by Hades. Demeter asks her daughter if she tasted anything underground; if so, she must spend one-third of the year with her husband Hades. Persephone confesses that she ate the pomegranate grain and is condemned to spending four months away from her mother and the other gods—during the time when the land is barren.

The myths of Cybele and Attis in the Near East, and Isis and Osiris in Egypt parallel the yearly rebirth of vegetation. Other Egyptian myths, dating from the fifth century B.C., tell of the phoenix, a bird which supposedly inhabited Arabia and was sacred to the sun god, Ra. The phoenix lived for 500 years or longer, then was consumed voluntarily by fire to arise from its own ashes to regain youthful life.

The serpent is one of the most common of all symbols of rebirth. During its yearly hibernation the snake sheds its skin and seems to be a renewed organism, a rebirth that at one time must have been believed literally. "The wisdom of the serpent, which is suggested by its watchful lidless eye," Dr. Henderson explains the title of his book, "lies essentially in mankind's having projected into this lowly creature his own secret wish to obtain from the earth the knowedge he cannot find in waking daylight consciousness alone. This is the knowledge of death and rebirth forever withheld except at those times when some transcendent principle emerging from the depths, makes it available to consciousness."

With reincarnation and transmigration of souls, the principle of death and rebirth is released from the circle of repetition to enter a cyclic, forward-moving process. The belief that the soul enjoys an indefinite series of reincarnations in a variety of life forms goes far back in the ancient religion of India. To the doctrine of eternal reincarnation was added much later, probably after 1000 B.C., the iron rule of karma, the reality principle of cause and effect plus the ethical principle of reward or retribution for earthly behavior. A person was punished for his bad acts by reappearing in some lower life status; he was rewarded with an elevated reincarnation.

The Hindu paradigm of ultimate reality embraces the unity of life and death, the basic unity of life in all its diversity, its underlying unity despite endless temporal changes, and the continuity of past, present, and future. This paradigm encourages emphasis of the cosmic essence and deemphasizes ephemeral manifestations. It leads to the most profound level of Eastern wisdom—transcendence of self—as the means to achieve ultimate happiness or the peace that passes understanding or mortal immortality. It is the yogi's lifelong pilgrimage for pure being, a mode of being transcending the human condition, final liberation from the suffering of human life; it is the Zen Buddhist's lifelong education to unlearn self-consciousness, to recapture the innocent, untutored, unconscious grace of animals; it was Buddha's quest for nirvana.

It is at precisely this point that Eastern religion poses its most serious challenge to the Western mind which seeks not negation but affirmation of self. Western civilization—from the works of its greatest artists to its prodigious scientific-technical accomplishments—is built on this opposite principle. In Western thought, happiness is achieved through realization of self; the greater the realization, the greater the satisfaction, achievement, benefits to all. The glorification of self is a defiant fist-shaking against the fear that self is *all*. "Do not go gentle into that good night. Rage, rage against the dying of the light," counseled poet Dylan Thomas. Schopenhauer, the philosopher who changed the course of Western thought on rationality, was influenced by reading a translation of the Hindu *Upanishads*. Here was the concept, venerable in the East, of layers of the soul from the waking state down to an essence inaccessible to the senses that inspired Schopenhauer to see the consciousness of higher organisms superimposed over the unconscious will of all life. The master yogi seeks to slough off the conscious self in order to attain the primal experience of the unconscious—conceived in the *Upanishads* as the final goal in man's search for the ultimate.

The Western mind, already suspicious that immortality may be a hoax, is hardly likely to think of everlasting life as anything but a consummation devoutly to be wished. The believer in the Hindu system who knows in his bones that it is the correct interpretation of all reality is sentenced to life, forever. There is no escape from the suffering, cruelty, ignorance, hatred, relentless cause and effect, the being born and growing in impermanent forms only to undergo ever-recurring death. The idea of an afterlife may have been a vague extension into the future for primitive men, but by the sixth century B.C., when Buddha lived, the mind had a much more substantial grasp of the concept of eternity.

The great question Buddha asked is: Why has fate been so cruel as to ordain that we must *not* die? In solving that problem, the immortal liberator of the Eastern mind showed his fellows how to die.

Siddhartha Gautama was an Indian rajah's son, born 563 B.C. north of Benares near the border of present-day Nepal. Because his father feared he might become a monk and leave no heirs, the prince was indulged with all manner of luxuries and shielded from life's unpleasant sights. Faithful to filial duty, Gautama did marry and provide his father with a grandson and heir. Nevertheless, the prince was dissatisfied amidst his riches.

Legend has it that one day while riding in the royal pleasure garden, he saw for the first time an old man "broken-toothed, gray haired, crooked and bent of body, leaning on a staff, and trembling in every limb." This was the first time Gautama had seen an old man and his first knowledge that old age comes to all. On subsequent rides he saw a sick man and a dead man. He went home troubled and depressed, and began thinking about the riddles of old age, death, and human fate.

One night when he was twenty-nine years old, the prince left his parents, his sleeping wife and child, rode with his servant to the border of his kingdom, took off his royal garments and ornaments, and sent them back to the palace with his servant. Gautama went on alone, with begging bowl and loincloth. The fugitive from pleasure sought to understand the meaning of life through study with religious teachers and asceticism. In particular, he sought how to achieve equanimity amidst the anxieties of existence, and to discover how one could break out of the wheel of karma and transmigration to achieve a final repose from the sorrows of life.

For six years he searched but found no answers in his philosophical discussions and asceticism. Thereafter he went into a forest to meditate. One night under a Bo tree, the wisdom for which he had been searching was revealed to him. He took his name from this Enlightenment, which in Sanskrit is called Buddha.

Buddha decided to go out and teach his salvation to the people and did so for the last 45 years of his life. This in itself was a significant departure from the prevailing Brahmanism which confined its highest teachings to the initiated few. Buddha also substituted a personal religion for one of formal ritualism and attacked the rigid caste system. These reforms are all of a piece with his most important concept: the means to break the iron law of karma.[1]

Karma was an instrument of the white-skinned Aryans who invaded India around 1500 B.C. and thereafter. The Aryans enslaved many of the dark-skinned inhabitants and imposed their language, Sanskrit, upon a large part of the subcontinent. In order to exploit their conquest and ensure its continuation, the Aryans developed the caste system whereby priests or Brahmans were considered the head; warriors the arms; tradesmen, bankers, and gentlemen farmers, the trunk; and servants and laborers—the bulk of the dark-skinned, conquered people—were the feet of a huge socio-religious organization. Karma appeared as an enforcement of the caste system, rewarding caste virtues and punishing sins against the system. If members of the lowest orders performed their menial jobs meticulously, they could hope for a social promotion. However, it might take hundreds or thousands of reincarnations (in the meantime there was always the danger of falling down to the level of

[1] Buddhism was deemed a heresy that existed in India for 1,800 years before being reabsorbed into Hinduism; but by that time Buddha's insights had infused new vitality into the ancient parent religion and spread throughout Asia as well.

insects or vermin) whereas the upper orders enjoyed the prospect of rapid advancement in their transmigrations.

This theocratic oppression coupled with the all-too-real hardships of low-caste life gradually transformed endless reincarnation from a life-reveling concept into a life-hating one in the minds of many Indians. Intellectual leaders of the oppressed majority began to cast about for an escape from eternal suffering. Everyone at the time believed he was tied to the wheel of rebirth by the innate desire which caused his earthly acts. Some of the most desperate Indians practiced debilitating austerities on the theory that they could break their will to live and thus win release.

This was the historical situation in which Buddha lived and although he himself was exempted by his station from these social degradations he chose to sally forth to confront the monstrous predicament of existence. He was to be the knight to slay the dragon of intolerable injustice.

Buddha first displayed the fruits of his enlightenment in the Sermon of Benares, the "Discourse on the Turning of the Wheel of the Laws." In it, he rejects self-laceration as an escape route, advocating the Middle Path to avoid the extremes of devotion to sensual pleasures or to asceticism. Then he proceeds to his fundamental tenets. Individual existence in this world is suffering. The cause of the misery is desire or attachment to the objects of sense. Peace of mind is attained through control of desire. Then Buddha extends this process of detachment into his great psychological, philosophical, and theological innovation. It is possible through right actions and thoughts, through concentration and the pursuit of saintliness, through self-purification to achieve a state of passionless peace, of perfect serenity. By so doing, one can wear down the forces of karma and escape the cycle of rebirth.[2]

This was nirvana. Nirvana is translated literally as "act of extinguishing." It means the going out of fire, especially the fire of desire, of anger, of greed. Unlike ordinary life, it is a state of permanence. "There is, O monks, a non-born, a non-becoming, a non-created, a non-caused. If there were not, there would be no refuge for that which is born, becomes, is created, is caused." Buddha refused to speculate on what happened to the saint in a state of nirvana after death. He said such speculation was useless. And, we might add, beside the point. For Buddha's gift was hope of release from the prison of existence.

The description of Buddha's death leaves little doubt that he had achieved his nirvana. It is recorded that the Exalted One passed through

[2] The Jain sect, which began too in the sixth century B.C., also was a protest against the caste system and offered a way to escape karma. Additionally, the Jains quite logically refused to kill any living thing, and the Jain monk carries a broom to sweep insects from his path.

four stages of rapture into a state of mind conscious only of the infinity of space to consciousness only of thought to consciousness of no special object. He then fell into a state between consciousness and unconsciousness and then no longer was conscious of sensations or ideas. One of his followers thought he was dead, but his time was not yet. The Buddha passed back through the states between consciousness and unconsciousness, and consciousness of no special object and of the infinity of thought and of the infinity of space. He entered the fourth stage of rapture, and the third, and second, and first; then the second and third and fourth stages of rapture. And passing out of the last stage of rapture he immediately expired.

Twenty-five hundred years ago, Buddha stated that the knowledge of perpetual existence is intolerable. The option, or at least possibility, of surcease an intellectual necessity. Sartre in the play *No Exit* offered the thesis that interminable, inescapable existence is, in fact, hell.

After Buddha, we have the paradox of men in the East going to extraordinary lengths to flee the predicament of perpetuity while people in the West began to strive no less assiduously to achieve the bliss of immortality.

Socrates died in 399 B.C., about 85 years after Buddha. Socrates was a political brawler too immersed in daily events to point toward life's culmination although he had faced death many times and heroically saved a friend's life in battle. Where Buddha sought the depths of the unconscious, Socrates sought the heights of rationality; where Buddha said, "Know the infinite," Socrates said, "Know thyself." They lived in different worlds and died different deaths—yet the parallels between the two men are remarkable.

At the time of Buddha's death, Athens and Sparta were busy fighting off the Persian incursions under Darius and Xerxes. Afterward, the Athenian fleet turned to trade, bringing great wealth to the city-state. With wealth came leisure, and with leisure science and philosophy. As astronomers probed the heavens and other men looked more closely at nature, philosophers began to examine the nature of men. Logic vied with belief, and natural explanations began to replace supernatural ones.

An early consequence of this was that the educated youth of Athens lost the faith of their fathers. Like old generals, Zeus and Apollo and all the mental residents of Mount Olympus began to fade away—although the cast was revivified with new names after Greece succumbed to Roman arms and Rome succumbed to Greek culture. Sophist Protagoras applied the Heraclitean doctrine of the flux of all things to the mind as

proof the gods could not be eternal beings. Indeed, men could not know
ultimate truth or certitude. Truth is relative, said Protagoras, man is the
measure of all things. Another Sophist, Critias, said 23 centuries before
Marx that religion is the invention of politicians. Twenty-three centuries
before Nietzsche, Sophist Thrasymachus said that might is the law of
nature and gratification of desire the natural right of the stronger.

Socrates also attacked the old gods, but he disagreed with the Sophists
as well, a position calculated to gratify his passion for debate. As a lethal
debater, Socrates had won his share of fear and hatred as well as ad-
miration during years of in-fighting in Athenian political affairs. He had
served as a hoplite, or heavy infantryman, in the Athenian army, as a
member of the democracy's Council of 500, and during a dictatorial in-
terregnum refused at the risk of his life to carry out an order that he
considered unjust. After the interlude of terrorism under the 30 Tyrants,
democracy was restored to Athens in 404 B.C. But in that year also, Athens
suffered final defeat after 28 years of war with Sparta. Political turmoil
was rampant; criticism of the government, not unexpectedly, was harsh.
Among the sharpest critics was Socrates. Is this any way to run a government, he complained, selecting and rotating the administrators by alphabet! The management of state is too important for amateurs. The best
men must be sought out and induced to rule, men must be trained to
govern. Justice, said Socrates in Plato's *The Republic,* is every man doing
what he is suited to do; the affairs of men will never be run properly until
we have philosopher-kings.

In the tumultuous times of the historical moment, this kind of talk
sounded like treasonous aristocracy. When a coalition of aristocrats did
try to overthrow the Athenian democracy and the revolution was put
down, even though the troublemaker Socrates had not taken part he was
put on trial for his life. He was charged with impiety—or atheism—and
corruption of youth; such a charge today would connote a dirty old man,
but at that time it meant that he had turned the heads of youth away
from the traditional gods. It was as good a charge as any to get him out
of the way, at least out of Athens.

At the end of the trial, the 510 jurors narrowly divided in favor of
conviction. According to custom, Socrates had the privilege of counter-
proposing a reduced sentence, which would be put to a second vote.
The closeness of the first decision—a swing of 30 votes would have
changed the verdict—and other factors convince historians that Socrates
could have left Athens with his life if he had chosen banishment. He
refused to compromise, offering to pay a small fine as an alternative.
Recognizing an insult when it saw one, the jury voted more decisively

to condemn him. Even then, through bribes by his friends and perhaps with the consent of the highest officials, Socrates could have been spirited away from Athens. He refused.

Plato was a young patrician, twenty-eight years old at this time, who had been converted to Socrates' religion: the search for truth and wisdom. Plato may have been Socrates' peer as a philosopher, may have excelled him—we cannot judge; certainly he carried Socratic initiatives to polished maturity and as a philosopher-writer was without peer in all history. Plato took it upon himself to justify Socrates' ways to men and did so with the *Dialogues*. But where the historical Socrates leaves off and the shining creation of Plato's mind begins, we are never sure.

Both Plato and Socrates wanted to prove something—that the state was wrong in charging that Socrates had left the youth without a faith, that the Sophists were wrong in contending there were no certainties. In choosing to lay down his life for the Athens in which he believed, Socrates also was following a tradition from the golden age of Pericles. In his famous funeral oration for Athenians who died in battle, Pericles said: "And then when the moment of combat came, thinking it better to defend themselves and suffer death rather than to yield and save their lives, they fled, indeed, from the shameful word of dishonor, but with life and limb stood stoutly to their task, and in the brief instant ordained by fate, at the crowning moment not of fear but of glory, they passed away." Athenian heroes could achieve a civic immortality, enshrined forever in the minds of the generations of their countrymen. Cowards were consigned to oblivion.

Plato sought a faith that would not dissolve with a crumbling Mount Olympus, but would last for the ages. He found the concept of ideas. The form of a table would exist even if one never were built . . . or all those in existence were destroyed . . . or no one was alive to see one. The idea of justice exists even if no one practices it and we know the concept of truth even if we cannot exactly grasp its elusive actuality. These absolutes always have existed and will exist eternally. The soul exists outside historical time and beyond physical space. Here 5,000 miles from Benares was pure thought.

The similarities hardly end here, as we see from the *Phaedo*, Plato's account of Socrates' last discussion with his followers before he drinks poison:

> "If at its release the soul is pure and carries with it no contamination of the body, because it has never willingly associated with it in life, but has shunned it and kept itself separate as its regular practice—in other words, if it has pursued philosophy in the right way and really practiced how to face death easily—this is what 'practicing death' means, isn't it?"

"Most decidedly."

"Very well, if this is its condition, then it departs to that place which is, like itself, invisible, divine, immortal, and wise, where, on its arrival, happiness awaits it, and release from uncertainty and folly, from fears and uncontrolled desires, and all other human evils, and where, as they say of the initiates in the Mysteries, it really spends the rest of time with God. Shall we adopt this view, Cebes, or some other?"

"This one, by all means," said Cebes.

There were also the elements of karma and reincarnation. Some souls have become so tainted, so attached to their physical bodies, so afraid to leave, that they hover about graveyards. And that is why people have seen ghosts and apparitions. "Of course these are not the souls of the good, but of the wicked, and they are compelled to wander about these places as a punishment for their bad conduct in the past. They continue wandering until at last, through craving for the corporeal, which unceasingly pursues them, they are imprisoned once more in a body. And as you might expect, they are attached to the same sort of character or nature which they have developed during life."

That was the scene as Plato, who had been prevented by illness from being there, later reconstructed it. The talk was considered, noble, as Socrates patiently explained his action and fortified his followers against death. Trusting in—betting on—his soul's warranty of immortality (what harm can be done by believing?), eager to pursue pure knowledge, master of his mind and fate, scoring the debater's point with the irrefutable logic of martyrdom, Socrates took his unruffled departure while his friends wept. Painlessly, the coldness spread up the legs through the seventy-year-old body. Nirvana, Athenian style.

Ever after, people spoke of meeting death philosophically.

It was quite another matter for the martyr in his early thirties at Golgotha. Crucifixion is slow death; in his case it took nearly nine hours. It is a painful death, particularly in the later hours of dying when the exhausted muscles degenerate into knobs of agony. Above all, it was degrading. This was treating the philosopher as animal, hanging a slab of meat on some spikes. No rapture here, no civilized chat with the acolytes, no purposefully selected *tour de force* to impress friends and foes. Most of the faithful never showed up, afraid for their own skins. Most of the people who did come were nasty hecklers high on the witch's brew of ignorance, hatred, guilt, and the adrenaline of attending a primitive death ritual. Jesus looked out on a scene of madness. They spit on him, but worse they mocked him, defied him to come down from the cross if he were who he said he was. Prove it.

There was the gall. He already had laid his case before them. With the parable of the Good Samaritan and the central thesis of the Sermon on the Mount—"Love your enemies, bless them that curse you, do good to them that hate you"—he had shown them how to break out of the Hebrew karma of an eye for an eye and a tooth for a tooth. He had divined the fracture in the human soul and told them they must heal it in order to enjoy spiritual health—"No man can serve two masters"; "If therefore thine eye be single, thy whole body shall be full of light." Hypocrisy is weakness. With the wisdom of the East, he had advised them to rely not so heavily on the conscious mind—"Which of you by taking thought can add one cubit unto his stature?"—but to consider the lilies of the field. With the parable of the Sower he deciphered life's great principle of ' evolution—to them that have shall be given, from them that have not shall be taken away—nearly two millennia before Darwin. Through the parables he tried to tell them about the kingdom of God. He told them where this kingdom was—within themselves. In so many ways he told them what it was—purity of soul, peace of mind, spiritual riches. His ministry—the acts of kindness and healing, his teaching—was to show them the way to this living nirvana, thinking they would follow. Those were his credentials. Instead they demanded magic.

Did Christ at this time construe a bitter irony in the advice he had given when he started out: "neither cast ye your pearls before swine, lest they trample them under their feet, and turn again and rend you"? Or did he doubt himself? Did he secretly hope for the verifying miracle?

He spoke with confidence when first upon the cross. "Father, forgive them; for they know not what they do." Later he could tell one of the thieves being executed with him, "Verily, I say unto thee, Today shalt thou be with me in paradise." But at the end, in the Gospel of Luke, it was: "Father, into thy hands I commend my spirit." And in John: "It is finished." Words of resignation and, in Matthew and Mark, despair: "My God, my God, why hast thou forsaken me?"

I am the resurrection and the life, saith the Lord: he that believeth in me, though he were dead, yet shall he live: and whoever liveth and believeth in me, shall never die.

Monotheism has long been identified as the unifying idea of the Jewish religion and its unique contribution to civilization. Here was no evolution away from, but a sharp break with, the primitive animism. The ancient Hebrews were very jealous of their God and knew that he needed devoted champions on earth—the expressions of an inarticulate deeper knowledge that they alone were caretakers of a precious idea. This pioneering concept was difficult to maintain, as the frequent backsliding and Old Testament adjurations for constancy attest.

But more was involved than a renunciation of polytheism. The religion was severed from nature and the religious tendency to believe in rebirth. Gone was the primitive belief in an afterlife—and gone, it should be noted, without qualms. The concept of an immortal soul—either individual or as an essence merged with the infinite—is nonexistent in the Old Testament. Body-mind-spirit were inextricably one animated body. The only immortality was in the continued existence of the Hebrew people and their religion—a corporate immortality. When one meets anxiety in the Old Testament, it is not a fear of death, but a fear of not having children. "I will make you a great nation," God promises Abraham and Israel. In this way, too, Judaism is a break with timeless, cyclical religions, for it is rooted in history, moving forward through specific times and events. Indeed, it is the fascinating story of the preservation of a vital identity through nearly 4,000 years of incredible vicissitudes.

The Hebrew people are traced back to Ur, one of the cities founded in the original urban civilization on the plain of Shinar between the Tigris and Euphrates rivers on the Persian Gulf. By 3000 B.C. the Sumerian cities were prospering with the use of metal, cuneiform, and well-organized governments. The civilization was conquered, subjugated, then revived once again under the leadership of Ur in 2200 B.C. only to go under to the conqueror Hammurabi, this time forever. Hammurabi built his capital Babylon on the Euphrates River and, like the phoenix, the Babylonian Empire was born out of the ashes of the Sumerian culture.

Within a few centuries, Hebrew and other tribes began swarming westward into Palestine and Syria, gradually dominating the area. The traditions in the first 11 chapters of Genesis have close Babylonian parallels—the extreme longevity of people, the wickedness of people, the great flood. And, of course, the Utnapishtim whom Gilgamesh visits is the counterpart of the biblical Noah. But where Utnapishtim was given immortality, the Judaic Noah had to die after 950 years.

The most serious Old Testament threat to the integrity and even survival of Judaic continuity came toward the middle of the first millennium B.C. After the 70-year monarchy of David and Solomon at the beginning of that millennium, the Hebrew state split into Israel and Judah, dividing while more powerful, imperialistic states began building up around them. The northern kingdom of Israel fell to the Assyrians in 721 B.C.; 30,000 inhabitants were exiled, were assimilated into their new environment, and disappeared from history as an organic entity. In 586

B.C. the Babylonians under Nebuchadnezzar overran and destroyed Judah. Again transplantation—the exile. But during this trial the Hebrew fathers kept the faith and exhorted their people to do the same.

Even as the Babylonian Empire was swallowing Judah, Babylon was to be devoured within a half century by the behemoth Persian Empire (which within another half century would crest on the shores of Greece). One way the Persians were able to manage their vast empire was through tolerance of minority groups, and in 538 B.C. Emperor Cyrus permitted a certain number of Jewish exiles to return to a small area in Palestine to rebuild the destroyed temple at Jerusalem. This was to become the nucleus that ensured survival of Judaism and led to the theocratic state that existed under Roman control at the time of Christ. For the majority of the Jews and their descendants, the exile went on for another century and more.

While granted a deliverance by the Persians, the Jews at the same time were exposed to Zoroastrianism, a religion seductively consistent with Judaic belief in some ways. Zoroaster, as the Greeks called him, or Zara-ushtra, as he was known to the ancient Persians, apparently lived in the sixth century B.C., and may have died just before the Persians conquered Babylon and the Hebrew captives, although he was first thought to have lived much earlier. Zoroastrians worshiped a supreme invisible God and practiced no idolatry. " 'In the mouth of two witnesses,' the spiritual worship of God was established," James Freeman Clarke writes in *Ten Great Religions,* "and not till Zoroaster took the hand of Moses did the Jews cease to be idolators. After the return from the captivity that tendency wholly disappears."

And other now familiar elements make their first appearance. The great principle of Zoroastrianism was that of dualism. There was a God of light and good and life, Ahura Mazda, and he was opposed by Ahriman, the prince of darkness and evil and death. Ahura Mazda was supported by six archangels called Immortal Holy Ones, and their individual names stood for Good Mind, Excellent Truth, Wished-for Kingdom, Devotion, Wholesomeness, and Non-Death. Beneath them were angels and lesser divinities. Ahriman led a company of archfiends and demons.

Like Judaism, Zoroastrianism was a historical religion. The world's history, according to Zoroaster, is a contest between good and evil, or light and darkness. This history has a definite time period—12,000 years, divided equally into four parts. During the first 3,000 years, the world is Ahura Mazda's spiritual creation. In the second period, he creates the material world which is invaded by Ahriman and his cohorts. The third period is marked by the contest between the two great rivals for the human soul. Implicit in this struggle is human free will—each person can and must make his own choice between good and evil. While this supreme contest goes on to the end, the fourth and final period begins with the arrival of Zoroaster to rally human forces for the good. This regeneration is to be carried on by three sons or descendants of Zoroaster to be born in succeeding ages. The last one is the Sayoshant, or Savior. At the end, there will be a final battle between the forces of good and evil. Ahriman and the forces of evil will be defeated and good will prevail forever. There will be a resurrection of all souls and a last judgment for consignment to heaven or hell.

Ever since the fall of Israel, Isaiah and other Hebrew prophets had been looking for the Messiah, the leader who would restore the Jewish kingdom to the power of David and the glory of Solomon. After the Persian captivity, the prophecies of a Messiah became associated with the apocalypse, the establishment of the kingdom of God after a final battle and eradication of the forces of evil. The Magi, the three wise men who followed the star westward to Bethlehem, came to pay homage to the Savior, whom they believed to be the scion of Zoroaster. Jews awaiting restoration of the physical kingdom knew he was not the Messiah.

With resurrection, immortality was introduced to the Jewish religion, and Judaism proved to be not particularly fertile ground for the alien seed. Resurrection was a special kind of immortality: it did not happen automatically, but everyone received it at one historical time, judgment day. This concept becomes fantastically complicated when one tries to mesh it with the Hebrew belief in the indestructible unity of body and soul. How were all these bodies to be physically reassembled? It is clear that no one, including Jesus, at that time had worked out a coherent theology of resurrection and afterlife. For one thing, the apocalypse still was sometime off in the future and did not demand immediate exegesis. For another thing, and more important, Jews were fundamentally concerned with life in the here and now. For himself, Jesus resolved the seemingly irreconcilable concepts of resurrection and the unfissionable unity of the animated body. If he were to be resurrected, he knew that it had to happen within three days.

The great historical rivers of the West had their confluence in Paul, who was born about the same time as Christ, in Tarsus, a city close to the Mediterranean Sea in the western half of Turkey. Paul was a member of the Greco-Roman world—a Roman citizen who spoke Greek and knew the Hellenistic mind. He also was a Jew inculcated in the faith of his fathers, and such a zealous guardian of that faith that he set out to preserve Judaic integrity from the Jesus heresy. History instructs us that Paul did accomplish his goal, after a mystical experience on the road to Damascus, by rechanneling the stream of Christianity into the gentile world where it became a flood.

If the life of Jesus had been captured on an imaginary motion picture film, all the frames in that film would not add up in importance to the final one when, after his cry of anguish, his head fell forward in death on the cross. That was the frame frozen for posterity. The minister of life was immortalized in the image of death.

It was reported that the corpse of Jesus disappeared from its temporary sepulcher, and afterward various followers reported seeing and holding conversations with the resurrected Christ on several occasions. These reports were not enough to convince or convert many Jews or Paul until he had his own vision on the road to Damascus.

But the Hellenistic mind for centuries had been cultivated with the faith of Socrates and the persuasion of Plato.[3] These people already believed in the immortality of an independent, preexistent soul which disengaged from the corruptible flesh at death, a concept inconceivable to the Jewish mind. Reports of the resurrection of Jesus were the first, glad confirmation of what they already knew. This was the Good News of the Gospels to be written in the final quarter of the first century—immortality is not myth after all. The proof is that Jesus lives.

> Now if Christ be preached that he rose from the dead, how say some among you that there is no resurrection of the dead? But if there be no resurrection of the dead, then is Christ not risen: And if Christ be not risen, then is our preaching in vain, and your faith is also vain.

To make sure there was no mistake, Paul explained the significance of Christ's resurrection in relation to the cause of death:

> For since by man came death, by man came also the resurrection of the dead. For as in Adam all die, even so in Christ shall all be made alive. . . .
> For when ye were the servants of sin, ye were free from righteousness. What fruit had ye then in those things thereof ye are now ashamed? for the end of those things is death. But now being made free from sin, and become servants to God, ye have your fruit unto holiness, and the end everlasting life. For the wages of sin is death; but the gift of God is eternal life through Jesus Christ our Lord.

[3] It is fascinating to realize that the concept of a cosmic principle which went eastward to shape Hinduism probably came westward through Persian Zoroastrianism to lay the groundwork for the concept of eternal ideas and Socrates' belief in one God which he opposed to the prevailing polytheism. Plato's *The Republic* describes a heaven, hell, and purgatory.

Of course, Paul was successful where Jesus failed. Few people were buying the message of the Savior of the living soul, but the purveyor of salvation after death found a ready market. Even the power of pagan Rome could not stand against the promise of immortality, and the Eternal City is a palimpsest for that struggle for the human mind. The Christian heroes in that crucial war were the martyrs who, not unlike the Assassins of the Old Man of the Mountain, were sure they were winning the gates to paradise in the next world.

There was an inherent conflict between the concepts of the Christian resurrection of the body at the last trump and the Hellenistic immortality of the soul now. But that was an internal misfit for the church fathers to square over the millennia. Paul explained it by saying the dead were asleep in Christ until the day of judgment, and the resurrection would come in stages:

> Christ the first fruits; afterward they that are Christ's at his coming. Then cometh the end, when he shall have delivered up the kingdom to God, even the Father; when he shall have put down all rule and all authority and power. For he must reign, till he hath put all enemies under his feet. The last enemy that shall be destroyed is death.

The two versions coexist still in contemporary Christianity. "The Order for the Burial of the Dead" in *The Book of Common Prayer* of the Episcopal Church begins: "I am the resurrection and the life, saith the Lord: he that believeth in me, though he were dead, yet shall he live: and whosoever liveth and believeth in me, shall never die.

"I know that my redeemer liveth, and that he shall stand at the latter day upon the earth: and though this body be destroyed, yet shall I see God; whom I shall see for myself, and mine eyes shall behold, and not as a stranger."

There was a resurrection in November 1922 near Luxor, Egypt. Archeologist Howard Carter discovered the tomb of an unknown Egyptian pharaoh. In February 1923 the sepulchral chamber was officially opened, followed a year later by the opening of the sarcophagus of Tutankhamen. The discovery yielded the only pharaoh to survive the centuries with his accompanying treasures intact. The mummy itself was ensconced in a nest of coffins. Court goldsmiths gave the king's face a weary and tragic appearance on the outer two coffins. But the exquisite innermost coffin, wrought of solid gold and shaped to the body, was graced with the face of a serenely beautiful youth who had transcended death.

The artifacts bestowed with the young monarch for his use as an immortal are a dazzling introduction to the splendor of New Kingdom

Egyptian civilization at its apogee. Superb statues, paintings, jewelry—golden daggers, a finely carved alabaster drinking cup, the glittering royal throne—priceless treasures because the craftsmanship excelled even the precious materials.

Tutankhamen died a young man, probably at the age of eighteen or twenty, in January 1343 B.C.—3,265 years before the discovery of his tomb by the Carter expedition. He ascended to the throne when he was nine or ten years old and ruled for about a decade during troubled times at the end of the magnificent 18th Dynasty. He was probably the late offspring of Amenhotep III and younger brother of Akhenaten, who ruled before him. Akhenaten, who was married to the beauteous Nefertiti, set out to reform Egyptian religion by replacing the ancient worship of a whole hierarchy of gods with one supreme God, the sun god Aten, who shone impartially on all people regardless of rank or station. Akhenaten destroyed existing idols and erased the plural word "gods." He is the first historical person associated with monotheism and there is reason to believe he exerted an important influence on the Hebrews who began their exodus from Egypt about 50 years later. Akhenaten perished mysteriously and the entrenched priests tried with equal zeal to eradicate every trace of the iconoclastic pharaoh.

Soon thereafter, the boy Tutankhaten assumed the throne of a land on the brink of revolution. Heeding his advisers, he restored the polytheistic religion and changed his name to Tutankhamen. Even so, he died in youth; we do not know the cause. At death a pharaoh was entitled to the most elaborate, meticulous preparations for immortality ever conducted by the human species.

Far back in the prelude to Egyptian civilization the concern with afterlife had led to experimentation with preserving the dead. These early people drew the knees of corpses under the chin in the fetal position, wrapped them in linen sheets or hides or mats, and buried them in shallow desert graves. The hot sand dried the bodies, preserving the soft tissues like durable old leather. What is probably mankind's first book, the hieroglyphic writings subsequently collected into *The Book of the Dead*, dates back to the start of Egyptian civilization, anywhere from 5892 B.C. to 4455 B.C. The book codifies the preparation of the person for death and immortality.

With the coming of that civilization, Egyptians began building tombs that gradually reached their climax in the middle of the third millennium B.C. with the pyramids, the most massive monuments humans ever have built. The Great Pyramid of Khufu, for Cheops, was some 750 feet square and nearly 500 feet high. It consisted of about 2.3 million stone blocks, each one averaging two and a half tons. The Greek historian Herodotus, who visited the pyramid in the fifth century B.C., said 100,000 men had worked for 30 years to complete the structure.

However, cadavers were not preserved so well when they were deposited in dank tombs instead of the hot desert. Even in the Great Pyramids few mummies survived. But preservation of the bodies was believed crucial for the immortal voyage, and centuries of trial-and-error experimentation led to the perfection of mummification by the time of the New Kingdom beginning in 1570 B.C. Tutankhamen, after death, underwent a process that took 70 days. Half that time or more was spent in dessicating the body with natron, a mixture of sodium bicarbonate and salt. Through an incision in the abdomen, all the abdominal organs except the kidneys were removed. The diaphragm was slit and the contents of the chest cavity except for the heart were withdrawn. The interior was washed with palm wine and spices, then temporarily stuffed with sand, straw, resin, rags, or dried fibers. The viscera were cleaned, dried, perfumed, preserved with hot resin, wrapped in packages, and placed in four jars for inclusion in the sepulcher.

The ancient Egyptians left the heart within the body because they believed it was not only the seat of the mind and emotions but recorder of the person's acts in life whereby he could be judged by the gods. The Egyptians believed the brain was of little importance. The bones inside the nostrils were pierced with a small chisel and a hooked wire was inserted through the nose to extract the brain matter, which was thrown away.

The cranial cavity was filled with resin or resin-soaked linen; the temporary stuffing was removed from the chest and abdomen, and they were filled with sawdust, myrrh, or onions wrapped in small linen bags; then the incision was crudely sewn closed. The body was rubbed with a mixture of cedar oil, cumin, wax, natron, gum, and possibly milk and wine, and then dusted with spices. To restore a lifelike appearance to the face, the cheeks and eye sockets were padded with linen, the eyelids closed, the nose plugged. Then the skin was coated with a thick layer of resin and the corpse carefully wrapped in linen. Such perfection was achieved in this embalming art that a corpse more than 3,000 years old still bears the stubble of a beard.

Not long after Tutankhamen's death, a military strongman, Horemheb, seized power. Horemheb set out to obliterate the name of Tutankhamen from the temples, the monuments, the archives—and the minds—of Egyptians. "To speak the name of the dead," said the ancient funerary inscriptions of Egypt, "is to make him live again." Horemheb meant to stamp out any such secular resurrection. Either the new ruler did not dare or saw no necessity to destroy the royal corpse. In time, the tomb itself was buried under that of a later pharaoh.

Horemheb did his work so well that ultimately he failed. The insignificance of Tutankhamen shielded him from the grave robbers who intercepted the legacy of every other pharaoh who has been rediscovered. We know very little of Tutankhamen despite the archeological detective work spurred by the twentieth-century discovery, but we must infer that he yearned for the immortality which was his birthright. Today, after 33 centuries of oblivion, his name is spoken and he lives again in human minds. People will continue to gaze with admiring wonder upon the golden countenance that masks the historical man. As long as civilization lasts, Tutankhamen will never die.

Undoubtedly, this is not the mode of immortality that the ancient youth had in mind. Nevertheless, social immortality is a form of survival coveted by many people today. Indeed, what person is so destitute that he does not hope to live on, after death, in the memories of friends and contemporaries! Of course, for most, the glow of memory will last for only a brief time before the person disappears in the river of history.

Human beings have found devices to circumvent such extinction. Perhaps they cannot build on the scale of the pyramids, but one can underwrite Rockefeller Center if one is a Rockefeller or endow a chair in medieval history if one's resources are more modest. A portrait by Rembrandt or Bachrach, a figure in marble, a bust in bronze preserve the impermanent body for public viewing. As for the personal essence, fame is the spur. "I have wrought a monument more enduring than bronze, and loftier than the royal accumulation of the pyramids," boasted the Roman poet Horace. "Neither corrosive rain nor raging wind can destroy it, nor the innumerable sequence of years nor the flight of time. I shall not altogether die." Neither will Judas and Hitler. Founding fathers live on through corporations, cities, states, and other immortal institutions. Indeed, civilization has been viewed as the materialization of human immortality.

With the advance of technology, the techniques of immortalization become more refined. Not only are the words of John F. Kennedy preserved on printed pages and in his own handwriting, but on phonograph records and audio tapes we can hear them as they were spoken with the original inflections along with the responses they drew. Not only is his image preserved in still photographs and on silver coins, but we can see him alive on film and with even greater verisimilitude on video tape. The body and personality of John Kennedy are resurrected for the two most important of our five senses.

Science-fiction writer Frederik Pohl envisioned carrying this electronic immortality to its ultimate realization, programming a computer with the person's experiences, education, beliefs—in sum, reproducing the person's mind before he dies. Then with voluminous tape recordings of the person's voice to serve as a selection bank, the computer could converse as if its progenitor were present. Over a telephone, a correspondent could not tell the difference between the original and the copy.

The most common immortality is the biological kind through one's children and grandchildren. With each generation, of course, a person's genetic heritage is inexorably diminished, but when we achieve cloning —replication from one cell alone—a person could reproduce replicas of himself identical to the last gene. Some people wrest a partial survival after death by donating kidneys, eyes, or other parts to living recipients. Even the follower of Democritus who believes that his body-mind dissipates in atomization after death can take comfort in knowing that the atoms are immortal and may one day help form some beautiful creature, perhaps of another species, in the reincarnation of life.

All these forms of immortality, however, suffer from a vexing deficiency: the person himself is missing. These pale substitutes for the conscious, experiencing self lack the allure of a persevering soul. But like the gods and goddesses of Mount Olympus at the advent of Athenian philosophy, the soul began to fade with the rise of science four centuries ago. The imperishable soul was excommunicated from the new method of thinking and consequently began to wither away.

This new wave of thinking was heralded by the publication in 1543 of *De revolutionibus orbium coelestium* ("On the Revolutions of the Celestial Bodies") by the Polish astronomer Mikolaj Kopernik, who took the Latinized Nicolaus Copernicus. In essence, *De revolutionibus* held that the sun was stationary and the earth and other planets revolved about the solar center. Actually, the heliocentric theory was not original with Copernicus, having been proposed by early Greek philosophers, and considered and discarded by Ptolemy, who in the second century A.D. had perfected the geocentric theory that the earth was the center of the universe. What was original with Copernicus was the arrival of an open mind, the willingness to reexamine the earlier solar concept and to subject the prevailing orthodox theory to later evidence, to prefer rational persuasion over tradition, authority, and the commonsense appearance that the sun obviously circles the earth. (Copernicus concluded that the heliocentric theory was a far simpler, and therefore more likely, explanation for the heavenly phenomena we see.)

When Galileo looked through a telescope in 1610, he *saw* that the

Ptolemaic system was incorrect. He could see the planet Venus in less than a full-face phase, and according to Ptolemy this should have been impossible. Galileo, moreover, devised the invaluable scientific tool of the controlled experiment for winnowing or isolating facts from the mixed components in all events. Here was a means of demonstrating proof (and incidentally reducing disputation and even authority to irrelevance).

The scientific attitude is apparent in René Descartes, the French philosopher-mathematician who formulated the first system of modern metaphysics. He determined to start from a point of absolute certainty and to arrive at that solid launching base by stripping away everything his intelligence could reasonably doubt. Descartes could not question his own existence or, more specifically, his mind that perceived that existence—"I think, therefore I am." Again, here is rejection of the authority of the past for what can be verified personally.

Descartes still was child enough of tradition to include an infinite God and a soul in his description of reality. But the God was necessary only to crank up the universe, while the unimportance of the soul became ever more apparent after Newton improved and synthesized Cartesian physics and Galilean mechanics. Does a perfectly functioning machine need a soul?

After the Inquisition chastised Galileo in 1633 for championing Copernican theory, scientists were content to leave the soul and afterlife in the hands of the Church. But church fathers were wrong about Copernicus, and it probably is impossible to overestimate the damage that their misguided interference in temporal matters did to Christian credibility in its own realm.

Scientists proceeded to follow the advice of Francis Bacon to advance science through its works. By the middle of the eighteenth century, the accomplishments not only seemed to justify the wildest expectations in the powers of science-and-reason, but corroded confidence in the unseen, unproved, in any matter one was asked to accept on faith alone. With the clairvoyance of genius, Blaise Pascal perceived early in the scientific revolution the irreconcilable nature of the confrontation between faith and reason. At sixteen Pascal wrote an important treatise on conic sections. At eighteen he invented a computing machine. With another man he invented the calculus of probabilities. After experiments in hydrostatics he formulated Pascal's Law, which says that pressure applied to an enclosed fluid is transmitted outward equally in all directions at right angles to the enclosing surface. At twenty-five he proved that mercury rises in a tube not because nature abhors a vacuum, the accepted explanation, but because of the weight of atmosphere. "Experiments," he said almost contemporaneously with Galileo, "are the true teachers in physics."

And then in his middle twenties Pascal renounced his blazing career in science and the bleakness of pure intellect for the comforting embrace of Christian belief. He retired to a convent, mortified his senses, and devoted the remaining days of his short life to refuting the arguments of atheists. Such was his brilliance that this effort, published posthumously as *Pensées*, won Pascal as great or greater fame in philosophy and letters than his earlier work in mathematics and physics. But this well-intentioned effort had the effect of introducing heretofore shielded beliefs in God, the soul, immortality, into the public arena where they became exposed to reason's redoubtable champion, Voltaire.

One century after Pascal's death, in 1762, Jean-Jacques Rousseau almost alone was trying to stem the rational avalanche, contending that feeling —the gut reaction—always took precedence when it came to an important decision in life. Even if reason did tend to undermine belief in God and immortality, Rousseau conceded, our feeling was overwhelmingly in their support—so why not trust our instincts in this case rather than succumb to arid skepticism?

Twenty years later, Immanuel Kant, the German philosopher who stood barely five feet tall, tried like an intellectual Atlas to hold up the crumbling immortal heaven. In his *Critique of Pure Reason*, Kant argued convincingly that science is limited to the field of actual experience, and its precepts do not reign in heaven and the hereafter. However, he had to acknowledge that religion, too, was helpless in proclaiming the nature of ultimate reality. The best that either of them could do was to fall back on hypothesis. In his follow-up *Critique of Practical Reason*, Kant contended less convincingly that the fact that each of us is imbued with a moral sense presupposes a reasonable God who grants us infinite time in which to achieve the virtue we strive after but fail to attain in this life. There should be immortality for moral reasons.

Kant's afterlife is a tenuous derivative of the vivid and specific hell and heaven of Dante's imagination, and hardly sufficient to quell the forces unleashed by the Enlightenment and triumphant in the French Revolution. In 1794 the king of France had been beheaded, the king of heaven routed, and just so members of the funeral cortège got the message as they trundled victims of the Terror into the cemeteries, Jacobin leader Joseph Fouché posted on cemetery gates the proclamation: "Death is an eternal sleep."

The immortal soul cannot be guillotined by fiat, of course, and it survived, but henceforth with a certain intellectual disreputability. Leading thinkers began to consider salvation in terms of this world. Leo Tolstoy, the incomparable Russian novelist, not satisfied with the

secular immortality he already had achieved, passionately wished to
be assured of spiritual survival. He followed the example of Pascal and
immersed himself in ritual and faith, hoping to seduce himself into
believing in his immortality. But it was historically too late for that.
He could not bring off the mental prestidigitation. Tolstoy then sought
to remove the sting of death of the ego by living what he considered
the central message of Jesus—giving up the self for others. By living a
selfless life, one infused it with meaning and frustrated death. The poet
Rilke would detoxify death's sting by making sure one does not die
with "unlived lines" in one's body. The French author Malraux believed that through art a person could negate the negation of death
and for a time at least transcend finite existence to touch the eternal.
One of the central pursuits of the existentialist philosophers has been
to find the unflinching mental fortitude to confront the nothingness of
death and the unpredictable timing of that nullity which robs life of
meaning and makes our individual lives absurd.

If science exorcised the once universal soul of our primitive ancestors,
one small tribe of scientists today is stubbornly investigating to see
whether the wraith should be reincarnated. Such a pursuit is a sign
that reality has proved to be more elusive than the mechanists cared
to believe in the heady flush of their first astonishing victories. In the
mechanistic universe, mental phenomena or psychology can be explained
in terms of biology and physiology, biological phenomena explained in
chemical terms, chemistry translated to physics, and physics reduced to
mathematics. And so we arrive at absolute certainty. But, paradox of
paradoxes, one starts with a totally materialistic world and ends with
pure abstraction. Where in this world is the gorgeous riot of flowers,
the loyalty of 50 years of marriage, the ideal of liberty, equality,
fraternity, or the dictum, Love thy enemy? How does one achieve happiness or even try to go about pursuing it? While science had assumed
the vestments of infallibility, it did not have all the answers. It developed the self-serving habit—both imperious and annoying—of picking
its shots, snubbing problems of great import with poor prospects of
solution. Sciences could, if they chose, simply ignore phenomena considered not in their purview.

Ghosts, for instance. A person who saw one of these either was
superstitious or hallucinating. But there were enough documented, unexplained psychic occurrences to make some people wonder, and try
to explain them scientifically. This study of unexplained psychic phenomena is called parapsychology, a perhaps not fully accepted and
certainly not well-manned branch of psychology. Its main claim to

validity rests on the extrasensory perception research of Joseph Rhine at Duke University. "ESP tells us that a human being is a more open system than we thought," says Dr. Karlis Osis, who studied with Rhine. Dr. Osis is director of research for the American Society for Psychical Research (ASPR) in New York City. And, ironically, it is a parapsychologist who pleads for fellow scientists to show the open-mindedness which once characterized the scientific enterprise. Psychology, he notes, "lost the soul, lost mind, lost consciousness. Now consciousness is back and so is mind."

The ASPR is trying to see if it is possible to learn anything, scientifically, about survival after death. Dr. Osis believes that there are enough clues that the personality is not completely limited to the body to justify the effort. "It would be odd," he mused, "if the ancients had read reality more accurately than we." Even if they were right, he added, their intuition "probably needs improvement, like their maps." We could find out one way or another about survival after death, he maintains, if we would put into the quest the kind of resources that took us to the moon. And think what that would mean about how we regard life and reality, he said. Instead of going to a hospital as we do now, hoping to glean a few more days of life, we would "go to get treatment for transition."

Transition. No one—neither parapsychologist, philosopher, priest, or prophet—claims that "afterward" one will ever again stuff a tumescent penis into the hot vaginal folds to experience the orgasmic transport. Severed from sense organs it is difficult to conceive of "seeing" the ineffable beauty of sunlight on leaves, sunlight glistening off water, sunlight spraying the opalescent sky from the evening horizon. Difficult to recapture the smell of apples, the wave of a friend, the aching pleasure of muscles that have won the race, the suffocating satisfaction of the deserved accolade, the invigorating rush of October air at twilight, the delicious, delirious exhilaration of tart champagne, the taste of fresh corn and lobsters and . . . .

It remained for the Spanish poet-novelist-philosopher Miguel de Unamuno, speaking with the liberated honesty of twentieth-century despair, to damn the salvation that had served humankind for so long. Unamuno's *The Tragic Sense of Life* impugns the mentality that insists on believing—since there is no better alternative—that half a loaf is better than none.

Commenting on Unamuno, the Spanish writer Arturo Barea wrote:

> Unamuno accepted the Christian teachings in the form of the Roman Catholic doctrine because they were bred into him and because he longed for faith, but these teachings could not lessen his despair and

rebellion. They could promise and guarantee him another life and the resurrection of the body, but never the continuation of his personality, of his ego. Neither a spiritual existence nor resurrected flesh would be he himself, his living self; nor would that other world be his world, that in which he was living. But he wanted, passionately, to remain himself in the flesh and in the world. Anything else would be nothing, or rather it would be something, but not he. And there was no remedy. The tragedy of Unamuno was that he had to protest against having to die and yet knew that the annihilation of his personal existence was implacably coming. His "tragic sense of life" made him equally incapable of resigning himself to his final death as an individual and of deceiving himself so that he could believe in a survival or resurrection of his individual life. No one can live without shielding his mind from this searing vision.

Unamuno finally articulates the despair and defiance that issued from the primal dread: the immortal soul is not enough!

III. Is It in an Elixir, a Fountain, a Testicle?

Alchemy is a chronicle of the search for physical immortality and a colorful tale as well of the long transition from myth and magic to science. The story begins in Alexandria in the first century A.D. Alexandria possessed a library of unprecedented wealth, including the legacy of Aristotle. The city was a crossroads and melting pot for ancient civilizations. Here the natural sciences and philosophical speculations of the Greeks met and mixed with astrology and astronomy, metallurgical skills and rites, and religious beliefs going far back into Egyptian and Babylonian civilizations—to give birth to Western alchemy.

Prehistoric men believed that minerals were formed even as living entities were: by fertilization of the male seed in the womb of mother earth. This was an ongoing process with minerals continually being made and growing. The evidence of the male and female principle in inanimate matter seemed to be confirmed by the alloying—the sexual union—of copper and tin in the matrix forge to make bronze. The miraculous property of fire [1] in the transmutation was equally obvious. Vulcan and Hephaestus were enshrined as the Roman and Greek gods of fire and metalworking. On earth, the smith was a very important person, providing weapons of conquest and defense.

Greek philosophers began to wonder: If bluish stone treated with fire becomes the red metal copper, what is the true nature of the substance? Are all materials but different forms of one basic element? Thales (ca. 640–546 B.C.) decided yes, and that the basic element is water. In the century after Thales, astronomers began to believe that the sky is not a semisphere over a flat earth but a complete (and hollow) sphere surrounding a spherical earth. This prompted the philosopher Anaximenes to conclude that air is the basic element of the universe. But Heraclitus, who lived from about 540 B.C. to 475 B.C., was convinced that flux, or change, is the basic characteristic of existence. Substances were continually changing forms and appearances. He opted for fire as

[1] Fire was a sacred symbol in the Zoroastrianism that blended with Babylonian beliefs after the Persian conquest.

the basic element. Empedocles couldn't decide who was right. He solved the problem by reasoning that all three were correct, and added a fourth element. Aristotle accepted and became instrumental in perpetuating the doctrine of the four elements—air, water, earth, and fire.[2]

Actually, Aristotle added a fifth element for the heavens—ether, from a word meaning "to glow," a characteristic of heavenly bodies. Aristotle considered ether to be incorruptible, eternal, and perfect in contrast to earthly elements. The fifth element was translated in Latin as *quinta essentia,* from which we get "quintessence."

Very early, men had divined that the sun is the ultimate source of life. From there it took no great stretch of imagination to believe that the golden radiance was the quintessence of life itself. Ra was the primordial Egyptian sun god. When gold first was discovered in Nubia, south of Egypt, about 3500 B.C., it was considered holy. Gold was a piece of the sun, God, brought down to earth, the immortal essence materialized.[3] It was not simply for appearance that Tutankhamen was encapsulated in gold. Pharaohs were sons of Ra and gold was the immortal mode. Obviously, these life-giving properties also endowed the yellow metal with great material value.

Silver, of all the metals, was second in importance only to gold, as the moon is to the sun. The Egyptian deity Horus—son of Ra, brother to the pharaohs—had one eye of gold, one of silver. And eventually, round gold and silver coins became small incarnations of the two most important spheres in the sky. In the mind and hermaphroditic world of the alchemist, gold represented the male principle and silver the female principle.

The alchemist was a Plato except that he believed the idea, the essence was a physical entity. The philosopher was transmuted into the alchemist when he became persuaded he could find truth through chemistry. But in the metamorphosis, the public man who influenced his fellows through his rational prowess turned into the clandestine, secular high priest, the initiate who jealously guarded his secrets. Hermes Trismegistus is the legendary founder of alchemy, and the term "hermetically sealed" suggests the tight preservation accorded the alchemist's arcana. Where the Greek philosopher had divested himself of religious beliefs to pursue pure ratiocination, the alchemist reabsorbed ritual and symbol and mystery. The snake that swallows its tail to form a ring is an important alchemical symbol; so is the egg with its yellow and white

[2] One can see what shrewd guesses these were, science writer Isaac Asimov points out, if one substitutes the terms "gas," "liquid," "solid," and "energy."

[3] In Babylonia, gold also was connected with the sun and with the god Enlil; silver was connected with the moon and the god Anu.

composition. Emerald has magical powers. The number 7—seven metals corresponding to seven heavenly bodies, the seven-storied mountain— and certain combinations of numbers possessed mystical significance, and so on.

The Greco-Roman alchemists of the early centuries A.D. devoted themselves to the search for the essence of all materials. Once they possessed this substance, they reasoned, they could then make any material they wanted. Particularly, they wanted to transmute lead, considered the basest of metals, into gold. One believed method to this goal was to extract the seed of gold in order to make it grow again. This elusive "genetic" substance became known as the "stone that is no stone," or the philosopher's stone.

With the Mohammedan conquest of Egypt in the seventh century, alchemy was imported into the intellectually burgeoning Arab world where the pursuit gained its final name. *Al* is the Arabic word for "the," and *kimiya* is Arabic for substance and art (the "chemy" also has been traced to Greek and Egyptian words). In Arabic, "alchemy" came to be used mainly for the art while the synonym *iksir*—or *al iksir*—referred to the substance. To Europeans the word became "elixir."

Jabir ibn-Hayyan—still conforming to the gold-silver tradition—concluded that the dry yellow powder sulfur was the male essence and the marvelous metal mercury,[4] liquid at normal temperatures, was the female essence which united to make all substances. Jabir sought the catalyst to blend sulfur and mercury into the required proportions to fabricate gold.

At the end of the eighth century, Jabir was chemist to the fabulous court of Harun al-Rashid, the caliph of *The Thousand and One Nights*. Baghdad was just blossoming into the commercial and cultural center of the new Arabian civilization that was being enlarged and enriched by Harun's military successes. Jabir gained his court position through the Barmecides, the caliph's viziers of the fabled *Arabian Nights*. Unfortunately for them, they were alien Persians who grew too powerful at the Baghdad court and soon after the turn of the ninth century, Harun had his grand vizier impaled and the other viziers banished.

We do not know what happened to Jabir after this purge, but whatever his fate he had had sufficient years and facilities to leave prolific alchemical writings and noteworthy chemical achievements. Jabir described ammonium chloride, distilled vinegar to obtain acetic acid— the strongest acid of the ancient world—and even prepared a weak nitric acid.

---

[4] The Latin word for mercury, *hydrargyrum*, translated to liquid silver, while the English "quicksilver" has the meaning living silver.

Late in the century and into the tenth century, Al-Razi concentrated on experiments to an even greater extent than his predecessor. This later alchemist not only believed that base metals could be transmuted into gold and silver, but that quartz and glass could be changed into rubies, sapphires, and other gems. However, Al-Razi's bent was toward medicine. A faithful follower of the Greco-Roman physician Galen, who lived in the second century, Al-Razi built and directed a hospital in Baghdad. His well-equipped laboratory contained beakers, retorts, crucibles, slides, steam boilers, cloth filters, hermetic caps, mortars and pestles, and other utensils. He prepared plaster of Paris and described how it was useful in making casts to hold broken bones in place.

Following Al-Razi, a century later, came Ibn-Sina, the most famous physician in all the centuries between Galen and modern times. Avicenna, as he was known to Europeans, rejected the notion of transmutation of metals because he believed it was impossible to purify the basic substance to a sufficiently high degree. Yet he did not reject the idea of an elixir, and envisioned such a substance in the context of medicine where it would have universal application. Thus grew the idea of a panacea, a cure-all . . . and an elixir of eternal youth.

During the twelfth century, the twin goals of alchemy—the search for an elixir of life and a means to transmute metals—filtered into Europe with returning crusaders and the progressive retaking of Spain from the Moors. Roger Bacon, whose life spanned most of the thirteenth century, possessed such prodigious knowledge that he set out to write a universal encyclopedia. A champion of experience and experiment as the route to knowledge, this philosopher-chemist-physicist-astronomer-mathematician was a precocious forerunner of the scientific method. Even so, Roger Bacon accepted the tenets of alchemy and believed that the lifespan of his day—usually not more than 45 or 50 years—could be trebled with alchemy's help.

Bacon reasoned that in the past persons such as Methuselah and Noah enjoyed great longevity, but this lifespan was eroded by immorality and neglect of hygiene. And so Bacon, who became a Franciscan monk in his late thirties, prescribed a morally and physically clean life. But he was inspired to hope for exceptionally long life by hearing of numerous cases where people by "secret arts" had added remarkably to their years. Bacon cited one Sicilian plowman who discovered a golden vessel hidden in a field he was furrowing. The jar contained a wonderful liquor which he drank and used to wash his face "and was renewed in mind and body beyond measure." Bacon himself, without the aid of such an elixir, managed to survive to the age of eighty.

With Theophrastus Bombastus von Hohenheim, who was born in

Switzerland the year after Columbus discovered America, the elixir-of-life branch of alchemy was approaching the doorstep of science. The name Bombastus may have been self-chosen. If so, the selection reveals a laudatory insight into his own character. The other name which he did choose for himself and by which he is known to history is Paracelsus, meaning "better than Celsus," Celsus being a Roman writer on medical matters whose works happened to be popular at the time.

Paracelsus, the son of a mining engineer, learned metallurgy as a boy and later searched for, and believed or said he had found, the chemical elixir for long life. Along the way, he learned about medicine "not only from doctors, but also from barbers, midwives, sorcerers, alchemists, in monasteries, among common people and nobles, from the wise and from the simple-minded." At thirty-three he was appointed a professor of medicine at the University of Basel and proceeded to burn the works of Galen in public. Paracelsus said he knew more than Galen and therefore didn't need his works; it was an inspired act of sacrilege for Galen's writings were revered as the Holy Bible of medicine.

Within two years Paracelsus was embroiled in what was to become a classic medical problem—the bill. He brought suit against the city council of Basel for medical fees owed him, and when he became too obstreperous in pressing his case, he was run out of town. Thereafter, he became a peripatetic physician who won a wide reputation for his remarkable cures and carousing. He died in a drunken brawl at the age of forty-eight.

While Paracelsus has been given such labels as megalomaniac, charlatan, and quack, he also pioneered the thesis that diseases have chemical bases and can be treated with chemicals. Today's arsenal of chemotherapy validates Paracelsus' contentions, while the sulfa drugs among others vindicate the alchemists' faith in the powers of sulfur.

Curiously, the search for a way to create gold seemed to take precedence over the search for an elixir of life in European alchemy. By the 1500s, kings and princes—especially in Germany—were devout patrons of alchemy. The measure of their devotion often could be correlated to their profligacy. What more practical, and satisfying, way to replenish a depleted gold supply than by making your own! By this time alchemists had learned many devices. The quantity of a given portion of gold can be increased by dilution and reduction in quality. Copper alloyed with zinc (which Paracelsus is credited with discovering) makes brass which looks like gold. In addition, certain alchemists were actually reputed to be able to make the conversion from lead to gold. Rudolph II, a Hapsburg Holy Roman Emperor of the late sixteenth century, maintained a stable of 200 alchemists, although his interest seemed to stem from intellectual catholicity as well as practical considerations. Rudolph also provided a castle for the work of the two most renowned astronomers after Copernicus, Tycho Brahe and Johannes Kepler, the latter doubling as royal astrologist. (Kepler's aunt was burned as a witch; his mother also was accused of witchcraft, but escaped the stake.)

While there was great demand for alchemists, some royal employers were exceedingly intolerant of failure. Frederick of Würzburg maintained a special gallows—painted gold—to hang his failures, alchemists who couldn't transmute. On one occasion, Frederick vented his especial pique by hanging the victim clothed in gold tinsel. The Elector of Bavaria executed alchemical pretender Marco Bragadino beneath Munich's brass gallows . . . by beheading. Woman alchemist Marie Ziglerin was burned at the stake by Duke Julius of Brunswick.

The severe penalties did not appear to daunt a long line of royal alchemists and aspiring mountebanks lured by that triumvirate so irresistible to con men—wealth, greed, and gullibility. After a long career as court alchemist and with his head still attached to his body at its normal length, a Pole named Sendivogius could not resist going before Emperor Ferdinand II and the royal court at Vienna in 1619 to fake a transmutation. To oohs and aahs in the palace hall, Sendivogius converted a half-silver, half-gold coin completely to gold. Later it was discovered that he had coated one half of a solid gold coin with a mercury amalgam which evaporated as the coin was heated. But by that time Sendivogius had moved on to a new jurisdiction.

Robert Boyle, an Irishman who decided, in the first break with Aristotle, that elements simply were irreducible kinds of matter, in 1661 dropped the first syllable of alchemy and thereafter in name and character the pursuit proceeded as the science of chemistry. At about that same time, the preeminent physical scientist Sir Isaac Newton hovered over alchemical fires for weeks on end trying to transmute lead into gold. But not even a Newton could produce this miracle at that point in history.

Dull gray lead and lustrous gold actually are quite close in structure. The nucleus of a gold atom is composed of 118 neutrons and 79 protons, the protons ordaining that 79 electrons orbit the nucleus. An atom of lead contains 126 neutrons and 82 protons girded by 82 electrons. Those three extra electrons separate lead from gold (the eight additional neutrons make lead somewhat heavier), giving lead its characteristic texture and appearance. If we remove the three electrons to reduce the total to 79, we will have transmuted lead to gold. But this electron transformation can be accomplished only by removing three protons from the nucleus and they are held in place by the most powerful glue we know—the nuclear force.

The secret of transmutation of elements lies in adding or subtracting protons from the atomic nucleus, but this requires tremendous force. A hammer blow cannot dent the shield of electrons to reach the nucleus. An alchemist's fire might break the bonds between neighboring atoms to melt lead and a hot enough flame might even dislodge one electron. But an atom stripped of one electron still is lead and the unpaired proton soon will capture a wandering electron to return to the original atomic integrity.

It took two and a half centuries of chemistry and physics and technology after Newton before Ernest Rutherford at Cavendish Laboratory in England achieved a transmutation in 1919. Dr. Rutherford bombarded nitrogen atoms (seven protons in the nucleus) with helium nuclei (two nuclear protons). The helium nuclei, moving at tremendous velocities, pierced the electromagnetic repulsion barrier in a few instances to fuse with nitrogen nuclei. The addition would have made a nucleus of nine protons, but one proton was lost in the collision, leaving eight. The eight protons attracted eight electrons, transmuting nitrogen into oxygen. In 1932 Ernest Lawrence in California succeeded in transmuting a number of elements in his newly invented cyclotron. With atomic energy in the 1940s, large-scale transmutations became almost commonplace.

The alchemist's dream could not be realized until science had attained a much more profound understanding of matter and had built far more sophisticated equipment than that possessed by the alchemists. The making of gold by nuclear fission or thermonuclear fusion would be prohibitively expensive; nevertheless our world abounds today with legions of alchemists who have learned how to make gold economically from baser metals. The auto or refrigerator manufacturer, for instance, starts with iron to make a consumer product, but his ultimate objective —like that of all businessmen—is to make money. The industrial farmer seeks to harvest a crop of greenbacks. The broadcaster perhaps has learned the consummate alchemy of making gold out of thin air.

Midas was the mythological alchemist. When the god Dionysus granted his wish that everything he touched would turn to gold, King Midas had to plead to be saved from his alchemical omnipotence in order to avoid starving to death. He learned that gold is not the universal value and to act literally upon that presumption leads to death.

As though alchemy were a predictable stage in intellectual evolution, it appeared independently in China, at least as early as 200 B.C.

Again, the same fascination with gold and with mercury, the liquid metal. The Chinese quintessential substance was cinnabar, the blood-red powder vermillion pigment which neolithic Chinese people buried with their dead. Cinnabar is mercury sulfide, a compound of the two male-female essences of Western alchemy.

The Chinese alchemist believed that through refining he could extract a supercinnabar and from that elixir make a superior gold. But this supergold was not an end in itself. It was a means to achieve something the Chinese alchemist considered more important: immortality.

What is believed to be the first passage written anywhere to refer to alchemy is found in the works of a first-century B.C. Chinese historian quoting the advice given to a Han emperor who lived from 156 B.C. to 87 B.C.:

> If you make sacrifice to the furnace, you will be able to transmute cinna-
> bar into gold. When the gold shall have been produced, you may make
> of it utensils for eating and drinking. Through using them your life will
> be prolonged, so that you may see the blessed immortals of the islands
> of P'eng Lai, which lies in the midst of the ocean. When you shall have
> seen them, and shall have made proper sacrifices to high heaven and
> broad earth—then you will never die.

Chinese alchemy grew from the roots of Taoism, the ancient Chinese folk religion that gained cohesiveness between 350 B.C. and 250 B.C. through several important writings on the precepts of the legendary Lao Tzu. Taoism's emphasis of magic and shamanism was a fertile environment not only for alchemy but for what evolved into a broad-scale regimen to attain immortality. These practices included, in addition to the search for the golden potion, a variety of physical disciplines. In part, at least, these techniques depended on the belief that through mastery of prolongevity techniques one could become a *hsien*—a saint-angel-sage who is immortal. When the *hsien* died, what the survivors saw in the dead body was something akin to the dead insect's husk, while the person himself had passed on to life everlasting. Through his arduous preparation, the *hsien* was believed to have perfected his embryonic self which survived forever. And so the physical techniques were based on this concept of going back to the womb, making of oneself the alchemical egg.

One important way to go about this was to strive for a reduction in breathing (since the embryo gets all the gases it needs without any respiration). In order to draw increased sustenance from the air, the Taoist adept learned to hold his breath for a great length of time, to guide the breath to inaccessible parts of the body, and, third, as the breath was about to be expired, to catch it in the throat and swallow it. This was known as "embryonic respiration" because it was deemed similar to what transpires *in utero*. The adept sought this so-called "nourishment by breath" in order to gain the perfect bodily harmony Lao Tzu attributed to the newborn.

To develop his powers of breath retention, the adept began by practicing holding his breath for a period of time equal to three, five, seven, and nine normal respirations. When he could hold his breath for a period equivalent to 12 respirations, he had completed a "small series." From there, he had to learn to add one small series to another until he had not breathed for 120 normal respirations, a "large series." At this point, it was believed, the adept was beginning to produce beneficial effects on his health. By this time, the adept's hands and feet tingled, the face became flushed, and he or she experienced a delightful intoxication. Taoists regarded this rarefied state as a rewarding stage in their pilgrimage to *hsien*hood. Pilots flying at high altitude have been taught to recognize this euphoria as the sweet prelude to death by anoxia unless the oxygen supply is restored quickly.

The Taoist seeking to become a *hsien* was exhorted to carry on his daily exercises until he could stop breathing for at least two large series. If he could hold his breath for 1,000 respirations, he would become immortal.

Gerald Gruman in *A History of Ideas about the Prolongation of Life* points out that this method of counting normal breaths is conducive to error—even the objective observer might become more excited the longer the adept held his breath and thus accelerate his own breath count. Gruman writes:

> Modern experiments show that, after training, certain persons can hold their breath as long as four and a third minutes; if we figure twenty respirations per minute, the upper limit of relaxed respiration, then this would amount to about eighty-seven respirations. The necessary training methods involve strengthening the will and building up the lung's capacity to hold air (and consequently oxygen); also helpful is preliminary "overbreathing" to decrease the amount of carbon dioxide in the body. All of these factors could have been utilized by the adepts. In addition, it should be kept in mind that the adepts were subsisting on a near-starvation diet and were practicing an almost trancelike quietism. Therefore, the body metabolism of the adept would be quite low, and, his use of oxygen being low, he might be able to maintain consciousness for five or six minutes (120 respirations).

As indicated in the passage, the aspiring *hsien* observed a stringent diet. Grains, meat, wine, and many vegetables were prohibited. As much as possible, the would-be immortalist tried to subsist on roots, berries, and other fruit. Ideally, he sought to live on air and saliva with the object of avoiding bodily excrements, the signs of impurity and mortality. "It is not surprising," says historian Gruman, "that the accomplishment of such a regimen demands the frequent use of medicines." Among these were old Chinese tonics prepared from cinnamon, licorice, ginseng, or sesame among others.

While abstemious in diet, Taoists strongly opposed sexual abstention as unnatural and unhealthy. This posed a dilemma for the Taoist adept who believed the way to immortality depended upon preservation of his *ching* or essence or sperm. *Ching* was identified with semen in the male and menstrual fluid in the female, perhaps because these substances were reduced by illness and disappeared in the aged. Furthermore, the Taoist believed that this essence of vitality could rejuvenate brain tissues. How the Taoist initiates solved this problem of having their women and keeping their semen led to some accusations of sexual gluttony.

The main technique was to employ *coitus reservatus:* the adept brought his partner to orgasm while stopping short of climax himself. The reasoning here was that in normal intercourse the penis is inserted strong and taken out weak. Enter a giant, come out a dwarf, and something is lost in the process. That something was *ching.* Now if the procedure were reversed, if the penis could be introduced as humble as possible and then withdrawn robust and proud, the apprentice *hsien* must be the beneficiary of more *ching.* Furthermore, this theory held that the partner's bodily emanations during orgasm also enhanced the adept's *ching.* Since male and female adepts were likely to stalemate, so to speak, in this *ching*-building encounter, they were considered unsuitable as sexual partners and assistance was sought from people not practicing to become immortals.

If one were serious about building up *ching,* he or she had to qualify as a marathon performer (and the fourth Taoist physiological technique, gymnastics, was designed to help in this assignment). Henri Maspero quotes the ideal: "He who is able to have coitus tens of times in a single day and night without allowing his essence to escape will be cured of all maladies and will have his longevity extended. If he changes his woman several times, the advantage is greater; if in one night he changes his partner ten times, that is supremely excellent." It was recommended that these partners be between fourteen and nineteen years old. A woman over thirty was to be avoided and one over forty was ineligible, as were women with hairy legs, cool bodies, thick skins, certain body odors, and masculine voices.

Now it was recognized that even a saint-in-training could not carry on this regimen without relief. But even when the adept permitted himself orgasm, he blocked ejaculation. As the *ching* "is about to be discharged, one quickly grasps with the two middle fingers of the left hand (the urethra) between the scrotum and the anus, one squeezes tightly while expelling from the mouth a long breath, at the same time grinding the teeth several tens of times." This action diverted the semen to the bladder from which it was excreted with the urine. The Taoist aspirant believed that in preserving his *ching* in this way he was distilling an interior cinnabar that eventually would enrich his brain. To facilitate this *ching*-to-brain flow, the Taoist adept also practiced hanging upside down.

The organized Taoist church sprang into existence toward the second half of the second century A.D., and in the first flush of religious fervor the believers interpreted literally Lao Tzu's advocacy of uniting the *yin* and *yang*, the female principle and the male principle. At the time of each full moon and each new moon, the Taoist church members assembled for group sexual relations (unmarried girls were exempted). At first, the Taoist priests tried to lead all the faithful to the state of immortality. Each church member was required to perform some supposed life-lengthening techniques and, says historian Gruman, "the Taoist religion assumed the aspect of a gigantic health cult. In time, however, a gap began to open between those who were able to devote only a small part of their time to such practices and those able to follow them wholeheartedly." After A.D. 600 Taoism began to decline over the centuries and the pursuit of immortality was confined to monasteries with their cult of esoteric priests. Taoism today is moribund.

The Taoist discipline offered the dietary, hygienic, and physical-culture rationale for humankind's first systematic attempt to achieve longevity and immortality. It was not the last time that people would identify their own chance for personal immortality with the carriers of species survival—the genetic germ cells. Actually, the reputation of semen as a rejuvenator predates the Taoists. Australian aborigines administer a potion of semen to dying or feeble members of their society. Havelock Ellis summarized the subject of semen as a rejuvenator in *Studies in the Psychology of Sex*.

The practice of gerocomy is based on the belief that one can extend life and youth through sexual diligence, but its rationale differs from conservation of *ching*. Gerocomy maintains that a man absorbs youth through close contact with a maiden. The eleventh-century Kapalika sect in India seemed to have enjoyed long life while striving for that goal through a series of sexual rites. One of these Chandella kings accepted a gift of maidens "because he wanted to live long." King David, when he was old, was given a fair damsel to lie with him. She "cherished the king, and ministered to him: but the king knew her not."

Roger Bacon, the prescientist-philosopher-alchemist, also recommended the rejuvenating breath of a young virgin, but the Franciscan monk cautioned against any accompanying licentiousness. Take it neat, he advised, and in this prescription he was reasoning by analogy: If disease is contagious, why not vitality? Many aged men and some old women, too, favor this December-May method of rejuvenation to improve the quality of their final years. They may add to the quantity as well, for experiments have shown that aging male rats perked up and survived longer than expected if a young female was put into their cage.

Dreams of gold not only motivated alchemists and their patrons, but explorers and *their* patrons, who happened to be the most powerful rulers of Europe. Two soldiers of fortune actually found conventional treasure. Cortez struck Aztec gold and Pizarro exploited the Inca bonanza. (Afterward, 500 mines in New Spain returned more than $2 billion in gold and silver to the mother country. Interestingly, mercury also was greatly sought after, because it was needed to extract silver.) The quest for golden El Dorado lured such hardy Spanish adventurers as Balboa, Coronado, De Soto, and Ponce de Leon. For their troubles, Balboa discovered the Pacific Ocean, Coronado what is now southwestern United States, and De Soto the Mississippi River. Ponce de Leon is remembered not so much for what he found but for what else he sought.

Soon after the turn of the sixteenth century—ten years after Columbus' discovery—Ponce de Leon was a leader in suppressing Caribbean natives and consolidating Spain's beachhead in the New World. During the course of these activities, he heard stories of gold on the island now known as Puerto Rico. In 1508 Ponce de Leon landed on Puerto Rico with royal permission to explore and colonize it. However, the following year, through some middle-echelon manipulations, jurisdiction of Puerto Rico was shifted to another Spaniard. Ponce de Leon fought for his island, both legally and militarily, but after two years lost out and was advised to pick another location to call his own.

By this time he had heard Indian stories of a fountain whose waters refreshed the weary and rejuvenated the aged. This wonderful fountain of youth apparently was placed on the island of Bimini in the Bahamas. On March 3, 1512 Ponce de Leon led a privately outfitted expedition from San German, Puerto Rico, in search of Bimini. He was now a seeker, in his own way, of both of alchemy's goals. By 1514 reports of the miraculous fountain were circulating back at the Spanish court and one correspondent was relaying these reports to the Pope with recommendations that they must be taken seriously.

Like the distant island of the immortals in Chinese legend, the fountain of youth is another immortalist theme of great antiquity. In the West it is traced back to the second chapter of Genesis, which mentions a river flowing out of Eden, and Psalm 36, which refers to a "fountain of life." In Greek mythology Zeus' wife, Hera, bathed each year in a spring which renewed her maidenhood. Hopes that there really might be such waters of rejuvenation revived with the Renaissance. Ponce de Leon's credulity and the inflation of his reputation during the remainder of the sixteenth century simply reflected the hopes and aspirations of the times (three centuries later a far more sophisticated set of human beings "took the waters" at the famous spas of Europe and the United States for what ailed them, including the ennui of age).

Ponce de Leon never did find the fountain of youth, of course, but in his search he discovered Florida where the aged still go hoping to regain their vigor. For himself, the legendary seeker of eternal life found death. Returning to Florida in a later expedition, the Spanish party was resisted by hostile Indians and Ponce de Leon suffered an arrow wound which proved fatal. He lived sixty-one years.

Luigi Cornaro, who was forty-four years old at the time of Ponce de Leon's death, was to exert a more prolonged influence upon European thought even though his objective was less ambitious and less dramatic than reversing the life process to restore youth. Cornaro merely wanted to live a long and happy life. At the age of eighty-three, he believed he had lived the formula and in 1550 sat down to write one of the first "how to" books, *Discourse on the Sober Life*. Buoyed by success, he added a second *Discourse* at the age of eighty-six, a third at ninety-one, and a fourth when was ninety-five years old.

The *Discourse* describes how he overcame a sickly childhood to attain longevity. One of the requisites, Cornaro maintains, is the proper attitude. One must enjoy life and old age if one is to survive. He comments that he wrote a comedy during his eighty-third year, an age when other writers deliver tragedies. After discussing his beautiful home and the lovely countryside around his native Padua, he goes on, "In the spring and autumn, I also visit the neighboring towns, to see and converse with my friends, through whom I make the acquaintance of other distinguished men, architects, painters, sculptors, musicians, and cultivators of the soil. I see new things they have done, I look again at what I know already, and learn much that is of use to me. I see palaces, gardens, antiquities, public grounds, churches, and fortifications. But what most of all delights me when I travel, is the beauty of the country and the places, lying now on the plain, now on the slopes of the hills, or on the banks of rivers and streams, surrounded by gardens and villas."

This intuition of the intimate relationship of a person's well-being and his environment was not limited to esthetic considerations. The Paduan countryside was rank with "the marshes and foul air once made fitter for snakes than for me. It was I who drained the country; then the air became good, and people settled there and multiplied, and the land became cultivated as it now is, so that I can truly say: 'On this spot I gave to God an altar and a temple, and souls to worship Him.'"

Continuing about what delights him in his old age, Cornaro writes, "And these enjoyments are not diminished through weakness of the eyes or ears; all my senses (thank God!) are in the best condition, including the sense of taste; for I enjoy more the simple food which I now take in moderation, than all the delicacies which I ate in my years of disorder."

Cornaro's key to health and longevity was temperance, particularly in diet. As one grew older, it was necessary to reduce the volume of food eaten. Not only the volume, but the kind: he ate only what agreed with his digestion. He cut back to small portions of bread, meat, broth with egg, and new wine. He also advised moderation in other things, guarding against too much heat or cold, fatigue, melancholy, and hatred. A person can have no better medicine than the temperate life, Cornaro said, and "no better doctor than himself."

The fountain of youth, the alchemist's elixir, the Taoist's apprenticeship were founded on primitive beliefs. With Cornaro, there is a transition. It is true that the Taoists chose a regimen of hygiene, and that Cornaro talked about preserving the body's "inner moisture." But in this philosopher of the practical, as historian Jacob Burckhardt called him, the fresh winds of the Renaissance are evident. There is a willingness to forgo the fantastic and to strive for what is realizable. There can be no greater tribute to Cornaro's rationale than to note that he lived to the age of ninety-eight and then, one biographer said, "died a very easy Death."

This exemplary, and long, life influenced the thinking of succeeding generations of Europeans, possibly because of the felicitous writing and possibly because people of those times did not have a clear notion of the limits to longevity. The famous Thomas Parr was reputed to have lived to 152 years and nine months, an age attested to at the autopsy by no less an authority than William Harvey, the medical scientist who first discovered the circulation of blood. A certain Henry Jenkins was believed to have reached the age of 169 years. Cornaro said that with proper living he saw no reason why the average person could not fulfill the natural human span which he set at 120 years.

With the dawning of the age of reason and the new concept of progress, men returned to their earlier, more expansive expectations, basing their hopes this time on science. The protean René Descartes dissected bodies, theorized on pathology, and wrote an important treatise on human physiology. These pursuits, apparently, were not simply the pastimes of an inquiring mind. Descartes knew he was in a race with time—his own allotted time—because so much remained to be discovered, and in his famous *Discourse on the Method* he prophesied: "we could free ourselves from an infinity of maladies of body as well as of mind, and perhaps, also even from the debility of age, if we had sufficiently ample knowledge of their causes, and of all the remedies provided for us by nature." Descartes could not quite bring himself to hope for physical immortality, but there were Methuselah and those other biblical Patriarchs affirming that a millennium was possible.

Descartes' faith in the enhanced chances of his own preservation were based on what he himself had contributed to the rational method and on his concept of the body as a machine. A biographer said that Descartes spoke so hopefully of extending his life that Queen Christina of Sweden got the impression that he sought to live forever. This influence gained strength, ironically, during the last months of the philosopher's life. Descartes died at the age of fifty-four. In fairness to this intellectual colossus who stood with one leg in the past and the other in the future, he said that as an alternative to prolonging life "I have found another, much easier and more certain, that of losing the fear of death."

Sir Francis Bacon, the father of modern science, had the same unbounded confidence in the future. Enough of this endless *talk*, Bacon counseled scientific philosophers. It is time for science to prove itself by its works. Nobody will take its word for anything until it does. Practical results are the only way to demonstrate truth. If knowledge is ever to become something more than mere ego-building ostentation, it must be made the means to improve the human condition. Once this course is adopted and given a few centuries of time, Bacon prophesied, who can predict what incredible bounty science will procure for humanity! The last three and a half centuries have served as demonstration that Bacon was the prophet supreme for our age.

But his envisioned task of improving the human lot was no undertaking for laggards or loners or inveterate speculators. It was a cooperative, corporate human enterprise to be conducted with unceasing
diligence. Nature was far more subtle and complex than people imagined, he said. What was needed was to amass a great inventory of
knowledge and to acquire that knowledge through the inductive method
—through specific experiments and firsthand observations of reality.
And this is where human knowledge can become human power. The
person who discovers the cause is master of the effect. When men learn
nature's hidden laws so that they can be turned to human purposes,
then knowledge is truly power. Punch the right buttons and nature's
cash register will open every time.

Where Cornaro avoided physicians, Bacon wrote out a prescription
for them. "Our physicians are like bishops," he said, "that have the keys
of binding and loosing, but no more." They tended to treat all ailments
with one remedy, usually physic. What they needed to do was to experiment more, collect and coordinate the results of research, learn more
about anatomy through dissection and if necessary vivisection. And
then Bacon introduced a new purpose into medicine. The doctor not
only was healer, fighter against disease, minister to the suffering, easer
of pain; he must now learn to be a prolonger of life. "This is a new
part . . . the most noble of all; for if it may be supplied, medicine
will not then be wholly versed in sordid cures, nor physicians be honored
only for necessity, but as dispensers of the greatest earthly happiness
that could well be conferred on mortals."

The beauty of Bacon's scientific method, its irresistibility, its *obvious-
ness* stood out in bolder relief with each new scientific achievement.
Progress *was* inevitable. There was no alternative, even if one contented
oneself with the slowest accretion and application of knowledge. At the
end of this road had to be utopia. Even such a wise, practical, scientific
man as Benjamin Franklin could write to the English chemist Joseph
Priestley that the time would come when "all diseases may by sure
means be prevented or cured, not excepting that of old age, and our
lives lengthened at pleasure even beyond the antediluvian standard."

If a Franklin could envision a lifespan in excess of a millennium, a
Marquis de Condorcet could offer in his *Progress:* "Would it be absurd
then to suppose that this perfection of the human species might be
capable of indefinite progress; that the day will come when death will
be due only to extraordinary accidents or to the decay of the vital forces,
and that ultimately, the average span between birth and decay will have
no assignable value? Certainly man will not become immortal, but will

not the interval between the first breath that he draws and the time when in the natural course of events, without disease or accident, he expires, increase indefinitely?" [5]

"In a word," asked the English philosopher William Godwin, "why may not man be one day immortal?"

This dizzying flight of reason was too much for Thomas Malthus, who fired off his famous *Essay on the Principle of Population*. There is no question as to the targets. The essay is subtitled: *On the Speculations of Mr. Godwin, M. Condorcet, and Other Writers.* Populations, Malthus wrote, are curtailed and contained by natural restraints. In the case of the human population, the mass executioners are disease, famine, and war (three of the principal regulators of animal populations in nature are disease, starvation, and predation). Even as Malthus issued the essay in 1798, Napoleon was starting out to make his contribution to population balance. The world wars and hydrogen bombs of the twentieth century were reminders of the Malthusian paradigm. But with successful management of infectious disease and the food supply, some people began to question the validity of Malthus' argument, only to realize that when traditional restraints are removed, population growth is thus decontrolled, posing the predicament of overpopulation with its own restraints. One way or another, the Malthusian view of reality dominated the main currents of thought and Mr. Godwin and M. Condorcet were demoted to historical foils.

Besides, the millennium never came.

On June 1, 1889 the respectable members of the Société de Biologie gathered in Paris to hear a lecture by Charles Edouard Brown-Séquard, one of the leading physiologists in the world. Brown-Séquard was something of a maverick among scientists. Even his origins were unusual. He was born on the British island of Mauritius to a French mother and an Irish-American sea captain father. Brown-Séquard apparently inherited his father's love for roving, moving through an extraordinary series of positions in the United States, England, and France; all were prestigious, including teaching at Harvard University, physician at the

[5] It is another one of those ironies of history that Condorcet, a brilliant mathematician and precocious humanitarian, wrote his *Sketch for a Historical Picture of the Progress of the Human Mind* envisioning a classless society and the intellectual and moral, as well as this wildly optimistic passage on the physical, perfection of individuals close to the termination of his life. As a Girondist deputy expelled from the National Convention and proscribed by the Jacobins, Condorcet wrote his most famous work while in hiding. In April 1794 Condorcet left his sanctuary, was imprisoned, and was found dead in his cell. He was fifty years old.

National Hospital for the Paralysed and Epileptic in London, professor of comparative and experimental pathology at the Faculty of Medicine in Paris. This career of change included three wives, the last one a young woman won in the autumn of his life.

Brown-Séquard settled down in 1878 when he was selected for the chair of experimental medicine at the College de France held by Claude Bernard, a difficult act to follow. Bernard had won such esteem for his neurological and physiological studies that he was the first scientist in France to be honored with a public funeral at Notre Dame Cathedral. Brown-Séquard's research—he published some 500 scientific papers during his peregrinations—included areas that had interested Bernard: internal secretions and the glands that produce them. Today we know they are hormones and the endocrine system, but Bernard and Brown-Séquard were just pioneering in the largely unknown territory.

On this June day, Brown-Séquard was seventy-two years old and feeling elated with his fitness. For the past several years he had been conducting dynamometer tests on himself to observe experimentally the onset of age. As he approached his seventieth birthday and during the succeeding years, he was able to record and measure muscular decline. He also suffered from fibrositis, fatigue, and sleeplessness—all of which apparently conspired to reduce his performance as a husband. During the spring of 1889, the aging physiologist began experimenting with extracts from various endocrine glands, an apparent continuation of work begun 20 years earlier.

The imposing, six-foot four-inch scientist had a reputation for dramatic presentation. In unscheduled introductory remarks, Brown-Séquard described for his colleagues the lassitude and physical impotence that had overtaken him. Then on May 15, just two and a half weeks earlier, he had cut the testicle of a young dog into small pieces, mashed the pieces with water, filtered the juice, and injected the extract into his leg. He repeated the process using a guinea pig testes, then administered still a third injection.

The transformation was remarkable, he told the assembled biologists. He had measured the muscular improvement on the dynamometer. Not only that, but he felt like a young man again, as though 30 years had been taken off his age. Then the *pièce de résistance*. In the past few hours he had faced the moment of truth. Whether Brown-Séquard spoke as detached scientist, as bravura performer, or as a triumphant man, his next revelation stamped the event indelibly. "Today I was able to 'pay a visit' to my young wife."

One can only speculate on the emotions with which this news was received by the Société members, many of whom were septuagenarians and octogenarians. A Paris newspaper, *Le Matin,* began a subscription fund for an Institute of Rejuvenation to administer the *Méthode Séquardienne.* In the service of aging Frenchmen, Brown-Séquard constructed "a fantastic Rube Goldberg type of machine with a belt pulley, tubes, alembic, aeration bladders, instrument dials: into it he fed bull testes, pulped, filtered through sand, ascepticized with boric acid, drawn off as a liquor. . . ."

If Brown-Séquard won popular success, he suffered professional disaster. A German medical publication hooted: "His fantastic experiments . . . must be regarded as senile aberrations." Its Vienna counterpart clucked: "The lecture must be seen as further proof of the necessity of retiring professors who have attained their threescore and ten years." One of today's leading gerontologists, Alex Comfort, points out that Brown-Séquard committed several unscientific *faux pas:* "This was a strictly scientific experiment—which makes it all the more interesting to notice in it the conspiracy, as it were, of all the old gerontological divinities: sexual rejuvenation, sympathetic magic (testicles are an old medicine for restoring virility), and, chief villain of the piece, subjective assessment of youth."

Brown-Séquard left Paris, and with one exception published no further scientific papers. His young wife deserted him. Slightly less than five years after his famous lecture he died from a stroke.

Subsequent researchers were unable to duplicate Brown-Séquard's rejuvenatory results. Possibly he experienced the placebo effect: it has been observed that some subjects will undergo an expected reaction even when given an innocuous substance, such influence does the mind have over the body. In his enthusiasm, Brown-Séquard overlooked Bacon's warning that nature is far more complicated than it appears and that any such simple solution—particularly in the area of aging which possibly is the most complex problem men have tried to understand—quite likely springs from that old human trait of wishful thinking.

With all the sensationalism and personal tragedy that went with Brown-Séquard's work, many historians have seen in it the launching of the science of endocrinology. And gerontologist Comfort says: "We can give a date to the beginning of truly experimental gerontology. It could be said to have been launched by a public lecture. On June 1, 1889 . . . ." After Brown-Séquard, the search for rejuvenation quickened.

In 1890 the Viennese physiologist Eugen Steinach began a series of experiments which he recounted 30 years later in his book *Rejuvenation through the Experimental Revitalization of the Aging Puberty Gland.* Steinach believed he could stimulate the hormone-producing part of the testicles by removing the sperm-producing part. He believed he could accomplish this by the sterilization technique practiced today—severing the vas deferens, the tube through which the sperm moves to the seminal vesicles to await ejaculation. Steinach reasoned that with no place for the sperm to go, the sperm-producing cells would degenerate to be replaced by testosterone-producing cells. The "Steinach rejuvenation operation" was a surgical fad until the 1930s when doubts of its efficacy led to its discontinuation.

Serge Voronoff, a cosmopolitan Russian émigré to France, became a rejuvenation specialist based on observations as physician-surgeon to the Khedive of Egypt, Abbas II, before World War I. Voronoff found that a disproportionate amount of his time went to treating eunuchs who guarded the king's harem. To Voronoff, these castrated men seemed to age more quickly than normal (a judgment that has been substantiated) and therefore were more subject to the degenerative diseases of senescence. Voronoff concluded that the absence of testicular hormones was responsible for the decline and began experimenting with animals—making gonad grafts from young to old individuals.

By 1920 he was sufficiently encouraged by his results to turn to the human species. Where Brown-Séquard had gone wrong, Voronoff theorized, was using extracts from alien species. His method was intra-species grafting, and so he began seeking human donors. French law forbade the use of cadavers. The attempt to use jailed criminals proved to be too complicated. He advertised for volunteers, assuring them they would not be hurting their own capabilities. Two men volunteered and their price was too steep for Dr. Voronoff.

Pragmatically, Voronoff settled for next best, anthropoid testicles. Such was the demand for this form of rejuvenation that hunters began looting the forests of French Equatorial Africa for chimpanzees and other anthropoids, shipping the live animals to Voronoff's villa-clinic on the Italian Riviera. Britain and Belgium, too, gave permission for the taking of anthropoids from their African territories to satisfy Voronoff's wealthy clientele (at least $5,000 a graft). Voronoff earned perhaps more than $10 million in his career—a figure matched by one John Romulus Brinkley who "operated" in rural areas of the United States and favored billy-goat testicles.

Brinkley was a barely disguised charlatan [6] whereas Voronoff believed he was contributing to science and human welfare. A conference of 1,000 surgeons in Austria in January 1928 agreed that "the gland transplantation operation devised by Dr. Serge Voronoff afforded transient regeneration." The jacket on his book, *The Sources of Life* published in 1943,

---

[6] Brinkley's persuasive powers may be gauged by the fact that he ran for governor of Kansas three times and once narrowly missed being elected.

reads: "I have responded to the needs of the world. I have opened a new prospect, which other scientists will increasingly extend and improve, present methods being perfected in proportion to the measure in which science shall continue to enrich human knowledge and modes of action." A few years later he died at the age of eighty-five in virtual disgrace and in sadness. The presumptive leader had looked behind him. No one was following in his footsteps.

The list of "youth doctors" is a long one. Paul Niehans, whose cellular therapy consisted of injections of cells scraped from the still-warm flesh of unborn lambs and whose patients included such long-lived persons as Pope Pius XII, Bernard Baruch, and Somerset Maugham. Dr. Ana Aslan of Romania with her procaine, or Novocain, injections. And perhaps most interesting of all, Elie Metchnikoff. Certainly he was the most distinguished, having won a Nobel Prize in 1908 for his work in immunity. Bacteriologist Metchnikoff, also a Russian who immigrated to France, had published his original findings as early as 1883. He conceived of the key immunological principle while engaged in marine biology research on the shores of the Mediterranean Sea.

"One day," he later wrote, "I remained alone with my microscope, observing the life of the mobile cells of a transparent starfish larva, when a new thought suddenly flashed across my brain. It struck me that similar cells might serve in the defense of the organism against intruders. . . . I said to myself, if my supposition is true, a splinter introduced into the body of a starfish larva, devoid of blood vessels or of a nervous system, should soon be surrounded by mobile cells . . . ."

Metchnikoff carried out the experiment immediately to find his hypothesis verified. And this introduced the concept of a body's defense against disease by an army of mobile cells—phagocytes, white blood cells —that devoured invaders. Such a revolutionary concept did not win ready acceptance. The great Robert Koch, for instance, opposed it. Metchnikoff was embroiled in lengthy, disagreeable conflict before Pasteur, then Lister, and finally the scientific world acknowledged that he was right. The sensitive Metchnikoff came away from the experience with the conviction that a scientist must persevere with his own ideas regardless of the opposition.

Metchnikoff's research led him to believe that the large intestine in the human being was the repository for poisons that passed through blood circulation eventually to debilitate the body, leading to aging and death. This theory was consistent with a belief he already held that aging was due to cell weakness or abnormality. He also noted that marine organisms without or with a simple digestive system had extremely long lifespans. Birds also have simple bowels that retain food products for minimal periods. Small birds like canaries can live up to 20 years in captivity, while the swan or goose lives to be 70 or 80 years.

The object, therefore, was to devise a bowel detoxification program in order to maintain youth and promote longevity. By the age of fifty-three and perceiving himself in failing health, Metchnikoff began applying his theories to himself. In large part his therapy consisted in eating no uncooked food along with great quantities of soured milk; later he emphasized yogurt, a specialty of the Balkans. Metchnikoff said that Bulgarian peasants were noted for their long lives and he believed that lactic acid produced by yogurt created an inhospitable environment for the toxin-producing bacteria in the large intestine.

The eminent scientist working at the Pasteur Institute in Paris became so encouraged by the improvement in his health and so confident in the youth-giving qualities of soured milk that he joined in a (nonprofit to him) scheme to manufacture the product. The factory advertised itself as the "sole provider of Professor Metchnikoff." This led to vociferous criticism in the press.

After 18 years of providing his large intestine with liberal numbers of lactic acid bacilli, Metchnikoff was as confident as ever in his regimen, but feared he was losing the relentless battle of intestinal poisoning. He died in 1916 at the age of seventy-one from congestive heart failure.

But by this time, the seeds of his belief had found fertile ground with surgeons. Sir Arbuthnot Lane, one of London's foremost surgeons, diagnosed a chronic form of poisoning which he attributed to intestinal stasis. The cure for "Lane's Disease" was removal of a section of the large intestine. Then, there was the auto-intoxication theory of disease and premature aging which required the same surgical remedy. By the 1930s this practice was fading into disuse although as late as 1936 a Montreal surgeon, Sir Henry Gray, was reported still pleased with what he called "abdominal spring cleaning."

Today only the popularity of yogurt has survived.

One other Russian—Alexander Bogomolets—is worthy of mention. In the 1930s and 1940s he experimented with a cytotoxic serum made from cells of connective tissue. His ACS serum was credited with accelerating the healing of wounds and fractures, but his hopes that it also ameliorated the ravages of aging were never substantiated.

As a result of these five or six decades of honest but ineffectual conviction and experimentation, and sometimes more shoddy practices, rejuvenation became the dirtiest word in the medical lexicon. Still, says gerontologist Alex Comfort, "It ill becomes us, with hindsight, to jeer at these pioneers." At least they were trying to do something about aging, he says, while most of their colleagues were singing its praises. But, Dr. Comfort states flatly, "the methods advocated by these experimenters have persisted only as medical history; they did not prolong the lives of their patients." Another leading gerontologist, Bernard Strehler, agrees that procaine, royal jelly, and other substances cannot be accepted as prolongevous ingredients. Neither, says Dr. Strehler, can they be ruled out. A trouble with all these therapies is that none of them was conducted with the rigorous scientific exactitude necessary to yield any definitive conclusion.

AN INVITATION TO HELP ATTAIN PHYSICAL IMMORTALITY

We invite you to join the Cryonics Society of New York. As a member of the first and largest Cryonics Society in the world you will have a unique opportunity to work for the attainment of the most profound objective imaginable—the indefinite extension of *your* life. Cryonics challenges the assumption that senescence and death are the inevitable consequences of life.

The Cryonics Society of New York (CSNY) is a non-profit, tax exempt organization dedicated to the extension of human life under increasingly better conditions. Our ultimate goal is the attainment of biological immortality—a life of youthful vigor untempered by physical limitations.

Several Cryonics Society groups were formed in the United States and France following a book written in 1964 by Robert Ettinger, *The Prospect of Immortality*. Dr. Ettinger, a physicist, proposed that corpses be preserved indefinitely through freezing. The prospect of immortality lies in the hope that the cadaver can be brought back to life. Such a resurrection is based on the presumption that medical and other sciences will advance to the point where they can cure or rectify whatever dispatched the person in the first place and thaw the body without "killing" it in the process. The hope also rests on the supposition that the freezing techniques do not inflict some "fatal" injury. The Cryonics Society of New York says, "At present, it is necessary to use unperfected freezing techniques after the patient has been pronounced 'dead' by a physician."

At the moment, the hopes and assumptions are untested and unproved. While at least 15 bodies are being preserved through cryonic suspension, there has been no attempt at reanimation (there has been very little elapsed time for the anticipated medical improvement: the first body was frozen in 1967). These bodies are being kept in what amount to oversize thermos bottles in which liquid nitrogen maintains a temperature of –320 degrees Fahrenheit. Blood is removed from the bodies and they have been perfused with dimethyl sulfoxide, which is intended to avert cell damage.

The new science of cryobiology—the study of life (and death) at low temperatures—already has achieved noteworthy accomplishments, freezing and successfully thawing both human blood and sperm. But when one extends this performance to the entire human being, one meets a complexity barrier similar to that which dashed the hopes of sex-gland injectors. Even though cryobiology has scored empirical successes, it does not know how or why extreme cold either protects or injures living tissue. Even with the preservation of spermatozoa, Professor J. K. Sherman of the University of Arkansas' School of Medicine said at a recent meeting of the Society for Cryobiology, 30 to 50 percent of the cells do not survive freezing. And these are relatively homogeneous cells, the professor of anatomy pointed out, whereas the human organism is composed of some 100 cell types, each with its own size, shape, organelles, functions, and life histories. These cells are interrelated among complex biological levels which extend from the total organism to the submolecular. "These heterogeneous cellular units are the foundation of life for the body. They plus the level of complexity, including environmental factors in the substances and fibers that surround these cells, create a complexity of diversity in form, function, and most important, sensitivity to stresses, such as the formation and dissolution of ice within and around the cells. Differential sensitivity from organism to organism, system to system, organ to organ, tissue to tissue, cell to cell, organelle to organelle, molecule to molecule is an established fact in biological science."

For all these reasons, Dr. Sherman believes freezing and thawing human beings at this time is premature and won't work.

The Cryonics people might be prepared to grant everything this medical scientist says except the absoluteness of his conclusion. In reply, Cryonics says to medical science: Let's get on with it. The sooner we gain this essential basic knowledge, the better. When we do, our clients at least will have a chance to benefit from it. Besides, what do dead people have to lose from Cryonic suspension?

Money. At the $1,000 yearly maintenance fee, Tutankhamen's [7] bill would have come to $3,265,000. But Cryonics is an expression of the faith that, given the expected rate of medical advance, people who die today won't have to wait nearly so long for immortality. The real kind.

---

[7] The Hope Knoll Cryogenic Cemetery Association at Appleton, Wisconsin, offers a burial service with or without reanimation. The nonprofit association says: "Through time immemorial, the human heart has yearned to be remembered by family and loved ones. In ancient times only kings and potentates could realize such hopes. Now, modern technology affords a vastly superior means of preservation which is available to all. Known as cryogenic entombment, extremely low temperatures are utilized to retard deterioration to an almost negligible degree. A cryogenically entombed person will deteriorate less in one century than in one minute at normal room temperatures. With optimum preservation assured, thought can be given to making arrangements so that loved ones can be viewed at any time in the future by friends, and descendant generations yet unborn."

IV. The Long Diagnosis

The aspiring immortalist and the physician make strange bedfellows. The physician traditionally has been a healer. Medicine seeks to ease pain, treat injury, cure or prevent disease, maintain or restore health, rehabilitate. The physician typically is a down-to-earth fellow who never has permitted himself to entertain grandiose visions; indeed, the concept of biological immortality is likely to appear most alien if not fantastic to people who must grapple professionally with disease and ultimately lose to death. While physicians may retard death, prolonging life per se has not been a medical goal, even with Francis Bacon's urging three and a half centuries ago.

But from the viewpoint of prolongevity seekers, the successes of medicine—no matter how modest the intent—are beacons shining toward the objective. Whatever medicine's goal, the common result has been the bonus of extra life. Even if medical fighters do look only one step ahead, they are leading humanity toward the promised land. Even with the process incomplete, we have come a long way from our hominid ancestors, few of whom survived a decade.

Medical historian George Sarton says that science—particularly medicine—is "the history of man's reactions to the truth, the history of the gradual revelation of truth, the history of the gradual liberation of our minds from darkness and prejudice." Truth is the word we use to denote a correct reading of reality. While truth often is camouflaged, it is delineated by the medical litmus test. In the medical context, truth is health and life; error is malaise, disease, and death. The question is: If we can learn the whole truth, how many more years of life can we expect?

The science of medicine began with Hippocrates, who said, "To know is one thing but merely to believe one knows is another. To know is science but merely to believe one knows is ignorance." The practice of medicine began long before Hippocrates with our primitive ancestors who misread reality in important ways.

In his attempts to interpret the ways of nature, savage man, untutored

91

because inexperienced, first of all confused life with motion [writes Fielding Garrison in his definitive *History of Medicine*]. [H]e was puzzled if not awed by the rustling leaves in the forest, the crash and flash of thunder and lightning, the flicker and play of sunlight and firelight, and he could see no causal relation between a natural object and its moving shadow, a sound and its echo, flowing water and the reflections on its surface. Winds, clouds, storms, earthquakes, or unusual sights and sounds in nature were to him the outward and visible signs of malevolent gods, demons, spirits, or other supernatural agencies. The natural was to him the supernatural, as it still is to many of us, but with this curious difference, that what we should qualify as supernatural was to him as natural as the light of day.

Starting from total ignorance it was not easy to explain the uncomfortable deviations from the norm of health and proper bodily functioning. Primitive people concluded that the unfortunate person had been inhabited, commandeered by an evil spirit.

A further association of ideas led our *primitif* to regard disease as something produced by a human enemy possessing supernatural powers, which he strove to ward off by appropriate spells and sorcery, similar to those employed by the enemy himself [Dr. Garrison writes]. Again, his own reflection in water, his shadows in the sunlight, what he saw in dreams, or in an occasional nightmare from gluttony, suggested the existence of a spirit-world apart from his daily life and of a soul or *alter ego* apart from his body. In this way he hit upon a third way of looking at disease as the work of offended spirits of the dead, whether of men, animals, or plants. These three views of disease are common beliefs of the lowest grades of human life.

Given the belief, the "cure" was to expel the undesirable occupant. This was the job of the witch doctor, the shaman, the medicine man. One seemingly reasonable way to go about this was by purging the system through bleeding, catharsis, diuresis, and emesis. In time the witch doctor commanded an extensive knowledge of herbs. Garrison says the knowledge began with observations on dietetics. "Prehistoric and primitive man, like the infant, was apt to swallow anything that seemed edible, and one of his first taboos was upon poisonous substances. This is borne out by the Mosaic code, with its interdictions upon ungulates, tardigrades (microscopic arthropods), smooth fish, reptiles and batrachians (frogs, toads, and other amphibian vertebrates), unclean birds, water contaminated by dead animals (Leviticus xii, 3-43), 'any thing that dieth of itself' (Leviticus xi, 9)." The Iroquois Indians, as the early French explorer Jacques Cartier reported, successfully treated the scurvy of his crew with the bark and leaves of the hemlock spruce and—to give one other example—the French at Onondaga in 1657 found the sassafras leaves prescribed by the same tribe "marvellous" for closing wounds of all kinds.

In addition to herb-doctoring, the shaman gained a crude mastery of bone-setting and even surgery. Neolithic skulls have been found in excavations all over the world with holes, about the size of a nickel or quarter. Researchers know the holes were not the cause of death because of evidence that the bone had grown in an attempt at healing. Some skulls bore multiple holes, one as many as five. This apparent first attempt at surgery (apart from cutting the umbilical cord at birth) still is practiced today to relieve pressures built up by tumors or other pathological states. In Neolithic times, the operation was performed to provide an egress for the demon closeted inside the skull. Trephining, as this operation is called, was probably used to cope with the particularly frightening disease, epilepsy. The seizure was so manifestly the occupation of the individual by an external power that this ailment eventually came to be known in early Greek civilization as the sacred disease.

The excised piece of skull bone frequently served as an amulet. It was believed that such a device would protect its wearer from future attacks by disease demons. But when these methods failed, the shaman resorted to exorcism—driving the devil out by incantations, prayers, fasting; or frightening the incubus with loud noises, wild dress, and threatening posturings. The theory was that if the situation became unpleasant enough, no demon would want to remain on the premises. This line of reasoning also led, in time, to scourging and beating the host to create the requisite hostile environment for the tenant.

If one is tempted to scoff at this stage of medicine, it is therapeutic to remember that the witch doctor probably enjoyed about the same recovery rate as physicians all through history until the past century or so. Russell V. Lee, one of the leading practitioners in the United States, told how this could be so. Third (in Dr. Lee's order), the shaman did possess a creditable mastery of natural remedies. Second, at least three-quarters of diseases that afflict people are eventually overcome by the body's own defenses, with or without the physician's help. And first, a large proportion of illness is psychosomatic. The very fact that the sick person believes that the doctor can produce a cure is a crucial factor. "The phrase 'bedside manner' is often used disparagingly, to suggest artifice and insincerity. But the fact is that a good bedside manner—the ability to inspire confidence and trust—is not only a comfort to the patient, but one of the physician's most effective weapons. Many illnesses are generated or intensified by anxiety, depression or loneliness—by a sense that no one cares. Through the centuries, the men of medicine have cared. Their sympathy and the faith they instill in their patients can work wonders."

As the centuries passed, the roles of the medicine man divided. The administering of the natural and practical remedies became the function of the forerunners of today's medical doctor. The treatment of disease through magic was taken over by religion. Under this arrangement, disease became associated with sin; God was the supreme healer. René Dubos writes in *Mirage of Health:* "The Jewish tribes believed that obedience to Jehovah's laws was a necessary passport to good health and that any transgression was likely to be punished by disease." The word "stroke" connotes an act of God in paralyzing a person.

In ancient Egyptian civilization, the remedies of the herb doctors were held in lower esteem than the magical medicine of the priests. The former were called upon to take care of the lesser ailments. The priests handled the important cases, those beyond the powers of rudimentary medicine, the bite of a venomous snake, for instance. The cleavage has persisted to our day. In all ages physicians have chafed at the popularity of quacks and quack medicines. A study published in October 1972 indicated that probably half the people in the United States would not rule out a claimed cure for cancer even if it were rejected unanimously by medical experts. Christian Science demonstrates the strength of faith healing, and its limitations.

Like his contemporary, Socrates, Hippocrates severed his discipline from religion. The sick person was not a sinner. Disease, even the sacred disease, was not a divine visitation, but had natural causes and must be dealt with by human methods. There were many diseases—not just various manifestations of one disease—and the physician could gain an understanding of these ailments through careful observation (in this, Hippocrates also removed medicine from philosophy with the Greek penchant for speculation rather than empiricism and his descriptions of tuberculosis, puerperal septicemia, epilepsy, and other ailments might, says Dr. Garrison, "with a few changes and additions, take their place in any modern text-book"). Diagnosis took on great importance and so did prognosis—telling the patient beforehand the course of his illness—replacing oracles and omens as a means of satisfying the Greek curiosity about the future.

Hippocrates accepted the theory of the four humors as the internal basis to explain health and disease. Just as the Greeks believed there were four basic elements and four basic qualities, so they felt there were four essential bodily fluids:

Blood was warm and moist like air
Phlegm was cold and moist like water
Yellow bile = warm-dry = fire
Black bile = cold-dry = earth

The source of the blood was believed to be the heart, the brain was the source of phlegm, the liver the source of yellow bile, the spleen the source of black bile. Health was the normal blending of these humors, disease the quantitative imbalance or improper mixture of the bodily fluids. For instance, if there were an excess of phlegm and it dropped down into the lungs, the person developed tuberculosis; if the phlegm went into the abdomen, the disease was dropsy, now usually known as edema; phlegm in the bowels meant dysentery; in the rectum hemorrhoids. Black bile was considered the greatest cause of evil. The humors came to be regarded as determining a person's temperament: the phlegmatic person was slow or slothful; the sanguine one loved music, wine, women, and laughter; the man with too much yellow bile was choleric or violent; while an overabundance of black bile caused melancholy.[1]

Hippocrates believed that changes "are chiefly responsible for diseases, especially the greatest changes, the violent alterations both in the seasons and in other things," such as our constitutions and habits.[2] He put

---

[1] Today bile denotes the yellow or greenish fluid secreted by the liver to aid digestion. And to be bilious means suffering from an excess of the liver secretion, but it also can mean peevish and ill-natured with its synonym choleric.

[2] It is illuminating and fascinating to learn that Dr. Thomas Holmes, a psychiatrist, and colleagues at the University of Washington School of Medicine have rated—quantified—the impact of stress in adjusting to changes in our daily lives. The scale below is based on hundreds of interviews, and in studies going back to the 1940s the researchers have found that a clustering of changes within a short period of time —200 life-change units within a single year might be a maximum level—represents a disruption a person cannot manage and sets the stage for the biological sequel: disease. It is worth pointing out that changes for the better contribute to stress impact as well as changes for the worse.

SOCIAL READJUSTMENT RATING SCALE

Rank	Life Event	Mean Value
1.	Death of spouse	100
2.	Divorce	73
3.	Marital separation	65
4.	Jail term	63
5.	Death of close family member	63
6.	Personal injury or illness	53
7.	Marriage	50
8.	Fired at work	47
9.	Marital reconciliation	45
10.	Retirement	45
11.	Change in health of family member	44
12.	Pregnancy	40
13.	Sex difficulties	39
14.	Gain of new family member	39
15.	Business readjustment	39
16.	Change in financial state	38

great faith in the body's natural healing power—*physis*—which eventually brought diseases to a crisis. At the crisis stage he observed that the body expelled pus and poisons (Hippocrates called the suppurative process "coction") and once this stage was passed successfully the patient recovered. Hippocrates' therapeutic strategy was to bring the patient to crisis with the best possible chance to survive it. To do this he used few drugs, but relied on diet, teas, fresh air, massages, and baths. The physician must help nature, he said, and take care that "his treatment shall at least do no harm."

While Hippocrates was transforming medicine into a science, he was humanizing the role of the physician, giving it the high ethical character it has upheld ever since. The Hippocratic Oath reads in part:

> I will use treatment to help the sick according to my ability and judgment, but never with a view to injury and wrong-doing. . . . Into whatsoever houses I enter, I will enter to help the sick, and I will abstain from all intentional wrong-dòing and harm, especially from abusing the bodies of man or woman, bond or free. And whatsoever I shall see or hear in the course of my profession, as well as outside my profession in my intercourse with men, if it be what should not be published abroad, I will never divulge, holding such things to be holy secrets.

17.	Death of close friend	37
18.	Change to different line of work	36
19.	Change in number of arguments with spouse	35
20.	Mortgage over $10,000	31
21.	Foreclosure of mortgage or loan	30
22.	Change in responsibilities at work	29
23.	Son or daughter leaving home	29
24.	Trouble with in-laws	29
25.	Outstanding personal achievement	28
26.	Wife begins or stops work	26
27.	Begin or end school	26
28.	Change in living conditions	25
29.	Revision of personal habits	24
30.	Trouble with boss	23
31.	Change in work hours or conditions	20
32.	Change in residence	20
33.	Change in schools	20
34.	Change in recreation	19
35.	Change in church activities	19
36.	Change in social activities	18
37.	Mortgage or loan less than $10,000	17
38.	Change in sleeping habits	16
39.	Change in number of family get-togethers	15
40.	Change in eating habits	15
41.	Vacation	13
42.	Christmas	12
43.	Minor violations of the law	11

Maimonides, a famous twelfth-century Jewish physician who practiced in the Arab world (where Jews were accorded equality denied them in medieval Christendom), expressed these noble thoughts in his Oath and Prayer: "The Eternal Providence has appointed me to watch over the life and health of Thy creatures. May the love for my art actuate me at all times; may neither avarice, nor miserliness, nor the thirst for glory, nor for a great reputation engage my mind; for the enemies of Truth and Philanthropy could easily deceive me and make me forgetful of my lofty aim of doing good to Thy children."

The Hippocratic Oath was sworn to Apollo, Aesculapius, Hygeia, and Panacea. Apollo was the chief god of healing in the Greek pantheon. According to legend, he bequeathed his talents to his son Aesculapius, who became so proficient in the art of healing that Pluto accused him of diminishing the number of shades in Hades. Aesculapius apparently lived as a physician about the twelfth century B.C., so that his reputation was generated by a real man. He became a god much later, about the sixth or fifth century B.C. The god's daughters were Hygeia and Panacea. Panacea also was a healer, and accomplished her art through the use of drugs. "For the worshipers of Hygeia," writes René Dubos, "health is the natural order of things, a positive attribute to which men are entitled if they govern their lives wisely. According to them, the most important function of medicine is to discover and teach the natural laws which will ensure to man a healthy mind in a healthy body." Hygeia (Health) was much more recent than Aesculapius, and symbolized a new medical concept with none of the shamanic overtones. She never fired the popular imagination, never was able to challenge the influence of Aesculapius— even as hygiene and public health today cannot generate the public enthusiasm lavished upon medicine.[3] "[T]he followers of Aesculapius believe that the chief role of the physician is to treat disease, to restore health by correcting any imperfection caused by the accidents of birth or of life," Dubos writes. "To ward off disease or recover health, men as a rule find it easier to depend on healers than to attempt the more difficult task of living wisely."

Hippocrates favored Hygeia. He observed the whole person and his particular situation, treated the patient rather than the disease. For Hippocrates, "health depends upon a state of equilibrium among the various internal factors which govern the operations of the body and the mind; this equilibrium in turn is reached only when man lives in harmony with his external environment." Dr. Lawrence LeShan was giving the essence

---

[3] It might be argued that the public demand for environmental improvement marks a change in attitude.

of the Hippocratic doctrine when he told the Second Conference on Psychophysiological Aspects of Cancer in New York City in May 1968 that "an individual does not just 'get' the malignancy, which starts on the cellular or immunological or endocrinological or psychological level. The entire organism eventuates toward cancer. His total biography, involving all its levels, moves in a direction leading to a total organism-in-an environment situation, which we term 'neoplastic disease.' The most dramatic aspects of this are, finally, the cellular disorganization, the inability to function on various psychobiological levels, and death." Dr. Arthur Schmale, Jr. told the same conference: "Cancer appears to be one of the diseases that frequently makes its first appearance in a life-setting of experienced hopelessness. Data presented at the previous conference indicated that carcinoma of the cervix could be predicted in asymptomatic women who had atypical and suspicious but not diagnostic changes in their cervical cytology. The dichotomy of cancer or no cancer was based on whether the women reported before their diagnostic biopsies a reaction to a life event(s) with feelings of hopelessness within a period of six months prior to their first atypical smear."

To Hippocrates (while he recognized that even the prudent person can become ill during an epidemic), disease was a signal that a person is not living correctly.

Despite Hippocrates' fine clinical descriptions and his profound interpretation of the states of health and disease, the Greeks were totally ignorant of the true functioning of bodily systems. It is almost impossible for us who start off with such hard-won knowledge to reconstruct this dense mystery of our own inner space. After all, men were trying to comprehend the workings of the most complex product of 3 billion years of trial-and-error evolution. Not the least of the problems was establishing absolute proof—how could one be sure he was right?

One obvious way to learn more about the body is to open it and study it systematically. Human vivisection, the cutting apart of living bodies for study, has never flourished, understandably. But neither did dissection of corpses in ancient and medieval times. Medical knowledge was blocked by the old human dread—fear or reverence for the dead. Men could slice, carve, gash, sever, puncture, mutilate, eviscerate, and butcher their fellows as long as they were living, but once dead no incisions were tolerated.

This prohibition left animal vivisection and dissection. Aristotle's anatomical—and other animal and plant—studies were so extensive that he is known generally as the father of biology and more specifically as siring zoology, botany, physiology, embryology, teratology (the study of genetic malformations), and comparative anatomy. (Aristotle taught that the heart is the central abode of life, of the mind and of the soul, the hearth from which comes animal heat and the blood.) Aristotle's love of learning passed through his pupil Alexander to one of the conqueror's commanders, Ptolemy, who seized Alexandria and Egypt upon the dissolution of the Alexandrian Empire. Ptolemy founded the great Alexandrian library and the world's first university whose school of medicine trained the ancient world's best physicians for more than four centuries. The dynastic Ptolemies defied the ancient taboo and permitted dissection of human bodies. Even with this advantage, however, there was no Open Sesame to truth. Erasistratus, credited as a founder of pathology, was misled by the very process of dissection into believing that arteries were conduits for air. Esmond Long in *A History of Pathology* writes: "Today we know that the elasticity of the arterial walls drives the blood on into the capillaries after death, and that air gets in only after the vessels are opened, an event inevitable in dissection. But Erasistratus knew nothing of capillaries, and believed in two circulations, one for blood from the heart and one for air from the lungs. These were the two important substances for the continuance of life, furnishing respectively nourishment and energy."

One of the accomplishments of Clarissimus Galen, who lived in the second half of the second century A.D., was to prove that the arteries carried blood. But Galen also believed that blood pulsed back and forth in the body in a tidal action, that the heart was a suction device, and that the blood passed from the right side of the heart to the left side through pores in the septum.

Galen may have been the most influential medical man who ever lived. He undoubtedly was an extremely talented physician, attending the Roman emperor Marcus Aurelius. After being summoned by the bivouacked emperor to one of the more barbaric reaches of the empire, Galen complained that such was not his style of medicine. Thereupon, Marcus appointed him to the sinecure of personal physician to his son Commodus. For the rest of Galen's life, from A.D. 169 to the turn of the century, the physician devoted his time to his grand enterprise. He set down all the medical knowledge there was in the most encyclopedic medical work ever written by a single man.

Galen not only rescued Hippocrates from neglect, but extended the Hippocratic position beyond the master's intent. The Greco-Roman authority gave such emphasis to the four humors and their correspondence to the four elements that they overshadowed the salubrious equilibrium so crucial to Hippocrates. "[H]e emphasized 'coction' or suppuration as an essential part in the healing of wounds," says historian Long, "to such a degree that his slavish apostles of later centuries, particularly the Arabs, instead of letting nature take its course in this respect, as did Hippocrates and Galen, went to all lengths to promote suppuration, and with them arose the notion of 'laudable pus,' the most pernicious concept that ever sullied medicine."

Galen brought Pythagorean numerology into his physiology and pathology; he admired Euclid and hoped to make medicine as exact a science as geometry. He reintroduced the theory of *pneuma,* a vital spark or spirit that animated bodily substances. The blood, he held, was imbued with "natural spirits" in the liver and "vital spirits" in the left ventricle of the heart; the vital spirits were converted to "animal spirits" in the brain. *Pneuma* is the seductive—but arid—theory of vitalism with which scientists have had to contend and overcome again and again. It surfaced most recently around the turn of this century as the *élan vital* of philosopher Henri Bergson.

Galen also incorporated another devilishly seductive theory—Aristotle's teleology, that everything nature does has a purpose. Fielding Garrison writes: "Galen, as Neuburger puts it, made his whole physiological theory 'a skillful and well-instructed special pleading for the cause of design in nature,' whereby he lost himself in *a priori* speculations 'to explain nature's execution before even her mechanisms had been demonstrated.' He never really sought *how* an organ functions, but in blind obeisance to Aristotle ('Nature makes nothing in vain') he reiterated the transcendental *why,* which Kant and Claude Bernard pronounced to be forever insoluble." (The Aristotelian confusion of result for purpose, effect for design is one of the most subtle—but most profoundly misleading—mistakes in the long human search to decipher reality. Evolution teaches us that nature *does* make things in vain. Nature is prodigal in its mistakes, making millions of errors in order to stumble upon—and *preserve*—one improvement. That is nature's strategy.)

This teleological cast to Galen's medicine—tying the goodness and design of nature to a Creator—won ready support from theologians. So medicine, which had been sanitized by Hippocrates, once again included philosophy and religion and a blend of truth and error that would take centuries of persistent scientific effort to sift.

Galen was no man to hide his light under a bushel. "I have done as much to medicine," he boasted, "as Trajan did to the Roman Empire, in making bridges and roads throughout Italy. It is I alone that have pointed out the true method of treating diseases: it must be confessed that Hippocrates had already chalked out the same road . . . but I have rendered it passable." Galen said he was the last word in medicine, and he was, for more than 13 centuries. During that time, men chose to read him rather than nature.

The physician-alchemist Paracelsus publicly burned Galen's works in

1526. But it was not until 1543 that the tradition suffered an intellectual roasting. In that year—the same year that Copernicus published *On the Revolution of Heavenly Bodies*—Andreas Vesalius published *De fabrica humani corporis* ("On the Structure of the Human Body").

Vesalius had studied the human body first hand, robbing graves, even stealing a corpse from the gallows. At Padua, where he was permitted to make public dissections at the medical university, Vesalius arranged with physicians to allow him to study their fatal cases and ingratiated himself with judges so that criminals were executed at times and in ways convenient to the dissector. During the course of these studies, Vesalius discovered that Galen (who had learned his anatomy from barbary apes, pigs, and other animals) erred repeatedly. "While written in Latin," Garrison says, "the *Fabrica* is truly vernacular in the sweeping scorn and violence of its language in dealing with Galenical and other superstitions. Although it completely disposes of Galen's osteology and muscular anatomy for all time and, indeed, recreates the whole gross anatomy of the human body, it has never been translated."

If Vesalius violated the tradition of Galen, the tradition wrecked the career of Vesalius. The inertial weight of conservatism is particularly heavy in medicine, testing all innovators. The young Vesalius (he was not yet thirty years old) was unprepared for the scorn and vilification poured on him. In a fit of indignation, this brilliant man destroyed all his other works in preparation, left Padua, accepted a lucrative position as court physician to Spain's Emperor Charles V, got married, and settled into the life of a courtier. He lived to regret this impulsive decision and yearned "once more [to] be able to study that true Bible, as we count it, of the human body and of the nature of man." It appeared that his wish would be fulfilled, for he received word on his way back from a pilgrimage to the Holy Land that after 20 years his old chair at the University of Padua was open to him. But he suddenly succumbed to an obscure malady and died alone on an obscure island in the Mediterranean.

After Vesalius, men could see with their own eyes where Galen was wrong. After Vesalius, too, men had a big clue to the true nature of the circulation of blood. "In the drawings which Vesalius had made, indicating the close proximity of the terminal twigs of arteries and veins," Garrison writes, "the truth about the circulation was literally staring in the faces of any observer who had eyes to see or wit to discover it." But medical investigators were blinded by Galen's words—blood ebbed and flowed between the closed and distinct venous and arterial systems through those imaginary pores in the dividing wall of the heart. (Vesalius questioned that, too, with a sarcastic: "We are driven to wonder at the handiwork of the Almighty, by means of which the blood sweats from the right into the left ventricle through passages which escape the human vision.")

Miguel Servetus discovered that "some" of the blood did not pass through the septum, as Galen contended, but circulated through the lungs. Servetus published this information in *Restitutio Christianismi* in 1553. The book offended leaders of the Reformation, particularly John Calvin. All but two copies of the book were burned at the stake on August 13, 1553 in Geneva along with the author.

Heironymus Fabricius, who succeeded to the chair at Padua that might have gone to Vesalius had he lived, discovered that the veins possessed valves which permitted blood to flow toward the heart, but closed and blocked flow in the reverse direction. Fabricius perceived the correct function of the valves, but, still a believer in the Galenic blood system, he thought the valves simply restricted excess blood flowing from the heart; the valves were to ensure that the upper parts of the body were not depleted of blood while the lower regions swelled from too much. And so scientific immortality passed from Fabricius to his pupil, during the years 1599–1603, William Harvey.

Harvey brought a fresh mind to the problem, even after he had read all the literature. Even so, when he began to study the living heart through vivisection of animals, he found the task of understanding the "motions and uses of the heart so truly arduous, so full of difficultes . . . that the motion of the heart was only to be comprehended by God."

One of mankind's landmark discoveries turned simply upon a reinterpretation of how the heart functions. With only one exception, all of Harvey's predecessors had believed that the heart operated like a suction pump, sucking in blood as it expanded. Harvey realized that the operative phase is the contraction which drives the blood out. From this position, he correctly traced the course of blood from the right side of the heart through the lungs to the left side and then out through the aorta.

Harvey then began to calculate what an enormous amount of blood was being pumped into the arterial system in a very short space of time. Too much to be replenished from the amounts being manufactured in the venous system (as contemporary theory had it) and so much that the tissues would become gorged "unless the blood should somehow find its way from the arteries into the veins, and so return to the right side of the heart; I began to think whether there might not be *a motion, as it were, in a circle.*"

Not so naïve as Vesalius, Harvey in putting forth such a novel theory "not only feared injury to himself from the envy of a few, but trembled lest he might have mankind at large for his enemies." Sure enough, wrote his only contemporary biographer, John Aubrey, "I have heard him say, that after his booke of the Circulation of the Blood came out, that he fell mightily in his practize, and that 'twas believed by the vulgar that he was crack-brained; and all the physicians were against his opinion, and envyed him; many wrote against him." But Harvey lived a long life, long enough to see his theory accepted.

During his distinguished career he was physician to King Charles I and in that capacity delivered one of science's most eloquent commentaries upon those affairs of men that fill up most history books. At the battle of Edgehill, the royal physician sat by the outskirts of the fight under a hedge reading a book.

Harvey never found the missing link between the arteries and the veins. A microscope was needed in order to see the capillaries. They were first observed by the Italian microscopist Marcello Malpighi in 1660, and later in the seventeenth century Anton van Leeuwenhoek in the Netherlands demonstrated that capillaries completed the blood network. Leeuwenhoek was a draper and janitor of the Delft city hall. Natural history was his avocation, natural history as seen through the lens of a microscope. This janitor had 419 lenses and 247 microscopes! "In the year 1675 I discovered very small living creatures in rain water, which had stood but few days in a new earthen pot glazed blue within." No one was to suspect the importance of these odd animalcula to the human species for another two centuries.[4]

In the meantime doctors were as helpless as ever in dealing with the major human ailments, perhaps less effectual than in Hippocrates' day because many physicians had forgotten his warning to make sure that the treatment "at least did no harm." Enthusiastic bleeding weakened and dispatched many a patient before his time, hospitals were centers of contagion, and many doctors were fearful to undertake surgery because the patient might die from the aftereffects: sepsis or shock.

In early Greek medicine four out of five people died after surgery. Down through the ages the practice remained highly risky and, if it is possible, grew even more painful. There was a Hippocratic aphorism, really of older origin, that diseases not curable by iron are curable by fire. This remedy took on great importance with the eleventh-century Arab physician Avicenna. With the development of chemicals and pharmaceuticals in the Arab laboratories, Avicenna considered medicine to be superior to surgery. He recommended that the two disciplines be sepa-

---

[4] A contributing factor may have been that Leeuwenhoek jealously guarded his method of grinding powerful lenses. The secret died with him. Such lenses had to be perfected anew, and it was not until the nineteenth century that scientists once again could see micro-organisms so clearly.

rated. Furthermore, he urged that the surgeon's knife be abandoned for hot iron. Wounds were to be cauterized by heat.

Avicenna's *Canon medicinae* took its place with Galen's works as the medical bible. The art of surgery became the province of barbers, wounds were treated with searing metal or scalding oil. This inhuman treatment persisted for more than five centuries until in the sixteenth century a French barber-surgeon made a battlefield discovery. While Ambroise Paré was treating wounded soldiers, he exhausted his supply of cauterizing oil. Wishing to give some aid, Paré applied a cold dressing of turpentine and oil of roses. "I expected to find them all dead in the morning," he later wrote. "Greatly to my surprise, I found that those whom I had treated with the salve had very little pain in their wounds, no inflammation, no swelling, and they had passed a comfortable night. The others, whose wounds had been treated with boiling elder oil, were in a high fever, while their wounds were inflamed, swollen, and acutely painful." Paré decided on the spot "that I would no longer cauterize the unfortunate wounded in so cruel a manner."

Gradually, surgery once again was reunited with medicine, an inevitable outcome as scientific discoveries showed the interdependence of the two callings. But surgery was stymied well into the nineteenth century. The operating table was a torture rack, promising health through pain.

This put a premium on speed, for the patient would die from shock even if he could endure the agony. A good surgeon was a fast surgeon. Among the best was Conrad Langenbeck, a surgeon-general of the Hannoverian army. It was said that Langenbeck amputated a shoulder while a colleague stepped aside for a pinch of snuff. Sir William Fergusson of Scotland worked with the sleight-of-hand of a shell-game operator. A visitor to his clinic was advised to "look out sharp, for if you only wink, you'll miss the operation altogether." England's William Cheselden was all-time champion for his division, cutting out a bladder stone in just 54 seconds.

Some operations require complete muscular relaxation. This is the way one Nathan Rice described the resetting of a dislocated hip-joint in *Trials of a Public Benefactor:*

> A pulley is attached to the affected limb, while the body, trussed up by appropriate bands, is fastened to another; now several powerful muscular assistants seize the ropes, and with a careful, steady drawing, tighten the cords. Soon the tension makes itself felt, and as the stubborn muscles stretch and yield to the strain, one can almost imagine that he hears the crack of parting sinews. Big drops of perspiration, started by the excess of agony, bestrew the patient's forehead, sharp screams burst from him in peal after peal—and all his struggles to free himself and escape the

horrid torture, are valueless, for he is in the powerful hands of men then as inexorable as death. . . . Stronger comes the pull, more force is added to the ropes, the tugs, cruel and unyielding, seem as if they would burst the tendons where they stand out like whipcords. At last the agony becomes too great for human endurance, and with a wild, despairing yell, the suffering patient relapses into unconsciousness. . . . The surgeon avails himself of this opportunity and . . . seizing the limb by a dexterous twist snaps the head of the bone into its socket.

Alcohol and opium were used as anodynes, but could not shut off all the pain. Cocaine also was used, and it was not extraordinary for the surgeon to try to dull his own recurring professional anguish in this way, and became addicted. Sometimes nicotine was tried, either by inserting a cigar in the patient's anus or blowing smoke into the rectum. Sometimes a bullet was inserted in the other end, and this is where we get the expression to "bite the bullet." A few surgeons employed hypnotism while one ingenious operator, it is said, induced fainting by delivering "a brutal remark."

In 1800 Sir Humphrey Davy of Penzance, England, experimented upon himself with nitrous oxide and stated that "it may probably be used with advantage in surgical operations in which no great effusion of blood takes place." Sir Humphrey's recommendation never was acted upon, although his notion of the exhilarating quality of the gas made it the laughing stock of traveling lecturers and entertainers.

On March 30, 1842 Crawford Long, a local practitioner at Jefferson, Georgia, removed two cystic tumors from a patient's neck without pain. The patient had been anesthetized by ether. Probably never before or since has such a momentous event taken place under more unlikely and obscure circumstances. Dr. Long, only twenty-six years old, had been the social ringleader at "tripping" parties for his group. The transporting agent of these occasions was ether. The physician noticed that during these jags his partygoers became insensitive to pain, and that observation led him to his unprecedented operation.

The country doctor proceeded to employ ether for all his operations, practicing an advanced form of surgery unmatched in the entire world. Local criticism against him mounted, naturally enough, and while he was a venturesome physician he was a cautious scientist. He kept looking for errors in his method—and never ventured to inform the profession about his discovery.

In December 1844 Horace Wells watched an exhibition of nitrous oxide at Hartford, Connecticut. In an unexpected development at the performance, a member of the audience under the influence of laughing gas gashed his leg, but obviously felt no pain. As a dentist Dr. Wells grasped the wonderful quality in any substance that could kill pain.

Wells, quite the opposite of Long, moved with dispatch. In short order he was manufacturing laughing gas and practicing painless dentistry. However, the nitrous oxide, not as powerful as ether, did not always work perfectly. Wells never tried to find out why or to achieve uniform perfection. Instead he hurried to Boston and through a former dental partner, William Morton, arranged a demonstration before the famous surgeon John Warren at Massachusetts General Hospital. Dr. Wells did not administer sufficient nitrous oxide and the "painless" tooth-pulling experiment was marred by humiliating screams. Wells returned to Hartford a failure.

Dr. Morton, meanwhile, who also had been searching for a way to deaden pain, was spurred by his former partner's efforts. Morton was now studying medicine as an apprentice to a well-known physician and chemist, Charles Jackson. To Morton's inquiries about a pain-killer, Dr. Jackson told him what was common knowledge at the time: that ether applied to the outside of a sore tooth eases the pain. When Jackson later added that medical students inhaled ether to get high, Morton was intrigued. However, he was discouraged by reading in medical books that inhaling large quantities of ether could be lethal. He procrastinated. Finally he experimented with a dog, and was encouraged. As his work advanced, he became more secretive, fearful that someone else would learn what he was doing and beat him to the goal. He went to borrow Dr. Jackson's equipment for administering nitrous oxide, being very circumspect about his intentions. During the visit Dr. Jackson recommended sulfuric ether as a possible anesthetic. Dr. Morton, dissembling, pretended he was quite ignorant of the substance. This stated ignorance was noted by third parties.

Afraid now that Jackson already suspected what he was up to, Morton screwed up the courage to render himself unconscious with ether for eight minutes. Now it was William Morton who stood before Dr. Warren, his colleagues, and students at Massachusetts General Hospital. This time the experiment was a quiet success. On October 16, 1846 Dr. Warren removed a neck tumor without pain to the patient. Not only was pain banished, but surgeons thereafter were granted the time necessary for their difficult task.

Morton at once embarked upon a scheme to make his fortune. Concealing the true nature of the gas, he took out a patent for "Letheon" under his name and included that of Dr. Jackson. He began manufacturing inhalation equipment and enfranchising Letheon agents in the United States and Europe. However, other surgeons at home and abroad soon were performing operations with ether and they objected, naturally enough, to paying more for Morton's brand name ether than the cheap generic ether. When U.S. army doctors ignored the patent in the Mexican War, the bankruptcy of Morton's venture was sealed. He next applied to the U.S government for a cash reward, both because of the army's use of his discovery and as a token of his benefaction to mankind

By this time—and with the likelihood of a handsome settlement in view —Drs. Jackson, Wells, and, finally, Long, came forth to claim that they were the discoverers of anesthetic ether. Jackson slyly paid an early visit to Europe to establish his claims with the most influential circles in medicine. Wells, too, went to the Continent. Returning to find his own claims rejected, he sought to discredit Morton by touting chloroform, which had just been used by Edinburgh obstetrician, Sir James Simpson.

Wells not only praised chloroform; he became addicted to it. His mind became unhinged. On the night of January 21, 1848 he approached a prostitute on lower Broadway in Manhattan and threw vitriol at her. He was arrested and taken to the Tombs prison. In a letter afterward made public, Wells wrote:

> I had during the week been in the constant practice of inhaling chloroform and on Friday evening last I lost all consciousness before I removed the inhaler from my mouth. On coming out of the stupor I was exhilarated beyond measure, exceeding anything which I have ever experienced, and seeing the phial of acid standing on the mantel, in my delirium I seized it and rushed into the street and threw it at two females. My character, which I have ever prized above everything else, is gone. My dear dear wife and child, how they will suffer I cannot proceed. My brain is on fire.

Three days later, Wells committed suicide by cutting his left thigh to the bone and severing the femoral artery. By his side was an empty vial of chloroform.

Establishing his just claim to the discovery of anesthesia became an obsession that robbed all pleasure from the last 20 years of William Morton's life. Everything else was sacrificed to pursue his petitions to Congress, lawsuits against the government, and defenses against the attacks of Jackson, Long, and other detractors. His lawsuits and petitions were unsuccessful. He was reduced to penury. Finally his health disintegrated. He died a broken man at the age of forty-eight.

Jackson, who also had believed that Morse capitalized on information he supplied to get undeserved credit for inventing the telegraph, continued to denounce the dead Morton in an unending stream of pamphlets, newspaper articles, reports to scientific bodies, and private letters. His hatred unquenchable, he turned to drink.

In July 1873—five years after Morton's death—Charles Jackson stumbled across Mount Auburn Cemetery to Morton's grave to gaze upon the monument donated by the citizens of Boston. The inscription read:

> Wm. T. G. Morton
> Inventor and Revealer of Anaesthetic Inhalation
> By whom pain in surgery was averted and annulled
> Before whom in all time surgery was agony
> Since whom science has control of pain

Jackson began flailing his arms and screaming. He was taken away forcibly to a mental asylum where he spent the remaining seven years of his life.

That left Crawford Long who first used ether but who does not get credit for discovering the anesthetic because he neglected to inject his knowledge into the professional mainstream. Each day in the last 30 years of his life was a drop of gall, reminding him of the glory that might have been.

Even with pain banished,[5] surgery remained a heroic—that is, extreme —resort, such was the fearful toll of infection (the chances of surviving an amputation in Great Britain were about one in two). "The operation was a success, but the patient died," is the black humor of that day.

At about the same time that William Morton demonstrated the efficacy of ether, Hungarian Ignaz Semmelweis was appointed in operational charge of the first obstetric ward of Vienna's most famous hospital, Allgemeines Krankenhaus. The maternity ward had gained such a notorious reputation for the high percentage of deaths from childbed fever that expectant mothers pleaded not to be taken into it. Puerperal fever, described by Hippocrates, is highly fatal.

The twenty-eight-year-old Semmelweis, a sensitive, dedicated humanitarian, was driven to frantic despair by the drama that unfolded relentlessly in his ward. The fear he saw in the eyes of the women, he tried to erase with hollow words of assurance. Once the fever began, the disease worked swiftly, painfully, surely. It struck the very human beings who deserved most to be saved. One month, the death toll in the ward rose to nearly one woman in five.

Semmelweis threw himself into a frenzy of work, pitting himself against the scourge. Every spare moment was spent with the new research

---

[5] For years afterward, there were those who campaigned against using any form of anesthesia to ease labor. They contended that the Bible said that woman must give birth in pain because of Eve's sin.

weapon medicine finally had at its full disposal—the postmortem. Carl Rokitansky, Semmelweis' superior and a leader in what was called the New Vienna School of Medicine, performed no less than 30,000 necropsies in his career. Furiously, Semmelweis pored over the corpses of puerperal fever victims. The autopsies, he knew, must contain the clue, somewhere, to the disease. Each day that he left the dissection room unenlightened he had to face the monstrous measure of his failure in the ward. To add to his frustration, the mortality rate actually dropped when he took a vacation leave, then rose again after his return.

Semmelweis was bedeviled by another fact. The death rate was much lower in the second ward where the patients were attended by midwives (who had to undergo a daily inspection even to their fingernails for cleanliness). The first ward was attended by obstetricians and student-doctors who divided their time with the dissection room.

The truth was revealed to Semmelweis after one of Rokitansky's assistants was cut accidentally during dissection and died soon afterward. The postmortem showed the same condition as those for the victims of puerperal fever. The contagion was one and the same! It was being transported from the dissecting table to the healthy women! This liberating truth bore a wicked sting of guilt: it meant that he, too, had been spreading death!

Thereafter, Semmelweis insisted that all obstetricians *wash their hands* in a chlorine solution before examining patients in the first ward. The mortality rate began to drop, but Semmelweis met with scorn and intense opposition from his fellow physicians. The indignity of a doctor being forced to wash his hands! Then the death rate began to climb once again, reinforcing the scoffers, until Dr. Semmelweis discovered that some students had deliberately disobeyed his orders. He dismissed those students. Then he was told the chlorine solution was too expensive. The budget didn't allow it. It must be discontinued. He tore through chemistry books and found a substitute, a chlorinated lime solution that was just as effective, but cost only one-fiftieth the price.

In 1849 the mortality rate from puerperal fever in ward one was close to 1 percent. Despite the indisputable success of his method, Semmelweis remained the target of abuse from fellow obstetricians. He quit Vienna to return to his native Budapest to write, when he was forty-three years old, one of the milestone treatises in the history of medicine, "The Cause, Concept, and Prophylaxis of Puerperal Fever," and also his scathing "Open Letters to Sundry Professors of Obstetrics." Whether from the strain of the ugly controversies or from brooding over his inadvertent role in the agonies of the first ward, Ignaz Semmelweis descended into insanity and was dead at forty-seven.

His example of clinical sanitation was not widely followed,[6] nor did it occur to anyone to extend his methods to medical practices across the board.

In Berlin, Rudolf Virchow was closing in on disease from another direction. The study of disease itself was Virchow's main focus. His teacher, Johannes Müller, had tried to determine the difference between benign and malignant tumors. Müller found the same cellular and sub-cellular structure in both. Having established the cellular character of tumors, he presumed that they originated from normal cells. At the same time, one of his students, Theodor Schwann, stated that all animal tissues are cellular. This great principle was announced in 1838.

Schwann misunderstood the method of generating cells. He thought that the cell nucleus and other parts were formed from a general tissue fluid. Virchow, the father of cellular pathology, set the picture straight— all cells come from cells, he said. "A new growth of cells presupposes already existing cells."

With Virchow's publication of *Cellular Pathologie* in 1858, men had a revolutionary new way of looking at the human body: it was a "republic of cells." The body is "a cell state in which every cell is a citizen," Virchow said, and disease is "a conflict of citizens in this state, brought about by the action of external forces."

Virchow believed that disease was deleterious changes in cell function-ing and that there were no specific disease causes. But this part of the theory was to be modified by Louis Pasteur and Robert Koch.

Early in his career, Pasteur was asked by a manufacturer of beet-juice alcohol to find out why some vats of beet juice turned sour. Pasteur's investigation led him to indict bacteria. In 1857 he published a paper declaring that microbes caused milk to turn sour, wine to ferment, and might also cause disease. Naturally the paper was greeted with skepticism and hostility.

As his investigations progressed, Pasteur realized he would have to

---

[6] Oliver Wendell Holmes, the American physician, author, and father of the U.S. Supreme Court Justice, had written a paper in 1843 *On the Contagiousness of Puer-peral Fever* three years before Semmelweis' appointment to ward one. Dr. Holmes urged that women in childbed should never be attended by physicians who have been conducting postmortem sections or attending puerperal fever cases; he contended that the disease could be conveyed from patient to patient. As a preventive measure, he recommended washing hands in calcium chloride, which Semmelweis used, and even changing clothes after leaving a puerperal fever case. The paper aroused violent op-position from some obstetricians. Semmelweis, of course, knew nothing of Holmes' paper, which had little practical effect on the course of events. Six years after Semmel-weis' initial achievement, Holmes returned to the attack with a monograph, *Puerperal Fever as a Private Pestilence*, in which he stated that one "Senderein" had lessened childbed fever by disinfecting the hands. Senderein was Semmelweis.

settle the question of the origin of microbes. The issue of spontaneous generation kept being destroyed and reborn like the phoenix. Men knew that frogs were generated in mud, and who could deny that maggots appeared spontaneously in putrefying meat? In 1668 the Italian naturalist Francesco Redi had shown that maggots grew from eggs deposited by flies by the simple device of covering a piece of meat with a fine gauze. The maggots grew on the gauze. With the discovery of microscopic organisms, spontaneous generation revived spontaneously. One century after Redi, another Italian naturalist, Lazzaro Spallanzani, proved that putrefaction would not take place if all the little animals were killed by heating and then no more were admitted from the outside. Still the theory would not die and in the nineteenth century even seemed to represent the rational scientific attitude. A single starting point for life suggested a divine creation. If life began once by natural laws, why not over and over, given the appropriate conditions?

After Pasteur had shown that specific organisms soured milk, fermented wine, caused beer to deteriorate, his critics charged that he had it backwards—the micro-organisms were the results, not the cause, of the fermentation process. In a simple but crucial experiment, Pasteur demonstrated by filtering air through cotton wool that microbes existed in the air, but none could generate in sterilized broth that was sealed from air. After two centuries the spontaneous-generation theory was vanquished forever and people's minds were freed to ask, when their bodies were attacked by infectious germs, *how did they get there?*

Pasteur followed this success with controlled heating of wine, with no harm to its quality, to destroy noxious organisms. Pasteurization, safeguarding milk from harmful germs, has been one of medical science's great gifts to all succeeding generations of children.[7]

By 1865 an English surgeon at the University of Glasgow, Joseph Lister, accidentally learned of Pasteur's work with heat sterilization. Lister had noticed that in simple fractures there was no infection. But in compound fractures that broke the skin "hospital gangrene" was a common companion. Something in the air, he reasoned, was responsible and the solution was to disinfect. Heating, as Pasteur had done, was unfeasible, but carbolic acid poured on wounds and sprayed in the air was miraculously effective. Hospital deaths plummeted. There was the usual quota of criticism, but by this time the medical world was receptive to antisepsis. The door was thrown wide open to the era of modern surgery.

In Germany Robert Koch returned from the Franco-Prussian war to practice medicine in a backwater town, and to break the monotony he

[7] At first, milk companies balked at pasteurization, saying it was economically unfeasible, that people would never pay for the added cost.

took up microscopic studies. In five years he had worked out the life-history of the bacillus that caused the cattle disease anthrax. When he showed his work to Germany's leading medical scientists, they called it the greatest bacteriological discovery ever made. Koch had perfected the tool for isolating specific microbes—growing them in a culture, fixing and drying bacterial films, and then staining them with dyes so that they were unmistakably exposed to human eyes. Koch soon added to this feat by identifying the bacteria that caused six infectious diseases in surgery.

By this time Pasteur had discovered the principle of vaccination. Vaccination had been used for smallpox since 1796 when Edward Jenner took some matter from the arm of a milkmaid who had contracted the milder form of cowpox and scratched it into young James Phipps. Dr. Jenner had observed that people who suffered from cowpox never got the more deadly smallpox. When he later inoculated the boy guinea pig with smallpox serum, the disease never appeared. Jenner became a national, an international hero: his government rewarded him handsomely (one basis for Morton's hope for a reward). We all wear Jenner's badge of immunity against smallpox, but at the time no one knew how to employ the principle of vaccination against any other diseases.

In Pasteur's laboratory some chickens were inoculated with cultures of chicken cholera which had not been used for some months. The chickens failed to develop the disease. They were then inoculated with a fresh, highly virulent cholera culture—and still did not develop the disease. Everyone was puzzled, and then Pasteur said, "Don't you see that these animals have been vaccinated!" Within the next few years, Pasteur perfected vaccines for anthrax, swine erysipelas, and rabies.

On March 24, 1882 Koch read a paper before a hall filled with scientists in perhaps the most dramatic presentation of its kind. The title of the paper was "The Etiology of Tuberculosis." The Sherlock Holmes of medicine had tracked down the bacillus that eluded every other investigator.[8]

When the oration was concluded, the audience sat in profound silence. Rudolf Virchow—the other giant of German science, the founder of cellular pathology who had contended there was no specific cause for consumption—left the room without a word. Paul Ehrlich, whose day was yet to come, later wrote, "That evening remains graven in my memory as the most majestic scientific event in which I have ever participated."

At the Tenth International Medical Congress at Berlin in 1890, Koch

[8] In the paper Koch laid down the laws since considered fundamental to establish the cause of an infectious disease: a germ (1) must be found constantly associated with that disease, (2) must be isolated from a lesion of the disease apart from other micro-organisms, (3) must reproduce the disease, (4) must be found in lesions of the artificially produced disease.

announced his belief that he had found a cure for tuberculosis, touching off almost hysterical rejoicing throughout the world. It was his one mistake. Results did not bear out his optimism, but his purported remedy, tuberculin, did prove to be a reliable means of diagnosis. In the institute that now bore Koch's name, Prussian army surgeon Emil von Behring perfected another way to prevent disease: counter the poisons given off by bacteria with antitoxins. Von Behring developed the diphtheria antitoxin, and another scourge of humankind was removed in spectacular fashion. "For a few eager months," says historian Esmond Long, "it seemed as if infectious disease was to be conquered through the use of specific antitoxins."

After all the centuries of groping, medicine had crossed a threshold. In the last quarter of the nineteenth century, investigators discovered the bacteria causing leprosy, gonorrhea, typhoid fever, lobar pneumonia, bubonic plague, meningitis, dysentery, whooping cough, cholera; pinned down the preeminent role of the fly as a disease vector.[9] Science finally had the tools and methods to deal with disease. Microbes could hide no longer from the hunters. Find the cause, and cure or prevention could not be far behind. Suddenly the ancient problem appeared marvelously simple. And uncannily reminiscent. Science had identified those demons that inhabit human beings. Now medicine men could exorcise them.

But still the medical millennium had not quite arrived. In addition to diphtheria, antitoxins were effective only against tetanus and snake bites (today we have added botulism). A vaccination for typhoid came quickly enough, but other vaccines required slow, dogged research. Of the vaccines commonly administered today, four (diphtheria, tetanus, typhoid, rabies), were products of that explosion of discovery, while a fifth (smallpox) came earlier. The others—for polio, measles, pertussis, influenza, TB, rubella—did not appear for another half century or more. And some

[9] One of the oldest folk intuitions was that flies transmit disease. Ancient Egyptians carried fly amulets. Beelzebub was the fly-god. The Bible tells of a "plague of flies" visited upon the Egyptians. In 1557 Ambroise Paré noticed that flies were disease carriers at the battle of St. Quentin. Joseph Leidy called attention to the same fact in his hospital work during the Civil War. In 1850 Nurse G. E. Nicholas noticed that flies and cholera appeared and disappeared together on board ship during the Levantine epidemic. In 1869 flies were shown to transmit anthrax. In 1886 flies were shown to transmit cholera. In 1888 Angelo Celi showed that flies transmit tuberculosis and that bacilli of tuberculosis, anthrax, and typhoid fever retain their virulence after passing through the intestines of flies. A report on typhoid fever in the District of Columbia in 1892 emphasized the importance of flies as disease vectors, connecting them to open privies and the epidemic houses. Walter Reed and other workers definitely proved the alliance of flies and typhoid in the Spanish-American War of 1898.

diseases, like pneumonia, were not susceptible at all to preventive vaccines. The pneumococcus and streptococcus bacteria together have at least 100 different strains; a vaccine against one or two of them would be hardly practical. More than 300 viruses are known to produce disease in humans; again, it is hardly practical to try to inoculate an individual against every one of them.

Cures, too, did not arrive automatically. There was one further development which spurred universal hopes for a panacea, but it proved to be more the final act of that remarkable epoch than the expected breakthrough. Paul Ehrlich, the last of those medical titans, is known as the father of both hematology and chemotherapy, while he won a Nobel Prize for his work in immunology (sharing the prize with Elie Metchnikoff). A thread through all of Ehrlich's work was experimentation with the effects of chemicals upon living tissue. He worked with various dyes because they were so visible. Early in his work, while staining tuberculosis bacilli, he noticed that certain dyes had a particular affinity for the bacteria. This led him to envision the existence of a chemical that would wipe out the invading pathogens without harming the host.

In 1902, some four centuries after Paracelsus, Ehrlich set out to find—to forge—a "magic bullet" chemical cure for disease. Like Paracelsus, Ehrlich was fond of Latin terms and made his goal nothing less than *Therapia magna sterilisans,* one chemical panacea to knock out all infecting microbes. He persevered with fanatical tenacity. He had to, for he had no precedent, no assurance of success, and the chemical variables from which to choose are virtually infinite.

Ehrlich experimented with trypanosomes, a protozoan member of the animal kingdom (and not known to give off a poison as some bacteria did so that there could be no antitoxin). In 1905 the minute spirochete of syphilis finally was isolated by a brilliant researcher, Fritz Schaudinn. The organism, *Treponema pallida,* also was a protozoan, Schaudinn said, possibly related to those on which Ehrlich had been experimenting. Syphilis was a target worthy enough for his bullet. Ehrlich struck upon one particular arsenical hydrocarbon compound and varied it 605 times. Every experiment failed. Either the chemical killed the host along with the parasites or the wily trypanosomes developed immunity, dashing initial optimism. In 1910 effort 606 succeeded! It became known as Salvarsan, the magic bullet to cure syphilis!

This was the climax to a career that won so many medals its owner couldn't carry them all if he could locate them. It was a triumph of science and mankind over one of the nastiest human afflictions. And it heralded a whole new kind of therapy. Except that Ehrlich's bullet didn't always kill every one of those spiral devils in the body. It sterilized the blood stream, dried up the chancres, enormously reduced the chances of contagion, but sometimes those spirochetes secreted themselves in tissues to cause trouble years later. Also the "606" itself was not safe for a percentage of the recipients, causing health complications. And finally, there were no follow-ups—no important antimicrobial drugs were developed for a quarter of a century.[10]

In the meantime the influenza pandemic of 1918 demonstrated that the human species still was vulnerable to its age-old but newly revealed enemies. Thirty million people died, with pneumonia collaborating to finish off millions of the victims weakened by flu.

Even Lord Lister's great innovation had its limits. Antisepsis had become asepsis—keeping hospital areas germ-free in the first place. But there was no way to make the trenches or forward aid stations in World War I aseptic; it was one thing to prevent infection, but once it got a foothold . . . doughboys, tommies, poilu, boche died by the thousands from gangrene, peritonitis, and other forms of infection. Typhus was their companion, just as it marched with Hannibal and Caesar. Even anesthesia had its limits: surgeons feared to open the chest. And there still was shock. By 1934 Lord Berkeley Moynihan, one of the great British surgeons of the era, said: "The craft of surgery has in truth reached its limit in respect both of the range and of safety."

The next year Gerhard Domagk demonstrated that sulfonamide cured streptococcus infection in mice and the year after that it was proved efficacious in humans. At last physicians had a drug to overcome the dreaded septicemia of childbed fever! The drug also was effective against gonorrhea and meningitis. Here was a versatile drug therapy of the kind Ehrlich envisioned. And interestingly it had been produced after eight years of research by a dye firm, I. G. Farbenindustrie. But the sponsors already had sulfonamide patented as Prontosil. Once again the attempt to capitalize on a crucial medical development was circumvented when researchers discovered that Prontosil broke down in the body to its active agent, sulfanilamide, which was unpatented. Sulfanilamide was not perfect, however. Some patients developed severe reactions to the drug; strains of streptococcus and gonococcus developed resistance so that it was not always effective.

But by that time, the sulfa drugs (a family of them were developed) were overshadowed by penicillin. The wonder drug was not a chemical, but an antibiotic—the poison given off by a common bread mold, a

---

[10] In another of those historic ironies, sulfanilamide was synthesized in 1908—two years before Ehrlich succeeded—and first used in the dye industry, but its therapeutic properties were not recognized for more than a decade and not exploited until the mid 1930s.

fungus, in the chemical warfare of the microbial world.[11] This poison very nearly met Ehrlich's ideal—nontoxic to most humans but lethal to the bacteria causing staphylococcus and streptococcus infections and meningitis: the dreamed-of cure-all. It overcame mighty pneumonia and handled the venereal diseases, syphilis and gonorrhea, with an ease that verged on the miraculous. Other antibiotics and chemicals, such as tetracycline, gave humans the pound of cure to supplement the ounce of prevention in the vaccines.

This armament was expanded by DDT, a chlorinated hydrocarbon insecticide. Another chemical of low toxicity to humans, DDT eradicated the typhus louse and Allied soldiers in World War II were the first to endure combat without suffering important casualties from that disease. Employed in all-out campaigns against the Anopheles mosquito, DDT drastically reduced the incidence of malaria.

With pencillin to control infection, World War II surgeons daily, hourly performed their own miracles, operating in combat areas on men mangled by the best that military technology had to offer. The war was a human laboratory, offering opportunities to attempt and perfect almost any kind of surgery and to learn about the last great surgical hazard, shock. It can take many forms, but mainly it was—simply loss of blood. Not just from obvious hemorrhaging, but pathological loss of serum into the tissues. This loss of fluid in addition to taxing the heart meant that poisons were not cleared from major organs. Blood transfusions, early and if necessary massive, and plasma were antidotes for shock. The treatment of various other kinds of shock has been one of the exciting surgical preoccupations of the postwar years. Technological advances such as the heart-lung machine and a battery of advanced, specialized anesthetics led in December 1967 to the historic heart transplant operation by Christiaan Barnard in Capetown, South Africa. In contrast to what Lord Moynihan estimated in the mid-1930s, a surgeon today is virtually unlimited in what he will dare, shying only from transplanting the human brain.

Kidney dialysis machines, insulin, lasers, radioactive tracers, cobalt rays, mental drugs . . .

From the perspective of a century ago, this surely is utopia. At the turn of the century, life expectancy in the United States was 47 years. Today it is about 67 years for men, 74 years for women. The "gradual

---

[11] Penicillin was first discovered accidentally in 1928 by Alexander Fleming but even though he recognized its antibacterial qualities he was unable to concentrate it in significant quantities and it languished for more than a decade. With the pressing needs of World War II, ways were found in the United States to mass-produce the drug so that by D-Day it existed in sufficient quantity to meet the needs of casualties generated by the invasion of mainland Europe.

revelation of truth" does not seem so gradual any more. Aesculapius is triumphant. Or is he? And is it the whole truth?

In the euphoria following the work of Pasteur-Koch-von Behring-Ehrlich-*et al.*, it was overlooked that disease epidemics in Europe had started to decline *before* the discovery of pathogens and counter measures. The mortality rate for tuberculosis in 1900 was just half what it was in 1850 *without* any cure. Something less dramatic than laboratory experiments but more pervasive had been taking place. A number of do-gooders, reformers, sanitarians—most of them unknown to posterity—began pushing to rectify some of the worst evils of the Industrial Revolution.

In English cities in the first half of the nineteenth century, one-half of the children died before the age of five from consumption, typhoid fever, dysentery, cholera, and other pestilences. Drinking water was sold by private companies that in London, for example, piped it directly from the sewage-browned Thames. Poor people in working-class districts were forced to worry about quantity more than quality. They waited in long lines for the water company to open the local tap for a short time each day or every other day. There was precious little water left over for washing. Malnutrition compounded the high cost of poverty.

In 1832 the British government commissioned Sir Edwin Chadwick, a lawyer, to study the living conditions of the poor. His report was not published for a decade, but it led to a great wave of sanitary, housing, and humanitarian reforms that started in England and spread through the Western world. Hundreds upon hundreds of pages documented the squalor and filth with which poor people lived.

Nothing was done at first about the Chadwick report, with slum land-lords and the water companies leading the opposition. But cholera epidemics in London in 1849 and 1853 frightened the public and augured a change.[12] At the same time, other reforms were in progress. In the same year as the Chadwick report, Parliament barred all women and boys nine years and younger from working in mines. Before that law, one of every three British miners ranged from four to seventeen years in age. In the United States hundreds of thousands of children worked six days, 72 hours a week.[13] In the 1850s New York City had the highest death rate

[12] The 1853 epidemic became particularly noteworthy because a physician, John Snow, traced the entire epidemic to one source—a busy public water pump whose well was contaminated from an adjacent cesspool to a tenement housing a cholera sufferer.

[13] Pennsylvania in 1848 was the first state to set a minimum work age for the textile mills—twelve years old. A number of other states followed, but the federal government was unable to pass national laws (that were not declared unconstitutional) restricting child labor until 1938.

in the Western world, followed by Philadelphia and Boston, all receptacle ports for immigrants seeking a new life.

The chief victims were the very young. In 1850 infant mortality in New York City was 18 per 100; in 1860, 22 per 100; in 1870, 24 per 100—just about one in four—before living conditions began to ameliorate and the toll began to decline. In 1898 the statistic still was 14 deaths per 100, but by this time the "name" microbial diseases were killing few of these infants. The big killer, causing more than half the deaths, was what is known as the pneumonia-diarrhea complex. By 1930 all other causes of infant mortality had dropped relatively little whereas the pneumonia-diarrhea complex had gone down more than 75 percent and dwindled to almost nothing in the years following.

This decline took place with no antimicrobial drugs. Even today only a small number of the pneumonia cases could be treated with drugs because of their viral origin. As for the diarrhea, there is no microbe, neither virus nor bacterium, that can be pointed to as *the* cause of the trouble. The most educated guess after seven decades of study is that the causative agents are simply the microbes that become our normal intestinal inhabitants as we grow up. The fact is that, except for a small percentage of the cases, "we have today no decisive treatments or preventives that we can put into the hands of a clinical physician confronted with an infant with the diarrhea-pneumonia complex," says Walsh McDermott, chairman of the Public Health Department of Cornell Medical College. This is hardly an academic point for the underdeveloped nations (where more than half of all deaths occur in the first five years of life) because "the truly great killer throughout two thirds of the world is that same pneumonia-diarrhea disease complex."

Why *did* the lethal infant disease disappear from New York City? Authorities are unable, today, to point to any one or two decisive measures, not even such beneficial reforms as pasteurization of milk and chlorination of drinking water. All we know, says Dr. McDermott, is that it was the result of many changes. "We do know that the first part of this period was one of lively social reform movement aimed at ameliorating the conditions in the New York slums. There were milk kitchens, visiting nurses, and the beginnings of well-baby clinics; there was the growth of pediatrics with Jacobi and Holt and the work of Park and of Lillian Wald. There were major campaigns against illiteracy and a big push in primary school education. There was a substantial fall in the birth rate . . . so that there were not quite so many infants and young children in the society."

Why do so many youngsters in underdeveloped countries succumb to the disease complex? This is Dr. McDermott's answer:

It may be recalled that the particular viruses and bacteria involved in this disease complex are not limited to the impoverished areas of the world. On the contrary they also are present in the affluent residential neighborhoods of an industrialized society. Indeed, they may be regarded as constituting some of life's inescapable microbial challenges. But in the overly traditional society the infant or two-year-old is wholly unprotected against these challenges and tends to receive them all at once. By contrast, in our society a set of structural and functional sanitary barriers have been erected whereby these individual challenges are stretched out over the whole childhood and adolescence of the individual. These barriers were developed in part unconsciously and in part by pediatricians and nurses; the barriers themselves are based soundly on biomedical science. They consist, in large measure, of the invention of a radically new kind of dwelling and of altering the events that go on within it. Among the structural changes are such inventions as windows that can be opened, central heating, hot and cold water, flush toilets, tables from which to eat, refrigeration, and paper towels. The functional change has been principally in the form of parents with at least enough education to enable them to manage the household machinery properly and to establish the hygienic practices within the home.

Tuberculosis as well as many of the other epidemic diseases was overcome first and mainly through cleanliness, sanitation, safe drinking water, wholesome food, clean air and sunlight, adequate and private living space, improved living conditions with a consequent improved outlook toward life.[14] As people came to understand the contagious mechanism of the disease, sufferers were isolated to sanitaria that specialized in the above conditions. Only later did drugs subjugate once omnipotent TB to its present state.

But, lo and behold, these are the therapies of Hygeia espoused by Hippocrates!

It would seem that the concepts of the body as a society of cells and disease as the invasion of germs should have erased forever Hippocrates' quaint notion of humoral fluids. Yet at the time Darwin was restating the Hippocratic doctrine that survival comes from fitness to the external environment, Claude Bernard was promulgating the complementary Hippocratic contention that the individual's health depends upon his inner equilibrium. The French physiologist was thinking very much in terms of fluids, having done pioneering work with the juices of the liver and pan-

---

[14] Max von Pettenkofer of Bavaria was such a champion of fresh air, uncontaminated land, and other public health measures that in order to prove his point against the contagionists he drank a brew of cultured cholera bacilli. This was in 1892 when he was seventy-four years old, and nine years after Koch had discovered the cholera vibrio. Von Pettenkofer survived this audacious test, duly impressing many people with the virtues of public health and of their protagonists.

creas. Bernard states: "The constancy of the internal environment is the essential condition of independent life." Internal environment in his native French is *milieu intérieur,* the expression that still denotes the biochemical interior.

Subsequent research confirmed that the healthy body does operate within narrow tolerances and seeks to maintain this biochemical balance. Harvard physiologist Walter Cannon earlier in this century showed that these processes are largely controlled by hormones and the autonomic nervous system. They seek to maintain the body's constancy in a process he called homeostasis. If external insults or emotional upset, for instance, disturb the equipoise of the temperature, blood pressure, oxygen, water, salts, and other components, then homeostasis, like some marvelous gyroscope, restores the original state through intricate orchestration of endocrine-biochemical signals.

The Russian psychologist Ivan Pavlov related this biochemical equilibrium to neural control. And, of course, more recent psychiatric investigations have established the intimate relationship between mental aberrations (and health) and the body's chemistry.[15] The long catalogue of psychosomatic illnesses and the case histories from the psychoanalyst's couch document very well the Hippocratic principle that inner harmony is a requisite for good health.

But what is most remarkable is that medicine is being forced into still another of Hippocrates' positions, and that is, that the physician must treat the patient, not the disease. What is so remarkable about the event is that while Hippocrates possessed the profundity to adopt this medical strategy he could practice it only with indifferent success. Medicine could come to this point only after conquering microbial disease . . . and only after the lessons learned from that experience.

Until the mind-expanding discoveries of Leeuwenhoek, Pasteur, and Koch, until the sanitary legacy of Semmelweis, Lister, and the champions of public health, until penicillin, DDT, and the other biochemical weapons, the association with disease pathogens was the most devastating experience in human history. These invisible destroyers were the true angels of death, the most pernicious of life's inscrutable evils. Time and again human intelligence intuited their existence, but there simply was an insufficient fund of knowledge and a lack of adequate tools to discover them and deal with them. Francis Bacon was wrong in saying knowledge is power. It requires knowledge and technology in tandem.

---

[15] At the forefront of biological science today, investigators are trying to determine the mechanisms by which the brain's hypothalamus directs the chemical supervision of bodily functions.

That was one of the lessons. Another consequence is that physicians were forced to expand their horizons to take an ecological perspective in order to comprehend epidemic disease. Initially, infectious disease may have been regarded simply as the invasion of our bodies by harmful germs and the indicated procedure was to kill the intruders with medicine. This still is a primary response, of course, but not the only way to deal with disease, as the discussion of the pneumonia-diarrhea complex informs. Contagious disease is an interaction of the human species with other species of organisms to the disadvantage of our species. For as long as we remain on this planet, we will coexist with millions of other species. The medical task is to explore all ways possible to intervene in or modify the interactions so that minimal or no harm is done to humans.

The fascinating story of bubonic plague illustrates the complexity of the problem and the sophistication with which contagious disease now is handled.

Plague swept from middle Asia via the Black Sea through Constantinople, Venice, Genoa, and other ports into Europe in the spring of 1346. The disease raced through the Continent like wildfire, an image used by Boccaccio to describe the scene at Florence. With incredible virulence, the disease attacked two-thirds of the population in eight years, killing 25 million people—one of every four persons in Europe.[16] The terror and decimation in many places crumbled the structure of society; charity for victims was displaced by fear, sufferers were shunned and abandoned. Thousands upon thousands of people fled their homes in mindless panic, but there was no haven. This calamity left such an impression that "plague" became the generic word for any epidemic, while the historic word "pestilence" came to mean plague unless otherwise specified.

Early in the pandemic, Venice and other ports instituted isolation procedures for incoming people and goods, from which we get the word "quarantine." A similar isolation was practiced voluntarily by some fearful citizens who sealed themselves in their houses, and by decree for those infected and anyone who had come into contact with them. Still, no one could contain this terrifying contagion nor could anyone understand how it was communicated.

With this ignorance as bona fide as ever, the plague disappeared from Europe in the eighteenth century never to return.

It was not until this century, though, that we understood the mechanisms of plague. The disease exists basically in wild rodents, with the

[16] Garrison puts the Black Death toll at one-fourth of the known civilized world of the time (60 million deaths).

main reservoir in central Asia.[17] The plague bacillus reaches human populations after a closely associated rodent population has become infected with the disease. These rodents have been rats. Bubonic plague is transmitted from rat to human and from rat to rat and from human to human by the rat flea, *Xenopsylla cheopis*.[18] So that is the mechanism for transmitting bubonic plague, the enigma that was so baffling for so long.

But why did the plague disappear from eighteenth-century Europe? The flea *X. cheopis* is a fellow traveler of the black rat, *Rattus rattus*. The black rat is a domesticated rat, a homebody who likes to live as intimately with humans as they will allow. In 1727 Europe was invaded by the larger brown, or gray, rat, *Rattus norvegicus*, that we are familiar with today. Although the humans who believed they owned the real estate were completely unaware of it, there was a rodent war for possession of Europe. The outcome never could have been in doubt because the Norwegian rat is fiercer than his smaller cousin. The black rat was evicted from his haunts, but the brown rat prefers to keep his distance from humans, given the choice. The newcomers occupied fields and barns, sewers, wharves, warehouses, slaughterhouses, and tenements too, whenever food and shelter were put at their disposal. Not only was this species of rat more removed from the human population, but its species of fleas are less effective carriers of bubonic plague. That probably is the paramount reason that plague vanished from Europe although Europeans' style of living underwent great changes between the fourteenth and eighteenth centuries and these factors may have been crucial as well.

Today we immunize people with a vaccine if they are going into a plague area. If the infection already has taken place, we combat it with streptomycin or aureomycin. We attack the fleas with DDT or other insecticides. We control rat populations and movements through rat-proofing, extermination, and sanitary measures. Modern civilization is virtually an entirely new environment compared to the medieval setting in which the plague flourished. (In this respect it can be seen that the current environmental campaign for clean air and pure waters is a new wave of the sanitary reforms that began in the nineteenth century.) It

[17] In March 1900 plague was diagnosed in San Francisco. The federal government moved to stop it, but indignant Californians, denying their state was infected, thwarted initial actions. With this delay the disease spread from rats to ground squirrels in California. Today the plague has infected 15 species of squirrels and 23 other kinds of wild animals, including cottontail rabbits, chipmunks, prairie dogs, wood rats, and harvest mice, and is now as far east as Kansas.

[18] An epidemic of pneumonic plague early in the century began when the disease was contracted by Chinese hunters from marmot (which suddenly had come into fashion). This version of the plague can be transmitted directly among humans through the germs sprayed by coughing.

is no longer acceptable to live with filth and rats and lice and go un-
bathed for months on end. And being bitten by fleas as a routine experience is unthinkable.

In sum, the factors for the disease involve a species of bacteria, the
plague baccillus, species of fleas, species of rats, the human species, and
how they interact. Temperature and humidity control or affect the proliferation of fleas. Experiments have shown that the fleas can jump no
higher than four inches and rats suspended in cages above that height
were not infected. So those fourteenth-century Europeans possessed a
countermeasure to plague well within their technological capability if
anyone had been inspired to strike upon it—stilts.[19]

The individual's resistance will influence the severity with which the
baccillus attacks, and this defense correlates to the history of his and his
forebears' exposure to plague. The reason bubonic plague was so lethal
in the fourteenth century is that it was the first time the European population had come into contact with the pathogen; the host's natural defenses were totally vulnerable. In the course of any infectious disease, as
the two populations continue to interact, they tend toward accommodation and the disease loses some of its virulence.[20]

Also involved in this disease equation is the environment in which the
interactions take place. Malaria does not prosper in temperate zones
because the Anopheles mosquito prefers warm temperatures; the mosquito also needs swamps or other bodies of still water in which to breed.
Plague rats breed in filth, and so on. Finally, there are the myriad forms
and acts of human behavior which can encourage or inhibit the spread
of infection.

A consequence of this ecological view of disease is the realization that
rarely is there just one cause of disease. Disease is the result, the con-
vergence, of a number of factors. "Thousands of people carry within them
the microbes of influenza, tuberculosis, staphylococcus infections and
other illnesses," say René Dubos, "but this single factor does not make
them develop the disease. However, inclement weather or starvation or

[19] In Vietnam when delta people were relocated in the highlands, they continued
their practice of building their homes at ground level. The native highlanders built
their homes on stilts so that their living rooms were about ten feet off the ground.
Unlike the natives who were generally free of malaria, the emigrants were subject to
the disease and resisted relocation programs, believing that evil spirits in the hills
did not like delta people. As it happened, the malarial mosquito there, Anopheles
minimus, rarely flies higher than ten feet.

[20] Smallpox, introduced into the New World by Europeans, took a fearsome toll of
Indian populations. Medical historians credit the conquest of Mexico to smallpox rather
than Cortez. To the north, Europeans deliberately gave contaminated goods to the
Indians (once they discovered the Indians' extreme susceptibility) in order to decimate
their populations and facilitate colonization.

even a family quarrel may provide the trigger that makes the disease flare up."

The physician is being driven toward this position of treating the whole patient and not the disease symptoms by still another historical evolution. Ever since Descartes split the human being into body and mind, physicians have been content to work within the framework of that division. If you had something wrong with your mind, you went to a mind doctor; the general practitioner took care of the body-machine. This was useful, probably necessary, given the primitive state of knowledge and the domination of microbial diseases which could be dealt with on that simplified basis. But modern civilization has conquered the ecological diseases. This is said with the knowledge that this newly won supremacy is not a permanent but a dynamic condition and must always remain so, since it concerns interrelationships of living, evolving populations of organisms. The time may come when so many organisms are resistant to penicillin that its usefulness will end. Some new mutant virus might infiltrate all our present defenses to ravage us like the medieval plague. The fast-mutating influenza virus infected more than 30 million Americans in 1968 (but killed only about 200 of its victims). A breakdown of civilization would leave us naked once again to our merciless disease enemies.

With that caveat, the fact is that relatively few people in modern civilization die from infectious diseases. Our very concept of disease is changing from the old-fashioned one of being sick in bed with the flu or strep throat. Health, as defined by René Dubos is "the ability to function effectively within a given environment. And since the environment keeps changing, good health is a process of continuous adaptation to the myriad microbes, irritants, pressures and problems which daily challenge man." Disease, says Jacques May, another authority on the subject, "is a biological expression of maladjustment." (A sign, Hippocrates said, that a person is not living properly.)

Most people in modern civilization die from what are called degenerative, but also might be labeled behavioral, diseases. Cirrhosis from undisciplined drinking. Obesity from overeating. Abuse of drugs. Smoking. Loss of physical fitness from sedentary work patterns. Highway accidents resulting from driving while intoxicated or because the driver is emotionally immature or untrained or because manufacturers have neglected safety or because the nation has persisted with a hazardous transport system. Accidents (highway fatalities account for not quite half the accident toll) are the preponderant cause of death for Americans younger than twenty-five years and still the leading cause of death for men until the age of forty-five. Suicide and homicide trail only accidents and cancer in the mortality of youths and account for nearly 2 percent of all deaths in the United States. The fastidious society that proscribes malarial mosquitos, plague rats, and typhoid carriers refuses to regard handguns as disease vectors: 21,000 Americans die each year from privately owned guns; since 1900 the toll has been 800,000 deaths in the United States. More young children in America are believed to die from child abuse than from any other cause. Even with venereal disease, which is microbial, the hard-core problem is behavioral.

The two main killers of humans in modern civilization—cardiovascular disease and cancer—are loaded with behavioral components. Smoking, of course, is closely related to both diseases. No one yet has figured out a way to measure exactly how stress contributes, but almost certainly the "rat race" is an element in both diseases. Atherosclerosis is probably associated with the rich and/or altered diet used by the affluent society during the past four or five decades. In order for a physician to find out what is causing biological maladjustment, he is being forced increasingly not only to examine the whole patient, but the patient's life-style and even beyond that complex to the cultural *milieu*—to discover that quite possibly society is doing something wrong.

In this century when cancer has risen steadily to become the number two killer [21] in industrialized societies—striking one in four Americans and killing one in six—the environment has become ever more conducive to malignancy. Australian Sir Macfarlane Burnet, who won a Nobel Prize for his work in immunology, comments:

"There is virtually only one thing in common among all the ways in which cancer can be experimentally provoked in animals or clearly demonstrated to result from environmental factors in man. None of the substances concerned would ever have been encountered except in some fantastically unlikely circumstances during the whole course of pre-human evolution. The first chemical carcinogens came only with the use of fire for domestic purposes. Since then we have first slowly and in the twentieth century at precipitous speed built a civilization on unbiological materials, i.e., materials that the mammalian body has not been adapted by evolution to deal with."

[21] This is not to imply failure in the war against cancer; quite the contrary. Before the turn of the century, the kill rate for cancer was close to 100 percent. By the late 1930s, the number of hostages being reprieved still were fewer than one in five (generally a person is considered cured if he lives five years without any symptoms of the disease recurring). Ten years later, one in four was being saved. In 1956, the ratio went to one in three, where it has remained. Authorities say that with present knowledge the ratio could be one in two. The victims who die needlessly are those who are not treated in time. Two million living Americans have been given a medical reprieve from cancer. Cancer and heart disease have become such common instruments of death, of course, because of the conquest of infectious diseases.

About 1,000 chemicals have been discovered, so far, to produce cancers in animals. Since human beings are animals, the syllogism is that these chemicals could cause human cancers, and so such carcinogens are banned from the consumer market. However, the jurisdiction of the Food, Drug and Cosmetic Act and the Food and Drug Administration does not extend to cigarettes, the agent responsible for the most dramatic efflorescence of cancer. By 1972 69,000 Americans a year were dying from lung cancer— 56,000 of them men, a rate 18 times greater than in 1932. While the female rate was much lower, it, too, was beginning to move upward, reflecting the recognition by manufacturers a generation earlier that women also have an equal right to contribute to the cigarette market. All told, the American Cancer Society estimates that nearly one American in six dies from causes related to smoking.

As apparent and as grave as such a threat is to its members, the response of society is ambiguous. For years, health spokesmen politely pointed to the statistical correspondence between cigarette smoking and lung cancer (the death rate for lung cancer is nine times as high among regular cigarette smokers as among those who never smoked; 20 times as high for those who smoke two packs a day or more; 92 times higher for smokers who work with asbestos; on average, a smoker at age 25 who smokes a pack a day or more can expect to forfeit six and half years of his life). To this, tobacco forces truculently retorted: prove it. Prove lung cancer isn't caused by X or Y or Z or a thousand other causes or combinations of causes—obviously a time-consuming if not impossible argument to refute scientifically. By 1972, the American Cancer Society no longer was observing such niceties, stating bluntly: "Most lung cancers are caused by cigarette smoking."

With all our knowledge of the cigarette-cancer alliance, our most accomplished institution for persuasion—advertising—is devoted to enticing people to smoke. If Madison Avenue finds nothing unethical or demeaning in selling cancer, neither have other purveyors of information. Newspapers and magazines gladly accept the advertising and so did broadcasters until prevented from doing so by circumstances beyond their control. But when it comes to benefiting from the tobacco industry's largesse, no segment of society excels the surrogate of the people and guardian of their welfare: government. The federal government alone takes in more than $2 billion from manufactured tobacco, making it one of the top three tax-producing commodities. Of course, there are other issues for lawmakers to take into account. What is the detriment to the economy? How many jobs would be lost if the tobacco industry were shut down? How would the functioning of government be affected by the loss of revenue? Could bootlegging be controlled? And (always unstated) who enjoys the profits and who gets the cancer? Like everything else, cancer prevention must be judged according to society's cost-benefit index. Still, a society conducting a crusade against cancer but unwilling to forego the leading carcinogen is patently schizophrenic.

If today's diseases are so entwined with how society functions, they cannot be regarded solely as medical problems nor even public health concerns, but the province as well of educators, sociologists, social workers, psychologists, religious leaders, philosophers, political leaders, and citizens. As we see with environmental and consumer affairs and in other ways that affect their welfare, citizens are influencing social mechanisms. Citizen involvement is bound to increase as people become more aware how closely interlinked are social patterns and the individual's health.

The story of medicine belies Norman O. Brown's statement that mankind "has no idea what it really wants." Mankind knows very well what it wants. Medicine is a concerted, unremitting, systematic effort to achieve death control. The enterprise has been so successful in this century that a baby born into modern industrial civilization has an excellent chance to live out his or her lifespan.[22] Let us grant, given this track record, that medical science finds the cures for cancer. The World Health Organization (WHO) says such a scintillating accomplishment would add only about two and a half years to life expectancy in the United States. WHO says a solution to cardiovascular diseases would make a more noticeable contribution—12 years for men, 15 years for women. However, this estimate may be too optimistic or simplistic, not taking into account the debilitating effect of aging. Gerontologist Edwin Bierman, in a report to the 1971 White House Conference on Aging, put the benefits from curing both cancer and arteriosclerosis "at barely five years." Old people, he explained, "would die a little later of something else." WHO conceded that heart diseases are so closely related to the aging process that their complete elimination is "impossible."

Looming behind the diseases is the disability for which wise old Hippocrates knew no strategy, and Panacea had no remedial drugs, and Aesculapius could not heal, and even Hygeia's therapy finally was unavailing.

---

[22] Today the odds are that nearly three out of four people in the United States will live to age sixty-five; two centuries ago in Europe three of four people were dead by age sixty.

V. What Is Aging?

We all know what aging is. Balding, graying, wrinkling, sagging, cane, spectacles, dentures, fragility, fraility, dependence. Ugliness, too. The old lady's legs are scrawny, rising past knobby knees to connect with a dumpy belly and the deflated hemispheres of her rump. The bikini is for her younger sisters. And if she dares flaunt her mottled skin and impoverished paps at a beach resort, and if she is not overlooked completely, she is regarded with disdain. "I grow old . . . I grow old . . . ," sighed J. Alfred Prufrock in his *Love Song*, "I shall wear the bottoms of my trousers rolled." That was poet T. S. Eliot's way of saying that the aging male's vanity keeps him also from wearing a bathing suit.

Who has not turned from a rigid old woman with strawlike hair, downturned lips and jowls, to a photograph of her a half century earlier, hardly able to suppress: "Why, you were beautiful!" It is just as startling to compare the old man with his thin shoulders and watery, rheumy eyes to the strong, virile, upright fellow he once was. It is as though the person has been etched by a morbid Jack Frost who works as imperceptibly as the earth turns so that the transition is impossible to detect in progress.

We all know some other things about aging, too. Aging is something that happens to us with time. The process is irreversible. The culmination is death. A person begins to age, the physician Galen believed, the moment he is conceived. Growing old, said one oldtimer, "is like living on an island that is steadily shrinking in size." Yet if old age is unwanted, it is the one undesirable condition about which we must change the comment to "There *with* the grace of God go I," or as Maurice Chevalier put it when he was asked if he minded growing old, "Not when I consider the alternative."

As the Greeks had done with the elements and qualities and humors, they assigned four ages to man: childhood (hot and moist), youth (hot and dry), adulthood (cold and dry), and old age (cold and moist). Hippocrates was the first to compare the stages of life to the four seasons. We recognize the analogy still. Walter Huston's wavery old-man's voice singing "September Song" is poignant not only for the sad-sweet lyrics but because that song was farewell for a venerable actor. His audience could identify with, and applaud, his gallant, graceful, undaunted perseverance into the gloaming of November and night of December.

William Shakespeare, that shrewd observer of the human scene, saw seven ages. First, "the infant, mewling and puking in the nurse's arms.

"Then the whining school-boy, with his satchel and shining morning face, creeping like snail unwillingly to school.

"And then the lover, sighing like furnace . . . ."

Fourth, a soldier "seeking the bubble reputation even in the cannon's mouth.

"And then the justice, in fair round belly with good capon lin'd . . . full of wise saws and modern instances."

That is the end of the adult plateau. "The sixth age shifts into the lean and slipper'd pantaloon . . . his youthful hose, well sav'd, a world too wide for his shrunk shank; and his big manly voice, turning again toward childish treble . . . .

"Last scene of all, that ends this strange eventful history, is second childishness and mere oblivion, sans teeth, sans eyes, sans taste, sans everything."

These representations imply something else we all know about aging. It is a process, continuous, going on within us at this instant. You were never as old as you are right now, ill-wishers like to remind us. If we survive, old age is our destiny just as the prune is implicit in the plum and the burnished apple shrivels into a crumpled ball. But the purple plum is implicit in the seed and the robust apple in the blossom. Is the process that produces the budding girl and fecund woman the same, then, as the one which turns her into the infertile dowager? We use the verb "to mature" to describe the ongoing process from birth till death. Yet we also call one growing and the other growing old or senescence. Are two separate and distinct processes at work? If so, are both normal? Is one normal, the other abnormal?

With the triumphs over contagious disease, other questions have grown more intrusive. Why does one man die from a heart attack at the age of forty-five while a Casals remains an incomparable cellist at ninety-five? If a Casals can be vigorous, still exquisitely coordinated at ninety-five, why must other men in Western societies expect to die before their eightieth birthday? Shouldn't it be possible to make old age more health-ful, more physically enjoyable à la Casals for the majority of people?

These are questions some medical, biological, and social scientists are asking today, and more. Science has verified what Francis Bacon so clair-voyantly postulated: if we can understand nature's laws, then they may be manipulated or amended or circumvented or repealed. Once only a superhuman Gilgamesh could swim at the bottom of the sea; today it is within the capability of less extraordinary humans who use scuba equipment. Until this century, men knew it was impossible to fly. And until this last instant in time, to walk on the moon was the achievement only of Jules Verne's imagination.

Is aging inevitable? Is it, indeed, irreversible? Before scientists can answer those questions, they must be able to answer this one: What is aging?

These are the stages in the human life cycle as seen by a developmental physiologist: [1]

1. *Embryonic.* This period embraces the first three months of prenatal life. The first week of life after fertilization is known as the ovum stage. This first trimester of life is characterized by rapid differentiation of cells into different types and establishment of organs and systems.

2. *Fetal.* For the remaining two-thirds of prenatal life, the organism is designated a fetus. The middle three months, the early fetal period, are characterized by accelerated growth, elaboration of structures, and the first functional activities. The late fetal period is marked by a rapid increase of body mass and bringing the organism to readiness for postnatal life.

3. *Birth.* Labor and delivery are the most profound and rapid transition the living organism is ever called upon to undergo. Externally, the individual moves from the womb to the outside world; internally, it switches from the placental to its own respiratory-digestive-excretory systems.

4. *Neonatal.* The first two weeks of postnatal life from birth include the changes just mentioned and adjustments in blood circulation.

5. *Infancy.* This period denotes the first two years of life following the neonatal weeks. The second two weeks of life are known as early infancy. Middle infancy begins after the first month and extends through the first year; it is characterized by rapid growth, maturation of functions, particularly of the nervous system, and ends with the assumption of an erect posture. Late infancy, the second year of life, sees a slowing of growth and increasing control of motor activities, such as walking.

6. *Childhood.* The early or preschool period from two to six years sees a further slowing of growth, rapid learning, milk teeth. Middle childhood, the first school period from six to ten years in girls, six to twelve years in boys. Late childhood, the prepubertal period blends into early adolescence.

[1] This outline is based on *Developmental Physiology and Aging* by P. S. Timiras (New York: Macmillan, 1972), pp. 2-4.

7. *Adolescence.* This begins with puberty, twelve to fourteen years in girls and fourteen to sixteen years in boys, and features changes in secondary sex characteristics. This is usually a period of maximum growth. Postpubertal, the next four years in either sex, is characterized by the maturing of sex-organ functions and the need for independence.

8. *Adulthood.* Between the ages of twenty and sixty-five years—prime and transition.

9. *Old age and Senescence.* From sixty-five years on.

It can be seen from this outline that definable stages occur in more rapid sequence at the beginning of the metamorphosis. Early developments take place more exactly "on schedule" within narrow time tolerances than later events. The discrepancies become more evident with physiological declines, both from individual to individual and among different parts and systems of the same person, so that age sixty-five is probably a more accurate social than physical demarcation of old age.

The spacing of these events has led investigators to see a lessening of hereditary guidance and a progressive increase of environmental influence through the life cycle. This shift begins immediately after the genetic union of the female egg and male sperm produces in the broadest and the most literal sense the *conception* of an individual—a biological potential that will be expressed one way or another through time and circumstances. In mammals, P. S. Timiras says in *Developmental Physiology and Aging,* "embryonal and fetal development is primarily dependent on genetic regulation, whereas environmental factors predominate after birth, when the individual is exposed to an increasingly complex biologic and social environment." But even before birth, environmental influences have a much more important role than was suspected until very recently. Indeed, one researcher found that birth weight, taken as an index to prenatal development, was affected more importantly by environmental than genetic factors.

While the influence of the past is readily seen in the genetic construction of the individual, the past also affects the individual's chances for survival and longevity environmentally through the mother's health and constitution: the end-products of *her* entire life.[2] So effective is the

[2] It is estimated that one in five pregnancies aborts spontaneously, a consequence of abnormal fetuses but also the physical condition of the mother. Women with such diseases as chronic high blood pressure, diabetes, and syphilis are prone to abort. Says the National Institute of Child Health and Human Development: "Evidence currently being accumulated suggests that in addition to other important factors, the state of a woman's nutrition before, during and after pregnancy (while nursing) may influence both the physical and mental development of her children. It has been suggested that in humans, maternal malnutrition during pregnancy may permanently impair the efficiency of children's protein synthesis."

uterine-placental system as shield and nurturing envelope that it took a thalidomide to shatter faith in its invulnerability, although studies as early as 1937 first confirmed a correlation between nutrition and prenatal development. Today obstetricians have a long inventory of environmental factors that can disturb development of the embryo-fetus, ranging from nutritional deficiencies to excessive hormones to fever to infections such as rubella or influenza to such drugs as penicillin (possibly causing growth retardation), streptomycin (deafness), tetracycline (impaired growth). In January 1973 the U.S. Public Health Service indicted cigarette smoking by pregnant women as a serious threat to the life of the fetus and child right after birth. The PHS report said 4,600 stillbirths in the United States a year can be attributed to the mother's smoking habits. The report to Congress said the new data indicate that a woman who gives up smoking by the fourth month of pregnancy eliminates the heightened risk for her unborn baby. It had been known for a decade that cigarette smoking by the mother was associated with lower infant weight at birth and premature births.

Weight at birth and length of gestation are two of the three key indicators to chances of survival at birth (the third is body length). Normal gestation is from 38 to 40 weeks, 266 to 280 days. The infant born before the 37th week of gestation or weighing less than five and a half pounds is considered premature. An infant's chances of survival decrease with reductions in weight and size at birth and in length of intrauterine life. The chances reach zero in births before the 28th week and when the newborn weighs less than two pounds. Deaths from prematurity usually occur because the respiratory, gastrointestinal, or thermoregulatory functions or the immune system are not well enough formed. But even if the premature infant survives in an incubator, the individual still may suffer long-term effects upon growth and development—although experts are not wholly sure about this because the types, degrees, and causes of prematurity are so numerous. It is as though nature draws up a huge scorecard listing every input—biological and environmental—as a plus or minus toward the individual's survival. Of course, some defects or environmental assaults can be lethal in themselves, but even infinitesimal items can assume weight in an aggregate.

Time also can be a crucial factor in the sense of when a challenge confronts an organism. A rubella infection usually is a mild affliction for the mother, but is catastrophic for the embryo. Experiments with mice indicate that LSD may do its harm to the human embryo between the sixteenth and twenty-second days of pregnancy, a time when pregnancy still may not be suspected, although it has not been proved conclusively that LSD causes chromosomal damage in human beings. Timing also is an important factor in when a pregnancy occurs in the mother's life. The third decade of a woman's life is optimal for child bearing, both in terms of the child's survival and its healthy development. After the thirtieth year in the mother's life, there are escalating risks of miscarriage, premature births, stillbirths, and neonatal deaths. Pregnancies very late in maternal life are associated with mental retardation, mongolism, and other nervous-system abnormalities.

All human embryos develop with such uniformity that the manufacture of a human being obviously is proceeding according to a well-laid plan. This act of creation is the preeminent marvel of life—and it may contain the secret of senescence. Each cell, each tissue, each organ, each system is formed in a systematic way, always in a standard order, on a tight schedule. The biggest mystery of biology today is how nature does this—how cells (or whatever process is the architect) know precisely when there are enough nerve cells, for instance, and thereafter to turn into skin cells or liver cells or blood cells, and then stop when there are enough of them, and finally to stop altogether when the organism has achieved its proper design (of course, cell manufacture for repair and replacement continues in some organs and so does body growth up to a point). Since it is known that an organism develops according to the blueprint contained in the DNA (genes and chromosomes), many scientists believe that cell differentiation and biological development proceed by a selective use of genetic information at different times. In other words, all the biological information available to the organism exists in the nucleus of every cell, but somehow each cell decides or is told to follow certain genetic instructions and to ignore others.

The regularity of biological development—the first baby teeth appear at about seven months, the first adult teeth at six or seven years, the reproductive organs mature last—shows that these events are programmed. Furthermore, in the embryonic and fetal stages, there are numerous examples of programmed aging and cell death (as there are in the individual after birth: red blood cells age and die in 120 days).

The prenatal organism makes, employs, and then disposes of a number of temporary organs. The young embryo undergoes an anatomic evolution that in the nineteenth century was thought to recapitulate the earlier phylogenic phases of our species—fish, amphibian, and reptilian manifestations before assuming the final mammalian form. Some of these embryonic organs turn into parts that are useful later; for example, the gills become the thymus and parathyroid glands. Some of the organs remain, but serve no purpose to the adult, such as the appendix. But most organs are removed through the programmed death of the cells—no less than 76 instances of cell degeneration have been counted in different phases of embryonic development. Cell death is one of the important mechanisms of cell differentiation (others are cell division, cell movement, cellular interactions, shifts in biosynthetic activity). The placenta is a good example of a temporary organ. That all-purpose substitute for the adult lungs, kidneys, intestines, and liver is made to last about 40 weeks. At the end it develops all the signs of aging tissue including a decline in function.[3] For this reason, delayed birth can become increasingly hazardous.

But is the programmed aging of the placenta a model for the senescence of the entire organism? Are the programmed cell deaths that figure in the morphogenesis of the embryo analogous to what happens to the aging human being? Is senescence programmed or does it come about, as some scientists believe, precisely because there is *no* program? Upon an answer to that question hinges the strategy to deal with biological aging.

The Hippocratic dictum that change (the more rapid, the more threatening) is related to morbidity and mortality is confirmed by statistics on the human life cycle. Most miscarriages occur at the very start of prenatal life in the early embryonic stage. Birth, the most traumatic transition, is attended by the highest incidence of infant deaths. Seventeen thousand children in the United States die from accidents each year, but five of every eight of these deaths occur during the first four years of life.

The decade between five and 14 years is the healthiest in the human lifespan. Resistance to microbial diseases is the highest, deaths from accidents and all other environmental challenges the lowest. "If we could stay as vigorous as we are at 12," says gerontologist Alex Comfort, "it would take about 700 years for half of us to die, and another 700 years for the survivors to be reduced by half again." Alas, there is no marking time at this way station. The teenager undergoes great internal changes including a spurt in physical growth and sexual development; he leaves home to go out into the world for the first time—and the death rate reverses direction, rising sharply.

There is a universal pattern to human mortality. It starts off high at

---

[3] The spawning salmon is an example of this accelerated, programmed aging in fish. After the salmon enters fresh water, the pituitary gland grows to double its normal size, slips the control of the central nervous system, and triggers a metabolic speedup that burns away almost all the fat on the fish. Says biochemist Andrew Benson of Scripps Institution of Oceanography: "It is as though all the glands were programmed to cause the combustion of fat simultaneously so that the whole machine runs out of fuel." At the same time, the fresh water stimulates production of a hormone that causes calcium to dissolve out of the bones, but sending it into the bloodstream. Both the pituitary gland and calcium changes occur in humans. "But in the fish," said biochemist Eberhard Trams of the National Institutes of Health, "the gland goes to hell in two weeks, a process that takes some 20 to 40 years in man."

birth, drops precipitously after the first year to a nadir between the tenth and fourteenth years, climbs steeply to the early twenties, levels off into the mid-to-late thirties, then resumes the rate of ascent begun in the teens. What is most remarkable is that this configuration holds for all societies, affluent or impoverished, industrialized or underdeveloped. The big discrepancies between high-survival and low-survival societies take place during the first half of life. In nonindustrialized societies, the rate of infant deaths starts at a much higher point and does not drop so far to the low point around the twelfth year. This means that the death rate for these countries remains appreciably higher all through childhood and middle adult life. But once past the age of about forty, *people everywhere die at a virtually uniform rate.*

A British mathematical analyst, Benjamin Gompertz, discovered this amazing regularity back in 1825. After the prime, the number of deaths in any population doubles every seven to eight and a half years, which means that statistically our chances of dying are 100 times greater at eighty-five than at the age of thirty-five. Moreover, this exponential increase has been found in captive species of rodents and *Drosophila* fruit flies, and is considered one of the fundamental characteristics of all living systems. However, while this rate of dying remains remarkably stable, the whole death-rate curve itself can be shifted in a longevous direction. This happened in the United States in the half century between 1900 and 1949. There is a consistent displacement to a lower level of mortality at all ages, even though the rates are parallel. These figures indicate that Americans were five years younger, physiologically, at mid-century than the members of the earlier generation.

While the death rate begins its long rise early in the second decade of human life, the individual does not reach his physical prime until the third decade. Thomas Cureton, a pioneer in the scientific study of physical fitness, has pinpointed the apex at the middle of the decade. At age twenty-six, physical ability begins to decline. This finding was based on an 18-item motor efficiency test for balance, flexibility, agility, strength, power, and endurance given to 2,200 adults. Gerontologist Joseph Still says the speed peak for sprinters comes early, between the ages of about eighteen and twenty-five, the peak for skill (the prime, say, for baseball players) between the ages of twenty-seven and thirty-seven, while the endurance peak for mountain climbers and long-distance runners is reached between the ages of thirty-four and forty-six. According to Cureton's chart, the decline in physical ability levels off after age 55, when it is roughly equivalent to that of an eight-year-old.

In measuring postprime declines, an observer is struck by certain general characteristics:

First, the various organs, systems, capacities decline at different rates.

Second, rates of decline can vary considerably between individuals and between lifestyles. Obesity and the use of nicotine can be seen to be aging multipliers. Not only do life insurance statistics show that obese people die at younger ages than lean people, but fat people age more rapidly. Dr. Nathan Shock reported that one study of more than 100 obese men in the twenty-five- to thirty-five-year decade showed that the greater the obesity, the greater the impairment. "Fifty percent overweight in a 25-year-old man was associated with functions of heart, lung and kidney and exercise performance found in normal men aged 50. Fifty-two of the originally obese patients reduced to and maintained their ideal weights for one year. At this time, their test results corresponded to those of their chronological age group (25 years). The other 55 patients who remained obese showed no change in their biological tests when repeated a year later." Similarly, smokers' lungs appear ten years older physiologically than nonsmokers' lungs. But the Surgeon General's study showed that the lungs of men who had given up smoking returned close to normal. A National Institute of Mental Health study of aged men revealed use of nicotine to be one of the two most accurate indicators of longevity, separating the short-lived smokers from the longer-lived nonsmokers.

On the other hand, there is evidence that exercise acts as an age reducer. It is no secret that physical work is nature's way of burning off the calories that make the fat that leads to obesity, which is an aging factor. In comparisons of two groups of men aged twenty-six to sixty, Dr. Cureton found that the group taking supervised exercise had a lower incidence of ailments and symptoms associated with the elderly than the general sample of men. Dr. Cureton found also that under certain conditions strenuous exercise can reduce blood cholesterol, triglycerides, and phospholipides which have been associated with heart disease. However, to be beneficial, exercise must be carried out consistently—an hour a day, 6 days a week through the course of the lifetime. The form of exercise found to be most effective is that which keeps the system steadily under pressure, such as jogging, swimming, cycling, or hiking.

Medically supervised exercise, especially for people who have suffered heart attacks or are suspected to be incipient cardiacs, is spreading as a new form of therapy. Facilities designed and supervised by physicians and physiologists have begun operating in Pennsylvania, California, Georgia, Alabama, Colorado, and New York. Clients are tested and then given a "dosage" of exercise to meet their needs and physical condition. "This is in far contrast to weight-reducing salons, where people come without evaluation and exercise without monitoring," said Herman Hellerstein, an associate professor of medicine at Western Reserve University. "Exercise therapy should be prescribed with the same precision as any other power-ful therapeutic modality like surgery or medication."

The University of California, Davis (UCD), is experimenting with the physical conditioning of older people, and Noel Johnson represents an extreme example of what can be done. When he was sixty-nine years old, Johnson, a retired aerospace shop supervisor, felt out of shape, had a touch of heart trouble, and physically could not walk for a mile. He became part of the UCD program and by January 1970 began training seriously. This meant, for one thing, running 150 miles a month. During the course of his training, he lost 40 pounds. In July 1971 Mr. Johnson, seventy-three years old, won three gold medals at the Amateur Athletic Union's U.S. Masters track meet at San Diego and was named the out-standing senior athlete at the meet.

Jack Wilmore, who supervises the physical fitness program, says, "In comparison to the average man, Mr. Johnson is probably at the level of the twenty-five-year-old man. He has approximately two to three times the endurance capacity of the man in his age bracket." Dr. Wilmore adds, "What Mr. Johnson has achieved is within the reach of others but certainly not any individual," although some other men in the program may excel Johnson's records when they reach his age.

Noel Johnson says he is taking the physical training program because "I just do not want to get old."

Says Dr. Cureton of the University of Illinois: "We have the beginnings of understanding in this area but, as an area of applied science which deserves development, we have a long way to go with the experimental work. It is quite probable that the fountain of youth for middle-aged people will be found in the wise use of leisure time to maintain their physical fitness."

Third in the observations of postprime declines, adulthood is a period of protracted stability and a person generally is unaware of the functional erosion that is taking place. One reason is that nature is so lavish with its endowments. Most organ systems are given up to four times the ca-pacity a person needs to survive. Even when function is cut in half, it is not fatal in many cases, nor even a handicap. A human being can survive with less than 40 percent of his liver, fractions of stomach and intestines, one lung, and part of one kidney. While this reserve capacity disappears and is not missed under normal circumstances, the individual becomes painfully aware of its absence when some crisis forces him to make de-mands that no longer can be met.

Fourth, the loss usually goes unnoticed also because it is gradual. In-deed, one of the many puzzling things about aging is indicated by scien-tists' inability to discover or define what are early signs of senescence.

While the incidence of death with age goes up at an exponential rate of 1-2-4-8-16-32-64, the functional decline advances at a linear rate of 1-2-3-4-5-6-7. The rate of functional loss is no greater between the ages of sixty and seventy than between the ages of thirty and forty. The relation between the two disparate progressions is that death is an index to the individual's weakest link.

Some bodily functions, to give the good news first, remain admirably constant. Volume of blood per body size and blood-sugar levels under resting conditions are two of them. Body weight and the deposition of fat increase with age, peaking in the sixth decade, and declining thereafter. Blood cholesterol follows a similar pattern, peaking in the fifth decade.

Most other indices go downhill. In the twenty-five-year-old, the heart pumps six and a half liters of blood a minute. At age seventy-five, this output is off 30 percent and by age eighty-five is down about 40 percent. Not only is the heart pumping less in advanced age, but the lungs take in less air. The amount of air that an eighty-year-old person can move through his lungs during a given 15-second period is 40 percent less than his twenty-year-old counterpart. This loss of maximum breathing capacity is one of the steepest of all physical declines. Not only are the older hearts pumping less blood and aged lungs taking in less air, but the older person's blood can assimilate far less oxygen per minute to distribute throughout the body. The blood of a twenty-year-old man takes up an average of 4 liters of oxygen a minute; by the age seventy-five the figure drops to 1.5 liters of oxygen a minute.

The cumulative, synergistic effect of these declines becomes clearly evident when the person is called upon to perform exercise or extra physical work. In the young person, the increased muscular requirements for extra oxygen and nutrients and for the elimination of metabolic wastes are met by accelerating blood flow up to 30 times the normal rate. The young heart can pump blood up to 35 liters a minute. But the oldtimer, with a reduced cardiac performance to begin with, is unable to come anywhere near to matching the emergency performance of youth. Not only do such demands stress the aging cardiovascular-respiratory system, but the aged person (as everyone knows) simply cannot do as much physical work. The strength of a man's grip at age seventy-five has fallen almost to half that of the thirty-year-old; the older man still can perform 70 percent of the physical work over a protracted period of time, but in the short bursts his capacity drops to only 40 percent. Of course, muscle loss also contributes to this declining function. The cells of muscles are unable to divide; thus there are no replacements in these organs throughout the individual's lifetime. The muscular loss is the most visible, being largely responsible for the decline in body weight and size that begins in the seventh decade. Body water is contained primarily in muscle and by the time a male has reached extreme old age (tenth decade), he has lost one quarter of that water content. "Most of the debilities of age," says gerontologist Nathan Shock, "apparently result from a loss of tissue, particularly through the death and disappearance of cells from the tissues." What remains, particularly the tissues that fill up the body—elastin and collegan—lose their elasticity and with it the suppleness necessary for high-grade physical performance. As a rule of thumb, gerontologists say that past the age of thirty-five most physiological functions decrease at a rate of about 1 percent a year.

Despite the decline in heart output and blood flow, nature mitigates the deprivation to the brain. At age seventy-five, blood flow to the brain has declined only 20 percent. To help the brain, other organs and particularly the kidneys are cheated. By age seventy-five, mechanisms constrict blood flow to the kidneys to one-half what it once was and by age ninety the flow is down to about 40 percent. This may be a reasonable trade-off, since the body does have two kidneys and each one has a tremendous amount of reserve capacity. However, this blood penalty plus concomitant attrition in the kidneys themselves (a 45-percent loss of filtration units and 30-percent loss of filtration function by age seventy-five) puts great pressure on the renal system, and after the cardiovascular system it is one of the most vulnerable points for human mortality (this is compounded by the fact that the kidneys become more susceptible to disease with age).

The inexorable kidney decline—starting in the fourth decade the decrease in function has been estimated at 2 percent a year—means that the organism cannot clear the system of metabolic wastes so quickly as in the younger person. The kidneys carry the major burden (along with the lungs, skin, intestines, endocrines, and central nervous system) in maintaining concentration of water and electrolytes in the body and in regulating the blood's pH or acid-alkali balance. In other words, the kidneys are a key governor of the homeostasis of the *milieu intérieur*.

The decline in renal and other homeostatic regulators means that various elements cannot be restored to their original values so quickly once they are disturbed. Although a steady blood-sugar level is sustained by the aged human, once the content is changed by a sudden infusion of glucose, the aged pancreas has great trouble in neutralizing the sugar. Many aged persons resemble functional diabetics, although they are not afflicted by that common degenerative disease. The indicated procedure in this case is not injection of insulin but reduction in the intake of carbohydrates and sweets.

The old person becomes sensitive to homeostatic decline when exposed to extreme cold or heat. Ordinarily, a person is able to maintain constant internal temperatures even into advanced age (another of the body's praiseworthy capabilities). However, the old person has difficulty sustaining inner heat in cold weather. Nor can the aging thermostat cope as well with heat. The body loses heat through circulatory changes and sweating. But aged skin with its atrophied, dried and rough tissue, loss of elasticity, partial loss of capillaries, and inability of remaining capillaries to dilate simply can't do the job. When inner equilibrium gets beyond homeostatic control, the outcome is death. Newswires carried the story of a man and wife in late middle age who on a romantic impulse one night drove from their home in the Los Angeles area into the desert to gaze at the full moon and ethereally luminescent landscape. But when they wished to return home, their car would not start. A letter written by the mother to her children under the burning morning sun gave pathos to the sequel. The couple could not survive one day in the unaccustomed heat. During any prolonged summer hot spell, death takes its tithe from the aged population.

Aging's first symptom usually is an annoying inability to read the fine print in the telephone directory. The lens of the eye consists of fibers manufactured by cells that keep producing the fibers. The new fibers coat the outer lens surface and prevent the elimination of existing fibers so that the lens gradually loses its elasticity and, sometime after the age of forty, the ability to focus on near objects. The lens also becomes less transparent. Our eyes no longer can see so well at the violet end of the spectrum, night vision declines, and glare becomes a troublesome problem; this combination makes it prudent for many aging people to forgo driving at night. The decline in focal flexibility ends at about fifty-five, but the accumulating lens opacity goes on, and by the late seventies or mid eighties most people have severe visual problems. The acuity of the other senses—hearing, smell, taste, tactile—have been deteriorating as well so that as the individual advances in age he moves into a thickening isolation from his external surroundings. Of course, there are bifocals, bright light bulbs, the use of more vivid colors, large print, hearing aids, false teeth, and the other means to keep up contact through the sensory fog, but it is obvious that the aged person becomes ever more vulnerable as he loses the ability to monitor and accommodate to the environment.

There often comes a point when the state decides that the aging person no longer is competent to drive an automobile and revokes his license. This not only adds a geographical restriction to the other elements of isolation, but imposes a hardship in procuring food and necessities that in some cases is insurmountable. If the person enters a nursing home, there is a further isolation from the world and circumscription of his life. One must acknowledge the insight of the simile that being old is "like living on an island that is steadily shrinking in size."

The phenomena of decline appear so randomly and can be explained so logically as results of stress, wear and tear, accidents, abuse, disease, attrition that one wonders if he is seeing any longer the fine hand of the genetic puppeteer. Yet there are two events late in the life cycle that evince "program."

One of these is cessation of the reproductive function in women. Menopause takes place almost as a mirror image of menarche, the onset of reproductive capacity in the first part of life. Just as the reproductive capacity is introduced by the development of secondary sex characteristics and begins abruptly, so the termination takes place abruptly followed by a fading of secondary sex characteristics. The reproductive cessation can be explained by the sharp diminution of primitive egg follicles over the years (indeed the possibility of pregnancy has been cut in half by age forty) until they disappear just at the time the ovaries are atrophying, but the suspicion of design is strengthened by the precision with which menopause arrives—age forty-eight or forty-nine is typical in Western industrialized nations. Male spermatogenesis follows the pattern of all the other functional declines—gradual and variable—with the most virile men still producing sperm in their ninth decade while fertilization is tied to density of spermatozoa in the ejaculate.

In females of almost all other mammalian species, the end of fertility coincides with the end of life. But in most other species, too, offspring are on their own rather quickly whereas human young are long dependent upon parental and especially maternal care. And so the divergence in the human female can be seen as obedience to the supreme evolutionary law—effective survival of as many vigorous offspring as possible. The lengthening dependence of children forced nature to change the strategy with the human species.

The most obvious evidence of genetic influence is the length of the cycle itself. With all our progress and prodigious accumulation of knowledge, Psalm 90 is as current today as when it was written: "The days of our years are threescore and ten; and if by reason of strength they be fourscore years . . . ." While life expectancy at birth in the United States has increased from forty-seven years at the turn of the century to seventy years today, this gain reflects death control in the first half (particularly the first year) of the lifespan. A great many more people live into their sixties and seventies. But at age sixty-five, life expectancy has changed little in the twentieth century: a gain of three and a half years for women, one and a half years for white men, two and a half years for nonwhite men.[4] But even these small gains might be deceptive. A U.S. Vital Statistics chart shows virtually no change for life expectancy for white males at age sixty since the founding of the Republic in 1789 except for a dip around 1900. In 1789 sixty-year-old men could expect about 15 years more of life, in 1963 about 16 years more.

Hardy people still manage to live to age ninety. But so few humans make it beyond that age that actuarial statistics are meaningless. The Administration on Aging says that some 13,000 Americans are older than 100 years. The Soviet Union, with a population of about 245 million people reported 21,708 centenarians in December 1971. The head of the Soviet Institute of Gerontology, Dimitri Chebotarev, says that in economically advanced countries the number of centenarians ranges between one in 10,000 and one in 20,000.

By age 110, virtually everybody is gone. The National Institute of Child Health and Human Development (NICHHD) says the aging process "often takes far less than the allotted 'three score and ten' years, and is almost always complete within 110 years." Gerontologist Alex Comfort in a 1961 article "The Life Span of Animals" wrote: "Birth certificates were introduced into Britain in 1837, so that now it should be possible to authenticate any age up to 124 years. There is no such certified record over 109 years, though in one instance absence of a certificate made an age between 111 and 115 highly probable." In a 1964 book, *The Process of Aging*, Comfort wrote: ". . . Pierre Jourbet, of Quebec, born 1701, died 1814. Jourbet's records were investigated in 1870 by the official statistician of Canada. This makes him (with 113 years 100 days) the present world titleholder for authenticated longevity." (Apparently commenting on this report in April 1970, Leroy Duncan Jr., chief of the Adult Development and Aging Branch of NICHHD, says, "The maximum lifespan of about 113 years appears not to have changed at all." Comfort set the maximum human lifespan at 115-plus. Gerontologist Bernard Strehler put the maximum at 118-plus. The scientists seem to be saying that human beings do not survive the twelfth decade, but . . . .)

Their scientific caution would appear justified. On April 22, 1971 the *New York Times* published a photograph of Mendieta Miguel Carpio of Vilcabamba, a village 8,000 feet high in the Andes Mountains of Ecuador. Miguel Carpio was 121 years old. The oldest woman in the village was 111 years old. Within two years, gerontologist David Davies of University College in London returned to Vilcabamba to discover a still older man,

---

[4] At age sixty-five, white women can expect nearly 16 more years of life, nonwhite women about 15 and one-quarter years more; all males can expect not quite 13 years more of life.

José David. By this time Sr. Carpio was 123 years old. With a population of 819 (about half of them adults), Vilcabamba had nine persons older than 100 years, an average higher than 1 percent.

Alexander Leaf, chief of medical services at Massachusetts General Hospital and professor at Harvard Medical School, visited Vilcabamba on the earlier expedition in 1971. He was satisfied that claimed ages in the village were confirmed either by Catholic church baptismal records or supported by the visible generations of offspring and testimony of aged friends and relatives. In a visit in the summer of 1972 to a small village in the foothills of the Caucasus Mountains in the southern Soviet Union, Dr. Leaf met Khfaf Lasuria. Madame Lasuria had no baptismal records, but she believed she was 141 years old. She had a son—by a second marriage—who was eighty-two years old, and she did not marry for the second time until she was past fifty. After interviewing the woman and cross-checking a series of dates, Dr. Leaf was satisfied to "accept some age between 131 and 141."

The Soviets acclaimed Shirali Mislimov at 167 years of age as the world's oldest person, but Dr. Leaf was not allowed to see him (on September 2, 1973, Tass reported he died at the age of 168). This Caucasus region—the mountains straddling the land area between the Black and Caspian seas and embracing the Soviet republics of Georgia, Azerbaijan, and Armenia—has the greatest concentration of aged people on earth, with upward of 5,000 centenarians. In Azerbaijan, the average is more than six per 10,000 and in Georgia nearly four per 10,000, but the preponderance of these longevous people reside in a region known as Abkhasia between the Black Sea and the mountains. The last available census in 1954 showed that 2.58 percent of the some 100,000 Abkhasians were older than ninety years—26 times greater than the average for the entire Soviet Union.

There is still a third place where human beings achieve exceptional longevity and that is in the remote, isolated land of the Hunzas, some 40,000 people who live in the Karakoram Mountains in Kashmir bordering on Afghanistan and China's Sinkiang province. There is no written language and no records, so that it is more difficult to certify ages and the oldest living Hunzakut claimed to be a mere 110 years old. "Yet," Dr. Leaf says, "I had the definite impression of an unusual number of very vigorous old folk clambering over the steep slopes that make up this mountainous land. It was the fitness of many of the elderly rather than their extreme ages that impressed me." [5]

[5] Herman Brotman of the Administration on Aging, an authority on aging statistics writes: "Although such a record may exist somewhere, I do not know who was the oldest American on verifiable record. Neither do I know who is the oldest person

Humans are blessed with the greatest longevity of all mammals. An Indian elephant is known to have lived at least seventy-seven years and so a pachyderm presumably could live longer, but the average is less. Forty years is an exceedingly old age for a horse; the average is thirty years for a small horse, twenty years for large breeds. Our closest primates, the chimpanzee has been known to live thirty-nine years and the gorilla thirty-six years although their averages are less (the gorilla does better in captivity, averaging twenty-six years to only fifteen years for chimpanzees). A spaniel has lived thirty-four years, but the average for most small dogs is seventeen years, and thirteen years for large dogs. And so it goes, down to the white laboratory rat with a maximum lifespan of four years and an average of three, the mouse with a maximum of three years and an average of eighteen months, and the shrew with a maximum of two years and an average of just one year.

Men have tried to discern the principle underlying this variety of lifespans. An obvious general rule seemed to be that lifespan increases with size. The trouble with this general rule is that there are so many exceptions. Small dogs live longer than large dogs, donkeys longer than horses. Whereas rodents and hoofed ungulates live shorter lives than they should, primates live longer and *Homo sapiens,* the complete nonconformist, lives three times longer than his body weight says he should.

In 1908 Max Rubner in Munich began to examine rates of energy expenditures for various animals, and found a reasonable uniformity of energy per pound per lifetime. This led Dr. Rubner to postulate that each organism is allotted a finite lifetime quota of energy. However, there was the human problem again. Anomalous *Homo sapiens* seemed to have nine times as much energy as any other species.

In the late 1950s gerontologist George Sacher discovered that brain weight is a more accurate predictor of lifespan than body weight. But when he put the two variables together and correlated brain size to body weight, he came upon an even more accurate index to mammalian lifespans. The greater brain size in relation to body weight, the longer a mammal lives. In closely related breeds of dogs or donkeys-ponies-mules to horses, the brain sizes are similar so that the smaller animals gain the advantage of their smaller bodies sizes. Dr. Sacher thought he might have discovered an exception to his rule among rodents: squirrels live much

---

living in the United States today." On May 21, 1973, the Social Security Administration wrote: "According to social security records, the oldest person receiving monthly benefits is Mr. Charlie Smith, 965 Laurel Street, Bartow, Florida. Mr. Smith is 130 years of age, based on a date of birth of July 4, 1842." Ordinarily, the Social Security Administration is not permitted to divulge such data, but Mr. Smith consented to the release. Mr. Smith, a former slave and one-time cowboy, was running a candy store that also served as his abode.

longer than rats; the gray squirrel, for instance, lives fifteen years compared to the rat's average three-year span. Upon examination, however, he found, "No squirrel has a brain as small as a like-sized mouse or rat." [6]

And so as the hominid brain was doubling in size over 10 million years and the human brain was doubling again over the last million years or so, our species not only was acquiring the intelligence capacity to deal more effectively and dominate the environment (thus realizing more of the individual's lifespan potential), but apparently expanding the lifespan itself through greater neural supervision of internal activities.

All this is not to exclude the very possibility that body size and rate of energy expenditure might have an important bearing on length of life. Gerontologist Albert Lansing points out that a mouse and an elephant each have approximately one billion heartbeats in their lifetimes; the mouse uses his at a much faster rate. And for good reason; the mouse metabolic rate is accelerated because compared to the elephant the little creature has an enormous body surface in relation to its size, requiring relatively more energy to maintain body temperature and homeostasis. This question of rate of living is open and under active investigation.

Every organization appears to have an allotted time, even stars, and in their case size is a determining factor. Each star has a finite amount of energy, and its active lifetime is determined by the rate of expenditure, and the rate of expediture is determined by size. A star ten times larger than our sun, which is about as large as a star can get, creates such intense heat that its much greater supply of hydrogen is consumed in a mere 10 million years. A star ten times smaller than our sun, which is about as small as a star can be, is cooler at the center and burns more slowly. It will go on for one trillion years. Our sun, a middle-sized star, has a lifetime of about 10 billion years (or another 5.5 billion years to go).

Size determines the manner of star deaths. Big stars end with a bang, supernovas that seed the galaxy with the elements for newer stars and solar systems. The smaller stars, probably including our sun, swell into red giants and then shrink into white dwarfs and slowly fade out. But so gradually will the sun expend its remnants of energy in this final stage that Freeman Dyson, a theoretical scientist who thinks about such matters, sets the length of time for the dying sun to cool to a darkened ash at infinity. This may be as close as we can come, conceptually, to immortality. Of course, other, ecological, events in the cosmos may disrupt this eternal continuity. "Time breeds disorder in both animate and inanimate chemical systems," says gerontologist Ber-

---

[6] Sacher's rule does not work for water-living mammals. Neither dolphins nor whales live as long as their great brain sizes indicate they should.

nard Strehler. "Living systems can, at best, only postpone or replace the effects of time and temperature."

The most effective living organisms that we know, measured by length of individual survival, are trees—conifers. The longest-lived species on earth, the bristlecone pine, has exemplars 4,600 years old. The sequoias and redwoods have maximum lifespans estimated at 3,000 years. The oldest deciduous tree that we know is the white oak with a lifespan of 600 years. These longevities bespeak an extraordinary accommodation with the external environment. At the same time, trees do not have to expend energy to kill their prey or labor for a livelihood or maintain the complex homeostatic networks of mammals. In addition to their highly efficient conservation of energy, another principle can be observed. Trees are not "steady state" organisms that stop growing at maturity: they continue to grow, adding another ring to the girth of their trunks until they die. Some fish have this same growth capacity, including the sturgeon which is believed to be the longest lived of all fishes. Its maximum lifespan is 100 years plus, perhaps 150 years, and it still is an open question whether it shows signs of aging or would do so if it lived long enough.[7] At the same time, rats keep growing, but it doesn't seem to be much help for their longevity. So the law would not appear to apply to mammals.

The longest-lived vertebrate that we know is a reptile, the Galapagos tortoise. One member of that species had an authenticated lifespan of 152 years and was believed to have lived at least 180 years. Box turtles older than 120 years have been reported. Reptiles are poikilotherms; that is, their internal temperature matches that of their surroundings. This is a drawback in some important respects. Like auto engines in midwinter, these animals are slow starting in cold weather and can be immobilized by a freeze. Because of this, many reptilian species are restricted geographically. At the same time, these "cold-blooded" creatures do not have to pay the energy price of homeotherms.

(It is germane to interject at this point that we are poorly informed on the subject of lifespans of other species. Except for records kept on a few domestic animals such as dogs and horses, it never occurred to anyone to study this subject systematically. Now that we are suddenly interested, we cannot have the information we desire instantly because it will require patient observation. This lack of such elementary knowledge is symptomatic of taxonomy, the science of classifying life forms. To

---

[7] This has led some investigators to see a quite logical connection between cessation of growth and senescence—when one stops, the other begins: or to regard senescence as simply another mode of development. This question also is under investigation.

suggest how vast is the subject and how colossal is human ignorance, three scientists began a paper on "The Origins of Taxonomy" with these sentences: "By current taxonomic standards, there are probably about 10 million species of organisms in the world, of which we have in the past 218 years described, at some level, 10 to 15 percent. For more than 99 percent of the described species, we know nothing more than a few morphological facts and one to several localities where they occur." Biologist Peter Raven, anthropologist Brent Berlin, and botanist Dennis Breedlove stated that, because of the burgeoning human population and limitations on taxonomic manpower, "it is doubtful that even 5 percent more of the world's organisms can be added to our inventory before the remaining 80 percent becomes extinct.")

However, as far as we know, the longest-living multicelled animal is an invertebrate, the sea anemone. Scientists can't be sure, but they believe this creature may have found a way to avoid death. The reason scientists suspect that the jellylike polyp may have learned how to live perpetually goes back to the fact that in the 1850s a British woman, Mrs. George Brown, gathered some of the creatures from the sea waters on the coast of Aran. In 1862, 16 of the anemones in their bell jar were given to a Miss Anne Nelson who tended them faithfully. In 1904 the anemones were studied by scientists who said at that time that the little animals had been living for about a half century in captivity. The anemones were placed in the aquarium of Edinburgh University where the species was identified as *Cereus pedunculatus* and where they were all found dead on the same day in 1940. The sea anemones had lived for about ninety years and during that time shown no signs of aging. Whatever caused their deaths, since they occurred so abruptly and uniformly, it is not believed to have been old age.

The sea anemone, while an animal, looks and acts like a plant, hence its floral name. It consists of a "stub" which becomes permanently attached to a rock or some firm surface and above the base a cylindrical body made up of clusters of jelly tendrils. The animal is carnivorous, but since it is stationary it must wait for whatever comes along. The tentacles surround or sting and paralyze prey which is then fed into a central mouth and gastric sac.

The sea anemone is a model of versatility. It can reproduce asexually by budding and fission as well as sexually by eggs and spermatozoa. When food is scarce, it does not die from starvation like humans and other animals—it cleverly shrinks in size until better times, when it grows again. But its chief device for living in perpetuity is the discarding of the jelly tentacles, which do have fixed lifespans, and replacement with new ones. So the organism is continually renewing itself.

This facility has led biologist-gerontologist Strehler to conclude "that *there is no inherent factor which automatically produces senescence in all lines of animals and plants*" (his italics).

Scientists at New York City's Aquarium are studying the sponge, another marine animal which may have acquired the ability to avoid senescence—or at least to live for a very long time, probably centuries. Sponges occupy a lower level of organization than sea anemones and are among the most primitive of the multicelled animals. In fact, sponges perform as an aggregation of single cells rather than as an organization of many cells, having no mouth, internal organs, or nervous system. Structurally, they appear close to one-celled animals, the protozoa.

At the level of the unicellular organism, individuals have found another method of escaping death. Bacteria, some yeast, and many kinds of plant clones achieve potential immortality—potential is all that is possible for any form of life since it is always subject to exhaustion of food, accidents, predation, or other environmental restrictions—by growing and dividing into two new individuals. Certain species of protozoa, one-celled animals, also seem able to divide indefinitely whereas other types after a long period will develop aging and mortality unless reinvigorated with sexual cross-fertilization.

There are four ways an individual can cease to exist, Dr. Strehler has observed: he can be eliminated (1) by environmental assault or the deterioration we know as aging; (2) by fission into two new individuals; (3) by fusion, as in certain slime molds, of individuals into a coalescence of protoplasm; (4) by replacement of parts until the entire individual has been changed. In terms of aging, Dr. Strehler asserts there are three categories of organisms: (1) those that do age primarily because they cannot replace parts as they deteriorate; (2) those that avoid aging of the whole unit by replacing parts as they wear out; and (3) those that never have an opportunity to age because they divide into new organisms before aging occurs. But nowhere in the variegated spectrum of life does the potential immortality of an individual appear to be an essential strategy of nature, although any such generalization must be qualified by our ignorance and by noting that giant tortoises do seem to age imperceptibly, and maybe certain fishes grow without ever showing signs of aging, and certainly the 4,600 years of the bristlecone pine is a respectable effort: who knows for how long a member of that slow-living species can go on?

It can be no coincidence that the conception of the wonderful one horse shay that fell completely to pieces at one time occurred to a physician (who was a professor of anatomy and physiology in the bargain), the same Oliver Wendell Holmes who was precociously wise about puerperal fever. Dr. Holmes had never seen a patient who disintegrated perfectly, so that all systems failed at the same time. And when one turns to causes of death, "old age" is unlisted. However, a few very old people do die from what doctors nominally call old age; that is, the person has been afflicted by so many diseases and undergone such general deterioration that the exact cause of death can not be pinpointed. "[O]ne of the main characteristics of the pathology of old age is the multiplicity of lesions," writes Dr. Timiras, a physiologist and physician. "Cases that come to autopsy reveal numerous lesions involving so many organs of the body that it is difficult to know which one was responsible for death; indeed, the pathologist is often perplexed as to how the patient managed to live so long with such a 'load' of disease." These lesions accumulate with advancing age so that somewhat like tree rings they become an index to age.

The association of senescence and disease is so intimate that the question keeps recurring: is aging a disease? Is growing old normal or abnormal? If old age is a disease . . . well, we have learned that there is nothing preordained about the power of disease. Roger Bacon thought aging was a disease and his hygienic regimen was really a form of preventive medicine. Galen regarded senescence as somewhere between illness and health, not a disease yet a physiological weakening of the person. Both old age and disease are characterized by decrease in homeostasis and so are indistinguishable by that measure. Dr. Hans Selye sees stress as the causative agent of both disease and senescence. And there is an obvious cybernetic relationship between the two. Growing old predisposes a person to disease, disease produces aging. Both lead to and end with death.

As people age an increasing percentage exhibit disease so that by age sixty-five, four out of five people are burdened with a chronic condition and about one in three suffers from three or more chronic conditions. Certain diseases such as kidney ailments, diabetes, arthritis, and rheumatism are strongly related to aging: they appear more frequently with advancing age. Cancer, too, is associated with the senescing organism, but the pattern is not a consistent correlation. Cancer peaks in the fifth and sixth decades, striking the largest percentage of women in their forties and the largest percentage of men in their fifties. After age sixty-five, cancer kills about one in seven, below the one-in-six death rate averaged for all ages. Of the people who live past eighty years, fewer than one in ten die from cancer.

If senescence has an executioner it takes the form of the cardiovascular diseases, especially those associated with the blood vessels. Arteriosclerosis, atherosclerosis, degeneration of the heart, cerebral hemorrhage, coronary thrombosis, hypertension. This constellation of diseases is closely correlated with senescence, taking an ever greater percentage of victims as any cohort, that is, any generation, advances in age and causing more than two out of three of all deaths: this is the way most people die in economically developed societies. Heart attacks and strokes are prominent in the earlier stages of old age; degeneration of the heart muscle, hypertension, and arteriosclerosis take over as the chief killers of those who reach the eighth decade. By age eighty, that upper biblical limit, death has eliminated most of the cohort. Only two percent of the population in the United States—one person in 50—is eighty years or older. In most industrialized nations, only one person in 250 is older than eighty-five years. The survivors of this winnowing are *de facto* the hardiest individuals. Most of the cancer-prone persons already have succumbed. Past the age of ninety, death is related to one principal cause, the one that has underlain most of the other cardiovascular fatalities— atherosclerosis. "Atherosclerosis dwarfs all other single causes of mortality in the United States and represents by far the major cause of death from cardiovascular diseases," says physiologist Timiras. Atherosclerosis is universal in almost all animal species and throughout all populations within a species. So if there is a central and unyielding mechanism for death, it is atherosclerosis.

Arteriosclerosis is a general term to describe the hardening of the arteries which characterizes most cardiovascular disease. This hardening is comparable to the loss of elasticity, increasing fibroid character, and rigidity of collagen in other tissues of the body. It is particularly injurious in the case of the arteries (rather than the veins) because the blood pressure is strong and because the peristaltic actions of the vessels assist the heart in circulating the blood.

One of the commonest forms of arteriosclerosis is a group of changes taking place in the inner lining of the artery known as atherosclerosis. Lipid materials, connective tissue, and usually calcium form what are called atherosclerotic plaques. These plaques cause the inner wall of the artery to become more rigid, rougher and thicker, gradually closing the passageway for the blood. The formation of the plaques sometimes causes hemorrhaging in small blood vessels feeding the artery so that the arterial wall becomes swollen with blood, blocking the artery. Sometimes the disturbed artery causes the blood to clot. The artery also can become occluded when a solid body made up from elements in the blood stream and called a thrombus forms over the roughened plaque surface. Tissue deprived of blood dies, and this is called infarction. When a coronary artery supplying the heart is occluded, a person suffers a myocardial infarction or what is commonly called either a coronary or heart attack. Sometimes a thrombus breaks off, traveling with the blood to block another part of the system in an embolism. Such a blocking of a brain artery is one form of stroke. Sometimes arterial walls become so weakened by atherosclerotic plaques that they blister. These aneurysms either burst or leak blood to cause death.

Atherosclerotic lesions can start early in infancy. Is atherosclerosis an expression of aging or disease? Or, how much of it is aging and how much pathological? We know that it correlates with age, the lesions accumulating as the person grows older. Yet we have reasons for suspecting that it is a disease with an etiology which could be changed if understood. Postmortems of GI's killed in the Korean War showed that young Americans—eighteen-year-olds, twenty-year-olds—already had atherosclerotic (aged or diseased?) arteries. Could it be disease in the young, but aging in the old? [8] The death rate from heart disease in the United States has nearly trebled since 1900. Is this because so many persons have been saved from the infectious diseases and thus become subject to the rigors of aging and, specifically, heart disease? Or have there been crucial changes in lifestyle during the intervening years?

Atherosclerosis has been associated with high cholesterol levels in the blood and with the high intake of animal fat in the diet.[9] The long-lived villagers in the Andes were virtually free of atherosclerosis. Dr.

---

[8] Russell Ross and John Glomset of the University of Washington School of Medicine suggest how atherosclerotic lesions could be both normal and pathological. They say that the migration and proliferation of arterial smooth muscle cells when there is an injury to the inner lining of an artery is associated with formation of a lesion. With healing of the endothelium, they hypothesize, the lesion regresses and goes away, so that normally there would be a continual appearance and disappearance of lesions. An artery would become diseased and manifest clinical atherosclerosis only when an imbalance developed in the complex biochemical processes of lesion formation-dissolution and more cholesterol was deposited in the arteries than was removed.

[9] P. S. Timiras in *Developmental Physiology and Aging* lists ten factors associated with coronary heart disease in the order of importance: (1) age; (2) hyperlipidemia —elevated cholesterol and blood fats (plasma triglycerides and low-density lipoprotein); (3) cigarette smoking; (4) hypertension; (5) obesity; (6) diabetes; (7) physical inactivity; (8) hyperuricemia; (9) family history of diabetes, hyperlipidemia; (10) electrocardographic abnormalities. The risks go up with age and when more than one of the factors appear in combination. One study indicated that a person with high cholesterol who smoked cigarettes and had high blood pressure was eight times more likely to suffer coronary heart disease than a person with none of the factors, five times more likely than a person with any one factor, two and one-half times more likely than a person with any two factors.

Two other key studies on heart disease and stroke list smoking and hypertension as the two most significant factors. The Framingham Study under the auspices of the National Institute of Health puts cigarette smoking first and hypertension second; the Cooperative Veterans Administration Study puts hypertension first and smoking second.

Leaf said that extensive cardiovascular tests of the some 400 adults revealed "there were only a couple of individuals with any atherosclerotic heart disease." The average blood cholesterol level was between 160 and 165, whereas the average for a fifty-year-old American man is 250. The Vilcabamba villagers consumed only 1700 calories of food a day (one study put it as low as 1200 calories) with only about 153 of those calories in the form of animal fat. A survey of 55 Hunza males showed a daily average of 1,923 calories. Because of the difficulty of keeping livestock in the mountainous terrain, they ate virtually no meat or dairy products and cooked with an oil made from apricot seeds. The Abkhasians ate a more liberal and varied diet of milk, vegetables, meats, and fruits with 30 percent of the calories from meat and dairy products. (They drink no coffee or tea, however, and few Abkhasians use tobacco.) And they did have signs of cardiovascular disease, but it did not take its usual toll, possibly because of their hardy physical condition. The more robust eating habits of people in the Caucasus is reflected in the fact that those eighty years and older still consumed between 1,700 and 1,900 calories a day. This is in contrast to the 2,400 calories a day recommended for American men over fifty-five years by the National Academy of Sciences and the 3,300 calories a day which is the average for Americans of all ages, with about one-quarter of that in the form of fat, mostly animal fat.

Gerontologist Bernard Strehler set forth the doctrine "that a species is optimally adapted to the environment in which it evolved. If this is valid, it seems likely that our ancestors were a lean and hungry lot!" But is diet the only difference separating Americans from these long-lived peoples . . . or from their American forebears at the turn of the century when heart disease was not the scourge it is today? In how many ways do contemporary circumstances differ from those that shaped the human organism during the eons of evolution?

To suggest just one change, it was a quiet world then, except for an occasional thunderstorm, lion, or waterfall. It still is quiet in the Andes valley and Asian mountains or in the Sudan where the Mabaan tribe lived in Stone Age isolation until quite recently. These people used neither drums nor guns. Not only do Mabaans experience no auditory decline but they show no rise in blood pressure into extreme old age. Samuel Rosen, a medical investigator from New York City, exposed some of these primitive people to the noise levels of a subway train and some of our power equipment. Involuntarily, the tiny muscles around the capillaries in their fingertips constricted, forcing the blood pressure to rise and the heart to pound more rapidly to overcome the resistance. This syndrome lasted for as long as 25 minutes after a five-minute noise session. One is tempted to wonder how long the din must last before high blood pressure becomes chronic.

But noise is one of the tangible signs of our progress. How many manufacturers have opted against reducing the noise levels of their products because they feared customers would regard quiet instruments as puny ones? Noise is good for business. So is planned obsolescence good for business. Restyling, creating a demand, was General Motors' inspired reply to Henry Ford's Model T, the car so beloved by Americans that he put it on the market unchanged year after year. Not only has planned obsolescence been successful, but change itself is enshrined on the altar of pragmatic America. So great is faith in the technique that the avant-garde now entertains an attack upon a fundamental institution of human evolution—the family—as obsolescent.

But change, according to Hippocrates, is harbinger of morbidity and death; it must be approached with caution. Morbidity and death have appeared in different guises in different ages. Leprosy, the scourge of biblical times, has all but disappeared. So has smallpox, the disease that reigned during the seventeenth and eighteenth centuries. Tuberculosis, the white plague of the nineteenth century, is in decline. Could it be that future shock is expressed morphologically today as atherosclerotic plaques?

Scientists simply do not know enough yet to say whether the fatty degeneration of the inner walls of arteries is abnormal pathology (in the young, for instance) or normal aging (in the old), or to sort out how much is senescence, how much disease, how much degeneration. In the meantime, most authorities do not equate senescence with disease. "[O]ld age," says Dr. Timiras, "cannot be regarded simplistically as a 'disease' but involves a complexity of physiological and pathological phenomena, both of which are subject to numerous environmental influences." Says the National Institute of Child Health and Human Development: "The aging process, a natural continuation of the developmental cycle, begins long before one normally considers himself old, or even middle-aged, and proceeds to whittle away at one's abilities until physiological competence becomes so poor, and resistance to environmental stresses so weak that the individual can no longer survive."

How one regards senescence is influenced by his hopes, his orientation toward life, his philosophy. Ana Aslan, the Romanian procaine therapist, said that she looked upon old age as virtually the same as disease. "I cannot agree with this assimilation of the two," commented Simone de Beauvoir in her book on old age, "disease is contingent, whereas ageing is the law of life itself." Carl Eisdorfer, who has served as director of the Center for the Study of Aging and Human Development at Duke University, says, "There is no necessary relationship between aging and disease."

Having stated this, it is possible that one disease may serve as a model for aging. The disease is progeria and the model hypothesis is the conviction of gerontologist William Reichel of Franklin Square Hospital in Baltimore. Progeria is so rare that only 52 cases have been reported in world literature. With progeria, a child grows old instead of growing up. The disease manifests itself by the age of three and what follows is a speeded-up aging process with all the symptoms of a normal lifespan, including high levels of blood cholesterol and arteriosclerosis, telescoped into a decade.

Dr. Reichel and colleagues described it this way: "The skin appears senile; there is no subcutaneous fat and the superficial vessels are prominent. The hair is straggly and grey, if present. Cardiac disease develops between the ages of 5 and 15 years, with the evolution of murmurs, cardiomegaly, hypertension, congestive heart failure, chest pain, and death. Death occurs between the ages of 5 and 27, usually between 12 and 18 years."

With Werner's syndrome, a similar affliction of forced aging, the victim usually survives into his thirties or forties. Werner's syndrome has been associated with inbreeding, as has one case of multiple progeria. Dr. Reichel believes Werner's syndrome is inherited as a single gene, which would mean that one particular enzyme is involved in this pathological aging.

If we learn what causes progeria and/or Werner's syndrome, Dr. Reichel hypothesizes, we may learn as well the secret to the aging process.

With all this, we know that there is more to aging than simply a physical decline from the prime of the third decade. Some lives represent a steady ascent in achievement, professional and personal capacity. When Winston Churchill was called to lead Britain and shepherd Western civilization in his supreme endeavor, he had reached the age that signals retirement for most men. Angelo Roncalli spent nearly eight decades in preparation so that in the last four and a half years at the apex of his life as Pope John 23rd he could transform the thought and traditions of the Roman Catholic Church.

The average age of the Man of the Year selected by the editors of *Time* over nearly half a century is about fifty-six years. Even more striking than the advanced age of some of the outstanding men—George C. Marshall, sixty-eight; Dwight Eisenhower, sixty-nine; Konrad Adenauer, seventy-seven; Pope John, eighty-one—is the scarcity of men in their twenties and thirties.

The philosopher Martin Buber could say that the years between seventy-nine and eighty-two were the happiest in his life. At eighty-one, Goethe could write about the pleasure of still being surprised. At eighty-five, Artur Rubinstein reflected, "Sometimes I feel bad to be still playing, taking up concerts that young pianists should have. I'm ashamed to be a survivor." But the aches and regrets of age disappeared when he performed. "At the piano, my sickness goes away and that makes me terribly happy." Picasso, in his eighties clasped New Yorker correspondent Janet Flanner and said, "We don't get older, we just get riper."

Obviously, these are human beings who have been most successful in meeting life's challenges. Gerontologist Joseph Still sees intellectual growth as a cumulative process, each realization of potential elevating the individual to a higher plain of performance. Dr. Still also sees successive stages in the kinds of intellectual performance:

> Memorizing ability is at a peak in childhood. From the late teens into the early thirties, creative imagination bursts into full flower. In the forties and fifties, if the individual has grown intellectually, he has learned the power of analysis, synthesis, organization; usually the teen-age poets and mathematics prodigies have by now become writers, scientists, business men, physicians, teachers or lawyers.
>
> Finally, the individual reaches the age of philosophy—the late fifties, sixties and beyond. If he has developed and matured intellectually, he has accumulated a vast store of knowledge and sufficient wisdom to deal with some of the great eternal questions. He becomes the philosopher, the statesman and the family adviser.

Sigmund Freud saw the individual's growth and development in sexual terms. There was the oral stage, the first year of life, in which the mouth is focal point for the young organism's gratifications. Aggressiveness is associated with this period. This was followed by the anal stage, roughly the second and third years, when the most important sensual pleasure shifts to the anal and urethral areas. Retentiveness is an accompanying trait. In the third year, this merges into the phallic stage which is characterized by intrusiveness in the male and receptiveness in the female. In the oedipal stage in the fourth and fifth years, the child takes the parent of the opposite sex as the object of sensual satisfaction and the parent of the same sex as a rival. Seductiveness and competitiveness are salient traits. At age six, the child enters a long latency stage during which he or she resolves the oedipus conflict by identifying with the parent of the opposite sex and satisfying sensual needs vicariously. During this period the child's conscience or superego is developed, internalizing the parents' moral and ethical demands. Finally, beginning at about age eleven, the young person enters the stage of puberty during which the infantile stages of sensuality are integrated into a unified genital sexuality and the individual takes another young person of the opposite sex as its object. Intellectualization and estheticism go with this final stage of development. By about age fourteen, the sexual unification is completed, Freud believed—and that was as far as he carried the "ages of man."

But a person does not age physically, intellectually, sexually in a vacuum. He matures in a social setting, and this is such an important part of the process that gerontologist Darrell Slover maintains that "the main problems are created not by aging but by society's response to aging." This is aging, sociologically:

First of all, there are changes in familiy life. Generally, there are fewer children in the family today. They go to college and leave home at the age of eighteen, so that there is a shorter period when children are at home and a longer period when the couple is left alone—an average of 25 to 30 years.

In middle age, a person reaches a point of career stabilization and increasing vulnerability. His chances of getting a new job diminish. The unlimited vista he held as a youth becomes narrowly confined.

In the sixties—

Retirement. This means a loss of one of the major roles in society, and along with that a loss of access to money, prestige, and security.

There is a loss of friends and relatives through death.

The meaning of time changes. Before, there was not enough time and too much to do, now there is too much time and not enough to do.

In the seventies—

Biological vulnerability: loss of motor skills and perceptual systems. The person becomes increasingly concerned about the well-being of his body.

Loss of ego integrity. The aged individual becomes increasingly concerned with evaluating his life. He reminisces, enters reveries, undertakes a life review in an effort to reach some resolution about his existence. This is a time for depression for those with poor careers.

Acute health and medical problems.

Widowhood and bereavement.

Psychiatric crisis.

Relocation. The aged person undergoes at least one major relocation and is ever more vulnerable to the stress involved with such change.

In the eighties—

Increasing dependency—financially, physically, emotionally. The penalty of being treated in this way lies in the fact that society values autonomy, productivity, and youth.

There is the possibility of senility, although this is not a natural part of aging but a medical event, a disability of the central nervous system. However, the tendency is to put grandma or grandpa in a bedroom and leave him there; but this enforces sensory deprivation and worsens the situation.

Dying and death.

These are the challenges of aging as seen by gerontologist Slover of Syracuse University. Dr. Slover has made this inventory not so much for descriptive purposes, but to help make each person aware of the eventualities he must face so that he can prepare himself to meet them.

Erik Erikson, a professor of developmental psychology among his other accomplishments, has encompassed all of the above psycho-social-sexual aspects in his paradigm of aging. Erikson's model not only is the most comprehensive, but the most optimistic, for it allows for the possibility of redemption. According to Erikson, there are eight ages of man. At each stage of ego development the individual must establish new basic orientations to himself and his social world; each stage holds the possibility for success or failure; failure at one stage does not ordain failure and decline at the next; personality continues to develop throughout the whole life cycle.

Erikson calls the first stage Basic Trust vs. Basic Mistrust. This is the first year of life when the ministrations and provisions tendered by the mother help the infant "to balance the discomfort caused by the immaturity of homeostasis with which he was born. . . . In his gradually increasing waking hours he finds that more and more adventures of the senses arouse a feeling of familiarity, of having coincided with a feeling of inner goodness. Forms of comfort, and people associated with them, become as familiar as the gnawing discomfort of the bowels. The infant's first social achievement, then, is his willingness to let the mother out of sight without undue anxiety or rage, because she has become an inner certainty as well as an outer predictability."

However, when care is inconsistent, inadequate, unloving, the child is likely to develop a basic mistrust of the world, a fearfulness and suspicion, that will characterize his later attitudes. This basic trust-versus-mistrust issue (like those to come) is not resolved forevermore, but is reopened and can be revised at later stages. While this promises a chance for repair, it also means that a person's earlier ego attainments can be undermined by later developments.

Stage two—the second and third years—is called Autonomy vs. Shame and Doubt. By this time the child has developed new motor and mental abilities and wants to use them—to climb, open and close, to pick and pluck and hold and let go. If the parents recognize this need and allow the child to proceed at his own pace, he develops a sense of control over his muscles, impulses, and himself. This is the sense of autonomy. If, on the other hand, parents are impatient with the child's fumbling efforts and insist on doing the maneuver themselves or are excessively harsh in criticizing mistakes such as wetting, spilling, or breaking things, the child develops a sense of shame and self-doubt. A diminished sense of autonomy will curtail the individual's self-reliance in adolescence and adulthood.

"There is in every child at every stage a new miracle of vigorous unfolding, which constitutes a new hope and a new responsibility for all," Erikson writes in *Childhood and Society*. "Such is the sense and the pervading quality of initiative." At the opposite pole in stage three—years four and five—is guilt. Initiative is a more active and more complete extension of autonomy: it connotes planning and attacking a task rather than just sitting back and defiantly protesting one's independence. Boys invade another's territory or prerogatives, girls think in terms of catching, either outright snatching or by making themselves more endearing. A child's sense of initiative is reinforced when the parents allow freedom for various self-initiated activities such as bike riding, skating, of tussling . . . and when parents answer their children's questions, thus encouraging intellectual initiative . . . and when parents do not ridicule childish fantasies. Inhibitory parental behavior in these areas, making the child feel silly or stupid, encourages a sense of guilt over self-initiated activities.

By stage four, the age period from six to eleven years, the child has developed enough so that he must relinquish his infantile fantasies—the oedipal complex with its desires for one parent and rivalry with the other is buried—and is ready to enter the real world. In any culture, however, this means schooling of some sort. The child now can employ deductive reasoning and follow rules so that he can play games where one takes a turn and obeys rules. In a simplified way, the child makes acquaintance with the tools and technologies that will be used in earnest in adult life. The theme of this stage is a sense of industry. When children are encouraged to build practical things, cook and sew, then praised and rewarded for their efforts, the sense of industry is enhanced. Parents who see such enterprises as mischief and "making a mess" encourage the alternative condition—a sense of inferiority or inadequacy. But by this time, the growing individual comes under other than parental influences. A child's sense of industry may be elevated by a perceptive teacher in school.

Childhood comes to an end with puberty and adolescence. The person undergoes a revolution physiologically. Psychologically, the person must begin to formulate an answer to one of the most difficult questions with which he will ever have to contend and one which well may be posed again later in life: Who am I? The oedipal family romance revives, but no longer can be satisfied with the fantasies of infancy, and so the person turns outward to "fall in love" with some young member of the opposite sex. But, Erikson maintains, this "is by no means entirely, or even primarily, a sexual matter—except where the mores demand it. To a considerable extent adolescent love is an attempt to arrive at a definition of one's identity by projecting one's diffused ego image on another and by seeing it thus reflected and gradually clarified. This is why so much of young love is conversation."

By the time one is a youth, he has experienced a number of roles—as son or daughter, student, friend, Scout, newspaper boy or baby sitter. The values one has been taught come up again for reassessment. The emergent person now not only has experienced his family and friends and local society, but has become acquainted with the concepts of an ideal family, friends, country. Idealism plays a natural role in the search for identity.

If the young person has developed with a sense of trust, autonomy, initiative, and industry, then he is better prepared to integrate his various roles and values and attitudes into a cohesive identity. Failure to achieve this objective of stage five, which includes the years twelve to eighteen, leaves the person with a sense of role confusion: a sense of not knowing what he is or where he belongs or what he should do with himself.

Up to this point it can be seen that Erikson's stages of life conform to those of Freud, although Erikson has not restricted them to sexual development. From this point classic psychoanalytic theory has nothing major to say about development in the life cycle. Erikson extends his paradigm to life's conclusion.

"The strength acquired at any stage," Erikson writes, "is tested by the necessity to transcend it in such a way that the individual can take chances in the next stage with what was most vulnerably precious in the previous one. Thus, the young adult, emerging from the search for and the insistence on identity, is eager and willing to fuse his identity with that of others. He is ready for intimacy. . . ." The person now must and should be mature enough that he can form a commitment without fear of ego loss. It is only at this point, Erikson says, that true genitality can be expressed. The earlier sexual experience is "of the identity-searching kind, or is dominated by phallic or vaginal strivings which make of sex-life a kind of genital combat." Now one is able to effect a loving relationship with mutual trust, a responsible love. To epitomize the goal of this stage, Erikson recalls that Freud once was asked what any normal person should be able to do well. Freud answered: to love and to work. And, Erikson reminds, Freud meant genital love, with emphases on both "genital" and "love." However, intimacy can be shared with friends, with teachers; it often is experienced by men in combat.

If intimacy cannot be established, a person is left with a sense of isolation.

In various ways all the preceding stages have been preparation for stage seven, the long period of adulthood. This is the central period of an individual's life and is the crucial period for the species as well for the stage is characterized by generativity. To Erikson "this term encompasses the evolutionary development which has made man the teaching and instituting as well as the learning animal." He goes on, "It has taken psychoanalysis some time to realize that the ability to lose oneself in the meeting of bodies and minds leads to a gradual expansion of ego-interests and to a libidinal investment in that which is being generated. Generativity thus is an essential stage on the psychosexual as well as on the psychosocial schedule." The individual becomes concerned with the welfare of young people and of future generations. He looks at the institutions of society which will guide the race. Productivity and creativity are typical expressions of this generativity.

Persons who cannot achieve this enrichment fall back into a self-absorption with their personal wants and needs. The alternative to generativity is "a pervading sense of stagnation and personal impoverishment." The person becomes self-indulgent and early invalidism may become a device for this self-concern.

The final stage of life turns out to be a culmination of all that has gone before. "Only in him who in some way has taken care of things and people and has adapted himself to the triumphs and disappointments adherent to being the originator of others or the generator of products and ideas—only in him may gradually ripen the fruit of these seven stages." It is more than simply sitting back to reflect on and take satisfaction in accomplishments of the past, although certainly that is an important part of it. It is a synthesis of vision that enables the person to feel a comradeship with distant times and different ways, yet value the dignity of his own unique course within the context of his particular culture and during an induplicable historical period. This means he now is able to accept his finitude, the completion of his own singular life cycle. Erikson call this ultimate achievement integrity.

"The lack or loss of this accrued ego integration is signified by fear of death: the one and only life cycle is not accepted as the ultimate life. Despair expresses the feeling that the time is now short, too short for the attempt to start another life and to try out alternate routes to integrity." Erikson brings his life cycle full circle by noting that Webster defines trust (the quality associated with life's first stage) as "the assured reliance on another's integrity." "[H]ealthy children will not fear life," Erikson concludes, "if their elders have integrity enough not to fear death."

With this paradigm of life, aging is not necessarily a descent into the valley, but, for some, an ascent to the summit. This model is an explication of Robert Browning's faith in "Rabbi Ben Ezra":

> Grow old along with me!
> The best is yet to be,
> The last of life, for which the first was made:
> Our times are in His hand
> Who saith, "A whole I planned,
> Youth shows but half; trust God: see all, nor be afraid!"

Aging, then, is a process so complex that we can gauge it only with a series of complementary and sometimes overlapping frameworks. There is chronological aging—how many hours, days, weeks, years an organism has lived since birth. When coupled with biological aging—the basic process in any living thing expressed in the rate of development and length of the life cycle of members of particular species—chronological age can tell us with great precision how "old" an organism is . . . as long as we are dealing with simple life forms. With more complex organisms, especially adult human beings, biological aging remains valid as a generality and chronological age is a reasonable indicator, but both diminish in reliability when applied to any specific case. A better indicator is measuring to see how well the bodily systems are functioning and how much reserve capacity they retain, the scientific equivalent for the conventional wisdom that a woman is as old as she looks and a man as old as he feels. Of course this physiological age can be influenced by pathological aging, the unhealthy or abnormal acceleration of degenerative processes by disease (presuming, of course, that physiological aging is not some kind of "deficiency" disease). Both of these kinds of aging are regulated or importantly influenced by psychological aging (what goes on inside a person's mind, how he regards himself and his situation) and by social or sociological aging (how he reacts to his social situation and how other people and society treat him).

Aging has been described as an organism's increasing loss of adaptability ("What times! What manners!" deplored an aging Cicero) . . . diminishing ability to survive stress . . . growing vulnerability . . . decline of bodily functions . . . erosion of reserve capacity . . . deterioration of homeostasis . . . as the measurement of cellular aging or the result of cumulative cell deaths. Aging is either a developmental process or what happens because there is no genetic-biologic programming—natural or abnormal, normal or diseased—and it culminates either in death according to nature's plan or, because there is no plan, no sustained defense against biologic errors and environmental accidents, in the entropy of existence.

We all know what aging is, but science does not, not completely, not yet. However, this ignorance may not last much longer, for science finally has begun to scrutinize the commonplace experience of aging.

VI. The Science of Senescence

Growing old is one of the few absolutes. Everyone accepts it. At the same time, an old person is a prophecy about youth which no one wants to admit. The twin attitudes appear to conflict, but they have reinforced one another in blocking human curiosity about aging. Unquestioning acceptance of the inevitability of aging generated a sense of futility which, combined with personal distaste for the subject, stifled the interest and support which is essential to scientific endeavor. As a result, gerontology—the science of aging and the aged—is itself young and immature.

Charles Brown-Séquard's experiments with animal testicular extracts in 1889 marked a beginning of scientific efforts to intervene in the aging process. He was followed by Steinach with his sex operation, Voronoff with his sex gland transplants, Metchnikoff with his fermented milk—it was Metchnikoff who first used the term "gerontology" in 1903—and Bogomolets with his cell serum (see pp. 83-88). But these men were trying to harpoon a whale of a problem with hypodermic needles and scalpels. There were wild emotional hopes at their promises and deep rejection at their failures.

In 1914 a Los Angeles physician, Ignaz Nascher, wrote a book called *Geriatrics* which inaugurated a change in medical and social attitudes toward the aged. Conditions that existed before this enlightenment were recalled by British physician Ivor Felstein:

> When I set foot for the first time in a typical old people's ward in a large, long-established Lancashire hospital, I felt that I had moved from the twentieth century back to an era when medicine was still in the hands of the alchemists and barber surgeons and the sick were mixed with the poor and the derelict in ancient hospices.
> As I recall, the main ward was reached through a heavy fake-panelled door with peeling green paint, on which no ward name or number was visible. Inside, the walls were grubby unplastered brick, thinly disguised with green distemper. High black iron beds jammed close together were parted only by pathetic old wooden or metal lockers. Cotsides on most of the iron beds belied the adult faces of the patients

occupying them. Bed coverlets were few and muddy grey in colour. Stone floors, dog-collared naked light bulbs and barred windows completed the picture. Most of the patients were elderly but a few were young people suffering from progressive diseases like multiple sclerosis and muscular dystrophy. The old ones were suffering from all kinds of medical conditions and were often confused and incontinent. The diagnoses on the patient's case sheet were most frequently headed by the term 'senile dementia,' irrespective of whether the patient's age was 50 or 90.

Physicians had to be taught that aged people could be cured of many of their ailments . . . that in some cases the aged showed their own peculiar symptoms, such as mental confusion, from relatively minor physical troubles that could be readily treated . . . and that, above all, "writing them off" as hopeless cases was a prescription for early death. From these discoveries developed the branch of medicine known as geriatrics. Geriatrics deals with the aged ill, with medical problems of the elderly. Gerontology is concerned with all the problems, all aspects of the elderly, the normal as well as what has taken place in preceding stages of the life cycle, the process itself. "I'm interested in the first week of life," said gerontologist Carl Eisdorfer, "because I'm interested in the aging process."

There was some gerontological research in the years preceding World War II, but modern gerontology began in the postwar years; most of the important work has been done in the past decade, with most of those contributions coming in the last half of the last decade. Scattered scientific interest in gerontology appeared in several Western countries in the 1930s and was sufficiently represented in the 1940s for the establishment of formal organizations. The American Geriatrics Society was founded in 1943 and today is the largest of all geriatrics-gerontological groups with some 8,000 members, most of them physicians. The AGS is dedicated to the clinical care of the elderly whereas the Gerontological Society, which grew out of the Geriatrics group in the mid-1940s is devoted to basic research in the psychology, sociology, and biology of aging. In 1950 the First International Congress of Gerontology at Liège, Belgium, was attended by scientists from 12 countries: Belgium, Denmark, Finland, France, Great Britain, Holland, Ireland, Italy, Spain, Sweden, Switzerland, and the United States. Out of that meeting grew the International Association of Gerontology, which holds a congress every three years, and which has some 35 member societies in 29 nations. These meetings and groups and their publications (The Gerontological Society publishes *Journal of Gerontology* and *The Gerontologist*) provided the vehicles for the intercourse essential to any broad scientific enterprise. Eventually, a few research cores, the production units in the scientific infrastructure, came into being. The Soviet Institute of Gerontology at Kiev was founded in 1958 and now is the largest in the world. The Russians specialize in the study of longevity. Fritz Verzár, one of the pioneers of modern gerontology, set up an Institute of Experimental Gerontology at Basel, Switzerland, in 1959 (when he was seventy-three years old). As its name indicates, it emphasizes experimental clinical gerontology. In England, the Nuffield Foundation has been a long-standing patron of gerontological research and sponsored that first international meeting.

In the United States, Duke University began large-scale and important gerontological research conspicuously early. In 1954 it began at its Medical Center what would become a long-term study of a group of aged people and the next year established a Council of Gerontology to encourage a many-faceted investigation of aging. The Duke approach is oriented toward medical psychiatry, but the group study has yielded valuable psychosocial as well as health information. An interdepartmental Committee on Human Development at the University of Chicago is a center for psychosocial gerontology with the emphasis on psychology. Syracuse University has still another center for pychosocial gerontology with the emphasis on environmental sociology. Syracuse reorganized its program into an All-University Gerontology Center late in 1972. An Institute of Gerontology at University of Michigan–Wayne State University specializes in the later stages of old age, and death.

The Gerontology Center at the University of Southern California, founded in 1965, conducts broad research and training, but is virtually unique among the universities for its molecular biology laboratory (similar work is carried out at Oak Ridge National Laboratory with other contributions from the biology departments at Brookhaven and Argonne National Laboratories). Gerontological research on an appreciable scale is being done at perhaps a dozen other universities. About 32 colleges give courses leading to gerontological research, while 37 give courses for people who wish to train in working with the aged.

The federal government began a gerontology unit in the National Institute of Health in 1940 funded by a grant from the Josiah Macy, Jr. Foundation. In order to study human aging and be able to work with aged persons, the Section on Gerontology was set up physically as part of Baltimore City Hospitals. In 1941, Nathan Shock, a physiologist from the University of California, Berkeley, was appointed leader of the unit and more than anyone else he has shepherded the science of gerontology to its present stage of development. One way he did this was by collecting all the literature on the subject, a massive amount of material because aging has so many manifestations and is related in some way to so many observations, speculations, tests, and experiments. Dr. Shock's bibliography now contains 83,000 different titles.

In 1958 Dr. Shock began administering a series of physiological, biochemical, medical, and psychological tests to 100 healthy men. Gradually, the panel was enlarged to more than 600 men ranging in age from eighteen to ninety-nine years. The participants were retested every 18 months if they were under seventy years of age, every year if older than seventy. This longitudinal study has yielded an important part of the information we have on what happens physically with aging, and is the basis for much of the data given in Chapter V.

In a longitudinal study, investigations monitor the course of development of the same subjects over a period of time. In a cross-sectional study, the researchers compare subjects of different ages at one time. The greatest advantage of a cross-sectional study, obviously, is that the researcher can get results quickly. However, in dealing with aging, there are drawbacks: each person ages at his own pace, affected by varying influences and showing individual effects. Furthermore, different generations culturally are subjected to dissimilar conditions. For instance, members of today's generation receive more education and higher incomes than members of earlier cohorts, and both factors can influence aging. With a longitudinal study, the investigator is not troubled by such variables, but he must be patient for his results. Fifteen longitudinal studies of aging are in various stages of progress in the United States; however, they do not employ standard measurements so that they cannot all be perfectly correlated.

In 1948 Dr. Shock's Gerontology Section was transferred to the National Heart Institute and seven years later was moved into the newly formed National Institute of Child Health and Human Development. In 1968 a $7.5 million Gerontology Research Center was completed in Baltimore. Dr. Shock's longitudinal program is conducted here along with research in molecular aging, cellular physiology, and behavioral gerontology.

One might suspect from the shuffling of the gerontology unit that federal authorities are not quite sure what to do with aging research. The suspicion is strengthened by the fact that although NICHHD is the main funding agency for in-house and extramural research in aging, important aging research is carried out and funded by the National Institute of Mental Health, Veterans Administration, Atomic Energy Commission, and the Health Services and Mental Health Administration. Suspicions blend into confusion when one learns that the government's main agency on aging—the Administration on Aging—has nothing to do with any of these groups and has access to virtually none (perhaps two-tenths of 1 percent) of the federal monies allocated for aging and the aged. The true Rube Goldbergian dimensions of federal strategy toward aging and the aged is suggested by noting that funds are disbursed through the departments of Health, Education and Welfare; Defense; Agriculture; Housing and Urban Development; Labor; Transportation; and through Action, Civil Service Commission, Office of Economic Opportunity, Railroad Retirement Board, and the Veterans Administration.

This diffusion of funds or proliferation of agents is a record of the mushrooming importance of the aged and the poverty of federal planning. The Administration on Aging, an outgrowth of the first White House Conference on Aging in 1961, was formed in 1965 to be the older Americans' surrogate within the Executive Branch. The AoA was placed in the Department of Health, Education and Welfare with access to the Secretary. But in a department reshuffle two years later, the AoA was swallowed up in a new Social and Rehabilitation Service and no longer reported directly to the Secretary of HEW. Anyone who has worked in a corporate structure knows what that kind of realignment means. If there were any doubts of the AoA's declining status, they were magnified in 1971 when some of the agency's important funding programs were taken away and given to the new voluntary agency, Action. At the same time, the budget called for only about $30 million of the $105 million authorized by Congress.

Only the Senate has a committee concerned solely with the aged—the Special Committee on Aging—and largely through its efforts funding for AoA was raised somewhat. In November and early December 1971, when the second White House Conference on Aging focused national attention, President Nixon announced to the assembled 3,500 delegates: "We want to begin by increasing the present budget of the Administration on Aging nearly five-fold—to the $100 million level." The loss of any access to the Cabinet was patched up by continuing Arthur Flemming as chairman of the White House Conference, appointing him as the President's Special Consultant on Aging and keeping him in a new Cabinet-level Domestic Council Committee on Aging.

In a preparatory report on the White House Conference, Chairman Frank Church of the Senate's Special Committee on Aging said: "Among the complaints that can be made about the structure of the Domestic Council Committee on Aging, are many that were directed at the President's Council on Aging.[1] Cabinet-level officers are not likely to spend hours in joint discussion of Conference recommendations; they may in-

[1] Established in 1962; its last report covered the years 1965–1967; now defunct.

stead send lieutenants with varying degrees of interest or concern in aging."

The stepchild status of aging has significant consequences in the area of research. For instance, in its "home"—NICHHD—gerontology must vie for funds with prenatal development and obstetrics, health of children, mental retardation, and family planning, all worthy areas of concern and mostly weighted toward the first half of the life cycle. Even so, one might presume that the Gerontology Branch was entitled to one-fifth of the Institute's resources. In fiscal 1972, only 6 percent of NICHHD's funds —$7 million—was assigned to aging. Aging research is an even smaller concern of the people who run the Veterans Administration or Atomic Energy Commission, and properly so.

The full insignificance of research in gerontology on the national priority list can be gauged by how much money is spent on aging research compared to funds allocated for other research and for the aged. A "Review of Government Supported Research on Aging" published in 1971 by the Institute of Child Health and Human Development in cooperation with other involved Government agencies states: "In fiscal year 1967 NIH spent $4,979,942 on the support of research on aging. This represented about 0.5 percent of the total expenditure of NIH on research in that fiscal year. NIMH spent $2,040,820, 3.0 percent of its research funds, on aging . . ." The VA allocated 2.9 of its funds, the AEC 3.5 percent of its funds. The average for five principal funding agencies came to 1.2 percent of their research budgets. "Thus aging research," the Review concludes, "viewed as a whole, is a greatly undersupported area—a gap area. Some aspects of aging are being studied less adequately than others and thus some imbalance exists. However, with the entire area so poorly developed, it does not seem appropriate to put much emphasis on imbalance."

Aging, as we have seen, is intimately related with disease and chronic vulnerability. In fiscal 1970 Americans spent more than $58 billion on personal health care. Twenty-seven percent of this amount went to help the aged, who composed only 10 percent of the population. Since more than half of all government funds devoted to health care go to helping the elderly, the state of health of the aged is a direct (financial) concern to every citizen. Gerontologists argue—some of them vehemently—that the United States is unnecessarily narrow in its attack upon the degenerative diseases and more emphasis should be placed on comprehending the aging process. "Cancer and heart diease are problems of aging," said Gerald Hirsch, a young molecular gerontologist at Oak Ridge National Laboratory. "They won't be solved without learning what aging is."

Paltry as the funding is for gerontological research, there is some question of how even that is allocated. Social gerontologist George Maddox of Duke University says that 75 to 80 percent of the money goes for biomedical research. Dr. Maddox says he does not underestimate biomedical problems, but "the wisdom of funding research which has the potential of increasing the life span without at the same time making an appropriate investment in knowledge about income maintenance, about effective use of leisure time, about factors which contribute to mental health, or about the social integration of the old is patently questionable."

For these various reasons, gerontologists united in their desires for their own government agency, a National Institute of Aging. This was the first and most urgent request of the Research and Demonstration Section at the second White House Conference on Aging late in 1971. Congress in 1972 approved with little opposition a bill creating such an institute within the Public Health Service, but President Nixon killed the bill with a pocket veto. He cited costs and duplication of work already carried out as reasons for his action.

Neglect of aging research can be laid to the scientific community as readily as to government. In fact, that is where Robert Finch put the responsibility when he was Secretary of Health, Education and Welfare in 1969. "I agree that the amount of research being done on the biology of aging appears to be small. The proximate reason for this is lack of interest among scientists in conducting such research. Last year only 103 of the 8,623 research proposals submitted to NIH were relevant enough to aging to be assigned to the Adult Development and Aging Branch, NICHHD. In that same year NICHHD received a total of 992 research grant proposals. Now, however, biological aging is coming to be considered a great threat to health . . . [but] . . . an adequate academic focus on the basic biology of aging does not exist."

Gerontology has been an unappealing field for scientists. There are very few sociologists who are exclusively or even primarily gerontologists. Instead, the aged invariably are considered as one segment of the whole sociological model. In medicine, physicians in the United States never established geriatrics as a medical specialty as it is in Britain. Psychiatry, with the impetus of Freud, has directed its attention toward youth. In psychology, gerontology has been a bit more fortunate in winning converts. But in biology, the rewards have seemed skimpiest of all. To the bright young researcher, the possibility of solving—of understanding—the aging process was assessed as remote. Human aging takes so long that an investigator either must work with short-lived animals (leaving something to be desired as a model for the more complex human being) or be prepared to devote a career among human subjects to discover if his research is on the right track—or the wrong one. Even if there were a solution, the chances were slim that it would be in some neat, dramatic form so beautifully suited for the popular imagination as, say, Immortality $= mc^2$. However, with the implications of the Watson-Crick DNA model and advances on both the molecular and cellular levels, the biology of aging now is beginning to open as an exciting challenge for investigators—and winning some recruits for gerontology.

Science and government are nothing more than specialized activities of society, animated by its attitudes and priorities. The subject of aging and the aged has seemed drab and depressing, whether we regard it as scientists, as citizens, or as human beings. Delegates to the White House Conference on Aging were disappointed at what they considered the lack of emphasis in the news coverage. By profession, news editors are sensitized to those stories that interest people and to those that turn people off. As a rule, this news judgment screens out the general run of stories dealing with the aged. Welcome exceptions occur when someone discovers extraordinary abuses in a nursing home or when a physician is caught cheating on Medicaid.

On the other hand, there is that other attitude: acceptance of the inevitability of aging. And so the ostrich society that doesn't want to think about growing old and assigns only a pittance of its great wealth for aging research at the same time spends more than one-fifth of the federal budget, close to $50 billion in fiscal 1973, on the aged. Most of this aid goes in the form of Social Security and, second, Medicare-Medicaid. Medicare-Medicaid, a belated result of the 1961 Conference on Aging, was the one big victory the aged initiated, although the intransigent medical industry was overcome only with the strength of labor unions.

Social Security, begun in the depression year 1933, was more economic than social in its inspiration and aimed at helping the young as much or more than the aged. The payments beginning at age sixty-five were intended to induce the older worker to retire—to open his job for a young worker. The true intent of Social Security is revealed by the restriction on income from work (but not from pension, dividends, interest) in addition to Social Security payments. Even though the older person has faithfully (since there is no other choice) paid his "contributions" over the years, he is penalized in receiving benefits if he earns more than about $38 to $40 a week ($2,100 in a year) and is entitled to nothing if he insists on keeping his full-time job.[2] Of course, the strategy worked (in many corporations, retirement became mandatory). In 1900 nearly

[2] After age 72, a person is entitled to full Social Security benefits even though he chooses to work full time, an option that has not gotten wide circulation.

two-thirds of older men remained in the labor force. By 1970 the percentage had dropped to one in four. The figures for women are 8 percent and 10 percent.

Social Security had another important effect. It fixed the age when a person is old.

There are in general two kinds of gerontologists. One, in the tradition of medicine and public service, is concerned with diagnosing problems of old people in order to remedy them; the goal is to enrich the later years through better health, by greater satisfaction, more happiness, by improving the quality of the living. Hopefully, this will add to the quantity: longer as well as better lives. This type of gerontologist usually is drawn from the ranks of physicians, physiologists, psychiatrists, psychologists, and sociologists.

Some things that these gerontologists have learned about older people:

One in ten Americans is sixty-five years old or older, more than 20 million of the 203 million total population in the 1970 census. The aged population grows by more than 300,000 people a year and is expanding at a more rapid rate than the total population. In 1900 there were only 3 million old people in a total population of 76 million. So while the population in general increased by about 260 percent in the twentieth century, the aged population grew by nearly 700 percent. The aged sector has gone up about 1 percent each decade since 1920. The number of people seventy-five years and older is growing faster than that of the decade between sixty-five and seventy-four years. In the 1960s the number of old people grew at nearly twice the rate of the total population while those seventy-five years old and older increased at three times the rate. Half of the aged are sixty-five to seventy-two years old, half seventy-three years old and older.

The proportion of older people will increase. The latest projections of the Census Bureau, based on the dramatic drop in the fertility rate, puts the percentage of people sixty-five years and older at upward of 12 percent in the year 2000. The extrapolation from present statistics is that there would be 28 million older Americans by A.D. 2000; if the population remained at the low census projection of about 250 million (based on a 1.8 child average), the aged segment would amount to slightly more than 11 percent of the total. However, Carl Eisdorfer believes there will be 40 million older Americans by the end of the century, or 16 percent of the 250 million projection. If the birth rate remained at a constant replacement level and if the death-rate-per-age level remained as it is today, then the population would come to an equilibrium with 15 percent of its members over sixty-five, 10 percent over seventy, 3 percent over eighty years of age. An improvement in longevity, of course, would add to these percentages.

The aged population is constantly changing, with a turnover of about 12 percent—one in eight—each year and of about 60 percent in a decade (the discrepancy between the two percentages is caused by the fact that large numbers of people who enter the category die within a few years while others live on through two or more decades). Each day, roughly 4,000 Americans turn sixty-five while 3,000 older persons die—a daily changeover of 7,000 people and a net gain of 1,000 elderly.

Power and affluence are commonly accepted as the indices to individual and societal success. But if survival is taken as the true indicator, then longevity tells us which people have met life's challenges most successfully, which societies perform most effectively for their people, and which people are most favored within a society. Your chances of living into old age are best if you were born in Sweden, the Netherlands, or Norway. Life expectancy in those three nations is close to seventy-six years for women, more than seventy-one years for men—a superiority of two years for women, four-and-a-half to five years for men. People in Denmark, Switzerland, Canada, United Kingdom, New Zealand, and Australia also can expect longer lives than Americans. "It is extraordinary," medical gerontologist Robert Butler wrote in 1969, "that in America where six percent of our Gross National Product is spent on health, which is both relatively and absolutely more than in any other nation in the world, we should be eighteenth in longevity for men and tenth in longevity for women."

While one in ten Americans is sixty-five years or older, only one in 30 of the some 9 million Spanish-origin Americans and one in 20 of the some 600 thousand American Indians are in that age bracket. Blacks formed 11.2 percent of the population in the United States in the 1970 census, but only 7.8 percent of the aged (there were 1.6 million aged or 6.9 percent of the Black population). If you are Black, the average lifetime is 63.7 years (1968 life expectancy). If you are white, the average lifetime is 71.1 years—a discrepancy of 7.4 years.

There is an identical discrepancy—of one-tenth of the lifespan—between the sexes. If you are a woman in the United States, you can expect to live 74 years; if you are a man, the figure is 66.6 years. In 1900 there were 100 older men for every 98 older women. With the improvements in public health, disease control, nutrition, and standard of living, the average lifetime grew longer and almost equally so for the sexes, for a while. In 1930 women showed an advantage of three and a half years. By 1940 it had grown to four and a half years. In 1950 the gap was five and a half years—female life expectancy 71.1 years, male 65.6 years. After 1950 probably because the gains from antibiotics and other health measures had been nearly exploited, the spectacular advance in average lifespan leveled off. It has remained nearly static for men—an addition of just one year for white males, two years for Black and other nonwhite men. Women, however, continued to show improvement: a gain of 2.7 years for white women, and 4.5 years for nonwhite women. In 1967 life expectancy for Black and other nonwhite women surpassed that of white males for the first time (the figures for 1968 were the same).

The consistent and growing disparity between male-female average lifetimes is now showing up more heavily in the composition of the aged population. In 1950 there were about 11 older women for every ten older men. By 1960 the discrepancy had enlarged to 12 to 10 and today is nearly 14 to 10 (according to the 1970 census there were 11.6 million elderly women and 8.4 million aged men, which works out to 138.5 women for every 100 men, and means that women composed 58 percent of the aged population to 42 percent for men) and is expected to keep widening (by 1990, there is expected to be 148 elderly women for 100 aged men, nearly a three to two ratio).

At the White House Conference on Aging, several women gerontologists and delegates in the Research and Demonstration section campaigned vociferously to approve a recommendation for increased gerontological emphasis on the problems of aged women. They argued that studies to date included a majority of men, but since there are more old women they should be given more attention. The reasoning and militancy seemed about to carry when a man gerontologist pointed out that there are more older women because so many men are having a problem living as long. He suggested that if there were to be a sex-emphasis in gerontological research, it should favor males. His suggestion encountered no enthusiasm, but it quelled the call for female-oriented research. One Black woman delegate had insisted earlier that greater attention be given to Black men who on average died 7.5 years before white men and Black women and nearly 14 years before white women. The section's final recommendations did ask more research for racial and ethnic minorities, but did not specify any sex. Leading a symposium soon after the White House Conference, gerontologist Walter Beattie, Jr. commented, "We're doing poorly by the white male."

Why *do* women live longer than men? Gerontologist Lissy Jarvik who conducts research at Columbia University's College of Physicians and Surgeons, believes without a doubt that there is a genetic basis. For one thing, she points out, it is not a human phenomenon but characterizes "every species studied." The male fruit fly lives 31 days, the female

33 days; the male spider 100 days, the female 271 days; the male rat 750 days, the female 900 days. Nor is it an American phenomenon. Women's life expectancy exceeds men's in every country in the world, she says, except Ceylon [3] where there is a high incidence of deaths at childbirth. She points out that 90 percent of diseases are more frequent in men. Dr. Jarvik, who has made extensive genetic studies at Columbia Presbyterian Hospital in Manhattan, believes the answer one day will be found either as some adverse factor in the male Y chromosome or a benign element in the female X chromosome, the section of the biologic blueprint that differs between the sexes.

A few miles south on Broadway, at Columbia University's Teachers' College, gerontologist Ruth Bennett refuses to accept a genetic basis for the difference "until all the adverse environmental conditions are controlled." Commenting on Dr. Jarvik's contention, sociologist Bennett said, "Genes set the limit for the species—that's as far as I'll go. She is an extreme geneticist—I'm an extreme environmentalist."

Anita Zorzoli is somewhere between the two extremes, ideologically not geographically, for she teaches biological gerontology at Vassar College in Poughkeepsie, New York. Dr. Zorzoli says there is a species of rat and a few other animal species in which males live longer, and that would seem to open the genetic door that Dr. Jarvik slammed shut (and yet the exceptions are so few that they call attention to the almost universal sovereignty of the rule of greater female longevity). Dr. Zorzoli says we don't know why women live longer, but she suspects it is due to the female estrogenic hormones. After menopause, she says, women suffer the same incidence of heart attacks as men.

Yet there are other anatomical differences aside from the celebrated ones separating men and women. The brain of the average white male in the United States is 1,426 grams. His body weight is 63,100 grams. The brain of the average white female is 1,312 grams while her body is 54,400 grams. On average, the male has a larger brain than the female, but she has a larger brain in relation to body size. The ratio of male brain to body is about 1 : 45, the female ratio about 1 : 42. Gerontologist George Sacher, we have seen, found that the larger the brain compared to the body (or the smaller the brain-to-body ratio) the greater the longevity in mammals.

With seminal inoculation, there are equal numbers of spermatozoa carrying female X chromosomes and those carrying male Y chromosomes. The male spermatozoa are more successful in running the vaginal gauntlet

[3] According to the United Nations *Demographic Yearbook 1971*, male life expectancy exceeds that of women also in six other countries: India, Pakistan, Jordan, Cambodia, Nigeria, and Upper Volta.

and perforating the ovum. Once this feat is accomplished, however, males lose the advantage. One study showed that when miscarriages and still-births occur, the aborted fetus is more likely to be male, with ratios as high as four to one during the second and third months of pregnancy; overall, there were four male to three female stillbirths. Even with this prenatal attrition, about 106 boys are born to every 100 girls. The higher male mortality rate continues through the lifespan. By age eighteen there are more females than males in the United States and, as we have seen, the disparity widens with advancing age. Women would appear to pos-sess some innate advantage which expresses itself more strongly (to turn Dr. Bennett's argument against her) as adverse environmental restraints —such as the hazards of childbirth and the rigors of primitive child-rear-ing—are removed.

Yet there is a social-cultural gulf between males and females. Boys are brought up to bear physical pain more stoically than girls; they learn soon enough that crying is for girls and "sissies." They must stifle their emotions. Child psychologist Bruno Bettelheim says studies show that boys in grade school are reprimanded nine times more frequently than girls. If the boy is at all observant, Dr. Bettelheim says, "he must come to the conclusion that while the school highly approves of behavior that comes naturally to girls, it rejects what comes equally naturally to boys. Thus, many boys are made academic failures by the very institution which should teach academics to them."

There is male machismo, the pride that takes offense at minute slurs and insists upon satisfaction at physical risk. There is the system of male competition inculcated early in sports as preparation for the more earnest struggles later in the business arena where the man must vie for the salary that determines the welfare of his family and his status in society. With few exceptions, only American males were killed in three wars during the past generation. Only males suffer from black lung disease and usually only men are subjected to asbestosis and industrial cancers. Overall, the difference in emotional attitudes means that men do not take care of themselves as well as women. As one study put it, if a woman gets sick, she goes to bed; if a man gets sick, he goes to work.

The above factors have not been assessed definitively. But in "Leading Components of Upturn in Mortality for Men, United States—1952–67" the U.S. Public Health Service has studied the less subtle reasons why men's longevity has fallen further behind that of women in the past two decades. Most of the surge in white male mortality between 1952 and 1967 that virtually negated all other health gains could be covered with two words: automobiles, cigarettes. Auto fatalities distorted the mor-tality statistics from age fifteen all the way up to age forty-five, and by that time lung cancer and later other respiratory ailments were taking their toll. In the younger years, there were increases in deaths from suicides and homicides; in the middle years, from cirrhosis of the liver; in advanced years, from coronary heart disease and other diseases of the circulatory system.

For Black and other nonwhite males, auto accidents and lung cancer also were the big killers. But in the younger years, deaths from suicides and homicides went up ever more sharply than for whites. The suicide rate in 1967 almost doubled that in 1952 for blacks fifteen through forty-four years old. In the twenty-to-twenty-four age bracket, homicides rose from about 80 per 100,000 in 1952 to 105 per 100,000 in 1967—more than one in a thousand the victim of homicide. Similar increases were registered through the years up to age forty-four. In middle years, there were increased deaths also from diabetes millitus, heart disease, and cirrhosis. In advanced years, there was an upturn in deaths also from leukemia, sickle cell anemia, heart and circulatory disease, diabetes, auto accidents, and homicide.

Certainly there are sufficient environmental factors in these causes for increased male mortality to bolster Dr. Bennett's contentions.

Marital status is another measurement of the aged populations and longevity. More than 92 percent of the aged people are or have been married. Remarkably, the difference between white American men and women in this respect is separated by only one-tenth of a percentage point. However, since there are over 3 million more older women than men and because 40 percent of the married older men are married to women younger than sixty-five, there is an enormous discrepancy in current status. More than two-thirds of all older men are married, approximately two-thirds of all older women are widowed (55 percent), single, divorced, or separated.

Geography, too, makes a difference. Most old people are concentrated in the most populous states—New York, California, Pennsylvania, Illinois, and Texas. However, the states with the greatest percentage of aged—and so presumably the places where one has the best chance for a long life—are rural states mainly clustered in the midwest (this is disregarding Florida, which leads all states with 14.5 percent of its population consisting of old people). These states in order of percentage-ranking are Iowa, Nebraska, Arkansas, South Dakota, Missouri, Kansas, and Oklahoma. Maine, Massachusetts, West Virginia, and Rhode Island also have aged populations at least 10 percent above the national average.

Clyde Martin, a behavioral scientist at the Gerontology Research Center, summarized all these statistics concisely. "You have the best chance for a long life," he said, "if you are a rural white married woman.

And the worst if you are an urban non-white unmarried male." Then, as a scientist will do, he cautioned that within this framework there are other variable factors that can affect longevity. And so we must look more closely at the older person.

Most people have a composite picture of old age: physical decrepitude, poor health, pain, senility, inmate of a nursing home or some other institution, impoverishment of spirit and finances, welfare, uniformity and rigidity of outlook, estrangement from the rest of society, ignored by their children, constricted world, sense of worthlessness, lack of satisfaction, hopelessness, misery.

This description is not random, but represents the mental model that social gerontologists have discovered is held by the public. Such is the fear of arriving in this forlorn state that one out of four people in a survey conducted by gerontologist Robert Kastenbaum wished to die at an earlier age than they expected to. But while there is truth mixed in, the stereotype is highly inaccurate. The real situation is far more optimistic, initial gerontological research has revealed, than the popular caricature.

How did we get this distorted conception of old people? Gerontologist Bernice Neugarten says that heretofore the mass media have been able to circulate reports only "from social workers who serve the poor, the lonely and the isolated, and from physicians and psychiatrists who see the physically ill and the mentally ill. Thus we base many of our current stereotypes on a picture of the needy rather than on a picture of the typical older person."

To begin with, old people are the least homogeneous of all age groups. This is so because the old person simply has had more time to evolve into his or her particular social entity: in other words, more chance to drift away from being a member of an age group and to become an individual. As in physiological aging, the person is a cumulative product of his or her decisions and actions and conclusions and particular answers to life's challenges. Thus there is greater opportunity for various discrepancies to increase from person to person the longer they live.

Moreover, the old person does not identify with aged people (it may be he does not want to associate with the pejorative image, indeed knows it does not represent him). There is no bloc of aged voters. Old people could exert considerable political muscle with about one in six votes if they decided to cast their ballots according to the dictates of an aged class. Although the old person is thought of as unbendingly conservative, he is just as likely to be liberal or independent or whatever his political bent has been before.

It may help to sort out myth from fact by noting that aged people have three major problems: (1) health; (2) reduced income; (3) the attitudes and consequent actions of society toward them.

As the previous chapter detailed, elderly people suffer physiological deterioration and are more vulnerable to disease. They are twice as likely as young people to be physically disabled and to require entering a hospital. Their hospital stays are more than twice as long as a younger person's. Per capita health costs for the elderly are $790 a year—more than three times the amount spent on the average person younger than 65 years. About four in five old people suffer from some chronic condition. Nevertheless, about nine of ten old people get around without any help. About one in 20 is maintained in an institution. In the past decade the average age of old people in institutions rose from seventy-seven to eighty-two years. Dr. Neugarten again: "Old persons are not dumped into mental hospitals by cruel or indifferent children. . . . few of them ever show signs of mental deterioration or senility, and only a small proportion ever become mentally ill. For those who do, psychological and psychiatric treatment is by no means futile." About 8 percent of the elderly suffer serious mental impairment of all types.

Skyrocketing health costs have hurt everyone, but since old people require more services, they are affected to a greater extent. The first White House Conference on Aging in 1961 recognized this primary problem of the aged, and American society responded with Medicare and, for the poor, Medicaid. These may not be total solutions, but they are far more than gestures. Medicare pays between 40 and 43 percent of the total health bill for aged Americans.

Poor health is a major cause for retirement, and an estimated one-half of all retired persons are unable to work for health reasons. Retirement means reduced income. So, obviously, these two problems interact with a vicious circular effect. In 1970 the median income for families with an aged head of household was slightly above $5,000—less than half that of younger families. The greatest hardship shows up among some 6 million old people living alone or with nonrelatives. Their median income was $1,950 compared to more than $4,600 for their younger counterparts and compared to the official 1970 poverty level, $1,850. Indeed, 47 percent of these people were below the poverty line. One in six families with an aged head of household also fell below the family poverty level of $2,330. These aged poor comprised nearly half of all Black families and nearly 80 percent of Black females living alone. One-half of all elderly Blacks are poor compared to less than one-quarter of aged whites.

One in four of all old people is impoverished, compared to one in nine younger Americans. Because of inflation and because the incomes of working Americans generally have kept ahead of the inflationary spiral, aged people have been losing ground economically. The numbers of elderly poor began increasing in 1968. And the situation is being exacerbated with a trend of easing workers in their early sixties out of the job market, so that they have economically depressed years even before they reach official old age.

Chapter One of a pre-White House Conference on Aging report by the Senate Special Committee on Aging is headed "The Key Issue: Retirement Income" and begins: "Inadequate income, as nearly everyone agrees, is the most serious problem facing older Americans." President Nixon told the Conference: "In addressing the challenges before us, let me begin where most of you begin: with the problem of inadequate income. If we move on this front, all the other battles will be easier. If we fail to move here, the other battles will be impossible."

The President urged passage of improvements in Social Security benefits, Congress complied, and the new scale went into effect January 1, 1973. Where the average retired couple had been receiving $244 a month, payments went up to $271—$3,240 a year. The average single person received $1,930 a year, just above the 1971 poverty line. Benefits were increased for workers who had paid relatively smaller amounts into Social Security, and the limit on outside work earnings was liberalized from $1,680 to $2,100 in a year. Furthermore, the new law, recognizing that inflation has become chronic, provides that starting in 1975 payments can jump 3 percent annually to match a corresponding increase in cost of living. This will ensure what already has occurred with Social Security: retirees will receive at a higher rate than they paid in.

Social Security benefits are not the sole means of support for most aged people. More than one-quarter of them still are working. Others receive pensions and stock dividends. Only one in seven married couples receives as much at 90 percent of its income from Social Security; among single aged, the figure is one in three. Nearly 70 percent of older Americans own their homes, and virtually all aged couples maintain their own homes. The average aged asset is $11,000 with the home representing $8,000 of the total.

The expansion of Social Security was a substantial national commitment, just how substantial most people did not realize until after the fact. It was the biggest tax increase—$7 billion—since the Korean War and meant that FICA taxes would escalate from the maximum $468 in 1972 to $702 in 1974. Yet there was virtually no taxpayer dissent. It signified that Americans were willing to assume the burden necessary for better benefits at their own retirement and for those who precede them as well.

The next question is: How far will the working middle-age groups be able to go in supporting nonproductive young people at one end and nonproductive old people at the other? Both categories have been encroaching upon the middle. With the child labor laws and then with more youths extending the period of their education, young people have been entering the job market at later ages. At the same time, older workers have been retiring at earlier ages. More than half the eligible people now are electing to retire at the age of sixty-two rather than waiting for higher Social Security benefits at age sixty-five. Gerontologist Beattie believes that within a decade the age for retirement will be sixty. In France, the retirement age (when workers are eligible for pensions) is sixty and in Italy sixty for men and fifty-five for women.

The trend toward early retirement is undermining one of the popular preconceptions about old age. Social gerontologist George Maddox of Duke University put it this way:

> In our cultural tradition work has been the central life task for men. A man's job has been his price tag and calling card, the regulator of his social life, and his opportunity for integration in communal life. To the extent that we accept this characterization of work, we are probably prepared to believe that retirement precipitates a crisis. This stereotype is not all wrong, but it is misleading.
>
> First, even a moment's reflection would make us wonder about those individuals who have spent a lifetime at routine jobs economically, socially, and psychologically unrewarding. Would not such individuals welcome relief from work, especially if an adequate retirement income were available? The answer is yes. Many blue collar workers who anticipate adequate retirement benefits not only look forward to retirement, they also, in increasing numbers, retire early when permitted to do so. White-collar workers, especially those who find some fulfillment in their work, are more likely than blue collar workers to be attached to their work. But even for the white collar worker, it is not clear that retirement precipitates a crisis that is severe or is sustained for any length of time.

This is not to say that in many cases there will not be problems with self-esteem or a sense of purposelessness and in adjustments to the use of time or to the home environment. Nor is it to deny that in an important sense the person is being removed from the mainstream of society. Furthermore, some people do not wish to retire at age sixty-five. And gerontologist Robert Butler observes, "we leave immune from arbitrary retirement political, judicial, and medical leadership (three groups that have an enormous influence on critical matters of life and death), and the self-employed."

With the break-up of the extended intergenerational family and the intense mobility of present American society, there is a popular belief that aged parents are deserted by their children. Gerontologists were especially concerned about this and aimed their research at the problem. This is what they found:

Gerontologist Maddox: "Research findings have been somewhat surprising. . . . the overwhelming majority of elderly parents have a child who lives reasonably close to them. Moreover, for the majority of elderly persons with children living, most of them have regular contact with at least one child."

Gerontologist Neugarten: "They [old people] are not necessarily lonely or desolate if they live alone."

Maddox: "We are very prone to assume that older parents expect and want a great deal of contact with their children. Some recent evidence suggests that we may overestimate these desires and expectations. Both children and parents are typically trained to expect geographical and social mobility. . . . One implication of this acceptance is the achievement of a sense of independence on the part of the old and young alike."

Neugarten: "[O]ld persons do not become isolated and neglected by their families, although both generations prefer separate households."

Maddox: "[T]here is evidence that neither parent nor child prefers to live in the same household if other arrangements can be made."

One other thing. There was a surprisingly large interaction between the generations, each helping the other with goods and services. Contrary to the stereotype of the aged parents showing complete dependency on their children, the flow of help was about even either way.

"Love Among the Ruins" Robert Browning called one of his poems, thereby gaining attention with a startling juxtaposition. To a young mind, sex among the aged is even more unlikely and if practiced, then somehow obscene. This attitude should be recognized for what it is: a hangover from Victorian times.

It is true there is a decline in sexual activity with age. One study showed that sexual life had concluded for four out of ten people older than sixty years. The segregation of the doers and the don't is not so much a matter of physiology—although poor health exacts a sexual penalty—as a matter of choice, or opportunity, and of the sexual patterns established in young and middle age. As in other areas, the older person is the unavoidable product of what he has been and done.

Kinsey's studies showed that there is a higher frequency of sexual acts among married people than among single persons. The availability of a partner becomes an ever more crucial factor as a person advances into old age, for the apparent first law for maintaining sexual capacity in old age is: one must exercise the right in order to keep the franchise. Although there have been fears that a woman's sexual apparatus deteriorates after menopause, Masters and Johnson say that this "may be corrected easily with adequate endocrine-replacement therapy [4] . . . but even more necessary for maintained sexual capacity and effective sexual performance is the opportunity for regularity of sexual expression. For the aging woman, much more than for her younger counterpart, such opportunity has a significant influence upon her sexual performance."

The Kinsey studies showed that a large part of a woman's sex drive during the years after menopause is directly related to sexual habits established earlier. In this sense, sexual performance is predictive. If a woman in her younger years has been inadequate sexually or has had unpleasant sexual experiences, menopause can serve as a reason for discontinuance of sex. The Kinsey material, on the other hand, "suggests that a woman who has had a happy, well-adjusted, and stimulating marriage may progress through the menopausal and post-menopausal years with little or no interruption in the frequency of, or interest in, sexual actively." Additionally, "social and economic security are major factors in many women's successful sexual adjustment to their declining years," say Masters and Johnson. "If satisfactory counseling of sexual content were made more available to sexually insecure, uneducated, or inadequate women in the premenopausal years, there is reason to believe that the unresolved tensions of the later years might be reduced or, to a large extent, avoided."

The lamp of a woman's sexuality can burn for as long as she lives, although it may be dimmed by the social and physiologic attrition of aging. But often enough the light goes out when a woman is in her seventies because by this time she is a widow or her older husband has become inert sexually and, Masters and Johnson note, "extramarital sexual partners essentially are unavailable to the women in this age group."

The sexual response of the human male wanes as he grows older. A comparison of men between the ages of forty and sixty with those older than sixty shows a reduction of sexual needs, intensity of pleasure, ability

[4] *Biology and the Future of Man,* the National Academy of Sciences' survey of the subject published in 1970, says: "There is a great need for a carefully planned study of the effectiveness of estrogens in relation to claims that they maintain youth, prevent osteoporosis (thinning of bones) and some vascular disorders, preserve sexuality, and reduce nervous tensions. Conversely the possibility that cancer, particularly of the breast, may be favored by prolonged estrogen administration must be examined." *Developmental Physiology and Aging,* p. 612, states: "Chronic treatment with estrogens has proven of value in alleviating many of the symptoms associated with the menopausal syndrome (Schleyer-Saunders, 1971) and, provided that nutrition and exercise are adequate, estrogen therapy may delay the onset of post-menopausal osteoporosis by ten years or longer (Davis *et al.,* 1966; Lutwak, 1969)."

to enter coitus successfully, and ability to bring it to a climactic conclusion. Of all the men Masters and Johnson treated for impotence, three-quarters of them were older than fifty years. However, as in other areas, the loss of sexual vigor varies from individual to individual and the function can be preserved into advanced old age. Masters and Johnson again: "[I]f elevated levels of sexual activity are maintained from earlier years and neither acute nor chronic physical incapacity intervenes, aging males usually are able to continue some form of active sexual expression into the seventy- and even eighty-year age groups. Even if coital activity has been avoided for long periods of time, men in these age groups can be returned to effective sexual function if adequate stimulation is instituted and interested partners are available."

As with women, the most important factor is regularity of activity. However, sexuality in older men is beset by a number of potentially important impediments, most of them psychological. They are, according to Masters and Johnson: (1) boredom with a repetitious sexual relationship; (2) preoccupation with career and economic pursuits; (3) mental or physical fatigue; (4) eating or drinking too much; (5) mental or physical troubles either with himself or his wife; (6) fear of performance.

This last category can begin with temporary sexual failure brought on by any of the other causes. For instance, an older husband is much more likely than a younger one to be rendered impotent by a wife who shows little sexual interest and concern. "Once impotent under any circumstances, many males withdraw voluntarily from any coital activity rather than face the ego-shattering experience of repeated episodes of sexual inadequacy," report Masters and Johnson. "There is no way to over-emphasize the importance that the factor 'fear of failure' plays in the aging male's withdrawal from sexual performance."

However, these experts on human sexual response say that with physical well-being, with proper marital environment and mental outlook, sexual capacity can be preserved beyond the eighty-year level. The study that showed that sexual relations had ceased for four couples out of ten by age sixty also revealed that the other six couples of ten continued to be active sexually until the seventy-fifth year. After that age, one couple in four still was warmed by the heat of sexual love.

The effects of age on intelligence are varied and may not necessarily be so deleterious as earlier research indicated. The nature of intelligence changes with age. The human organism starts out with a fresh biological mechanism for acquiring information and processing it into knowledge. Initially, this intelligence is extremely flexible and absorptive, excelling at abstracting principles from a variety of phenomena and capable of rapid calculations. At the same time, the brain starts off with none of the information which the mental apparatus is designed to collect and process.

The acquisition of information, the methods of learning, and the choice of information inescapably impose their own structures upon the mind. It is as though at the outset the native intelligence is open to infinite courses, but by the nature of things only one route can be lived. Two processes are taking place simultaneously. The mind is filling with information which makes intelligence more structured and less flexible. Unavoidably, the mind becomes more organized along certain lines. A forest will not be regarded in the same way by an artist, an ecologist, and a lumberman.

Dennis Bromley, a British psychologist who specializes in aging, calls attention to this transition by noting the different age periods for peaks in various kinds of creativity. Achievements come early in mathematics, which is highly abstract and open to the greatest inventiveness. Chemistry and biology come later, followed in more advanced years by history and taxonomy, the science of categorizing life.[5]

Dr. Bromley divides intelligence into fluid abilities and crystallized abilities. "Fluid abilities are those inborn psychobiological capacities which are fundamental to normal intellectual functioning"—attention, memory, representation, symbolism, abstraction, generalization, and relational thinking. "Crystallized abilities, on the other hand, are those culturally based intellectual capacities which children acquire through their formal schooling and home background and through their life experiences generally," such as vocabulary and grammar, conceptual systems and mental skills. There is a good deal of evidence, says Dr. Bromley, "to show that fluid abilities mature early and then decrease steadily, whereas crystallized abilities mature late and can be maintained fairly well, especially among people who regularly exercise these mental functions." Test values for vocabulary and information go up and stay there into advanced old age while other parameters are dropping.

This should augur well for old writers and, indeed, George Bernard Shaw wrote some of his best plays in his seventies and Boris Pasternak completed his great novel, *Dr. Zhivago*, when he was sixty-five years old. The combination of intellectual strengths late in life also leads to the peak of many careers in philosophy, statecraft, the Church, and education.

We may sometimes forget that our intelligence is biologically based, quite dependent upon the physical condition of the brain and nervous system. The brain starts out with 10 billion neurons. These "thinking" cells are not to be replaced. When one cell dies, it physically reduces the

[5] See gerontologist Joseph Still's stages, p. 155.

intellectual apparatus. Postmortems show that the brains of older people weigh less, have large internal spaces, fewer neurons, more senile plaques, and more abnormalities of all kinds than the brains of younger people (of course, the brain like the other organs has a margin for safety and can sustain some physical loss without mental impairment—how much is not known). Moreover, the brain is closely associated with and dependent upon the blood circulatory system. Studies by Frances Wilkie and Carl Eisdorfer at Duke University correlated drops in intelligence levels with high blood pressure. Studies by Lissy Jarvik and others have shown that sharp intellectual declines presage death within the year; in this way, such intelligence tests can serve as early warning indicators of death. What is happening, Dr. Jarvik believes, is arteriosclerotic deterioration within the brain.

Still, as we have seen, the brain is the most favored of organs in being supplied with blood, and the latest studies show it can bear up well. Dr. Jarvik and associates have been taking part in a long-term study of aged twins that began in 1947. They found that on average most intelligence test scores remained stable between the ages of sixty-five and seventy-three and then began to show accelerating declines between the ages of seventy-three and eighty-five. However, there were many inconsistencies, both among individuals and among various tests taken by the same individual. Some subjects' score remained the same or even improved during the later years. "These results," reported Drs. June Blum, Lissy Jarvik, and Edward Clark, "lead to the conclusion that a life-span investigation of intellectual changes should be approached in terms of individual differences in specific abilities and not in terms of 'global intelligence.' To ignore the individual variations is to fall into the perennial trap of lumping the aged together as having outlived their usefulness—instead of recognizing it is the individual, not the age, that makes the difference."

Most of the earlier data showing appreciable intelligence declines with age had come from cross-sectional studies where the aged, a less-educated generation, compared unfavorably with younger cohorts. But in another longitudinal report conducted at Duke University, says Carl Eisdorfer, "we demonstrated that over the ten years between sixty-five and seventy-five, declines in intellectual performance occurred only in those individuals in whom hypertension was a problem. Thus under this close inspection the accepted intellectual decline in this older population was associated with sickness rather than age."

The Duke research showed that old people do not lose the ability to memorize or to learn. However, they tested poorly under time pressures. At first this was interpreted as meaning that the old person could learn as well as a young person, but needed more time. Now Duke research-ers theorize that the oldsters are reluctant to hazard quick answers. They are not as achievement-oriented as young people, less inclined to strive, more familiar with functional losses. In short, the lowered per-formance may have the same psychological cause as the great sexual crippler—fear of failure.

Finally, to look at one other facet of old age: old people do not regard their lot as poorly as do young people. In general, an older person has a clearer sense of identity than a younger one. The tendency to admit shortcomings drops with age, and so does the tendency to hold a negative perception of oneself. While the number of old people who feel they have good or excellent health drops below the 50 percent mark, most old people feel they have better health than other people their age and are more inclined to give themselves better health ratings than their physicians do. As a person grows older, he regards lack of education as less of a shortcoming. Feelings of inadequacy both as husbands or wives and as parents are fewer in old age than during earlier periods of life. Old people are less likely to feel older and slightly more likely to feel younger than their age than younger people. A person is much more likely to regard himself as old if he is retired and if she or he is a widow or widower.

In attitudes toward life, older people are less likely to feel a sense of mastery over conditions of their lives than young people; at the same time they are more likely to emphasize the responsibility of the individual for his destiny, whereas younger people are more likely to stress environ-mental influences. Consequently, old people are more likely to blame individuals while young people want to change conditions. The tendency to doctor oneself and resist going to a hospital steadily increases with age. So does the tendency to take a more pessimistic view of things.

Life satisfaction in a general sense begins to decline in early adult-hood and these feelings become intensified in relation to specific oc-currencies in old age, such as losses of health, important roles in life, or independence. However, there is no diminishing in the feeling of worth or contentment to be drawn from work or family life. One study showed that the percentage of people feeling "very happy" remained almost constant from youth to old age. Similarly, the number of worriers and nonworriers seems to remain the same regardless of age. In another study, morale went down from age sixty to past age seventy-five. One's job becomes a primary source of satisfaction with advancing age. More employed old people had high morale than their retired counterparts, but socioeconomic status and good health—in that order—were more im-portant factors affecting morale; so that a greater percentage of retired old people with high socioeconomic status and good health had higher morale than working old people with poor health and/or low social status. When the three factors—high status, good health, and employment —coincided, 75 percent of the old people in one study rated their morale as high.

There are few psychosocial theories of aging. Erik Erikson's developmental stages of the life cycle (see pp. 157-161) are widely accepted although they have been subjected to little testing. Within gerontology, Elaine Cumming and William Henry in 1961 proposed the disengagement theory of aging. This theory suggested that as a person progresses through the sixty's and seventy's he withdraws psychologically and socially from his fellows and society reciprocates in this disengagement. The individual's withdrawal is a developmental or intrinsic process as he becomes more preoccupied with the self and cuts his emotional investment in his surroundings. Robert Havighurst, Bernice Neugarten, and Sheldon Tobin of the University of Chicago tested this thesis in a widescale survey known as the Kansas City Study of Adult Life. They found the disengagement theory to be a substantially accurate description of what happens. They detected the beginnings of psychological disinvolvement in the fifty's followed by social disengagement in the sixty's and seventy's.

But is the description a prescription? Is this the proper way for people to go about growing old? Conventional wisdom argued an opposite course: resist the shrinkage of your social world, maintain the activities of middle age as long as possible; when one is forced to retire find substitutes for work, and substitutes for loved one and friends who die. This "activity" theory said that the way to age optimally is to remain active, adhering to the patterns of middle age. Disengagement theory said to seek a natural equilibrium rather than an unnatural disequilibrium.

Havighurst and team decided to test the conflicting theories by introducing a new criterion: the individual's happiness. They rated a person high on satisfaction with his life when he (1) took pleasure from his daily activities, whether sitting in a rocking chair watching TV or heading a community fund; (2) regarded his life as meaningful and accepted responsibility for his past life; (3) felt he had succeeded in achieving his major goals; (4) held a positive self-image; (5) had an optimistic outlook.

The study found in general that people who are socially involved are happy, and this relationship becomes even stronger in people seventy years old and older. "In other words, those older persons who are highly engaged in various social roles generally have greater life satisfaction than those who have lower levels of engagement. At the same time the relationship is not a consistent one. There are some older persons who are low in social role activity and who have high life satisfaction; and vice-versa, there are others who are high in activity, but low in satisfaction."

People do not grow old in a single pattern, and individuality or personality counts for more than lifestyle in any particular instance. The people who aged most successfully—the majority of the seventy-year-olds in the study—divided into three patterns of aging. One pattern was called the *reorganizers* and in some respects they were optimal agers in American society. These people substituted new activities for lost ones, gave time to community affairs, the church, or other groups. One retired school teacher was selling insurance and making more money than ever. A second group of well-integrated personalities was called the *focused*. They were selective in their activities, devoting their energies only to roles they deemed important and eschewing all other activities. One seventy-five-year-old emeritus professor still taught (only the courses she wanted to), was glad to have her husband home to free her from chores, seldom saw her children and preferred it that way. A third pattern for well-integrated personalities with high satisfaction in their lives was called the *disengaged* because they had reduced their social roles and were inactive. They remained interested in the world, but not the whirl of activities; they felt high self-regard but chose to lead a relaxed life at home, gardening a little, helping their wives, and visiting their children and grandchildren.

Next was the group with "armored" or "defended" personalities. These were ambitious people who drove themselves. They had medium to high levels of happiness. One pattern for this type of personality was known as *holding-on:* "So long as you keep busy, you'll get along all right." Life satisfaction was keyed to the ability to keep busy. The other lifestyle was called *constricted*. These people were busy defending themselves against aging, guarding against new experiences, following elaborate rituals to maintain health.

The third personality type, "passive dependent," included two patterns of life. The *succorance-seekers* were highly dependent upon one or two persons in their lives. As long as a spouse or child took care of all the old persons's needs, he or she lived with medium levels of activity and satsifaction. The small number of *apathetic* had few activities and little interest in the world. Life was hard and there was not much that could be done about it. One woman's activities were limited to meeting her physical needs and caring for two cats.

Finally, there were the "distintegrated" or *disorganized* persons who had gross psychological impairments. They managed to keep themselves in the community either because of protective families or the forbearance of people around them. One example was a paranoid, isolated man who did some janitorial work in a rundown building in exchange for a room in the basement.

Two other, psychological theories about aging deserve attention. One is the foreshortened life perspective proposed by Robert Kastenbaum of Wayne State University. In effect, this theory says that as a person ages he becomes ever more oriented toward his past and ever more surely avoids thoughts of his future because so little is left and what there is may be preponderantly unpleasant. Dr. Kastenbaum calls this the psychological loss of the future. He has found that a majority of people are past-oriented by age forty, and virtually everyone is by age fifty-five. Exceptions are those people who have earned the competence to be able to look forward to new achievements.

The foreshortened life perspective is not limited to the aged. Dr. Kastenbaum and John Teahan studied a group of hardcore unemployed men who were taking an employment rehabilitation program at a public utility company. After six months, 14 of the men still were working at the plant while 15 had quit or had been fired. The future perspectives of the unsuccessful ones "foresaw fewer good years ahead and predicted shorter life spans (20 years, on the average) than the men who held onto the jobs. All of these so-called 'hardcore unemployed' were young adults and all were black. These results lead us to speculate that being young and black in our society is the functional equivalent of being old and white." A foreshortened life perspective at any age, says Dr. Kastenbaum, "is likely to increase the probability of premature death."

Robert Butler, a research psychiatrist and gerontologist who has conducted studies for the National Institute of Mental Health, says that the aged use the past—survey it, reflect on it—as a preparation for death. This is a natural process, he says, as the person tries to derive a sense of order from his life experiences. Dr. Butler calls this process the life review. It is this inner impulsion which causes so many people to write autobiographies at the end of their lives: the books are a by-product of this search for a synthesis and summation that goes on in almost everyone as he nears completion of his life. The process can bring a sense of resolution and composure—and a harvest of wisdom. By spurning the collective knowledge, judgment, and skills of the aged, Dr. Butler says, American society is wasting a precious resource.

Well, what can gerontology tell us about living longer, better lives? Anita Zorzoli, a biologist, emphasizes diet. "For myself, I maintain good quality nutrition: adequate protein, carbohydrates and fats with the accent on protein. Supplement with vitamins. Life-lengthening occurs in youth. One must avoid obesity in order to live well. Maintain your body in a lean state. I don't agree with the large-scale intake of milk in the American diet. I believe strongly in low fat, low cholesterol." So for Dr. Zorzoli: (1) proper diet; (2) exercise regularly; (3) don't smoke.

Ruth Bennett, a sociologist, emphasizes mental activity, being alert intellectually, keeping an interest in your life, environment, world. She says that for an aged person, physical exercise is not nearly as helpful, if at all, as mental exercise. There is, she says, a correspondence between intelligence and longevity. So for Dr. Bennett: (1) stay active mentally; (2) proper diet; (3) no smoking.

Robert Kastenbaum, a psychologist, simulated with students in one of his classes conditions under which old people must get along in American society. His object was to have young people preexperience what it is like to be aged. Since slowness is one of the characteristics of age, he forced these young people to perform certain tasks under unreasonably speeded-up schedules. The result was "aged" behavior. The subjects made more errors in their decisions, and in ways discernible in older people. "Some fumbled and became impulsive and anxious. Others withdrew into passivity—just seemed to give up. Most lost themselves in routine—settled on one rigid decision strategy and stuck to it, even in the face of evidence that the strategy was not working." In other tests, subjects were given important roles and then systematically eased out of them or designated elders in mock social groups where they were ignored and held in low esteem. As one might suspect, the young people were dismayed, deflated, irritated, angry at the way they were treated.

This lesson illustrates that one of the most onerous parts of being old results simply from social discrimination. Columbia University, where Dr. Bennett teaches, will not allow a student to matriculate if he is older than sixty years. Isaac Presler went to work as a sales clerk in Macy's Department Store when he was fifty-six years old. He worked for 18 years, established an excellent record, retired at the age of seventy-four, and asked for a pension. Macy's gives pensions to employees with more than 15 years service, but only if the 15 years are completed before age sixty-five. Presler took his case to the New York Division of Human Rights, claiming discrimination because of age. New York's Human Rights Law is designed to comply with mandatory retirement rules and applies only to people between the ages of forty and sixty-five. The agency told Presler it could not help him. With the aid of distinguished law professor Telford Taylor and Legal Services for the

Elderly, Presler appealed all the way up to the U.S. Supreme Court. In April 1972 the high court refused to hear the case. Human rights end at sixty-five and justice defers to the supreme law of the land—mandatory retirement, which a worker violates at his own risk. Why must retirement be mandatory? And why dictated chronologically since, we have seen, time is a crude indicator of human old age? The Soviet Union, a more regimented, totalitarian society, allows greater personal freedom in this important area than the United States—there is no mandatory retirement law in Russia. (Two reasons for this are lack of manpower and low birth rate.)

Since longevity would seem to depend on both individual and societal actions, it would be well at this point to consider two of gerontology's most definitive research contributions. One is a longitudinal study by the National Institute of Mental Health in 1955–56 and 1962, and a follow-up in 1967, at the Philadelphia Geriatric Center. This study began with 47 men aged sixty-five to ninety-one years. The median age was seventy-one years. The researchers wished to start with a sample of totally healthy subjects. However, this proved to be impractical, so the study was begun with 27 healthy subjects and 20 who were essentially healthy in that they showed no symptoms but did have mild abnormalities usually related to arteriosclerosis. The study monitored more than 600 characteristics of each subject's physiological state, health, and behavior.

Also in 1955 Duke University began a longitudinal study of aged people. This sample included women as well as men and some younger subjects. The age-span began at sixty and went as old as ninety-four years. The basic panel included 256 subjects, each coded for 788 pieces of information. Most of these data fell into medical and social categories with the remaining one-fourth psychological and psychiatric/neurological. Three reexaminations were held, the latest on which findings are based in 1967 (although the study is continuing). A U.S. government report says the two studies complement each other, "and where findings are similar, their validity may merit much confidence."

By 1967, 24 men in the NIMH-Philadelphia Geriatrics Center study had died and 23 still survived. The average age of the survivors by then was eighty-one years. Only six of the 20 men with mild arteriosclerosis—30 percent—survived whereas 17 of the 27 completely healthy men—63 percent—survived. The men who died were not significantly older than the men who lived. The two groups, survivors and nonsurvivors, gave investigators an opportunity to evaluate characteristics in relation to longevity. They reduced the differences to 15 important factors. These were the most significant:

Chronic cigarette smoking was one of the key differences. Even among men who were virtually identical physiologically in the first test, the smokers were nonsurvivors and the survivors were nonsmokers. Survivors performed significantly better in virtually all forms of intelligence tests. Survivors reported themselves more involved in social relationships, were less affected by environmental loss, were more resourceful in meeting needs and pleasures, had higher self-esteem, and scored higher in what was called Organization of Behavior to measure the amount of planning and the complexity of daily activities.

Organization of Behavior and cigarette smoking together were found to be the key indicators, as good as all 15 measurements together, with an 80 percent accuracy in separating the quick and the dead. Men who scored high on Organization of Behavior and who did not smoke were most likely to live.

The Duke study—which included both sexes, did not exclude unhealthy people and therefore was more representative of the aged population—found four significant predictors of longevity. In order of importance, they were: (1) work satisfaction, a person's feeling of general usefulness and ability to perform a meaningful social role; (2) happiness, a person's general satisfaction with his life situation; (3) physical functioning; (4) use of tobacco (as a negative factor).

For men in their sixties, work satisfaction and tobacco use were the only two really important factors, coinciding with the NIMH longitudinal study. For men in their seventies, physical functioning—in other words, the person's general health situation—took over as the most important indicator of living or dying, followed by work satisfaction and happiness. By this time, smoking no longer was a prime determinant.

For women of all ages above sixty, the degree of happiness was the foremost predictor of longevity. For women in their sixties, it was followed by physical functioning, work satisfaction, and use of tobacco. But when women were in their seventies, there were only two significant determinants—happiness and work satisfaction.

Intelligence, rated by performance I.Q. tests, was the fifth most important signpost toward long life or early death. For Blacks, it was the most crucial determinant. There was only one other for Blacks—use of tobacco.

Professor Erdman Palmore summed up: "These findings suggest that, in general, the most important ways to increase longevity are:

"1) to maintain a useful and satisfying role in society,

"2) to maintain a positive view of life,

"3) to maintain good physical functioning, and

"4) to avoid smoking.

"It is significant," wrote Dr. Palmore, "that the first two most important factors (for the total group) are these social-psychological dimensions rather than some measure of health or of mental abilities."

So. Along with keeping healthy and trim through proper diet and exercise, and not smoking cigarettes, the objectives for the aging person are to be busy at rewarding work, fulfilling a role or roles that bolster self-esteem, and thus to take satisfaction from life. However, these are precisely the goals that contemporary American society makes difficult to achieve with mandatory retirement, reduced roles, reduced opportunities, reduced economic status, reduced social status, compounded by the American penchant for rating people by their income and consumption. It takes a redoubtable ego to withstand this assault on one's sense of worth.

The onslaught does not end here. The recent changes in society all work against the aged. The break-up of the multigenerational farm and rural families, the evolution of the nuclear family, the new mobility and almost routine job relocations all sever the older generation from their families. The rapidity with which new knowledge becomes available is causing problems of job obsolescence even for middle-aged people and makes the oldtimer a relic as far as transmitting job skills. Not only is American society youth-oriented, it is future-oriented, or perhaps, more correctly, it is youth-oriented because it is future-oriented. It sees few utilitarian uses of the past. Congress obligingly rearranges national holidays for the convenience of merchants, employers, and workers. As landscape designer Ian McHarg has pointed out, all highway builders know the economy of a straight line, but none knows the value of history. Since aged people are both oriented to the past and no longer producers, it is difficult to resist the utilitarian conclusion that they are obsolescent. Older people are sensitive to this judgment: delegates to the second White House Conference on Aging seized on the theme that they do not intend to be members of the "throwaway generation."

If old people are both economically useless and economically dependent (the utilitarian reasoning proceeds), then they are being maintained at the sufferance of the producers, who pay the income tax and Social Security bills and who are therefore entitled to set the rules. This line of argument is presented explicitly in an article about Social Security by *New York Times* Washington correspondent Edwin Dale, Jr. in the *New York Times Magazine,* January 14, 1973. The article is entitled "The Security of Social Security: The Young Pay for the Old." An accompanying artist's sketch shows four young people, glum or glowering, stuffing money into the opened foreheads of four old people. In the text, Dale says that now that Social Security has been put on a pay-as-you-go basis, any pretense that it is a contributory fund has been removed. It is revealed for what it is: a tax levied on the young to support the old. Therefore, any raises in benefits—such as the legislated escalation to match inflationary rises in the cost of living—will in effect mean new taxes on the young. They should have something to say about that, Dale suggests. "The choice is whether to raise taxes on the young at all and, if so, what to spend money on. The answer is not necessarily higher cash benefits for the aged." Dale says that unspecified "many people feel that there are higher priorities for new federal funds than cash benefits to the aged: services, food and cash for poor children, for example. Some people even prefer more spending on defense."

Perhaps ever heavier commitments to Social Security are not the proper solution to maintaining old people. Perhaps such a broad-scale approach will become financially untenable. Pensions won by school teachers and other municipal workers in New York City have been cited as undermining the city's financial integrity. But the point with Social Security is that it is the carrot which society has used along with the mandatory retirement stick to drive older workers from the job market in order to give young people access to well-paid work. And perhaps that makes sense, too, on the theory that unemployed young people can be more troublesome than unemployed old people. But for society to turn around as though it had no complicity in the matter and assume a stance of objectively debating how much should be doled out to its older "wards" is schizophrenic.[6]

It is clear from gerontological research that an individual's longevity is to an important extent dependent upon his social context. Indeed, society is an elaborate, cooperative apparatus human beings have erected in order to promote their survival. For society to become a major limiting factor to survival is a basic contradiction. William Bevan of the American Association for the Advancement of Science, in an editorial in *Science*, says that "the key to the problems of the aged is not national resources or the know-how of the medical and behavioral sciences. It is a fundamental change in national attitude." And Nathan Shock, who has contributed substantially to enhancing the chances of longevity, once gave voice to the dilemma of such a pursuit. "If I had my way," he said, "there would be nothing done to extend longevity until we get a clear conception of what the role of the aged should be in society."

The concluding paragraphs of the report on the NIMH–Philadelphia Geriatric Center longitudinal study are addressed to some of these prob-

[6] Or, in Dale's case, perhaps just poor reporting. The true purpose of Social Security is one of the nation's best-kept secrets. Gerontologist Ruth Bennett says the child labor laws finally succeeded for the same reason—to open up jobs.

lems. "Changes in cultural practices," the report says, "even though they would be difficult to bring about and would require much time, might be very important." As examples, the authors suggest that women marry men more nearly their own age and that far greater attention be paid to grief in the elderly with early medical attention for those who become sick while grieving.[7] The longitudinal report says that different levels of government and institutions will probably have to provide services usually provided by the family because of geographical dispersal. And it says that the nation's economists, business managers, and labor unions will have to give more attention to employment and retirement practices for the aged.

Gerontologist Carl Eisdorfer is optimistic. He believes that "by 1990, the American lifespan will be pushing 80." One of the big reasons for his confidence is that the present crop of old people-to-be are smarter, better educated, more affluent than those who have gone before. They will be better able to meet their problems more successfully, get what they need from society. And, as many gerontologists point out, awareness of the problems ahead itself serves as a safeguard. If the middle-aged person sailing along at full steam is alerted that ahead lie doldrums, that he is racing toward deflated status and a Sargasso sea of time, and that he had better sit down with his wife to plan how they will live their retired future together and how they will meet expenses for what they want, then a person's chances of meeting the challenges of old age improve.

Dr. Eisdorfer believes there is need "for a whole new creative approach. A G.I. Bill for the aged. A Peace Corps for the elderly where the corpsmen already would be thoroughly trained." The idea is that instead of inducing idleness, which is alien to many people and which is unproductive for the nation, a sense of purpose would be restored to elderly people who would once again be contributing to society. The federal Retired Senior Volunteers Program is a step in this direction, providing out-of-pocket expenses for old people who volunteer their time for community work.

The California Commission on Aging found an untapped pool of workers in the state's aged volunteers. Commission Chairman Mrs. A. M. Russell reported some of the things these volunteers did: "Some teach crafts at regularly scheduled classes at convalescent homes. Some tape talking books. One woman works twenty hours a week as motor pool dispatcher for the Red Cross. A group of men show movies each week at the Veterans' Hospital. Another group help run a glaucoma screen-

[7] The work of Dr. Austin Kutscher and others in this area was cited in Chapter I, pp. 24-25.

ing clinic. Some teach defensive driving courses. Some send cookies to Vietnam (Operation Cookie Pak sent 361 boxes in three months). Some seniors drive others to doctors or visit the ill in hospitals. Others contact and arrange for speakers, plan trips, deliver meals on wheels or serve as guides in civic centers."

Mrs. Russell told of their first volunteer, referred by his physician. "Ernest B. is a courteous dignified man of seventy-five years who is completely alone. No one seemed to need him despite his ability to speak five languages, play and teach several musical instruments, teach chess and gourmet cooking. . . . Such skills could not be wasted. He is now teaching piano to blind students at Braille Institute and is aiding the City Schools Volunteer program tutoring language students. Life is once more worthwhile for Mr. B."

Gradually, opportunities for oldsters to fill jobs paying money were introduced into the program and, gradually, the undertakings became more ambitious. One senior group took over the operation of a Greyhound Bus Terminal that was going to be discontinued. Another group contracted to provide a complete program of recreation therapy for a 200-bed convalescent hospital. But there is an important difference in the kind of work older people want, Mrs. Russell said. They "want jobs that, one, use their experience with or without retraining and, two, provide a positive image of important contribution to society, to education, or to the needy."

Director Walter Beattie, Jr., of the All-University Gerontology Center at Syracuse University, says we need to make a new approach to the production and distribution of services, for the aged offer a great potential as providers as well as consumers of services. Longevity, he says, is forcing a redefinition of many of our concepts related to the life cycle. Dr. Beattie says we must move away from the eighteenth-century economic view of man to a twenty-first-century view of continuing participation in society. This means moving away from segregated leisure villages to communities where the generations are integrated and interdependent. Social planning is essential and so is a coherent social policy based on a nondiscriminatory high quality of living throughout the lifespan. Our concept of education must change from the nineteenth-century youth-oriented preparation for work and life to a new concept of continuing education as a means of meeting needs and changed circumstances as they arise. "There is a tendency to deal with aging outside the family. We must think in terms of strengthening the family in order to cope with aging. In Sweden, payments are made directly to the family to give in-home care. In the United States, we have forced the wife to go to work."

William Reichel of Franklin Square Hospital in Baltimore, a practicing geriatrician and a member of the Board of Directors of the American Geriatrics Society, states that "all attempts should be made to keep elderly citizens in the community close to home or at home. The costly and difficult chore of institutional care, whether it is in a hospital or nursing home or in extended care centers could be ameliorated by better selection of patients for institutions and by more effort to keep the aged at home or close to home."

Dr. Reichel believes this goal can be accomplished with a threefold strategy. At the hub of each local medical network would be a community hospital which serves as a center to orient family physicians to geriatric medicine, to train physician assistants or nurse practitioners in geriatrics, and to diagnose the health situations of the elderly. A Geriatric Evaluation Clinic was set up at Franklin Square Hospital "to make the proper clinical evaluation of older persons to avoid wrong placement and to keep the elderly as close to home as possible. Many elderly thought to have an incorrectable mental illness have been found on proper medical, psychiatric, and neurological evaluation to have a variety of medical problems including hypothyroid states, electrolyte imbalance, and drug overdosage. Many of these persons seen in this clinic have been returned to the home and none of our patients studied have necessitated state hospitalization."

The second component in the plan are family physicians who not only think of their patients at their present ages but keep in mind that one day the patient will be sixty-five years old and therefore stresses preventive medicine for the diseases of old age. "What America needs most for its total medical care and for its geriatric care is an increased number of family doctors."

Family physicians are simply too busy to carry out the necessary home care for the elderly, but this could be done by creating a new class of physician assistants or nurse practitioners. Overburdened physicians are simply going to have to change and allow other people to help them, Dr. Reichel believes. Franklin Square Hospital has set up such a physician assistant training program in conjunction with a neighboring college. New York State has taken a giant step in this direction—one that is being watched with interest by many other states—to train nurses for more responsible roles in the community.

But Americans have put their faith in technological solutions and most trends seem to be away from what these gerontologists advocate: away from the family to the agency, away from the mother to the day-care center, away from the parent to the child expert, away from the family physician to the specialist, away from the integrated community to the golden-agers community, away from the home to the institution. Seven new nursing homes open each day! The number of these establishments grew from fewer than 7,000 in 1960 to 23,000 in little more than a decade.

But perhaps solutions will come from an American tradition that predates the technological mystique. In Philadelphia, Margaret Kuhn at the age of sixty-six founded a group in 1971 called the Gray Panthers. The group's purpose is to liberate the old. Among the group's members are young people, whom she calls "cubs." She said the empathy between the generations was "curious and wonderful."

With funds from the Presbyterian Church and the United Church of Christ, the Gray Panthers have lobbied in Washington for tenants' rights in old-age homes and won concessions from a Philadelphia bank to pay utility and other bills so that its aged customers would not have to carry much cash. They had been the targets of muggers.

The Gray Panther leader scorns the "paternalism" of homes for the aged, shuffleboard and the "assinine" activities of "those damned golden age clubs," and the stereotype of the elderly as "fuddy duddies" who cling to the past. The former church worker was planning to experiment with different lifestyles, such as using a big old house in Philadelphia as the living quarters for old people and students. "It all has sexual overtones and undertones," she said, but "it would be a new community that the church ought to bless."

It appears that today's elderly do have a role. Never before have there been so many aged people, such a large leisured class, so many problems. Whether they wish it or not, today's old people are pioneers on a new frontier.

Yet it is not wholly unexplored territory. There are a few communities with great numbers of old people who live to very ripe old age: Vilcabamba village in the Andes Mountains of Ecuador, the Hunza people in the Karakoram Mountains of Kashmir, and the Abkhasians living near the Caucasus Mountains in Soviet Georgia (see pp. 142-143 and 151-152).

There is a strong temptation to dismiss these models as irrelevant since they are so anomalous to human experience. For instance, it might be pointed out that these are all mountain people, and living in such elevated places could produce special conditioning of the respiratory-vascular systems. Except that the Abkhasians are not so elevated topographically. They are spread over land that rises from the Black Sea to the Caucasus foothills 3,000 to 4,500 feet in elevation. And the Nagir people living high in the Karakorams adjacent to the Hunzas are not notably long-lived.

It also could be pointed out that Hunza and Nagir people rarely intermarry, indicating that longevity is a matter of genetic heredity. An early American gerontologist, Raymond Pearl, in the 1920s bred long-lived and short-lived fruit flies. Other studies of animals under controlled conditions showed that longevity is strongly influenced by parental longevity. For years the standard, ironic advice for achieving a long life has been "to pick long-lived parents." The Ecuadorean village also is isolated, but the Abkhasians are a conglomerate of many ethnic stocks. Still, Dr. Alexander Leaf of Harvard Medical School found that most old Abkhasians were born of long-lived parents. "There is no known gene for longevity," Dr. Leaf writes, "there is only the absence of 'bad' genes—those that increase the risk of fatal disease."

Yet a mass survey in Russia of people older than age eighty and cited by Dmitri Chebotarev of the Soviet Institute of Gerontology in 1969 showed that only between 28 and 40 percent (percentages varied in different areas) of the subjects "were found to have blood relatives who attained extreme old age." The Duke longitudinal study showed almost no correlation between the mother's and father's age at death and the person's longevity or predicted longevity. "My interpretation of this finding," writes Erdman Palmore, "is that the main effects of genetics on longevity occur at ages before sixty (when our subjects entered our study). That is, inherited diseases and other genetic imperfections probably relate to early death before age sixty. But for those who have survived sixty years, any residual genetic effects are washed out by the overwhelming weight of sixty years of environmental influence." Dr. Palmore says the trouble with human studies linking longevity to the age of parents is that none of them has separated genetic from environmental factors. A person inherits more than genes from his parents; he also gets a set of attitudes, beliefs, values; a style of living; and the same environment in which to live.[8]

What the three long-lived communities do share in common is they are rural, the people work in agriculture, there is no age for retirement, and the aged enjoy high social status. Physical activity is a way of life, both working in the fields and tramping up and down hills. As we have seen (pp. 151-152), the Ecuadorean villagers and the Hunzas have low cholesterol, low fat, low meat, low dairy-products diets and extensive

---

[8] Judging parents' ages, particularly the one of the same sex, probably is the most common indicator people use to gauge their own life expectancy. Lyndon Johnson, whose father died after a heart attack at the age of sixty, had his own and his family's medical history fed into a computer, which predicted that he would not live beyond age sixty-four. Mr. Johnson met that deadline, dying at sixty-four. But who has done the definitive study of self-fulfilling prophecy? His last years were marked by psychological stress, resumption of cigarette smoking, build-up of weight—and atherosclerosis.

testing showed the Vilcabamba villagers all but free of arteriosclerotic disease. The Abkhasians, again, are an exception, eating meat and dairy products—and carrying all kinds of cardiovascular diseases. A Soviet gerontologist and heart specialist who has studied these oldtimers believes that they do suffer heart attacks but they go unnoticed. Exercise has so strengthened the heart-lung system that the superior oxygen supply to the heart overcomes local blockages that would be crippling or fatal to an average person. Recent research has shown that sudden death from atherosclerosis and heart disease is much less frequent among middle-aged people who are physically active (who also are not obese and don't smoke cigarettes).

Abkhasians themselves attribute their long lives to diet, work, and sex. Work in the fields begins in childhood and continues throughout the lifespan. As they grow older, workers set a slower pace and curtail their hours. A Soviet scientist studied 21 men and seven women over the age of 100 and discovered that on average they worked four hours a day on the collective farm. One woman, 109 years old, was paid for 49 full workdays during a summer. Competitiveness in work is not native to Abkhasians. However, that is beginning to change; the Soviet Government is encouraging competition in order to increase production, and the younger men now work more rapidly.

Another custom is beginning to change. Some young people are marrying in the mid-twenties instead of waiting until at least thirty, as the custom has been. One 102-year-old man told anthropologist Sula Benet that he had waited until he was sixty to marry because while he was in the army "I had a good time right and left." The reason Abkhasians delay sexual gratification and marriage is that they believe they must conserve their energies because they expect to live long lives. To them, youth extends to age sixty or eighty. Medical scientist Leaf also noted this striking expectation of longevity and wondered: "Are we in the United States perhaps a mortality-ridden society, programming our lives to a shorter existence?"

An active interest in the opposite sex is believed essential for vigor and vitality. At 117 Gabriel Chapnish gave his recipe for long life: "Active physical work, and a moderate interest in alcohol and the ladies." In studies of 15,000 people older than eighty years, Soviet scientist G. E. Pitzhelauri found that with few exceptions only married people lived to extreme old age. He believes that marriage and a regular, prolonged sex life are very important to longevity.

Not only does the older Abkhasian keep working, but he does work that both he and his society consider important. He feels he is needed and so does everyone else. He is contributing to the economy of the community. The aged are regarded as wise because of their long experience, and their word often is family law. Abkhasians are extremely proud of their ability to live long lives. "Each of the elderly persons I saw," says Dr. Leaf, "lived with family and close relatives—and occupied a central and privileged position within this group." Abkhasians of all ages are integrated into an elaborate and tightly knit kinship network so that one person has scores of "brothers" and "sisters" in his own and other villages. Even though these people may be quite distant relatives, still they consider themselves brothers and treat each other that way.

The high degree of integration in their lives and the sense of group identity, anthropologist Benet believes, gives each individual a strong feeling of personal security and continuity so that the Abkhasians persevere amidst the changing conditions imposed by the larger Soviet society. "My own view is that Abkhasians live as long as they do primarily because of the extraordinary cultural factors that structure their existence: the uniformity and certainty of both individual and group behavior, the unbroken continuum of life's activities—the same games, the same work, the same food, the same self-imposed and socially perceived needs. And the increasing prestige that comes with increasing age." She says that there is no hypocritical discrepancy between what children are taught and the way adults behave. "Since what they are taught is considered important, and the work they are given is considered necessary, children are neither restless nor rebellious. As they mature, there are easy transitions from one status in life to another."

Abkhasians, it would seem, corroborate the Duke longitudinal study and its predictors for longevity: work satisfaction, happiness, and sturdy physical condition. They testify to the ancient wisdom expressed in Ecclesiastes: "Live joyfully with thy wife whom thou lovest . . . and in thy labor which thou takest under the sun." And all are consistent with Freud's dictum on what any normal person should be able to do well: to love and to work.

In our incandescent civilization with its variety of stimuli and swiftly changing patterns, life burns more quickly. Of course, industrialized societies do not value longevity and have been intolerant of it. We emphasize quality rather than length of life, choose enrichment rather than continuity of experience. Our image of extreme longevity is repugnant. Swift's immortal struldbrugs are grotesque and miserable, wishing only to be able to die; Aldous Huxley's 200-year-old man in *After Many a Summer Dies the Swan* is a hideous regression hidden from the world. When a Western writer such as James Hilton does write positively about ageless people who live happily ever after, his idealized Shangri-La is placed in Hunza country.

The most successful lover that we know, Casanova, was finished at sixty. Then he savored his experiences in his mind and spent his last years writing them down to prove to the ages that his pen was mightier than his sword. When 117-year-old Gabriel Chapnian was told that Americans rarely attain his age, he replied, "Hmm . . . too literate!" Would we relinquish the soaring intellect, forgo the pursuit of success or knowledge, give up peering into electron microscopes or programming computers, trade the stimulation of our communications or the febrile pleasures of flight and television to move closer to the lifestyle of the bristlecone pine, if that is the choice? Would we, really, steer away from the rapids with their exhilarating velocity, danger, promise, to some placid backwater? We have fled the quiet countryside, evacuated the boondocks to be where the action is—although the dropout rate is growing.

And we *have* sought longevity in our fashion. Fearing death, we have followed the men in white and the makers of patent medicine. Admiring youth, we have followed Ponce de Leon and Helena Rubinstein. Craving immortality, we have followed alchemists and rejuvenators. Not Methuselah, but Adonis. Long life is not good enough unless packaged as eternal youth.

Moreover, it may be possible that no choice is necessary. Perhaps we can eat our cake and have it. At least a baker's dozen of items have preceded longer life on industrial civilization's shopping list—power, wealth, health, knowledge, avoidance of labor, comfort, travel, communications, beauty, pleasure, leisure, diversion, art. We take pride in how successful our science and particularly our technology have been in giving us these things. Is it unreasonable to conjecture that the technological know-how which took us as far as the moon can take us further along the life cycle than a peasant society is bringing its people?

In an attempt to answer that question we must turn to the second kind of gerontologists.

VII. Biological Gerontology

Social gerontology studies old people; biological gerontology studies rats, rotifers, bacteria, brains, pancreases, cells, parts of cells, molecules, parts of molecules, atoms. Social gerontologists are concerned with the plight of the aged; biological gerontologists are motivated by intellectual curiosity. Aging, says biochemist F. Marrot Sinex, "is one of the major things that man has wondered about since we first meet him in his written record. His mythology, his religion and now you might say the religious side of his technology is directed to finding the meaning of the mortality of man. Now there's a meaning about the mortality of man which is rooted in biochemistry and molecular biology. I think it would be fun to find out what that meaning is."

Where social gerontology wants theories but has come to some conclusions, biological gerontology has produced theories but wants results. Nevertheless, it is on this front that scientists entertain hopes for a breakthrough. Here fountain-of-youth visions are alive and well. Soar along the rainbow with biophysicist Robert Sinsheimer of the California Institute of Technology as he expounds on the promise of the new genetics: "Even the timeless patterns of growth and maturity and aging will be subject to our design. We know of no intrinsic limits to the life span. How long would you like to live?"

If this is fantasy, it is a social gerontologist, Ruth Bennett, who says matter of factly that "it is just as difficult to change society as it is to change genes."

The centrality of biology to aging is obvious. The loss of reserve capacity, loss of cells, loss of functioning, loss of vigor, gain in susceptibility to disease, gain in the likelihood of death—in other words, the basic ills of old age—are biological. It has been said that nature deals the cards and each person plays his own hand. The aim of psychosocial gerontology is to help each individual play his hand well. Biological gerontology says, "Let's change the cards."

Of course, humans have been intervening in biological processes since witch doctors administered therapeutic herbs and cut holes in the skulls of epileptics to liberate the devils within. The Taoist alchemists who quaffed golden elixirs were practicing their brand of biological gerontology. Today's gerontology, however, is heir to all the knowledge won not only in biology and medicine, but in chemistry, physics, and technology as well.

When August Weismann examined death scientifically, he made a startling discovery—it was not an innate part of life. Weismann was born in 1834 at Frankfurt, Germany, and began his career as a physician with a broad scientific education. Attracted to biological research, he took up insect embryology, but a period of poor eyesight as a young man forced him away from the microscope. This fortuitous development turned his attention toward general problems of biology and shaped his whole future work. This was the decade after Charles Darwin had published *The Origin of Species,* and Weismann became a champion of evolution in Germany. For many years he was a natural scientist, collecting specimens and facts, and then returned to insect embryology.

Weismann's interest focused when he began to investigate heredity— at a time when the Mendelian principles still were unknown. Weismann discovered that there are two different kinds of cells—the sex cells which transmit life and all the remaining body, or somatic, cells which do not possess this faculty. He observed that after the fertilized egg of the round-worm *Ascaris* divided, only one of the two resulting cells possessed the ability to reproduce a roundworm. After a second division, making four cells, still only one cell carried the thread of life. It was the same with the third division and eight cells. This process took place in all animals Weismann observed.

In one-celled organisms, however, after the cell divided both resultant cells retained the power to reproduce and thus carry on life. In them, this power went undiminished. These organisms, Weismann concluded, are potentially immortal (potentially because the line could be ended by all manner of environmental troubles).[1]

"Let us now consider," Weismann wrote in 1891, "how it happened that the multicellular animals and plants, which arose from unicellular forms of life, came to lose this power of living forever."[2]

Weismann chose to search for his answer through the lens of evolution,

[1] As we have seen (p. 148), science today believes that some unicellular species are potentially immortal whereas others occasionally require sexual reinvigoration in order to avoid senescence and death. But there is no scientific quarrel with Weismann's belief in the immortality of life that began some 3 billion years ago and continued without interruption through countless individuals and evolving forms.

[2] Still another example where science has validated myth; in this case, the uncanny intuition in Genesis and other myths that immortality preceded death.

which is really nothing more than a mental instrument using educated observation and deduction. Weismann proceeded to give one of the brilliant demonstrations of the rational process. His starting premise was that evolution always seeks to promote life through the maximum number of vigorous individuals.

These individuals are continually appearing through reproduction. Therefore, reproduction is one of the essential qualities of life. Reproduction and new individuals recur in the unicellular realm without death, and for an excellent reason. "Normal death could not take place among unicellular organisms because the individual and the reproductive cell are one and the same; on the other hand, normal death is possible, and as we see, has made its appearance, among multicellular organisms in which the somatic and reproductive cells are distinct."

Evolution encourages the formation of more complex organisms. Complex organisms come about through the differentiation of cells into specialists, each performing a particular job to benefit the whole organism. The power to reproduce a new organism was confined to the sex cells. The somatic cells lost this power; they could only reproduce themselves. In time they lost the ability to reproduce indefinitely, becoming subject to the wear and tear of time.

Death, for Weismann, is closely bound up with the differentiation of cells—the principle of the division of labor. Death comes about through external agencies and because it serves the purposes of evolution. Our lives are finite "because the unlimited existence of individuals would be a luxury without any corresponding advantage." Furthermore, "worn-out individuals are not only valueless to the species, but they are even harmful, for they take the place of those which are sound."

This line of reasoning leads to the conclusion: "Death itself, and the longer or shorter duration of life, both depend entirely upon adaptation. Death is not an essential attribute of living matter; it is neither necessarily associated with reproduction, nor a necessary consequence of it."

In this assessment of life and death, August Weismann dealt with subjects—particularly the characteristics of cells—which are crucial to the biology of aging today. To pursue just one aspect of his argument, there is some evidence linking length of life to the advantage of the species.

An English investigator, A. D. Blest, studied five different species of moths in the rain forest of Panama. Three of the species were protectively colored, camouflaging their members from predators and enhancing chances for survival until reproduction was accomplished. On average, these moths died 13 days after the end of reproduction. Soon after laying their eggs, they became hyperactive and flew themselves to death. The other two species of moths were vividly colored, exposing their members to the surveillance of predatory birds and monkeys. On average, these moths lived for 45 days after laying eggs. A hormone inhibited the death-flight pattern and caused these older moths to remain largely immobile in plain view. The brilliant moths were nasty tasting, so that each old moth seized and rejected by a predator served as an object lesson protecting the younger members of the species. The protectively colored moths, on the other hand, were sweet tasting to the insect-eaters. The sooner these moths were gone, the less chance was there for enemies to decipher the camouflage.

The giant land tortoise of the Galapagos and some other islands in the Pacific Ocean is the longest-lived animal we know (see p. 146), and there is a very good species reason for this longevity. Although these creatures lay eggs each year, the attrition is fearsome. The parents must bury the eggs so deep to protect them from the equatorial sun that the hatchlings usually are trapped below ground at birth. Only once or twice in 20 years is there sufficient rain softening the earth to enable the newborn to escape to the surface. When that happens, the competition for food is so fierce that perhaps just a few times in a century will the survivors of this natural lottery reach the long adulthood necessary to continue the cycle and preserve the species.

The human species has a prolonged postreproductive life—indeed we are singular in this characteristic—and there is a good evolutionary reason for that, too. Chances of an infant's survival are linked to parental survival through the long period of childhood dependency. And there is reason to believe that the extended survival of tribal elders with their accrued knowledge and wisdom also conferred a survival advantage for the group as human evolution turned into social pathways.

A conference in 1962 at Princeton, New Jersey, on aging at various biological levels dealt extensively with the relationship between evolution and senescence. At one point, gerontologist George Sacher of Argonne National Laboratory recapitulated: "From the standpoint of evolution, the one irreplaceable material that has to be conserved and which has to be maximized is the genetic potential of the species. From this premise, the argument can be developed that the progressive degradation of the genetic information in the germ plasm during a typical individual life history is what ultimately determines the course of somatic aging. This is explicitly a Weismannian view of aging. But it was stated in various ways by Professor [Theodosius] Dobzhansky at the beginning of this conference. In other words, Weismannian thinking has been assimilated into present-day genetics and evolution."

Dr. Sacher subsequently referred to a theory of aging proposed by British Nobel laureate Peter Medawar that sees senescence of the individual as an oversight of evolution, since nature is concerned only with survival of species. Aging, according to this thesis, results from the running out of genetic program. Errors creep into the repetition of genetic information, variations go uncorrected, accident damage is not properly repaired, losses go uncompensated. Alex Comfort, director of the Medical Research Council Group on Aging at London University, has espoused this theory. In addition to being a gerontologist, Dr. Comfort is a prolific writer who has been virtually the only popularizer of biological gerontology. And so his simile for the Medawar theory is probably the most widely known model for aging:

"[W]e probably age because we run out of evolutionary program. In this we resemble a space probe that has been 'designed' by selection to pass Mars, but that has no further built-in instructions once it has done so, and no components specifically produced to last longer than that. It will travel on, but the failure rate in its guidance and control mechanisms will steadily increase—and this failure of homeostasis, of self-righting, is exactly what we see in the ageing organism."

Bernard Strehler in his 1962 book, *Time, Cells, and Aging*, concludes a discussion of evolution and aging by saying that in general he concurs with Comfort that senescence "is essentially a result of the lack of sufficient selection pressure to foster the development of immortal races . . . ." Dr. Strehler, like Weismann, says he sees no inherent property of cells or complex organisms to prevent *their organization into perpetually functioning and self-replenishing individuals. On the other hand, the evolutionary dereliction is probably so manifold and so deeply ingrained in the physiology and biochemistry of existing forms, including man, that the abolition of the process is a practical impossibility."* (Dr. Strehler's italics.)

The Medawar-Comfort-Strehler explanation of aging parallels Weismann's explanation for the appearance of death. What is different is the point of view. Weismann sees aging and death simply as facts of life and, if anything, useful agents in the service of species. The latter-day scientists see aging and death as nature's "failure" and "dereliction." The nineteenth-century biologist looked at senescence and death from the viewpoint of species, evolution's vehicle for extending life. The twentieth-century biologists regard senescence and death from the viewpoint of the individual, with an implication that something should be done about them.

In 1908 German biologist Max Rubner proposed what came to be known as the "rate-of-living" theory of aging. Rubner observed that among a variety of animals there is a consistent relationship between metabolic rate and lifespan: the greater the former, the shorter the latter. Man and mouse each expend about 700 calories per gram of tissue during their lifetimes. Because the mouse has relatively so much more surface through which heat can escape from its body, it must use its energy at about 30 times the rate of humans—and lives about one-thirtieth as long. Animals that hibernate are long-lived, indicating a link between longevity and reduced metabolism. A small mammal like the bat is known to have lived more than 22 years. The desert mouse which estivates during the summer outlives his laboratory relative by more than four times. Women's metabolic rate is about 10 percent less than that of men, and women in the United States live approximately 10 percent longer.

Gerontologist Raymond Pearl tried to test this rate-of-living theory on human subjects in 1928. The theory seemed to imply that people who did more physical work would have a higher metabolic rate and thus use up their lives more quickly than those who took it easy. As we know, exercise promotes physical fitness and delays physiological decline whereas sedentary habits produce opposite effects. Pearl's experiment was inconclusive.

Another series of experiments, however, have seemed to support a correspondence between rate of living and energy intake or use. The first of these experiments was conducted in 1917 by Jacques Loeb and John Northrup with *Drosophila* fruit flies. Loeb and Northrup could increase or shorten lifespans of these flies by lowering or raising environmental temperatures at a certain stage of the insect's development. Dr. Northrup found also that he could extend a fly's period of growth through starvation.

In 1927 Clive McKay at Cornell University began experimenting with dietary restriction on laboratory rats. Five years later he published his first results. With the exception of Alexis Carrel's "immortal" chicken tissues, McKay's experiments are the most famous in biological gerontology, which is something of a commentary on the subject. McKay put one group of control rats on a diet of protein, minerals, and vitamins with unlimited calories. Most of the animals lived the normal lifespan of about two years. The oldest survivor lasted 969 days, about two years and 8 months. A second group of rats were given a drastically low caloric diet from the outset of life to periods up to 1,000 days. The reduced diet curtailed growth, but it also maintained most of the characteristics of youth. These rats, older (and smaller) than the longest survivor of the normal group, were spry, had normal levels of intelligence, and still had glossy coats although their bones had lost some calcium. If the low rations were continued for 1,150 days, most of the rats were unable to grow to normal size. But when a normal diet was restored at 1,000 days, the animals grew to full size. The oldest survivor lived just over four years, or about twice as long as the average rat.

In the mid 1960s, Charles Barrows, Jr. of the Gerontology Research Center began experimenting with both diet and temperature. He worked with rotifers, tiny aquatic animals smaller than a pinhead. The uniformity of the experimental subjects could be assured because rotifers are parthenogenic and many identical individuals can be derived from a single egg. Also they are poikilothermic, "cold-blooded," so that they take on the temperature of their environment.

If the rotifers were maintained in water heated to 95 degrees Fahrenheit, they uniformly lived for 18 days. They laid 40 eggs from the fifth through the twelfth days, then lived six days and died. When environmental temperature was reduced to about 76 degrees Fahrenheit, the lifespan of all rotifers was nearly doubled to 34 days. The gain was entirely in postreproductive life. With the lower temperature maintained, Dr. Barrows started reducing the rotifers' food. Those whose nutrition was cut roughly in half lived for 55 days—three times the original lifespan. This time, however, the added days all were added to the reproductive period. Rotifers still laid 40 eggs, but they were spaced from the fifth day through the thirty-third day. There was a similar correlation for enzyme activity. It showed a marked change at the time the egg-laying ceased in all cases.

The rotifers apparently operate under two distinct regimes—a period of fertility which can be regulated by nutrition but is unaffected by environmental temperature and a period of maturity which responds to temperature but not nutrition. But the great theoretical lesson Dr. Barrows draws from his experiments is that contrary to the Comfort-Medawar hypothesis that aging results from a lack of program, "there is a program for the total lifespan [of] organisms and those environmental conditions which alter the length of life do so merely by altering the rate of occurrence of specific events."

What practical lessons can be drawn from all these experiments? We already have noted that actuarial tables show that overweight people live shorter lives than people with normal weight and noted also that extremely long-lived people in remote areas exist on low-caloric diets. So, in affluent societies, prudence would indicate eating less rather than more, within reason. However, it must be noted that experimental diets had to be practiced on the young from birth and had to be drastically low enough to retard growth in order to achieve their doubling and tripling of longevity. These laboratory animals lived in protected conditions and were not exposed to stress. Dr. Barrows says that such a drastic regimen could hardly be transferred to human infants. It would be moot whether such undernourished, undersized youngsters could survive their childhood to enjoy their theoretical bonus years. However, underfeeding without starvation and malnutrition of essential vitamins and proteins probably is a very important strategy.[3]

As for lowering temperature, Roy Walford at the University of California at Los Angeles also found a longevity-producing effect in another poikilotherm, the annual fish, *Cynolebias*. By reducing water temperature about 10 degrees Fahrenheit, Dr. Walford was able to double the fish's lifespan. Bernard Strehler of the University of Southern California cites other reports of long-lived fish in cold lakes and findings that the desert mouse with a lower temperature than his laboratory cousin lives four times as long. Furthermore, Dr. Strehler says, the temperature relationship to aging is very similar to that for the rate of oxygen consumption in most systems—use of oxygen is cut in half with each reduction in body temperature of about 15 degrees Fahrenheit. He says that dogs have been maintained at body temperatures of about 92 degrees without apparent harm. Even in normal humans, he says, body temperature fluctuates by one or two degrees each day while some persons have a lower than average 98.6 degrees without any difficulties.

"It follows, therefore," Dr. Strehler concludes, "that a decrease in core temperature of 2 to 3 degrees centigrade (about 3 to 5 degrees Fahrenheit) is very likely to have no noticeably adverse effects and this small decrease would be expected to add about 20 to 30 useful years to the life span . . . ." He would reset the body's thermostat in the hypothalamus for a cooler, and presumably longer, existence.

If the Strehler hypothesis is correct, according to Carl Eisdorfer, people could sleep in special waterbeds or bedchambers to chill them at night. "It's just a technical problem," he said, "no more complicated than setting up a renal dialysis unit in someone's garage." But if the goose-fleshed sleeper turns up the electric blanket, would he forfeit those added years?

---

[3] Cancer researcher Robert Good has reported that rats, mice, and Australian aborigines on low protein diets show strong resistance to cancer. However, the protein restriction must be severe enough to retard growth and be maintained through life. Morris Ross at the Institute for Cancer Research in Philadelphia confirmed McKay's findings on the relationship between low caloric diet and longevity; Dr. Ross is critical of the way McKay carried out his experiments in other areas. Dr. Ross writes: "His conclusions on the role of dietary protein and those by the few subsequent workers in this field, should be examined carefully since they are open to question. These studies were so designed that it was not possible to separate the effects of the protein component from that of caloric intake. Furthermore, different dietary components were used, and in some experiments, were not carried out to term or there were insufficient numbers of animals for a critical assessment." Dr. Ross also has found a relationship between protein in the diet and cancer, but the correspondence was not consistent for different types of cancers: some tumors occurred with high protein intake, others with low protein intake, and still others when there was a moderate amount of protein in the diet.

And, would longer life be a sufficient temptation to entice people from Miami Beach to Antarctica?

Charles Barrows, who conducted the rotifer experiments, is not rushing out to buy a supercooled waterbed. All the temperature–life extension experiments were done with cold-blooded animals whose body temperatures naturally match their environment, he points out. "Reduced temperature in homeotherms reduces life."

In the meantime, the search for an aging clock goes on. Lissy Jarvik, a geneticist, believes there is one and believes it will be found in the genes. Denham Harman, a chemist-medical researcher, believes it lies in cell oxidation.

If there is such a timepiece and if it is found, then maybe someone will figure out how to change its rate or keep it from running down.

In 1941 when the world was absorbed with war and violent death, a Finnish-born chemist working in the United States published a radically new concept of the cause of aging. Johan Bjorksten was employed by a manufacturer of film, and it struck him that "a strange resemblance is apparent between the 'aging' or progressive tanning of photographic or of hectograph duplication films and the aging of the human body. Both processes involve protein reactions, leading to reduced hydration, loss of elasticity: all the earmarks of slowly, but inexorably, progressing tanning reactions." Dr. Bjorksten followed this in January, 1942 by stating: "The aging of living organisms I believe is due to the occasional formation, by tanning (cross-linkage), of bridges between protein molecules, which cannot be broken by the cell enzymes."

The parenthetical words gave their name to the cross-linkage theory. The phenomenon that Dr. Bjorksten described is apparent to anyone because it takes place readily and steadily in collagen. Collagen is the most common form of protein in the body, composing one-third or more of all human protein. Collagen is one of the important, and extracellular, components of the body's connective tissue which fills in and supports various organs and structures. At birth, collagen and connective tissue are plastic, giving the newborn infant its rubbery texture. With age, the collagen becomes tougher, more crystalline, more rigid, more brittle, less elastic, less soluble. Fibers within the molecules grow thicker, moving from random patterns to line up parallel to one another and, most important from Dr. Bjorksten's point of view, more and more molecules become bound together with chemical links. A certain amount of these processes are beneficial, giving the adult anatomy a firmer structure than the bouncing baby. However, also with age, enzymes which normally break down the chemical cross-links to maintain the tissue freedom of youth become less active, and so the cross-linking spreads its petrifying effect.

Dr. Bjorksten described it in this manner: "The effect is like what would happen in a large factory with thousands of workers, if someone slipped a pair of handcuffs on one hand of each of two workers, to tie them together. This obviously, would reduce their ability to do their work, and if the process were allowed to spread through the factory, even at a slow rate, it would ultimately paralyze the entire operation unless means were found to remove the handcuffs faster than they were being applied."

A cross-linking theory of aging also was proposed by the Swiss gerontologist Fritz Verzár and molecular cross-linking has been widely verified. However, its significance is undecided. One thing that troubles researchers is that cross-linking in collagen, where its effect is unmistakable, does not involve cells. It is difficult to accept that such a central process as aging is an extracellular occurrence. As for cross-linking in vital molecules, experiments have not been able to determine that such events are harmful . . . or cause aging. So the question remains open: Are cross-links a cause, a result, or a characteristic of aging?

Dr. Bjorksten has sought a chemical, including a soil bacteria enzyme, to break the molecular handcuffs.

Another chemist envisions aging as "a natural consequence of how we use energy": aging brought on, at least in part, by adverse, irreversible changes that take place during the lifelong process of oxidation. Denham Harman was a research chemist with the Shell Oil Company when he read an article in the *Ladies' Home Journal* about the Russian rejuvenationist, Alexander Bogomolets. Dr. Harman then read a book by Bogomolets about prolonging life. Harman's curiosity was further stirred by Carrel's experiments with "immortal" cells. Chemist Harman left Shell to go to medical school. After that training, he embarked on a new career —to find out what causes aging.

At first, he was totally baffled; aging was an enigma. But in November 1954 he connected his earlier chemical research on oxidation with what might be taking place within the biological machine. Namely, an unwanted by-product of cell metabolism: random, destructive chemical reactions caused by free radicals.

Free radicals are unmated atoms or parts of molecules cut loose (in this case) in the human body. These unattached particles with their open electrons are eager to unite with almost anything at hand and do so. Often, free radicals contain oxygen and set off a tiny chemical reaction that will trigger a second reaction that will set off a third in a firecracker chain. This so-called auto-oxidation serves no bodily function, but instead can inflict molecular damage, particularly, it is believed, to cell membranes. "It's like tossing sand into machinery," Dr. Harman says.

Sometimes, instead of setting off oxidation, free radical reactions may fuse two molecules unnaturally. This is the cross-linking phenomenon which is the basis for Johan Bjorksten's hypothesis for aging. Dr. Bjorksten says that free radical reactions cause only about 10 percent of all the cross-linking which takes place in our bodies and therefore are minor contributors to the aging process. Professor Harman says, on the other hand, that cross-linking is too general a concept to be useful, like saying that aging is a chemical reaction. Dr. Harman has been testing over the years his theory that free radical reactions cause the biological degradation and, again, took his lead from nonlife chemistry.

Free radical oxidants are key actors in the spontaneous combustion of oily rags, the formation of smog, the drying of oil paint, and making butter turn rancid. Industrial chemists have devised substances called antioxidants to block these undesirable volatile reactions in such things as rubber, chicken feed, and cornflakes. Dr. Harman experimented at the University of Nebraska with antioxidants in the diet of mice and found that three substances [4] did lengthen average lifespans, by nearly one-third in some cases. Maximum lifespans were not extended.

A. L. Tappel, a professor of nutrition and biochemistry at the University of California, Davis, had been studying these phenomena as long as Dr. Harman and came to the conclusion that unsaturated fats in the body are the culprits. It also occurred to Dr. Harman that in 1900, when heart disease and cancer were not the killers they are today, 30 percent of an American's calorie intake was in the form of lard, a saturated fat, and olive oil, a fat that is only moderately unsaturated. Then in the 1950s came the stampede to substitute polyunsaturated fats as a step toward countering heart disease. So in 1971 Dr. Harman decided to test his suspicions on two types of mice and a species of laboratory rat. When fat was increased to 20 percent of the diet, animals on lard and olive oil averaged longer lifespans than those on corn oil and safflower oil. For the rats on the 20 percent fat diet, those fed safflower oil lived an average of 24.8 months, those on corn oil 26.6 months, those on olive oil 27.8 months, and those on lard 29.8 months.

Dr. Harman deduces from this that it would be beneficial for Americans to cut down on fats in general and polyunsaturated fats in particular. But Dr. Tappel says that polyunsaturated fats are our major source of the important natural antioxidant, vitamin E. Dr. Tappel advises: "To sup-

---

[4] 2-MEA (2-mercaptoethylamine), BHT (butylated hydroxytoluene) and Santoquin (a quinoline derivative).

press atherosclerosis, a diet rich in polyunsaturated lipids appears appropriate. A proper balance between polyunsaturated lipid and biological antioxidant intake is necessary."

The National Research Council of the National Academy of Sciences recommends 30 milligrams of vitamin E a day. Dr. Tappel says surveys have shown that the average person gets only 7 milligrams a day from cereals, milk, fish, muscle meats, vegetables, and the vegetable oils. He believes in dietary supplements and is reported himself to be taking a gram a day of vitamin E.

The use of vitamin E leads into a maelstrom of medical controversy and the latest national health fad. So much emotion swirls around the subject that it is difficult to sort fact, fiction, hope, and conservatism. Vitamin E—vitamins are organic compounds necessary for life which the body cannot make—has been known for more than half a century. It has been extensively investigated. Yet it is the least understood vitamin and the object for the wildest claims (both logically compatible). Wilfrid Shute, a physician who heads the Shute Foundation for Medical Research in London, Ontario, has championed the cause of vitamin E. Dr. Shute believes that modern milling methods have removed vitamin E (as well as a host of other important ingredients) from wheats and other grains, creating a dietary deficiency. This is the reason, Dr. Shute contends, for the upsurge in heart disease in the twentieth century. And his research foundation is used mainly to treat victims of heart disease with vitamin E.

Other proponents of vitamin E have expanded the catalogue of the ills it cures—sterility, impotence, miscarriage, high blood pressure, diabetes, and many more. When aging is added, it easily qualifies as a modern panacea. The extreme claims, made on talk shows and in crusading books, have led to a national popularity rivaling that of vitamin C. The General Nutrition Center in Pittsburgh featured a "Vitamin E Rejuvenation Kit" which the store manager called a "fantastic seller. We can't keep it in stock."

The medical community, however, has not been sold. *The Medical Letter,* an independent publication that evaluates medical research for some 50,000 subscribing physicians, stated that with one minor exception vitamin E has "no established value in preventing or treating any common human disorder." A report compiled for the publication by a committee of medical experts said there is no well-defined vitamin E deficiency state in adults and "little unequivocal evidence that vitamin E is of nutritional significance in man or is of any value in therapy."

Dr. Harman says that the latest information indicates that if a person loses vitamin E along with vitamin C and thymine, body fats become more unsaturated and burn up more quickly in those nasty free radical reactions. Dr. Tappel calls vitamin C a multiplier of vitamin E's anti-oxidant effects. But whereas Nobel laureate Linus Pauling has summarized evidence that large doses of vitamin C may promote longevity (as well as shorten colds), Dr. Tappel believes supplementary doses of vitamin C are unnecessary.

A Beverly Hills physician who wrote to the National Institutes of Health for advice on vitamin E was referred to the Gerontology Research Center in Baltimore. The center in turn referred the physician to his local medical society, the Food and Drug Administration, and the literature.

What is needed, gerontologists say, is a thorough testing of possible anti-aging agents. Dr. Harman believes the time is ripe for stringent tests with human subjects. He admits such a procedure would be costly, "but cheaper than a battleship." What Dr. Harman envisions is a longitudinal study with 1,000 people or more, all older than forty years. Their physiological, medical, psychological, and chemical history would be exhaustively checked and then they would be followed through to the end of their lives as closely as possible, being checked for hand grip strength, intelligence, fatty acids, and everything else. Varying diets, particularly with different degrees of fats, could be tested in different groups (although such regimens would have to be obeyed exactly, and that would be the most difficult part of such a study). After five, ten, or twenty years, however, Dr. Harman believes that researchers would have much better notions about who is "old," what constitutes being old, who is aging more rapidly or more slowly than the norm, whatever that is.

Alex Comfort in England doesn't believe human guinea pigs would stay still for such rigorous and chronic testing, so he has devised an abbreviated battery of tests, 59 in number, ranging from counting gray hairs to taking tissue biopsies. Hopefully, he feels researchers could spot age changes in three to five years. However, Fritz Verzár of Switzerland questions Dr. Comfort's selection of tests. At the same time, Verzár fears that an exhaustive measuring of every conceivable physiological change would simply yield an avalanche of confusing information. "Felix Bernstein 50 years ago compared changes of visual accommodation of the crystalline lens with the person's time of survival. We do not even know whether lens-collagen ages in a similar way as other collagen in the body, in the arteries, in the corium or in the articulations."

It so happens that at the time Dr. Verzár was making that statement Robert Kohn and C. R. Hamlin at Western Reserve University were conducting experiments with human collagen that would give them an aging yardstick. Hamlin and Kohn purified collagen taken from the diaphragms of five people who had been killed in accidents. The ages of the subjects were twenty-two, thirty-three, forty-two, fifty-seven, and sixty-seven years. By measuring how long it took the enzyme collagenase to degrade 50 percent of the samples, the researchers discovered that collagen is increasingly resistant to enzyme action with age. Not only that, but the rate of "indigestibility" is so consistent with age that it becomes predictable: a laboratory could receive a sample of collagen from an unknown donor and tell how old he is within a year or two. This discovery would seem to indicate that it does not matter how a person behaves or what he eats, his collagen is going to get progressively tougher by the calendar.

As for measuring anti-aging drugs, F. Marrot Sinex of Boston University says *that* could begin at once at the Food and Drug Administration's new national laboratory at Pine Bluff, Arkansas. Two ingredients Dr. Harman would like inspected are the flavinoids in citrus fruits and ginseng, a plant extract which the Chinese have been using in tea for 4,000 years. Ginseng, it will be recalled, was one of the herbs favored by the Taoist adepts in their training to become immortal. Dr. Harman says that ginseng has been helpful in extending the lives of fruit flies. It also has slowed the degeneration of human cells no longer able to divide.

Bernard Strehler would welcome tests of royal jelly and procaine, the local anesthetic (known by the brand name Novocaine) used by Ana Aslan in Romania and claimed to be effective in improving an array of disorders related to age. Experiments by English, Canadian, and American scientists failed to substantiate Dr. Aslan's findings, but now it is believed that the Westerners were using not quite the same preparation as the East Europeans.

Among a variety of other candidates from the anti-aging pharmacopoeia are the immunosuppressants. These drugs first gained prominence when medicine turned to transplant operations. All too often these brilliant surgical accomplishments exhumed the grim humor of the nineteenth century when infection was rampant: the operation was a success, but the patient died. The immune system which protects the body from foreign invaders—usually but not always alien protein—attacks the transplant, often resulting in severe bodily reactions and rejection of the new organ.

Immunosuppressants, as their name indicates, are drugs that dampen the immune response. Roy Walford of the UCLA Medical School experimented with two immunosuppressants on strains of short-lived mice and found that average lifespans were lengthened by ten weeks. Another experiment with a synthetic hormone had an even more dramatic effect upon mice, quite possibly for immunosuppressive reasons.

Dr. Walford is especially interested in the effects of immunosuppressants on longevity because he is a proponent of the immunologic theory of aging. Australian Nobel laureate Macfarlane Burnet first suggested the theory in 1959. Failure of the immune system now is believed to allow the spread of cancer. Cancer, as we know, is an age-related disease. Dr. Walford believes that other age-related diseases such as diabetes and senile plaques which form in organs and are one of the characteristics of atherosclerosis also are allied to immune failure. In fact, he sees aging as the gradual failure of the immune system.

After birth the body undergoes an elaborate biological self-identity screening tagging native components for future reference. This process of distinguishing self from non-self is called selfing. Once this inventory is completed, the newly formed defense system wipes out all trespassers that somehow have gained admittance to the body (the skin and mucous membranes at the natural gateways make an excellent first line of defense). The internal security system, highly resourceful and flexible, is what is called a person's resistance.

The key agents of the immune system, the second line of defense, are lymphocytes—lymph cells—which are manufactured in bone marrow. Apparently these are the sentinels which must identify foreign agents in order to activate the immune response. There are two kinds of lymphocytes: those which are processed through the thymus gland and which are responsible for maintaining the body's biological uniqueness (they reject such foreign matter as transplanted organs and, presumably, home-grown cancerous cells); and those which are antimicrobial.

If the foreign incursion is local, the patrolling lymphocytes (which make up about one-quarter of the blood's white cells) call upon another type of white blood cell, phagocytes (eating cells). Phagocytes surround the invading bacteria or viruses and literally eat them up. Lymphocytes also may help to isolate the units. We become aware of such a local skirmish when we see an inflammation. The pus issuing from an open wound is composed of the dead bodies of phagocytes, which are short-lived even if not victims of the defense operation.

If the phagocytes cannot contain the raiders and they break out of the tissue beachhead to enter the bloodstream, a general alarm goes out. All foreign units (native ones, too, for that matter) have specific configurations or surface marks called antigens. These antigens in some way trigger recognition in the lymphocytes in the first place. Now the second type of lymphocytes begin to manufacture antibodies—specific protein agents designed to hook onto the particular antigens of the invaders. It is believed that this marvelous defense system of improvisation can machine-tool at least 100,000 kinds of antibodies; nobody knows what the maximum number is, but it must be enormous, since our bodies may encounter millions of types of organisms during a lifetime.

The antibodies combine with and straitjacket the germs, not only immobilizing them physically for their dissolution by cell-eaters but contributing to their breakdown chemically. When the struggle becomes generalized, other mechanisms restrict the flow of blood to the body's surface, reducing the loss of heat. This forces up the body's temperature which, in turn, speeds phagocytosis, and enzymatic chemical processes. Fever, as Hippocrates knew, is the sign that the body has marshaled its defenses in an all-out battle; soon must come recovery or defeat.

There are two main ways in which the immune system can fail. One, which Dr. Burnet suggested, is that the immunologic surveillance deteriorates. It is known that the thymus develops early and ages early; presumably it may be making fewer lymphocytes or making inferior sentries. As a result, the monitors don't recognize every alien agent, whether foreign or domestic in origin.

Researchers at the University of Texas Medical Branch have discovered a significant decrease in the amount of thymosin, a key hormone produced by the thymus gland, in the blood stream between the ages of twenty-five and forty-five years. "This direct evidence," says Director Allan Goldstein of the school's Biochemistry Division, "provides a testable hypothesis that decreased immunity with age is due to a defect or inability of the thymus gland to produce thymosin." Dr. Goldstein adds, "We know that the injection of mice with thymosin increases their immunity and resistance to disease, and we have good reason to suppose it will do the same in man."

The immune breakdown could come about in another way. Defective lymphocytes begin mistaking friends for foes or else manufacture "confused" antibodies which attack native cells. This civil war is known as autoimmune disease (rheumatoid arthritis is an example). When Dr. Walford fed immunosuppressants to short-lived strains of mice and they lived longer, the assumption was that these mice were congenitally susceptible to autoimmunity but the suppressants delayed the self-destructive syndrome.

According to the immunologic paradigm, aging is a biological identity crisis from which we never recover. However, Dr. Walford does not view this condition as the primary cause of aging. He believes it is brought on by a precedent cause or causes.

Most investigators are seeking this first cause in the smallest and most basic unit of life, the cell.

Alexis Carrel lived as strange a career as any of the searchers for physical immortality. He received his medical doctorate in his native France in 1900 and early showed a genius for surgery. However, he found little interest for his work in France and in 1904 he went to Canada to raise cattle. Soon he was lured to Chicago and physiological research. He developed a method for suturing blood vessels end to end and then the first successful procedures for transplanting these organs. For this pioneering work, Carrel was awarded a Nobel Prize in 1912, the same year that he was appointed to the staff of Rockefeller Institute for Medical Research in New York City. In World War I he perfected a new method for sterilizing wounds that saved many lives. In the 1930s he collaborated with Charles Lindbergh on a germ-free pump known as the first artificial heart. After publication of an immensely popular book, *Man the Unknown*, in 1935 Carrel probably was second only to Einstein as the best-known scientist of the time.

Man the Unknown, a melange of science and Carrel's personal beliefs, preached a faith in racial superiority which apparently was not challanged in those confused times but which stands out conspicuously in today's retrospective. Sprinkled through the book are such dogmatic comments as "Men of genius are not tall. Mussolini is of medium size . . ."; and mental diseases are to be feared more than physical diseases "chiefly because they profoundly weaken the dominant white races."

Carrel returned to France shortly before the beginning of World War II and after the fall of France joined the Vichy government as director of a new Foundation for the Study of Human Relations. Identified as a collaborationist, Carrel was accused after the liberation of France of advocating the elimination of "biologically unfit" people. He denied the charge. He died in Paris less than three months after the city was retaken from the Nazis.

Almost all of this is forgotten now. What Alexis Carrel is remembered for is that in 1912, the same year that he received the Nobel Prize and began an illustrious career at Rockefeller Institute, he took some tissue from the heart muscle of a chicken embryo and kept it alive in a culture. The culture was carefully fed, kept clean, and when the tissue grew too large, parts of it were cut away. The chicken tissue still lived when Dr. Carrel died in Paris in 1944. The cells were as robust as ever two years later when scientists terminated the experiment. It had proved its point, they believed, having lived three and a half times the lifespan of a normal chicken. Carrel's fame, his significance, rested on his demonstration that somatic cells taken from a mortal organism—Weismann to the contrary—are themselves immortal. Other researchers noted this same indefinite longevity with mouse cells *in vitro*, that is, in culture.

The issue seemed settled until Leonard Hayflick sought to duplicate Carrel's experiment in the 1960s. Dr. Hayflick, now at Stanford University, found that his embryonic chick cells could live for only about one year in their culture. Every other investigator who tried the experiment got the same results. What Dr. Hayflick believes happened is that Carrel's experimental culture was fed a crude extract taken from embryonic chicks that inadvertently included new, youthful cells. With the new cells eliminated from the more stringently conducted later experiments, the tissue immortality disappeared.

In the case of the mouse cells, Dr. Hayflick says, another mechanism was at work. These cells are not normal. "It has been found that when normal cells from a laboratory mouse are cultured in a glass vessel, they frequently undergo a spontaneous transformation that enables them to divide and multiply indefinitely. This type of transformation takes place regularly in cultures of mouse cells but only rarely in cultures of the fibroblasts of man or other animals. These transformed cell populations have several abnormal properties, but they are truly immortal: many of the mouse-derived cultures have survived for decades." One strain of tumorous cells used in cancer research by Professor Henry Harris at Oxford University originally was taken from a mouse in the laboratory of the German medical scientist Paul Ehrlich in 1907—in human terms, that would be a millennium ago.

In the case of human cervical tissue kept alive since 1951, the culture was taken from a woman, Helen Lane, who died from cancer. These famous HeLa cells have chromosomes of abnormal numbers, shapes, and sizes. They behave like cancer cells, and when injected into laboratory animals produce tumors. Many of the transformations that have now been found as well in the cultured cells of other vertebrates and insects —cells that keep reproducing indefinitely—Dr. Hayflick concludes, are indistinguishable from cancer.

Dr. Hayflick's interests, however, were directed not toward abnormal cells that divide indefinitely, but normal cells. How long do they go on dividing? It is impossible to study this phenomenon *in vivo*, in the living body, so he was forced to go to cell cultures. For his experiments he chose fibroblasts, these are common building-block cells found in various kinds of tissue, from the human lung. He discovered that fibroblasts from human embryos will divide an average of 50 times. When the cells are taken from subjects between birth and the age of twenty, the cells will divide about 30 times. When the donors are older than thirty years, the fibroblasts will divide no more than about 20 times. Embryonic cells taken from short-lived animals can divide no more than about 15 times with the capacity decreasing in adults. Weismann appeared vindicated.

Dr. Hayflick froze some of the embryonic human cells in liquid nitrogen at 190 degrees below zero. Years later some of these cells were reconstituted and resumed their dividing. They had "remembered" exactly where they were in their progression and went on dividing until the string was out. This consistency seems to shout "program."

Extensive experiments conducted and cited by George Martin, Curtis Sprague, and Charles Epstein at the University of Washington Medical School in Seattle verified that cultured human cells have limited growth potential. This potential varies in different cell types. Skin cells can replicate more times, for instance, than marrow cells. But all cell doublings are limited. Skin cells from a nine-year-old boy suffering from progeria, the disease that simulates speeded-up aging, reproduced only twice compared to 20 or 30 doublings for a normal child his age. Another strong indication of an inborn aging factor or "program."

Dr. Martin and his colleagues measured precisely the increasing inability of cells to divide with age. Judging from skin cells taken from donors ranging from fetuses to age ninety, the researchers discovered a 0.2 drop in the number of cell divisions per years of life. This steady erosion of growth potential, they believe, is a signal of cellular aging.

Dr. Hayflick disagrees. "What does us in now, as far as clinical aging signs are concerned, I believe to be those things that change in the cell during that period of time prior to its loss of ability to divide—or to function. It's those earlier events, say, 10, 15, or 20 doublings before the loss of division potential, that manifest themselves as what we call age changes." The end of cell division after 50 doublings, he believes, may constitute the maximum lifespan limit which humans have not achieved.

Robert Hay of Wright State University agrees that Hayflick and Martin have demonstrated satisfactorily that cultured cells have limited lifespans and that Martin's work suggests that this phenomenon has some relation to human aging. However, he points out that *in vitro* the cells live for less than two years, while in the human body they can survive for more than a century. He believes that this discrepancy is the most significant factor to be considered. His work indicates to him that no matter how fastidiously a scientist maintains a culture, it is a poor environment for a cell. Deficiencies in the culture affect the cell's ability to manufacture the protein materials it needs to function properly.[5] It is this loss of cellular metabolic function, Dr. Hay feels, that points the way to the secret of aging.[6]

---

[5] Also it is not clear if this limit on division is what happens in the body. Skin and intestinal cells appear to reproduce hundreds or thousands of times.

[6] James Danielli, at the State University of New York at Buffalo, found that amoebas kept on an adequate growth diet multiplied indefinitely, but if the food supply were reduced to a maintenance diet for two weeks and then switched back to the more ample food supply, the one-celled organisms lost their immortality. Their lines had limited lifespans. Similarly, if a small part of cytoplasmic matter from a limited lifespan amoeba were put into an immortal one, the latter became a "spanned" animal.

And so as in a Chinese box puzzle—a box within a box within a box within a box—the searchers go deeper into the cell.

The cell is the basic unit of life. In order to appreciate the scale of life on this level, a red blood cell is about ten microns across and three microns thick. A micron equals 1/1000 of a millimeter. A millimeter is 1/25 of an inch, so that a red blood cell is about 1/2,500 of an inch wide. Most bacteria are about ten times smaller in size, that is, one micron or 1/25,000 of an inch, although some bacteria are only 1/150,000 of an inch. The largest chemical molecule is only 1/1,250,000 of an inch so that the smallest cell, the smallest organization of living matter, is seven or eight times the size of the largest organization of non-living matter. Viruses, which bridge the chasm between the living and the nonliving, also bridge the size gap. The largest viruses are bigger than the smallest bacteria, while the tiniest viruses are smaller than the largest nonliving molecules.

From one cell, the fertilized ovum, the human being develops into an adult with some 60 trillion—60,000,000,000,000—cells. These cells in aggregate form four kinds of tissue—epithelial, connective, muscular, nerve —and individually appear as about 100 different types with different capabilities, functions, and behavior. Nerve cells conduct, muscle cells contract, kidney and digestive cells secrete, liver cells process incoming raw materials into substances needed through the system. In addition, cells must maintain themselves. Most cells do this by growth and reproduction through dividing, a process known as mitosis. Skin, intestinal, lung, red, and white blood cells typify the kinds of cells that renew themselves frequently through mitosis. The skin forms a new layer of cells about every four days, the lining of the intestines is replaced even more frequently, while the lifetime of a red blood cell is four months. When a person is wounded, the skin and blood cells produce a great many more new cells in order to replace the lost blood and to heal the broken surface. So prodigious is the normal turnover in the body that every day we discard and renew about 1 percent of our cells.

Other cells, such as those of the liver, kidneys, pancreas and other endocrines, skeleton, and heart muscle fibers, show only a limited or erratic ability to reproduce—although the liver can regenerate itself if some of the organ is lost to disease or excision and parts of the kidneys also can replace themselves more or less on demand.

Then there are certain types of cells that do not divide at all. These include cells of the muscles, the nerves, and the brain.

Cancer almost always is associated with the dividing cells, usually starting with the hyperactive reproducers in the skin or epithelial lining of interior organs. Cardiovascular diseases, too, are associated with mitotic cells.

There is a dramatic difference in behavior between a cell alone in a culture and cells in a community. Alone, the cell is mobile and given to growth and reproduction. However, when the surfaces of two cells come into contact, there is an immediate change. The cells become immobile and reduce the manufacture of protein so that there is a cessation to growth and reproduction. This suppression of growth could be an explanation for a cell's century-long duration in the human body compared to its two-year lifespan in culture. A cancerous cell ignores these external signals, pushing its way over other cells and, of course, growing and proliferating without regulation.

All cells have a membrane, a cytoplasm, and a nucleaus: the three forms of protoplasm, the most basic material of life. The plasma membrane, only a few molecules wide (too thin to be seen with a light microscope but clearly visible in an electron microscope), is not a static wall, but a malleable sheet capable of regulating traffic in and out of the cell. The cell membrane is very sensitive to its environment, and the touch of a hormone, for instance, can jolt the cell into a new mode of activity so that it begins making a called-for substance.

The cytoplasm is a jellylike mass that occupies most of the cell around the nucleus. It resembles a stockyard wherein are most of the materials and parts needed for whatever the cell may want to manufacture. A number of key subunits, called organelles, are embedded in the cytoplasm and each is contained in its own membrane. Among the most important organelles are ribosomes, mitochondria, and lysosomes. Ribosomes are little workshops for making proteins. Almost all living material is composed of protein. Protein, in turn, is made by an orderly assembly of lesser molecules called amino acids. The nearly self-sufficient cells can fashion almost everything they need to survive. However, our bodies cannot make ten of the 20 amino acids; this explains the necessity for including protein in the human diet, and the havoc of malnutrition even when there is an adequate calorie intake in carbohydrates and fats.

Mitochondria are the power units of the cell. There are 1,000 of them in a liver cell. In these sausage-shaped organelles, energy is extracted from nutrients, packaged in a compound known as ATP and then sent to fuel the thousands of chemical reactions taking place elsewhere in the cell. Because 90 percent of the oxidation in the body takes place in the mitochondria, Denham Harman suspects that these sites may be the sought-after aging clocks. The faster the oxygen is used and broken down in these energy-producing units, the greater the number of free radicals formed and the more intense the resultant damage: this is the way, according to Harman, that higher metabolic rate translates into shorter lifespan.

Dorothy Travis at the Gerontology Research Center has observed changes in both mitochondria and lysosomes in the heart cells of aging rats. Lysosomes represent the security force for the cell. They are sacs containing enzymes which attack and break down viruses or other large molecules coming into the cell. Ordinarily these centurions are sealed off from the rest of the cell by the lysosome membrane. However, if the membrane is ruptured or breaks down, the released enzymes turn upon the cell itself and destroy it. In fact, this is what happens after a person dies—his tissues are dissipated by these "self-destruct" units.

Dr. Travis has noted that lysosome activity begins to increase in aging cells and she has observed rows of lysosomes attached to aged mitochondria like the scaffolding of building wreckers. It is as though upon a certain signal the cell begins to shut down shop and dismantle the parts. Lysosomes begin to grow more active in rat cells between 12 and 18 months, and we know rats live an average of 24 and a maximum of 36 months. Possibly the trigger is the breakdown of mitochondria and lysosome membranes by the constant battering from free radical reactions as suggested by Dr. Harman. Whatever the cause, this could be the mechanism for cell death which begins before the person himself dies and which leads to the emaciation of very old age and accompanies the fall-off in physical functions. Dr. Travis is trying to induce increased lysosome activity in young cells so that she might better understand how to stop it and thus ward off cell death.

For years researchers had observed bits of inert brown pigment that collected as nondividing cells grew older. Dr. Travis says that this tell-tale pigment now has been fully identified as residues of cell parts that are not totally broken down. Whether this accumulated debris interferes with a cell's viability—is a cause of aging—long has been a subject for speculation and controversy.

The nucleus is the cell's headquarters. It is the site of the chromosomes, DNA, genes. Physically, DNA is found in chromatin, a material that also contains basic proteins called histones, acidic proteins, and some RNA. DNA is the cell's biological link to the past and the future, containing the chemical master plan for both the cell and the entire organism; it directs what the cell shall do. How this is accomplished is the most fascinating story modern science has to tell.

The story does not yet have an ending, but it begins in a monastery garden at Altbrünn, Austria, in 1854. This was five years before Charles

Darwin published his theories on the origin and evolution of species, but the questions of evolution already were in the air. How did species come about? How could two sisters be so similar, dissimilar, and a blend of various characteristics? The most educated explanation for heredity came from animal breeders who accounted for it as a mixture of bloods and referred to hybrids as half-bloods, quarter-bloods, and so on.

With a heart as stout as his body, Gregor Mendel at the age of thirty-two set out to solve the riddle of heredity. Afterward he had to admit that it took a bit of courage to entertain such aspirations—particularly, it could be added, for one of such humble station in the commonwealth of science. Mendel chose as his Rosetta stone to decode the strange language of heredity the equally humble garden pea.

The Augustinian monk spent two years collecting 34 varieties of peas to make sure he had pure strains and then in 1856 began to cross-breed contrasting varieties—plants with round peas were crossed with plants with wrinkled peas, plants with yellow peas united with plants with green peas, and so on. When these hybrids ripened, one of the characteristics in each pair had disappeared: all peas were round, none wrinkled; all in the next group were yellow, none green. The following spring, Mendel interbred the hybrids. This time, the less dominant trait reappeared: three of every four peas were round, the other wrinkled. There was a consistent 3:1 ratio.

The next year, 1858, Mendel allowed his pea plants to reproduce by self-fertilization. Those one-quarter of the plants with wrinkled peas all brought forth wrinkled peas. The original trait of the great-grandparent reasserted itself in pure form, undiminished, undiluted by its association with the dominant round peas! Of the other three quarters of the hybrid plants—there were 565 of them with round peas—193 plants produced all round peas and 373 plants bore both round and wrinkled peas in the same 3:1 ratio.

From these and other consistently similar results, Mendel saw that when hybrids were mated, three-quarters of the offspring exhibited the dominant characteristic and one-quarter the recessive. But he further deduced that only one-quarter were pure dominant while the other three-quarters retained both dominant and recessive traits, so while the recessive quality was masked, nevertheless it persisted and could be expressed again at a later time. While the apparent ratio was 3:1, the actual ratio was 1:2:1. One purebred dominant, two hybrids with both qualities, and one purebred recessive. The qualities persisted evenly and undiminished.

As long as the paradigm for heredity was analogized to a vat of paint with an endless blending of tints and colors, it was impossible to understand how heredity worked. The door to comprehension was opened when Mendel showed that heredity is not a blend but a *mosaic* of *discrete* units.

Even though his discovery may seem elementary enough for today's school child to grasp, its difficulty may be gauged by the fact that the great Darwin also worked with peas . . . also noted the uniformity of the first generation . . . also observed generations with 3:1 ratio . . . but could not penetrate the mystery. What the encyclopedic naturalist lacked was Mendel's combination of botany and mathematical logic.

In February 1865 the resident monk reported his revolutionary findings to the Brünn Society for the Study of Natural Science, hardly the most august body in Western science. The following year his lecture was published as a monograph in the Society's *Proceedings* and, as per custom, shipped to Vienna, Berlin, Rome, St. Petersburg, and Uppsala to gather dust on book shelves.

Mendel was disappointed at the lack of enthusiasm, even notice, that his discovery engendered. So he wrote about his experiments to one of the leading botanists of that time, Karl von Nägeli. It so happened that Nägeli also was trying to learn the secret of heredity, but he could find little value in what Mendel told him. There were no attempts to repeat Mendel's experiments.

For his part, Mendel followed Voltaire's advice and tended his garden. Further experiments led him to the threshold of discovering an important elaboration of his theory that gradations in a certain quality can be explained if it is governed by two hereditary units. However, in 1868 Mendel was appointed abbot and soon all his attention was devoted to resisting efforts by secular authorities to tax the monastery.

When he died in 1884, a huge crowd of scientists, professors, churchmen, and citizens came to pay tribute to Gregor Mendel, their beloved clergyman. Later, in the disposing of his effects, his scientific papers were burned.

In Mendel's case it is possible to measure how far he was ahead of his time. Thirty-five years. In 1900 three scientists independently experienced the thrill of discovering the basic hereditary law of distinct units of transmission, only to have their exultation dashed by rediscovery of Mendel's dust-ridden monograph. The three scientists manfully admitted Mendel's priority and their names are known today only to specialists. The triumphant practicality of Mendel's arithmetic even relegated the brilliant Weismann to the shadows in history's hall of fame. In 1922, on the 100th anniversary of his birth, the world paid tribute to Gregor Mendel, the scientist.

A good deal of other information about heredity had been accumulated during the years that Mendel's knowledge remained concealed.

The material DNA had been duly noted in the nuclei of cells. So had tiny, threadlike bodies which were called chromosomes, "colored bodies," because of the way they stained from certain dyes. Weismann had shown that heredity could be transmitted only through germ cells. This in itself had a profound impact upon the thinking about heredity. In a tradition that went all the way back to Hippocrates, it had been assumed that semen is derived from all parts of the body. A logical assumption with this concept is that acquired characteristics can be passed on to offspring. If a man works hard to develop his biceps, then his son will inherit large biceps.

In 1802, before Darwin was born, a Frenchman, Jean Lamarck, proposed a well-thought-out theory of evolution, citing the graduated complexity of species from the most primitive to human beings. The observed changes in anatomy could come about, Lamarck believed, through constant use which encouraged development of an anatomical part and disuse which led to atrophy: thus evolutionary change was brought about through acquired characteristics. This earlier theory of evolution brought no outcries from religious leaders and virtually no response from anybody else. Lamarck, too, was ahead of his time. A contemporary leader of French science dismissed the theory as the naturalist's "new piece of madness."

But the hypothesis of passing along acquired change is seductively persuasive and even Darwin believed it to be an instrument of evolution; of course, he did not have access to Mendel's knowledge of how heredity worked. Although Darwin correctly emphasized selection as the major means of evolution, he suggested that hereditary particles continually pass from all parts of the body to the reproductive organs. In this way he theorized that modifications of somatic cells would enter the hereditary stream.

Convinced that germ cells were isolated from body cells, Weismann was a vigorous opponent of the Lamarckian view and in this respect was more of a Darwinian purist than Darwin himself. In order to disprove the theory that changes in somatic cells could bring about hereditary change, Weismann experimentally mutilated adult rats in a succession of generations. Always the offspring were whole and unchanged.

With the rediscovery of Mendel's hereditary laws serving as a keystone, the other blocks of information could be fitted into their places, and investigators could begin to construct the most complex model in all science—the representation of life itself. To begin with, Mendel reinforced Weismann and undermined Lamarck. All right, if inheritance is as unvarying as Mendel's units indicated, how *did* changes come about? In 1901 a Dutch botanist, Hugo De Vries—he was one of the scientists whose discovery was swallowed up by the rediscovery of Mendel—proposed the mutation theory. This was based on long-time observations that once in a while a plant or animal "degenerates" or deviates from the norm. De Vries suggested that occasionally there was a random, spontaneous alteration in one of the hereditary units and in this way evolutionary forces continually had the opportunity to experiment with biological changes.

In 1903 Wilhelm Johannsen further clarified the distinction between the invariance of inheritance and the obvious diversity of individual traits. At the same time he distinguished the influences of heredity and environment whose subtle interplay had confused Lamarck and his followers. In experiments with bean plants, Johannsen showed that the size and weight of beans were not ordained by heredity, but could be affected by the environment in which the parent plants grew. Plants in poor soil grew small beans, those in rich soil grew large beans. With this important qualification, hereditary units could be viewed as potentials which could be expressed more or less depending upon the circumstances of the individual. Thus the man who exercised did develop large biceps, but what he passed on to his son was exactly what he himself inherited—a potential for well-developed biceps if the son made use of them. Johannsen suggested the important distinction between genotype and phenotype, the total biological potential passed on through a species and the particular expression of this potential in any individual.

Weismann had suspected that chromosomes were the carriers of inheritance, and in 1902 Walter Sutton formally proposed that Mendel's hereditary units were located in these elongated structures usually found associated in pairs. Just before the cell divided, the pairs lined up end to end, all joined together in a row. Then they reproduced themselves and with mitosis each set of chromosomes went with one of the daughter cells. That's what happened in somatic cells. In germ cells (where the process is called "meiosis"), there was no chromosome reproduction. One member from each pair joined the separate rows facing one another. When these rows separated with cell division, the mature sex cells carried only one-half the normal complement of chromosomes.

The somatic and immature sex cells of every animal species contain a specific and characteristic number of chromosomes. The smallest possible chromosome number is two, in the roundworm *Ascaris* with which Weismann had worked. The largest number, 224, is found in a moth. In humans, there are 46 chromosomes, distributed in 23 pairs. In the female, each member of a chromosome pair is identical. In the male, 22 pairs are identical; the 23rd contains both an X and a Y chromosome, the Y containing the male sex characteristics. In the female, this 23rd pair contains two X chromosomes. The difference between X and Y divides the female from the male.

In 1909 Johannsen named Mendel's hereditary units "genes," for the Greek word for race, from which the science of genetics takes its name. Starting in 1910 Thomas Hunt Morgan and a small group of his students at Columbia University began mapping chromosomes—trying to locate where specific trait-causing genes appeared in each chromosome—through ingenious cross-breeding experiments with the fruit fly *Drosophila* melanogaster. The virtue of *Drosophila,* the best insect instructor mankind has ever had, is that it does not live long and reproduces rapidly, so that investigators can observe many generations in a relatively short time span. Even so it took five years of eye straining and patient record taking in the famous "fly room" for the Columbia gene hunters to amass their initial findings.

Drosophila has four chromosomes and by the time Morgan and his students were finished, they had a good idea of the positions of various genes. Their work further strengthened the gene theory. Dr. Morgan envisioned genes as a string of beads on a thread. In 1933 he received a Nobel Prize, the first worker in genetics so honored.

Later work with *Drosophila* showed that each specific gene has a characteristic rate of mutation, although these spontaneous changes are rare occurrences. In 1927 one of Morgan's former students, Herman Muller, proved that genes can be altered by x-rays. These studies verified the mutation theory proposed by De Vries and earned a Nobel Prize for Muller. Today it is known that a gene will mutate once in every million cells; for some genes the rate is less frequent, for others more, depending on the species. Of course, the mutation must occur in gametes, or sex cells, in order for the change to be passed on to future generations. Mutations in somatic cells disappear with the individual.

Despite all this new-won knowledge, scientists still did not know what genes were made of, what they looked like, or exactly where they were located physically. The problem was one of size. Where researchers had been dealing with cells, now they were probing into parts of cells and molecules. Where cells are measured in microns—1/1,000 of a millimeter or 1/25,000 of an inch—molecules are measured in angstroms—1/10,000,-000 of a millimeter or 1/250,000,000 of an inch. The scientists were being forced into a world 10,000 times smaller than the cell and they did not have the equipment to take them there.

In the 1930s and 1940s, technology perfected a whole new generation of biological tools, and genetics largely marked time until it was re-equipped. Some of the analytical tools that enabled researchers to "see" the molecular denizens of cellular life include:

High-speed centrifugation—by spinning cellular material at speeds up to 100,000 times gravity and higher, submicroscopic particles will separate out according to their mass and weight, each at its own "g" rate.

Electrophoresis—in this operation molecules are separated by virtue of differences in their electrical charge.

Chromatography—this method takes advantage of varying chemical properties in different substances. By immersing them in various solvents, different molecules will migrate certain measurable distances through solids, such as chalk. Chromatography was particularly helpful in deciphering enzymes and mapping the linear arrangement of their parts, the amino acids. For years, enzymes were enigmas—"black boxes" with unknown purposes. Gradually, biochemists began to unravel their role as catalysts to various cellular chemical activities. Ordinarily, the body's chemicals would take so long to react together that life processes would proceed at a pace perhaps better measured on the geological time scale. On the other hand, if the chemicals possessed the volatility to carry out the biological processes spontaneously, the body would go off like a Fourth of July pinwheel. Instead, nature arranges through the tiny protein enzymes for just those reactions the body wants when it needs them. It is as though, for instance, a matchmaker enzyme spots a carbon dioxide molecule and a molecule of water, introduces them, gives each of them a stiff drink, escorts them to a motel room and then lets them do what they otherwise would not have gotten around to doing for years—make carbonic acid. In this pairing, the enzyme would have to be carbonic anhydrase. Biologists found that for each particular reaction, there is a specific enzyme. It began to dawn on them that this finding implied a huge number of enzymes. The first enzyme to be isolated was urease in 1926. Today, about 1,500 enzymes have been isolated. It is believed that the human body has 150,000 different enzymes, all very similar in appearance but no two kinds exactly alike and each with a different assignment.

This biochemical knowledge passed into genetics when experiments in 1941 confirmed earlier suspicions that enzymes were linked to genes. The increasingly sophisticated concept of genetic control at that time became known as "one gene, one enzyme."

At about this time biological laboratories began getting a powerful new optical instrument, the electron microscope. It had been invented more than a decade earlier in Germany, but took that long to come into general use. Where the light microscope illuminates an object with a beam of light, the electron microscope illuminates the specimen with a stream of electrons. Where the light microscope was useful in observing the behavior of cells, the electron microscope could look at organelles, and finally its power of resolution was pushed to the molecular level. A light microscope cannot separate two points if they are any closer than about 2,500 angstroms. An electron microscope can resolve all the way down to 2 or 3 angstroms—the distance between atoms is 5 angstroms. While their power of magnification was not so great at first, it has been enhanced over the years, so that the most powerful electron microscopes can enlarge an image 360,000 times (compared to a maximum 2,500 times for a light microscope). However, if a picture—called a micrograph—is made of the image, this can be enlarged another ten times photographically, now making the magnification 3,600,000 times. By manipulating these two techniques, a micrograph finally was made of a DNA molecule in 1969. This picture had been magnified more than 7 million times.

In order for electrons to pass directly through the specimen under observation, necessary for a clear picture, the object must be sliced thin. The thinner, the less blurring and distortion. An ultramicrotone can cut cell material only 100 atoms thick—sections thinner than a wave of light so that they are literally invisible when viewed from the side!

The early electron microscopes did not project objects in three dimensions as the later models did, simply a flat, two-dimensional image. But investigators were beginning to suspect that the form of a molecule had a crucial bearing on what it did and the way it performed. In order to divine the structure of the big protein molecules, the researchers turned to x-ray diffraction, a method which had helped show how smaller (and simpler) molecules were shaped. In this technique, a flow of x-rays is sent through the molecule and the silhouette is recorded on a plate on the other side. From the patterns formed by the rays that passed straight through, those that were blocked and those that were diverted by collisions with the atoms of the structure, the researcher tries to reconstruct the intervening object.

With these new tools, with the expanded fund of biochemical knowledge gathered about proteins, and with the movement of nuclear physicists and chemists into the life sciences, molecular biology was ready to commence with the post-World War II world.

Nucleic acids had been identified as far back as 1872 as complexes with proteins. It had been known for decades that DNA—deoxyribonucleic acid—resided in the cell nucleus. No especial importance was attached to this because proteins also existed there and proteins were attracting the scientific attention as the material of life. By the early 1940s biochemists knew that while RNA was located both in the cytoplasm and the nucleus, DNA was a major constituent of the nucleus. However, investigators did not consider DNA as a carrier of genetic information because they believed it was simply a monotonous repetition of four basic parts, called nucleotides.

In 1944 Oswald Avery and his associates at Rockefeller Institute took dried and purified DNA from one strain of pneumonia bacteria and injected it into the cells of a different but similar strain. The original bacteria were virulent, the second strain harmless. After the inoculations, the harmless bacteria were transformed into pneumonia disease agents.

Scientists in general, even Avery, were unwilling to accept this evidence linking DNA and the long-elusive genes. Some thought that the DNA extractions may have been contaminated with other cellular material, particularly proteins. Furthermore, it was not known at that time that bacteria could breed sexually, so that such an experiment seemed to have little meaning for other species. And besides, everyone had that prejudice against monotonous, useless DNA.

But doubters were converted into believers in 1952 when Alfred Hershey and his assistant, Martha Chase, showed that a particular DNA virus could take over a bacterium and replace the cell's genetic information with its own. Nucleic acids also were the stuff of life! The race was on to find out what DNA was all about.

James Watson, a young Ph.D. in biology from Indiana University, and Francis Crick, an English physicist turned biologist studying for his doctorate at Cambridge University, were decided long shots in the DNA sweepstakes. The favorite was Nobel laureate-to-be, chemist Linus Pauling. As it turned out, Pauling was instrumental in the outcome, but did not win the prize. Pauling's earlier work led the eclectic Watson and Crick to think of the DNA structure as a spiral. X-ray crystallography by nuclear physicist Maurice Wilkins caused Watson to refine his model to a structure composed of two spirals twining around each other.

In 1953, at the same Cavendish Laboratory where Rutherford had achieved the first alchemical goal by transmuting elements, Watson and Crick patched together bits of metal and pieces of wire into the famous model of the double helix—the molecular blueprint for life. The spines of this molecule were on the outside. The two helices served as the sides of a ladder. They were connected at regular intervals by rungs. Each half of a rung consisted of one of four chemical bases called nucleotides: adenine (A), thymine (T), cystosine (C), and guanine (G). These bases always were paired—A joined only with T, and C only with G—and were weakly held together by a hydrogen atom. If upon superficial inspection the limited number of nucleotides seemed predisposed to repetition, it could be seen upon closer consideration that by varying their order, the four bases could in fact store the genetic library.

Since one nucleotide always attracts its opposite number, the mirror images of each side of the molecule suggested to Watson and Crick how DNA duplicates itself. Breaking the weak hydrogen bond at the middle of each rung, the DNA molecule simply opens like a zipper, separates, and then selects matching bases from the surrounding chemical soup to reconstitute the open side of each ladder.

There were Nobel Prizes for Watson, Crick, Wilkins, and also for Arthur Kornberg who by 1956 found an enzyme crucial to DNA replication. He named it DNA polymerase. Dr. Kornberg placed a single-stranded DNA molecule, the four bases (A, T, C, G), some other chemicals, and the enzyme in the same brew: they proceeded to produce a new double helix. The Watson-Crick model worked!

Understanding how a cell could reproduce its genetic material provided clues but not complete answers to how one of the materials of life, nucleic acids, directed manufacture of the other, proteins. Scientists already suspected that a single-stranded nucleic acid, ribonucleic acid (RNA), was involved in the process. RNA also is made up of four bases like DNA; three of them identical. Scientists discovered that there are three kinds of RNA. One is messenger RNA, which is made when one section of DNA pulls apart and the exposed nucleotides put together, in order, their opposite-number RNA constituents. When the transcription is complete, the newly formed ribbon of RNA is detached and the strands of DNA rejoin. The messenger RNA then migrates to a ribosome which contains another type of RNA and moves between its large and small globule sections, somewhat like a piece of tape through a tape recorder.

In the meantime, units of the third kind of RNA—transfer RNA— have been roving through the cytoplasm like scouts, linking with specific amino acids and escorting them to a ribosome assembly plant. There the tRNA waits until its call number comes up on the mRNA message, takes its position on the assembly line at the same time depositing its amino acid into its proper niche in the growing protein chain. This protein synthesis is known as the translation of genetic information. Most of the proteins being formed are enzymes to start up, shut down, or in some way control the cell's chemical functioning.

One nagging question still remained for life scientists. How could four nucleotides in the DNA call for 20 amino acids in proteins? A physicist, George Gamow, likened the four bases to the four suits in a deck of cards. Obviously, there could not be a one-to-one relationship. If the cards were dealt in pairs for each amino acid there could be only

16 combinations at most. Still not enough. Dr. Gamow reasoned that the nucleotides must be taken as a trio. With three bases per unit, 64 combinations are possible.

At the National Institutes of Health, an unknown biochemist, Marshall Nirenberg, discovered that a piece of RNA composed only of a single one of the four bases always produced a protein chain with a single amino acid, phenylalanine. Nirenberg concluded that the triplet with the three same bases was the code word, or codon, for phenylalanine. With that one clue, he and other researchers worked out the codons for all the amino acids. There was room for redundancy; in some cases six different codons called the same amino acid. A few triad combinations summoned no amino acids. This was puzzling until the decoders realized that these codons were punctuation marks, signifying when instructions ended or a new message began. A Nobel Prize for Dr. Nirenberg.

And so men learned the language of life. The four nucleotides are the letters of the alphabet. All words are a trinity of letters. There are about 60 words and a few punctuation marks in the genetic dictionary. The great DNA molecules in the chromosomes in the nucleus of each cell contain the total library of information. This information is dispatched in a series of messages. The messages, from conception until death, write the book of life for each individual. In the beginning was the word.

Genes—Mendel's hereditary units and Morgan's beads on a thread—now became segments along the DNA ladder. The human genome, which is the word for the totality of genetic information in the cell, contains about 6 billion nucleotides. Divided by three, that still leaves 2 billion code words. But we still don't know how many code words make up various genes or, to put it plainly, how many genes we have. In the National Academy of Sciences' *Biology and the Future of Man*, the figure is given as at least 1 million genes, but James Watson said in March, 1973, that "we still do not have even an order of magnitude for the number of human genes . . ." Human beings also consist of and employ perhaps one million different proteins. Discretion being the better part of valor, molecular investigators started with bacteria, which have about 6 million nucleotides and about 2 to 3 thousand proteins.

Working with common intestinal bacteria, Jacques Monod and François Jacob at the Pasteur Institut in Paris found that when *Escherichia coli* were in a medium without lactose, they rarely manufactured the enzymes required to break down the sugar. Within about two minutes after lactose was added to their medium, however, manufacture of three lactose-degrading enzymes increased a thousandfold and remained at that level until the lactose was gone. This is what Monod and Jacob believe happened:

The three producer genes make the enzymes reside side by side on the DNA column so that they encode the mRNA strand in a single operation. Located beside these genes is an operator segment of DNA, beside it is a promoter segment, and beside it a regulator gene. Completing this paradigm is a protein molecule called a repressor. When no lactose is present in the cell, the repressor protein is bound to the operator segment of DNA. When lactose appears, one of the incoming units is fixed to the repressor protein and that causes it to withdraw from the operator segment. Once the operator segment is unbound, it permits the promotor segment to summon the RNA polymerase enzyme which opens the producer genes to synthesize mRNA to manufacture the breakdown enzymes. These mRNA's last only a few minutes, but their fabrication goes on indefinitely until the last traces of lactose disappear from the cell. When that happens, the repressor protein returns to its binding position on the operator segment, thus shutting off manufacture of lactose-breakdown enzymes. The function of the regulator gene is to keep synthesizing the repressor protein which acts simply as an on-and-off switch. For Drs. Monod and Jacob, Nobel Prizes.

This operon model, as it is called, suggested to all investigators the cybernetic sophistication involved in cellular regulation. For one thing, it was clear the DNA did not call all the shots. Regulation was a two-way street between the nucleus and the cytoplasm, and this in turn could be affected by what happened outside the cell. This realization spurred a new interest in hormones, the Paul Reveres of the intercellular network. It confirmed the importance of environment as well as heredity on the molecular level.

Investigators began to see that regulation of intracellular activities could take place at a number of control points—where the genetic information is translated into protein at the ribosomes, by subsequent modification of existing enzymes, and through degradation of proteins —in addition to the transcription of RNA. Researchers began to envision an even more elaborate DNA-protein regulatory system for humans than the one employed by bacteria. These models suggest that a single regulator gene, in a chain of command, affects a number of operator genes and thus controls batteries of producer genes. Bernard Davis of Harvard Medical School says that such human traits as behavior, temperament, intelligence, and physical structure are determined by polygenic coordination. "Indeed, man undoubtedly has hundreds of thousands of genes for polygenic traits, compared with a few hundred recognizable through their control over monogenic traits."

Possibly the most significant discovery was that not all of a cell's genetic information is used at any particular time. Much of the information, perhaps most of it, lies dormant. Some of it may *never* be expressed in an individual's entire lifetime—and if it is expressed, it is by mistake. In 1967 investigators isolated another repressor protein in that bacterium, *E. coli.* This repressor kept the lambda virus, which has become a part of *E. coli's* DNA, turned off. However, when the lambda repressor was destroyed or inactivated, the virus genes went into action, producing virus protein particles that killed the bacterium.

Robert Huebner and George Todaro at the National Cancer Institute believe that a similar event or events have happened to human DNA. Down through the eons of time, various organisms were attacked by cancer-producing C-type RNA viruses. In what may have been the best defense strategy at the time, these viruses were incorporated into the DNA where their effects could be suppressed. "Evidence from sero-epidemiological studies and from cell culture studies supports the hypothesis that the cells of many, and perhaps all, vertebrates contain information from producing C-type RNA viruses," write Huebner and Todaro. "Carcinogens, irradiation, and the normal aging process all favor the partial or complete activation of these genes." Thus the potential for cancer is part of our heritage, a part that normally is not called forth.

Roy Britten and David Kohne have found that certain sequences of DNA are repeated thousands of times in higher animals and the correspondence of these repeated sequences is greatest between species close on the evolutionary tree. Certain of these repetitions may have occurred hundreds of millions of years ago when the DNA was a common genetic blueprint for innumerable species that have separated since. As the species split off, their own DNA undergoes mutations so that gradually some of the old sequences are erased and/or new ones are added. In this way DNA is a palimpsest for each species' biological past and a record of evolutionary history.

What makes this concept of gene regulation so attractive is that it offers a plausible explanation for differentiation. Britten and Eric Davidson stated: "Cell differentiation is based almost certainly on the regulation of gene activity, so that for each state of differentiation a certain set of genes is active in transcription and other genes are inactive." They based their assertion on the fact that all cells (except mature sex cells) have a complete set of the genetic code, evidence that much of the DNA in higher organisms is inactive, and that different types of RNA are made in different kinds of cells.

Taking cues from the cell's cytoplasm and external environment, the genetic master plan switches on banks of genes and turns off batteries of others: a fertilized ovum becomes an embryo becomes a fetus becomes an infant becomes a child becomes an adolescent becomes an adult. Then declines and dies.

Molecular researchers in aging now are scrutinizing the DNA-RNA-protein circuit. The route is circular because protein enzymes, repressors and inducers, govern the behavior of genes and RNA as much as the nucleic acids regulate the proteins.

In 1963 Leslie Orgel, then at Cambridge University in England, proposed the error theory. In order to produce good protein, he said, the genetic message always must be reproduced accurately. This means it must be transcribed correctly from the DNA template to the mRNA and translated accurately from the mRNA to the tRNA in the ribosomes. In addition, the tRNA must always select the proper amino acids. These processes further depend upon the existence of perfect enzymes—RNA polymerase for the synthesis of mRNA, and tRNA synthestases to affix the right amino acids.

Like everything else human, Dr. Orgel suggested, an error might crop up somewhere along the line. As a result of such an error, an incorrect amino acid would be inserted into a protein molecule. In many cases this might affect just one molecule in an inconsequential area. However, if the fault occurred in enzymes that were integral to the tool-making operation itself, the results would be a series of defective proteins that would cause further disruptions in the system. In the end, an "error catastrophe" would cause the death of the cell.

It is remarkable that this modern theory, built on the pinnacle of molecular biology, has the same premise for death as the primitive African myths—the message that failed (see p. 10).

Some experimental work has tended to support Orgel's theory. A study of ovalbumin protein taken from a chicken and laboriously analyzed molecule by molecule showed that an erroneous substitution of amino acids occurred about once every 3,000 times. When amino acid analogues—that is, synthetic amino acids with a slightly changed composition—were fed to fruit flies, the flies died sooner than controls. On the presumption that defective enzymes are more prone to be deactivated by heat, experiments have shown that there are greater numbers of heat-sensitive enzymes in senescent cells than in young ones. Cells also produce enzymes that repair damage to DNA, and tests with radiation exposure show that the work of these repair proteins declines with age.

Also, it appears that in cells that keep dividing, many of the errors are eliminated through turnover and the evolutionary principle of "survival of the fittest." Half of the DNA is being renewed with each division. With cells that do not divide, it is to be expected that errors have a greater tendency to be locked into the system. Bernard Strehler and Roger Johnson of the University of Southern California found evidence in the brains of aging dogs that DNA information necessary to make protein is lost. Brain cells do not divide.

Since most of the apparatus for making proteins exists in the cytoplasm, that part of the cell logically might be a more likely place for the errors to occur. The transfer of cytoplasm from an old cell has been found to cause a young cell to age prematurely. And a similar transfer from spanned amoebas has caused other strains of amoebas to lose their potential for reproducing indefinitely (see p. 221, note 6).

Bernard Strehler believes that protein synthesis breaks down in the translation stage in the cytoplasm. (The lost DNA information in the aging-dog experiment coded for the specific type of RNA that is found in ribosomes.) With about 60 code words for 20 amino acids, the message for any single protein can be written millions of different ways. Dr. Strehler believes that what happens with differentiation is that each kind of cell calls the amino acids through its own particular combinations of codons. Each type of cell speaks its own language.

This would mean that each differentiated cell is vastly limited in the genetic information it can read, or translate, into protein. If messages are garbled, it cannot switch to a backup system. Moreover, the cell's "reading" ability may be reduced—and this time disastrouly—in an unintended way. A "side" effect of differentiation is "that as cells mature they may shut off the ability to read, or decode, certain code words."

The essence of Dr. Strehler's theory "is that a highly deterministic set of instructions, that regulates where and when each gene will be active, is present in living things. During early life this set of instructions, choosing among different cell languages, causes maturation; but as maturity is approached some materials necessary for very extended life (or immortality) can no longer be manufactured. Consequently, animals age because the storehouse of materials manufactured during development gradually deteriorates. As these materials deteriorate, the functions they support also deteriorate, until a point is reached where some environmental or internal challenge can no longer be overcome and death ensues."

Heretofore, "program" and "lack of program" have appeared as irreconcilable opposites. This either-or viewpoint was suggested in Thornton Wilder's *The Bridge of San Luis Rey:* "Either we live by accident and die by accident," says the Franciscan monk Brother Juniper, "or we live by plan and die by plan." The narrator then phrases it this way: "Some say that . . . to the gods we are like the flies that boys kill on a summer day, and some say, on the contrary, that the very sparrows do not lose a feather that has not been brushed away by the finger of God."

But it is apparent from Dr. Strehler's concept that thinking of senescence and death in terms of program versus lack of program can create a false antithesis. The explanations can be complementary. If there is a lack of program, it is the consequence of genetic program. If there is a lack of program, it is part of the evolutionary program—deliberately encouraged or at least allowed to persist by default.

In restrospect we can see that August Weismann from his lesser vantage point of 80 years ago penetrated deeply into the mysteries of life and death. What we have learned from molecular genetics strengthens his contention that aging and death are intimately linked with division of labor—the differentiation, specialization, and interdependence of cells in complex organisms. We know that the specialized human germ cells have forfeited their ability to reproduce themselves and go on living indefinitely. This is so because mature sex cells have only one-half the normal complement of chromosomes: they are deficient in genetic instructions for cell reproduction. They must unite with a germ cell from the opposite sex in order to restore the chromosomal integrity. In that way, they regain the capacity to reproduce and thus sustain the potential for immortality.

However, contrary to Weismann, somatic cells have not lost their capacity either to reproduce the entire organism or to reproduce indefinitely. In the mid 1960s Professor John Gurdon, a biologist at Oxford University, removed the nucleus from a frog's egg cell and inserted in its place the nucleus from an intestinal cell. With the somatic nucleus the ovum had its complete set of chromosomes: it was fertilized. The cytoplasm of the ovum provided the environment essential for differentiation to begin. The cell proceeded to develop into a tadpole and another frog. Of course, the frog bore the genetic heritage of only one parent and so was a clone.

That experiment terminated further belief that somatic cells had lost the ability to recreate an entire organism. The ability is there but it is suppressed or in some way not expressed. In its own cytoplasm, that particular frog cell chooses to reproduce as an intestinal cell.

Similarly, we can infer that somatic cells have not lost their potential for immortality; they simply choose not to exercise it. We might never have suspected that this latent capacity was preserved through the billions of years of evolutionary transition were it not for cancer. If those cells cultured by Dr. Hayflick are allowed to become aged so that the end of reproduction is imminent and then they are infected with Simian Virus 40, they undergo a cancerlike transformation and continue to divide indefinitely. Researchers everywhere have been able to keep cancer cells living *in vitro* and through successive transplants in new animals without end. That is what cancer is by definition: mutinous cells that ignore the body's discipline and keep growing indefinitely.

For all these years we have been transfixed by the medium, but what a message cancer cells bring! The elixir is not an impossible dream. The fountain of youth exists. Fruit still grows on the tree of life. Paradise is not lost. We can return to Eden, theoretically. Achieving the goal, like going to the moon, becomes a problem for technology.

VIII. Prognosis

The next question is: When?

Prediction is an uncertain business, as weather forecasters remind us daily. On the other hand, scientific forecasters say that if something is possible, and if it is a boon for mankind, then it will be achieved, probably sooner than expected.

Arthur Clarke, a highly knowledgeable writer of science and science fiction (*2001: A Space Odyssey*), is a prognosticator with a track record. Back in 1945 he predicted that communications satellites would orbit the earth in fixed positions, just as they do now. Where Clarke was mistaken was in not foreseeing that the development would come so soon in his own lifetime (if he had, he says, he would have tried to take out a patent). In his first novel in 1947 he set 1959 as the year for the first rocket to hit the moon (exactly correct), but set a manned landing on the moon in 1978. Again too conservative.

In a book written in 1962, *Profiles of the Future*, Clarke estimated what scientific accomplishments would happen when. He predicted humans would achieve immortality about the year 2095.

In 1964 T. J. Gordon and Olaf Helmer, a consultant to and a staff member of the Rand Corporation, experimented with the Delphi method of forecasting future events. The Delphi system seeks to get as specific a consensus as possible from a spectrum of experts. This technique avoids open, group meetings where stronger personalities may dominate opinion and cause bandwagon effects. Instead, selected experts are sent questionnaires asking when they believe an event is likely to happen and why they believe so. On the basis of responses, a second round of questionnaires presents reasons that might cause respondents to revise their prediction or elicit a further defense of their original estimate.

The Gordon-Helmer inquiry refined and narrowed the range of forecasts through a series of four questionnaires. The entire panel consisted of 82 experts, about half of whom were connected with the Rand Corporation (whose business is, of course, to make educated visualizations of likely and contingent futures). The experts were divided into six groups. The panel on scientific breakthroughs was asked when there would be "chemical control of the aging process, permitting extension of life span by 50 years." The earliest anyone expected this to happen was 1992, the latest about 2065. The important date, representing the midpoint of all the estimates, was 2023.

Later in the 1960s A. Douglas Bender and three colleagues conducted a Delphi study on the future of medicine for the pharmaceutical firm, Smith, Kline and French Laboratories. A preparatory study included only scientists from Smith, Kline and French. The second study used a panel of outside experts with specialists from internal medicine, medical genetics, molecular biology, and other medical areas. That survey was published in January 1969.

In the first study, the consensus was that "ability to control the aging process permitting significant extension of life span" would be achieved before the year 2017. In the second study, the year was 1993.

With each successive Delphic study, the estimated year for a breakthrough on aging advanced.

An even more startling progression can be seen in Bernard Strehler, who is one of comparatively few scientists who concentrate on relating advances in molecular biology to gerontology. In his 1962 book, *Time, Cells and Aging,* Dr. Strehler concluded pessimistically that the evolutionary process of aging is so deeply ingrained "that the abolition of the process is a practical impossibility." In 1971 he predicted we would understand the aging process within five to ten years, and be able to do something about it—restore function—in ten to 30 years. Two years later Dr. Strehler qualified this prediction to the setting up of an Institute of Aging and increased public support for aging research. "If the institute is established and adequately and imaginatively funded and administered, it seems likely that by the year 1983 we will understand, in depth, the details of cellular and bodily aging."

A similar ten-year estimate comes from William Reichel, for years a cellular investigator at the Gerontology Research Center. Because of pioneering studies of progeria, the disease which simulates aging but at an accelerated pace, Dr. Reichel believes that senescence and cellular death are closely programmed, and that we may well be able to alter the timing of that program. "My first thought is—we're not ready for this yet. We must learn more in the next decade. The biggest hope lies in advanced molecular biology." What is required before we can reach the next breakthrough stage, he believes, is the same methodical accretion of knowledge that followed Darwin and Mendel and now has been going on for 20 years since Watson and Crick. Because of his conviction in this enforced hiatus for tangible results, researcher Reichel decided to return to his other specialty, geriatric medicine.

One reason for the optimism that genetic change can be brought about is that scientists see a feasible method for accomplishing such an end. It is called "transduction." Transduction operates naturally when a virus invades a cell to insert its DNA into the cellular genome. Scientists already have taken a gene from bacteria and transplated it into human cells . . . in a laboratory flask at the National Institutes of Health. The vehicle for the transplantation was a type of virus that first preyed on the bacteria, which happened to possess a gene that was ineffectual in the human cells. Then the viruses were placed in a solution with the human cells and the culture was heated to body temperature. Afterward, molecular biologists Carl Merril, Mark Geier, and John Petricciani at the National Institutes of Health observed that the human cells had absorbed the gene in question because they had gained the power to manufacture a crucial enzyme that was missing before.

The next giant step would be the insertion into the human body of tailored genes, either occurring naturally or synthetic, to compensate for whatever deficiencies are discovered.

It is interesting that the one-decade forecast holds for this, too. Gerald Hirsch, a young molecular gerontologist at Oak Ridge National Laboratory, writes: "I think that in the near future we will find the means to insert genetic information into some cell types (10 years). My guess is that cell division will be required to do this, hence it will be possible to insert genetic information to correct defects which appear in males, since their germ cells are continually dividing. However, the task of correcting the same types of genetic defects in females, so that their offspring will be permanently 'cured' is formidable (but *not* impossible) since the female's eggs are formed during her own development and before her own birth."

There is another possible answer, of course, to that question of when. Never.

Bernard Davis, Adele Lehman Professor of Bacterial Physiology at Harvard Medical School, writes: "My general view is that our success in conquering most infectious diseases, and in developing elaborate means for improving health in many other diseases, combined with our fantastic rate of advance in understanding molecular and cellular biology, have given rise to a most unrealistic set of extrapolations in the medical area. I have very serious doubts that research will lead to dramatic changes in so deep-seated a product of evolution as the aging process."

"As of today," gerontologist Nathan Shock wrote in 1970, "there is no youth pill . . . and it is doubtful whether any single substance will be found to reverse the accumulated changes of a lifetime."

If we do find out how to turn on the right regulator genes, if we do learn how to reset the aging clock—if—there still might be an insuperable barrier to indefinite longevity: the brain dilemma. Brain cells do not reproduce and hence cannot replace themselves. We are born with some 10 billion neurons and as they die our brains are diminished. Studies have shown that some parts of the cerebral cortex of a ninety-five-year-old person have only one third or one fourth as many cells as the brains of a newborn child and a twenty-one-year-old person. Harold Brody of the State University of New York at Buffalo, who did the original research on the disappearance of brain cells, says that at the observed rate of attrition the brain would be completely gone in 250 to 350 years. However, Dr. Brody says we have no way of knowing if the cell loss would continue to the vanishing point or how great is the margin of safety—just where the critical threshold is.

If, on the other hand, the rejuvenatory process started brain cells subdividing, something equally incalculable could happen. Those cells do not divide apparently for a very good reason: they store our memories, experiences, knowledge, learning as well as operate voluntary and autonomic nervous systems. New brain and nerve cells presumably would "forget" what their predecessors knew. If the person survived the neurological havoc, he might not be able to retain his identity. He would be changing continually like the sea anemone, so that while the same organism lived indefinitely, he would not have a continuity of memories and experiences and personality. He would forever be turning into somebody else.

Dr. Strehler has an answer for that one, too. "What we want to preserve," he said in July 1971, "is the sense of self—the memories and behavior patterns and responses." Suppose every 200 years we regenerated a new brain and imprinted it with all our experiences, thoughts, feelings, beliefs, memories—the whole storehouse. In other words, the "person" was transferred to a new package. Listening to Dr. Strehler, fixed by his piercing blue eyes, it took an act of conscious will to be reassured that this was not science fiction but science science.

"Would that be immortality?" he asked.

If we resourceful human beings manage to crack the brain barrier, at least one hurdle will remain still, the more prosaic one that occupies social gerontologists: the civilization that kills its youth on the highways and condemns its aged to pointless existence, that undermines marriage and the family, that either brings out the cancer that's in us or puts cancer into us, that profits financially from tobacco and sex and amphetamines and heroin and handguns and jet fighters, that dotes on violence, that admires predators, that does not dare nor does it know how to renounce war. In short, the social arrangement that militates against extended life. In this context, social gerontologist Ruth Bennett's assessment "it is just as difficult to change society as to change genes" assumes a prophetic meaning.

A biological breakthrough will force a new militancy, a new crusade. "Make the World Safe for Immortality," will be the cry.

Or else.

Part Two

QUESTIONS

IX. The Ecology of Immortality

It is curious that, since the striving for immortality has been such a pre-occupation of mankind, so little thought has been given to what a world of immortals would be like. There has been no planning on the part of governments, insurance companies, or pension programs for even a modest extension of lifespan. The lack of foresight becomes understandable if one realizes that the drive for immortality is the work of the unconscious mind—the human core, *desire*. It is not rational thought but irrational wish. Our rational, conscious mind has not examined this territory for the very good reasons that there has been no need to and it has never been told to do so.

The cerebral cortex does its job by trying to read reality correctly, to discern truth. The unconscious mind, Freud told us, does not know that it is not immortal, hence we ordinarily do not feel mortal and it is virtually impossible for each of us to envision his own death. However, the human cerebral cortex has disabused its hosts of this misconception. With the tutelage of science, this superb reader of reality has become our genie obediently executing our wishes. And now this magnificent servant may be able to satisfy the innate craving for more life.

Difficult as the truth is to discover in the profusion of appearances, this mental instrument has even greater trouble trying to identify consequences. Human beings have had to learn each lesson the hard way. Which berry was poisonous, which was edible. Some lessons were so subtle that it took millennia to learn them. Ecologist LaMont Cole, speaking of irrigation in the earliest civilization of the Tigris-Euphrates delta, wrote:

> At this stage man could hardly have been expected to anticipate that irrigation without adequate drainage would cause the water table to rise and produce waterlogged soils inimical to agriculture, or that evaporation of water moving upward would deposit a crust of salts on the surface, or that insidious erosion by wind and water, so slow as to be barely perceptible, could eliminate the fertile topsoil, ruin the plant cover, and end in violent erosion and gullying. These things had to be learned empirically and at great cost, for they were probably the princi-

pal factors causing the collapse of the great Babylonian Empire and other civilizations of the Middle East and Mediterranean regions.

In other words, the same practice that brought the flowering of the early Mesopotamian civilization caused its downfall. What began as a blessing ultimately proved to be a curse.

Molecular genetics has been a crowning achievement of biology or what today are called the life sciences. At the apex of this achievement is our knowledge of DNA, the biological thread of life. "That is why," wrote Nobel laureate Jacques Monod, "Mendel's defining of the gene as the unvarying bearer of hereditary traits, its chemical identification by Avery (confirmed by Hershey), and the elucidation by Watson and Crick of the structural basis of its replicative invariance, without any doubt constitute the most important discoveries ever made in biology. To which of course must be added the theory of natural selection, whose certainty and full significance were established only by those later discoveries."

Garrett Hardin, an ecologist at the University of California, Santa Barbara, also made a survey of great moments in biology. "History will show, I think, that the two most important dates in biology in the twentieth century (so far) are 1953, when Watson and Crick published their paper on the structure of DNA; and 1962, when Rachel Carson published *Silent Spring*. The importance of the former is universally recognized; of the latter, not." Dr. Hardin said that in 1969. In the few years since then, the importance of ecology has impressed itself upon the public.

Ecology is, literally, the other side of biology. Eugene Odum in *Fundamentals of Ecology* wrote that it is convenient to say that life is organized on ten levels: (1) biosphere; (2) ecosystems; (3) communities; (4) populations; (5) organisms; (6) organ systems; (7) organs (8) tissues; (9) cells; (10) protoplasm.

Ecology, he said, is largely concerned with the upper half of this spectrum. "Since introductory biology courses usually stop abruptly with the organism, and since in dealing with man and higher animals we are accustomed to think of the individual as the ultimate unit, the idea of a continuous spectrum may seem strange at first. However, from the standpoint of interdependence, interrelations and survival, there can be no sharp break anywhere along the line. The individual organism, for example, can not survive for long without its population any more than the organ would be able to survive for long without its organism. Similarly, the community can not exist without the cycling of materials and the flow of energy in the ecosystem."

It is equally obvious that molecular and cellular biologists concentrate on the bottom of the spectrum while biochemists usually confine their investigations to the lower half. This double focus in the way that we look at life goes back to a division in the human psyche and experience. On the one hand are the aggressiveness, daring, full-speed-ahead dynamism that have enabled us to become the dominant species on the planet. But we have also learned that sometimes there is a paper-thin line separating bravery from foolhardiness, audacity from stupidity. Human success depended no less on the ability to learn from past mistakes and to imagine future consequences in order to avoid being ambushed, mousetrapped, conned. Craftiness vouchsafed experimentation.

The emergence of ecology at this moment in history is a reassertion of this second set of human traits. In this sense, ecology is the science of wariness; the wisdom accrued from bitter lessons, from learning things the hard way. The prodigies of molecular science encourage one to glory in how much we know. They elicit human confidence, pride, a sense of omnipotence. Ecology, on the other hand, reminds us of how much we don't know. It prompts apprehension and humility.

The molecular geneticist and biochemist see that life has a chemical basis. They know of no fundamental reason why, with the proper application of chemistry, we humans will not be able both to create life and to extend it, perhaps indefinitely. Heretofore we have regarded these powers as properties of the gods. And so this branch of science seems to be offering the godhead. However, if we accept the definition of the Jain sage who replied when Alexander asked how a man could become a god, "by doing what is impossible for a man to do"—then paradoxically the godlike status recedes at the moment of attainment.

Ecology, too, aspires toward a godlike power. Ecology, said ecologist Frank Fraser Darling, is "a science of identifying causes and consequences." The ultimate goal of ecology is omniscience. Ecology aims to be a predictive science that will give us a way to foretell the consequences, all the consequences, of our actions. In plain English, to reach a point where we know what we are doing.

The difficulty of the task was attested to by Herbert York, a physicist who advised the United States government during the missile-rattling phase of the Cold War. "You know, it just isn't possible to predict that DDT is going to make a pelican's eggs have thin shells. It just can't be done. I would challenge anybody who would have predicted that he would have been able to tell you what the Los Angeles smog situation would be. The point is that the human mind is really limited in what it can do. I am perfectly willing to make a prediction that if one learns how to do genetic engineering, that this is going to cause problems. But what are these problems?"

"No one could have foreseen," says Nobel biologist Peter Medawar, "the speed and scale with which advances in medicine and public health would create a problem of overpopulation that threatens to undo much of what medical science has worked for." The intended aims and the unexpected consequences of American entry into the Vietnam conflict—from inflation at home to My Lai in South Vietnam—illustrate the state of the art at the moment . . . even in a situation where eventualities were subjected to exhaustive study. Indeed, it appears likely that human beings may never master comprehensive prediction, and René Dubos explains why: "Any attempt to shape the world and modify human personality in order to create a self-chosen pattern of life involves many unknown consequences. Human destiny is bound to remain a gamble, because at some unpredictable time and in some unforeseeable manner nature will strike back. The multiplicity of determinants which affect biological systems limits the power of the experimental method to predict their trends and behavior." Unlike the laboratory, there are too many factors to be considered in the real world. Godhood remains a remote estate.

Nevertheless, making the effort is the best we can do. We already have seen the rewards of the ecological perspective and the understanding it can introduce. We need all the wisdom we can muster because we are approaching another fork in the evolutionary road.

Evolution proceeded biologically until the human brain reached its present dimensions. Since then evolution has occurred along cultural lines. The coming decision is both social and biological. We can consciously influence what direction we take, but in order to do so we must exercise our option to decide. There will be little likelihood of rescinding the decision once made: evolution goes only one way, down the selected road.

The promise, the commitment of biological gerontology is to make the phrase "and they lived happily ever after" come true. However, molecular biologists cannot be expected to guarantee the happiness part. Their training qualifies them only for "and they lived ever after," which is another state of affairs.

From an ecological perspective, the prospect would elicit a question. "We're immortal, so what else is new?" If ecology has a basic law, it was stated by Garrett Hardin: "The practical implication of an ecological system is just this: *we can never do merely one thing.*" Barry Commoner postulated four laws of ecology, but added that in a way the first three were summed up in the fourth: "There is no such thing as a free lunch." Here is awareness that an action produces not only intended effects, but unwanted "side" effects and that there is a cost as well as a benefit to each action.

We look into the mirror and it reflects back, as ever, our image of mortality. But let us step through the looking glass into a future where people have the capability to live indefinitely. We must go this time not as a flight from reality into fantasy, but as a new Lewis and Clark expedition into uncharted country, as scouts far down an evolutionary road, in order to bring back a report to the main body of our fellows.

Some people might protest that the choice of indefinite lifespan is sensationalism, extending the argument *ad absurdum*. To answer such objections before we start: Alex Comfort is widely quoted throughout gerontology as forecasting a more modest 20 percent extension of lifespan by 1990—15 extra years. But Comfort adds, "Bearing in mind the rate of growth in biology and the intensification of the research effort that would surely follow the first and minimal human demonstration, one bonus could lead to others. . . . What is clear is that even a slight breach in the primeval human certainty that we will die between the ages of 70 and 90 will produce vast changes in our self-estimate. Show once that aging can be pushed back and, like the generation that has lived with the pill, we shall never be able to go back to the old attitudes."

Bernard Strehler has written that one way to control the rate of aging "lies in the reactivation of the controller genes that affect one's ability to make specific substances or cells needed for indefinite existence. Because the nature of these controller substances may be more simple than was previously supposed and might well be inserted in a very precise manner, the chance for a chemical modification of the maximum lifespan is probably closer to realization than most persons anticipate. . . . If we did not age—that is, if we kept the physiology of a fifteen-year-old indefinitely—the average human life-span would be in excess of 20,000 years."

Finally, we have seen in great detail that the human desire for eternal youth is deep, venerable, unflagging. Immortality, not merely some reasonable extension of lifespan, is the great expectation. Paul the apostle could only see life as through a glass, darkly; but Paul the prophet clearly foresaw that "the last enemy that shall be destroyed is death." It is time to take this motivation seriously and to begin to survey its implications.

To begin with, the form in which the elixir comes will influence our prospects for longevity. For example, there is Dr. Norman Orentreich, a busy plastic surgeon in New York City who conducts aging research on the side. He has been experimenting with plasmapheresis, a legacy from Alexis Carrel. It is like kidney dialysis except that this filtration supposedly would wash the aging toxins from the blood. Aside from inconvenience, this system would be too expensive for most people (kidney dialysis costs some $20,000 a year). The beneficiaries would be the

wealthy unless the government tried to finance such a project in order
to dispense its blessing equitably. In that case, Fort Knox would be
emptied, the U.S. Treasury bankrupted, Dr. Orentreich would become
as rich as J. Paul Getty, and the rest of us would still be as poor as
church mice—a condition not conducive to longevity.

However, Dr. Comfort assures us that the elixir "will not be luxury
medicine." Like Dr. Comfort, Dr. Strehler assures as that the elixir will
preserve us in a state neither too young nor too old, but just right. Dr.
Strehler has written a paper, "Ten Myths About Aging," in which he
demolishes fallacies about aging which he says derive from misinformed
opinions and have the important effect of slowing public funds into aging
research. He feels it is self-evident that extending healthy life means
there will be no increase of enfeebled people in society.

As for society itself: "Added years of comparative youthfulness will
not add to social problems; it may modify some problems, but the opportunity for second careers, the greater opportunities for travel and
personal enrichment, and most importantly the postponement of the
background concerns about senile illness and death will, or can, produce
a more healthful, composed and coherent society." The social worry Dr.
Comfort entertains is whether the breakthrough on aging "will catch us
unprepared to iron out preventable personal and economic side effects."

Here, then, are some of the themes on the benefits to be conferred by
extending youthful life. In general, it offers an unprecedented opportunity for personal fulfillment. The person who wants to be a mother or
father and a lover and a teacher and a researcher and a writer and a
traveler and an expatriate and an athlete and an artist and a guru will
have time enough for all these careers. The saying "Art is long and time
is fleeting" no longer will be valid.

One's first reaction to this is: Is that *all* there is to more life, simply
more of the same? No, this process will lead to the accrual of knowledge which, it is maintained, will lead to wisdom. This is the conclusion
of *Extended Youth,* a book on aging research by technological forecaster
Robert Prehoda:

> The conquest of aging . . . would give man the added years of youth
> to realize his most ambitious dreams and to achieve an education beyond
> the scope of any degree of learning possible today. If the conquest of
> senescence is the key to unlimited human knowledge, then it will also
> allow all of man's reasonable expectations of science to be achieved: the
> control of unlimited sources of energy and raw materials, the discovery
> and colonization of planets circling distant stars, and the transformation
> of our society from a pattern of war and struggle to an era of utopian
> peace. Most important of all, men would have adequate time to strive

to uncover the secrets of the natural universe and incorporate them into a philosophy that could serve as a foundation for a civilization of never-ending progress.

Music up and out, the screen goes black, the house lights go on. We put on our coats against the cold and go out once again into the real world. Francis Bacon, says René Dubos, "certainly contributed to the modern world its most characteristic aspect and its most lasting illusion when he created his utopia of happiness based on application of scientific knowledge." And in his book *The Dreams of Reason,* Dr. Dubos explains why utopias are mirages and are impractical as models for anything except the most immediate future—or as catalysts to bring about desired changes. They do not take into account such human characteristics as jealousies, emotional tensions, and all the rest; they assume acceptance of a common political philosophy; but most important they are mental efforts to freeze the Heraclitean flux, to dam the torrent of evolution. This cannot be done; even "the responses of the human mind cannot help being modified by changes in environment; however well organized society may be, these changes are inevitable, and their effects are to a large extent unpredictable. Even the dogs most carefully prepared by Pavlov lost their conditioning when their environment was suddenly altered."

The psychological impact of indefinite life extension upon each of us seems almost impossible to calculate and undoubtedly would vary with the individual. Would the thwarting of the death instinct and removal of inevitable death to some remote future cure the human neurosis divined by Norman O. Brown? Would we gradually deemphasize the past and future to settle into an eternal now? If we did, would this mean an end to seeking an ersatz immortality through achievement—an end to building monuments, writing poems, acting on behalf of posterity?

"Every gain in our ability to stave off death," Dr. Comfort says, "increases our respect for life—our own and others'." Yet in the twentieth century when the average lifespan has increased dramatically in Western societies, we have seen orgies of slaughter—two world wars, genocide, Stalin's purges, Hiroshima. Perhaps a breakthrough on aging will serve the cause of peace. Would a soldier be willing to fight for his country if he were jeopardizing 20,000 years? What cause would justify exposing a patriot to such a sacrifice? What if the situation pitted a force of soldiers from Western nations backing a just United Nations cause against the legions of a pushy dictator from a poor nation—where the fighters from the industrialized nations had access to the elixir but their foes did not? Which would be the more effective, aggressive combatants? How much would we have to pay our policemen? Would the human reservoir of courage drain away to be filled by caution?

"Greater love hath no man than this," said Christ, "that a man lay down his life for his friends." What would happen to this highest test of human fidelity? It is a quality shared by other mammals—the parents will fight to the death to save their young. Would the conditionally immortal human parent any longer be willing to make such a sacrifice? Or would he rationalize that there would be time enough to breed anew?

"Had we but world enough, and time," said the seventeenth-century poet Andrew Marvel to his coy mistress, and he would spend 100 years admiring her eyes.

> Two hundred to adore each breast,
> But thirty thousand to the rest;
> An age at least to every part,
> And the last age should show your heart.
> For, Lady, you deserve this state,
> Nor would I love at lower rate.
> But at my back I always hear
> Time's winged chariot hurrying near;
> And yonder all before us lie
> Deserts of vast eternity.

It is the scarcity of time that elevates her charms. Scarcity confers value. When wilderness was plentiful, we despised it. Now that wilderness has grown scarce we are trying desperately to preserve what remains. Suddenly millions of human beings, who had never thought about it before, hunger for wilderness as a priceless asylum for renewal. What would an eternity of time do to the quality of love? Will life still be precious?

What will we be like as free-floating organisms who no longer must work against the pressure of a limited timespan? Would we grow psychologically flabby, like the muscles of an astronaut in space?

It seems almost impossible to gauge the psychological effects of adding increments to the lifespan. One reason for this is what is known in ecology as the density-dependent factor. This rule simply is: no matter how good something is, there *always* comes a point where there is too much of a good thing. One thousand autos in the United States was an interesting novelty. One million autos, a cherished luxury. Ten million autos, spreading the enjoyment democratically. Fifty million autos, making things a bit crowded and polluted but a necessity. One hundred million autos, a menace to health and environment. Two hundred million autos, intolerable.

As the elixir mass-produces years for the human lifespan, where is the transition point? Will it take 1,000 years of musical beds; 10,000 years? Will it take 100,000 TV talk shows before each additional viewing becomes a drop in the Chinese water torture? At what stage will the sparkle of life effervesce into ennui?

Albert Rosenfeld, a science writer, has suggested a solution for this kind of problem. "Presumably no one would be required to go on living, but those who wanted to would have the option." This seems reasonable enough and indeed seems to parallel the Jain's reply to Alexander's question; How long is it good for a man to live? "As long as he does not prefer death to life," said the sage. However, it must be remembered that the Jain wise man was considering the natural conditions under which we now exist. In the brave new world, we will not be old, not be decrepit, not prodded by pain, still youthful, independent, vital, vigorous. With the biological metamorphosis comes a subtle but nonetheless drastic change. The way things work now, nature takes care of our demise. But in the promised new order the individual must deliberately choose to end his life—either through outright suicide, by exposing himself to hazards such as driving while drunk, or simply deciding to stop taking his longevity pills. But this is aberrant behavior. It goes against the instinct of self-preservation bred into us by the whole tide of evolution, goes counter to our bolstering ethics and morality. Nothing less than an act of antilife is required. How intense must the provocation become, how awful the hell, before the healthy person will opt for self-annihilation? Will death be any less cruel under such circumstances than it is now?

There is another factor to be considered under these altered circumstances. Anyone who has had to settle a squabble or cut a pie to distribute among his children knows how deeply ingrained is the human sense of fairness. Each one is content with his lot as long as everyone else gets the same. It strains credulity to believe that most human beings, no matter how distressed, will voluntarily yield such a precious commodity as life with the knowledge that their fellows do not intend to do the same. The alienated people will live if only out of resentfulness, a sense of violated justice. This produces numbers of people who are living unhappily ever after. And that produces an unstable situation. Discontented, desperate, vengeful people who no longer fear and even welcome death are the stuff of troublemakers, revolutionaries, assassins. These types are notorious for interfering with other people's longevity.

Moreover, with escalation in a person's lifespan goes inflation in the price on his life. Threats of murder and assassination will carry an infinitely higher impact and along with extortion and kidnaping will be more lucrative enterprises. What price will a person set on his own immortality? The criminal entrepreneur will be quick to revaluate this commodity.

It becomes apparent that biologists, for all their prognostications and good intentions, cannot add a day to the lifespan without the cooperation of society. The elixir of life would have little meaning for participants in World War III. Barring such an extreme event, society still must provide an environment and facilities compatible with continued existence.

The Center for the Study of Democratic Institutions held a conference on the extension of the human lifespan at Santa Barbara, California, in April 1970. The conferees took as their premise a modest increase in the lifespan of ten years. Drs. Strehler and Comfort were sanguine about such an event, but Byron Gold, acting director of the Administration on Aging's Program and Legislative Analysis Division, had this to say:

"While I am willing to accept the virtual certainty of the extension of life by science during the next 50 years, I am not at all sanguine that that American society during that same period of time will be willing, or even able, to deal with the rather profound social changes which will inevitably accompany the extension of life. . . . The history of American public policy concerning the elderly does not give much cause for confidence that, once life is extended, the resources necessary to make life something more than a struggle to stay alive will be devoted to those citizens whose lives have been extended."

Is another decade or century of marginal life a gift? Were the discoveries of Mendel, Watson and Crick, Jacob and Monod meant to provide an additional 200 years of shuffleboard? Clearly there would have to be a revolutionary change in the role of the aged.

And that's what would happen, says Richard Kalish, a professor of behavioral sciences at UCLA—for economic reasons. In a follow-up paper, he wrote, "I suspect that a sudden and unexpected increase in life span would bankrupt every retirement fund in the country and would seriously threaten the present structure of the Social Security system." Dr. Strehler has presented the positive economic consequences of extended lifespan: increased national productivity and the opportunity for each individual to extend his productive life. But there is a negative aspect: the individual no longer would have a choice in the matter. Continued work will be compulsory and dreams of leisure will fade in the light of the new economic reality. Retirement will have to be postponed and employees continue working because the middle-aged population would be unable to support a swollen, unproductive aged segment.

Workers would have to continue contributing to the national productivity for X more years, depending upon how many years were added to the lifespan.

Suspension of retirement would mean that the fellow who has worked faithfully for a quarter of a century and finally has a shot at the presidency of his company now must wait another two, five, or X number of years because the fellow ahead is not stepping down. But does this match the dismay of the worker who has been able to endure his hated boss only because his own or his boss's retirement was imminent? "The prospect of adding a decade to the average life of upper echelon managers, university professors and deans, and legislators at the state and national levels, without providing concomitant flexibility and awareness," said Dr. Kalish, "would induce me to outlaw all biological research for at least 100 years."

The dislocations hardly stop at the top. Promotions are blocked all down the line in a massive societal logjam. Society once again is faced with the problem that Social Security was engineered to remedy—providing openings for the young people flooding into the job market. Obviously there would have to be a transition into some sort of "steady state" arrangement. But how would the at least temporary stagnation affect people's attitudes? It's one thing to have to carry on when you are president of General Motors and quite another when you are working on the Chevrolet express assembly line. Of course, the rotation of jobs and the second careers mentioned by Dr. Strehler would be one solution to the tedium. But would the people with the high-paying and stimulating jobs be willing to rotate? Would Dr. Strehler take his turn in the Chevrolet plant and Dr. Comfort do his stint at garbage collection as the decades roll by?

The whole point in the mobile social-economic system we have evolved is to work your way to the top, not to be bottom. If there is one predictable occurrence, it is that people who have acquired the sinecures and prize positions will use every stratagem, artifice, ingenuity—and power—to keep their positions.

This leads to some of the most troubling of all questions in the event of extended lifespans. How will we be able to deal with the human love of power over other human beings? How will corporation presidents be dislodged from power once they are released from mortality? A considerably more frightening prospect develops when this question is transferred to the political realm. It would be illuminating to know how many votes there would have been to bestow the gift of extended life on Josef Stalin—if the balloting were restricted to the Soviet politburo. Indefinite life for the dictator would mean truncated lifespans for everyone he disliked or feared or suspected. Uncle Joe, like a queen bee, would go on and on while the workers and drones lived finite spans. Perhaps a subordinate could survive through obsequious servility. If a man has been a spiritual eunuch for a thousand years, can the molecular geneticists provide him with a new pair of balls?

Consider the power that will derive to the elixir itself. Eventually everyone will become dependent upon the pill, the treatment, or whatever, for life. Talk about addiction! Talk about a captive market! The manufacturer literally will hold the power of life and death. So will the governmental regulators. And the nations in which the product is made. And the workers who could strike and halt manufacture. With a product so precious, so potent, we can imagine the power plays, secret deals, machinations. For the first time, the power of life and death over vast numbers of people will devolve into a few hands not through overt bloody action or nuclear holocaust—merely by withholding. For these longevous people would exist only with the acquiescence of the dispensers. Would anyone willingly relegate such awesome powers to today's captains of industry?

"Let us not fail to note a painful irony," warned Leon Kass, who is executive secretary of the National Academy of Sciences' Committee on the Life Sciences and Social Policy. "Our conquest of nature has made us the slaves of blind chance. We triumph over nature's unpredictabilities only to subject ourselves to the still greater unpredictability of our capricious wills and our fickle opinions. That we have a method is no proof against our madness."

Dr. Comfort assures us that the elixir will be cheap. Can he also allay our fears that such power will not be abused? It is not cost of manufacture that sets the price, it is demand. The market for the elixir of life would bear a handsome tariff, don't you think?

Nor have the economic potentialities of such a product been overlooked. The Gottlieb Duttweiler Institute for Economic and Social Studies held an international forum on the Control of Human Aging at Zurich in September 1971. "Perhaps the most significant aspect of the meeting," wrote Gerald Leach of the *London Observer*, "is the number of people from the pharmaceutical and food industries who are here. They are the first to admit that when the biologists pull it off, there will be huge profits to be made from marketing age-slowing pills or foodstuffs."

The life insurance industry also stands to make an initial windfall, but once it dawns on people that they don't have to worry about providing for "after they're gone," the policy-writers would have to diversify in order to avoid a crash. But what about inheritance? What about all the people who have been mentally including their just legacy in plans for the children's education or a new home? What will happen to colleges that depend upon death bequests? How will the federal government compensate for the drying up of inheritance taxes? And how will it control the swollen family fortunes? Indeed, how will this turn in events effect that peculiarly human trait, acquisitiveness? As it is now with our brief tenure on the planet, people believe they "own" patches of the eternal earth. Will the grip become more spastic when they don't have to give it up? Will the gift of extended life encourage philanthropy or avarice?

Then there is the question of who will benefit from this gift of life. A biological anti-aging breakthrough will not help the millions of youngsters in deprived areas who die from the pneumonia-diarrhea complex. Such a breakthrough will benefit the haves of the world, certainly at first—those people with the intellectual, financial, and social resources to take advantage of and enjoy the extra life provided for them. Today's inequities will be compounded. Death is the great equalizer, the last equalizer. Even though a woman is a ravishing beauty who marries into power and wealth, she must die. Even though a man earns a Nobel Prize for his benefactions to mankind, he must die. Even though a Stalin has the power to liquidate millions of his fellows, he must die. Not only loved ones, but hated ones, neurotic ones, defective ones are removed. There is a certain safety and comfort and justice in this equality. But already, within limits, some people are more equal than others. The immediate effect of removing the lid will be to exaggerate the inequality.

Presumably the benefits of longevity will gradually seep to the less fortunate, as have automobiles and television sets. But by that time, and probably long before it, we all will be painfully aware of overpopulation. Drs. Strehler and Comfort both say a one-shot boost in longevity of ten to 20 years would be perfectly manageable population-wise. Of course, Dr. Comfort was overlooking his expectation that once biologists get the hang of it, they will parlay the breakthroughs.

It does not take a biological wizard to figure out that if new bodies keep arriving while the veteran inhabitants drag their feet in shuffling off to the great beyond, this place is going to fill up faster than it is now. Even without a lifespan increase, overpopulation looms as an imminent crisis for the species.[1] Overpopulation is another antidote for longevity,

[1] Calculations from the United Nations *Demographic Yearbook 1971* show that approximately 125 million persons were born that year while 50 million persons died —a year's gain of 75 million people for the world population. Elimination or postponement of those deaths would expand the increase by another two-thirds.

but, again, it is selective. The haves will be the long-lived survivors. With a prolonged spate of this, however, the have-nots could become restless and nasty.

One solution would be for the haves to use their nuclear weapons to clear a space for their own burgeoning populations. *Lebensraum* has been a cause for conflict ever since ape-men fought over the remaining groves in the receding African forest. This solution, while imaginable, is unthinkable. And only a temporary solution at that, since the inevitable human surfeit would reappear.

Shipping people to colonize the universe could hardly be expected to dent the population of stay-at-homes.

There is euthanasia, of course, but that practice conflicts with open-ended longevity.

No, there is only one solution if we intend to go on living indefinitely. Far down this evolutionary road the bill will come due for biological immortality on a finite planet: an end to children.

There will have been preparation for this eventuality. Even with the modest extension of lifespan assumed at the Santa Barbara conference, forecaster Robert Prehoda advanced the universal one-child family as the ideal way to reduce population. Gerald Feinberg, a physicist at Columbia University who has given much thought to the implications of future developments, points out that if we extend our lifespans to 200 years, even with two children, child bearing and rearing will occupy only a minor part of our lives. Even in the artificial lake of a live-forever society, there still would be a trickle of newborn coming in to replace those who go over the dam at the other end, but most people no longer would associate with children or young people.

No attempt will be made here to explore this bleak extremity, but the meaning of the loss is suggested in this passage from Erik Erikson: "The fashionable insistence on dramatizing the dependence of children on adults often blinds us to the dependence of the older generation on the younger one. Mature man needs to be needed, and maturity needs guidance as well as encouragement from what has been produced and must be taken care of."

Will some savage, as in Huxley's *Brave New World,* perceive the loss of innocence that now refreshes our lives and world? Will he search his human ingenuity for a way back to the natural paradise of the twentieth century?

For by then, it will not be nature's way, but man's way. The vehicle for continuing life will have shifted from the species to the individual. When we say women and children first to safety in time of danger, we tacitly acknowledge the overriding importance in the way that life is transmitted. If the emphasis is shifted to the individual, then women lose their privileged status and children are unnecessary. It becomes everybody for himself. And a good argument could be made that the molecular gerontologists should be first into the lifeboats, for by then society will be so dependent upon them and will have invested so much in their expertise, et cetera, et cetera.

Now we are reaching the end of the evolutionary road. In order for life to be carried forward by the ageless individual, he must continually renew himself intellectually and psychologically—just as his cells are doing physically—in order to keep adapting to the changing environment. Can we do that indefinitely? A pessimistic answer is indicated by none other than Johan Bjorksten, one of the champions of the conquest of aging. Dr. Bjorksten was explaining why it takes so long to modify scientific opinion—up to 50 years after an obviously better explanation is made available. "The reason for this long time lag is that some of the leading scientists have committed themselves to the old theories and have become so emotionally involved that they use their established authority to resist, to the limit, acceptance of the new theory. Max Planck, the great physicist, said that the only way for a new theory to become accepted is for the adherents of the old theories to die."

Such a practiced visionary as Arthur Clarke says: "Death (though not aging) is obviously essential for progress, both social and biological. Even if it did not perish from overpopulation, a world of immortals would soon stagnate. In every sphere of human activity, one can find examples of the stultifying influence of men who have outlived their usefulness. Yet death—like sleep—does not appear to be biologically inevitable, even if it is an evolutionary necessity."

If the conquest of death is biologically attainable, would we human beings give up this ancient dream voluntarily? Even if to persist risks terminating the species? *Is* the price too high? After all, we, the members of the final generation, would be the ones taking this last fling.

X. Dialectic

"If we are indeed facing a sudden new extension of the life-span, with a dramatic new increase in the proportions of the old, will industrialized societies be more ready than before, and better prepared? The problems will be enormous," says social gerontologist Bernice Neugarten. "If the average life-span were to go beyond 100, especially if this were to occur in the relatively short period of a few decades, the effects upon the social fabric are presently unforeseeable. Few social scientists and even fewer biological scientists have given serious thought to the social implications."

Extending the human lifespan is not the problem that concerns Ewald Busse, who has served as director of the gerontology center at Duke University and as president of the American Psychiatric Association. "What worries me is *then* what would we do? Let's not get caught again in scientific advances without sensible planning to cope with advances in technology."

When it comes to the wider issue of genetic engineering, foreboding has been expressed by James Watson, one of the fathers of the genetic revolution. Unless questions raised by the possible uses of our new powers are dealt with now, he has said, "the possibility of our having a free choice will one day suddenly be gone."

Leon Kass is a molecular biologist who has been speaking out from within the National Academy of Sciences about the potential consequences of biological engineering. Heretofore, Dr. Kass has pointed out, our interventions have been restricted to external nature. To tamper with our own intrinsic nature is to embark on a blind adventure. "Thus, engineering the engineer as well as the engine, we race our train we know not where."

"I am as worried as anyone about the idiotic misuse of technology," Alex Comfort says. "But the potential misuse of aging research doesn't keep me awake at night. If it did, I wouldn't devote my time to it." What bothers Dr. Comfort is the "possibility of anguished and unproductive argument between a naturalist view (that turnover is a good in itself, which should not be 'resisted' by the individual out of a selfish desire to survive) and the general humanist position, that the quintessence of respect for people is to preserve them as individuals as long as possible. This argument has been obscured in the past by the imperfect character of the attainable preservation. Fortunately for the humanist view (which I, for unconscious as well as conscious reasons, hold to be the right one), the Rubicon of an initial systems breakthrough is highly likely to be passed before the argument becomes general. Thus, as in the case of birth control, Hudibrastic arguments will come too late, long after general-public acceptance."

There are several confusions and assumptions in the above statement which must be delineated if we are to come to grips with the issues raised. To begin with, it is crucially important today for everyone to know, and for scientists to remind themselves, what is the purpose of science. The purpose of science is to *understand* nature.

"[I]t was not until about four generations ago," historian Lynn White, Jr. writes in "The Historical Roots of Our Ecological Crisis," "that Western Europe and North America arranged a marriage between science and technology, a union of the theoretical and the empirical approaches to our natural environment. The emergence in widespread practice of the Baconian creed that scientific knowledge means technological power over nature can scarcely be dated before 1850, save in the chemical industries, where it is anticipated in the 18th century. Its acceptance as a normal pattern of action may mark the greatest event in human history since the invention of agriculture, and perhaps in nonhuman terrestrial history as well."

By definition, to say that knowledge must be used automatically to intervene in natural processes—to substitute control of nature as the purpose—is a perversion of science. Moreover, there is a key omission in the abbreviated version of "science discovers—technology implements." The equation should be "science discovers—society decides if the knowledge is to be used and if so, how it is to be used—technology implements." Dr. Comfort chose an apt metaphor in crossing the Rubicon because he is talking about the usurpation of authority. The legitimate arbiter of the use of scientific knowledge is society—our duly elected representatives, our various institutions, ordinary citizens, you and I. The significance of the ecological-consumer revolution is precisely this awakening by society to the realization that while science and technology are in bed together, the public is out in the cold. The price of a laissez-faire attitude toward science and technology is chemical hot dogs, mother's milk laced with DDT, and a glut of dangerous drugs. Society now shows a determination to resist this kind of tyranny.

There is yet a further assumption in Dr. Comfort's statement, the "inevitability" thesis. Scientific information must be used, shall be used "because it is there." The SST affair shows that society is becoming more discriminating in what it accepts as inevitable.

Having said this, there can be little doubt that a scientific breakthrough on life extension will be put into effect; it will be inevitable. Even though I suggested unpalatable consequences of a lengthy prolongation of lifespan, I imagine that I, too, will be on line along with everybody else when biologists start handing out more life. We'll all be back for a second helping, and a third, for just as long as it lasts, smiling sweetly, "Don't mind if I do." *Todos queremos mas* goes a Spanish song, "we all want more." We will have unleashed a process unstoppable by any social restraints because it will be propelled by the self-interest of each of us.

It is because of this irrestistibility that we should consider such a prospect now—while it is still academic—and wonder how we can deal with it. And try to keep our options open to use new information wisely. Any process that is out of human control is under the control of nature. Overpopulation and underevolution are two more obvious natural restraints. Presumably we would be able to guard against them somehow. The enemy most feared by a fighter pilot is the plane coming out of the sun. Ecological disaster, almost by definition, is the consequence we cannot foresee. It is its nature to be a Trojan horse. Like irrigation to ancient Babylon, the Trojan horse first appeared as a gift.

Is human imagination equal to canvass the possibilities? "We have always quested for immortality," said Jonas Salk, "but are we asking how long a person *should* live?" No one is asking that question, he said. His answer is that a person should live as long as the capacity built into his genes. But Dr. Salk did not go on to wonder what it means if immortality is built into his genes.

James Carse, chairman of the History of Religion Department at New York University, who recently taught a course on "The Meaning of Death," has thought about such a possibility. Dr. Carse, an existentialist, says, "Immortality must be avoided. Death is the source of meaning. If you could live forever, life would be meaningless. Death is the source of man. There is no self without death."

It is true that biographies would have no endings. There would be no summation to people's lives. We would just go on and on. Would such a state be the death of meaning? Would we, eventually, lose track of who we are? If Dr. Carse is correct, then here is a true dilemma. For loss of self is the great penalty of death. Preservation of self is the point of immortality, isn't it?

A half century ago, Alfred North Whitehead foresaw the central dilemma of our times. Whitehead was a brilliant British mathematician who wrote the monumental *Principia Mathematica* with Bertrand Russell and then later in his career became a philosopher and came to Harvard University. In the Lowell Lectures delivered in 1925 and published in the book *Science and the Modern World,* Dr. Whitehead saw that science had won the field from religion and philosophy. The weapon system of victory was the strategic insistence that truth could be got at only through the method of quantitative, verifiable objectivity coupled with the tactical persuaders: the works of technology.

The strategy, Whitehead knew, was vulnerable; but he also knew that it was protected by the tangible achievements, which were invulnerable because so highly valued by most people. The general success of science, Whitehead said, has "made it impervious to criticism." Science, religion, and philosophy, it must be remembered, are abstractions for different methods of thinking and of looking at reality. But the intellectual triumph of science produced a very real consequence. Ever greater proportions of the brightest people enlisted under the banners of science. The out-gunned defenders of the other faiths were further intimidated. The rout was completed with big battalions. In the half century since Whitehead spoke, we have seen the steady attenuation of religion while philosophy has retreated out of sight of most people and today has little bearing on lives in Western societies (the effect of Existentialism in France is an exception).

So when philosopher Whitehead spoke at Cambridge, Massachusetts, in 1925, it was a last stand, the Sioux at Wounded Knee. He clearly grasped the historical forces unleashed when the visions of Copernicus, Galileo, and Vesalius exploded against the stationary world of the sixteenth century. Once started, nothing could quench the passion for new truths about nature and reality, although as human beings will, people in entrenched authority resisted the challenges every step of the way. Treaties were negotiated, jurisdictions staked out. But once scientists were able to put into practice the advice of Francis Bacon, science became irresistible. Enough of this eternal talk, Bacon had told the philosophers. It is time to put knowledge to work for human welfare —by your works shall they know you. Those who could became scientists, those who could not remained philosophers and theologians.

Philosopher Whitehead stood up against the juggernaut, knowing he could not stop it and suspecting it might bury him. Still, with the philosopher's slingshot he hurled words at the armor, and struck the chink in impervious science.

This weakness is so subtle that until recently it escaped the attention of almost everybody. It did not matter as long as science *was* successful. Only when clinkers began showing up along with the good works did science itself publicly confess to Whitehead's indictment.

Science does its job, Whitehead said, whatever the job is—isolating an effect, discovering a cause, establishing a relationship—by simplifying. This makes sense because the sheer bulk of phenomena, the overwhelming numbers of factors are too great for the human mind to grapple with *in toto* (in this regard, it can be appreciated how computer technology has extended scientific capability). Simplification is achieved either by arbitrarily circumscribing the area of investigation or by abstracting; that is, sloughing off extraneous factors until only essentials remain—until a Koch, for instance, has eliminated all the microscopic organisms except the bacillus that causes tuberculosis.

The flaw in the method does not show up as long as the situation remains relatively simple. The troubles appear when one starts applying limited scientific truth to complex situations, particularly to large ecological systems and human affairs. Not only do the chances for erroneous conclusions increase, but even if an investigator has accurately postulated a truth, it is unlikely to be the whole truth. There is the constant hazard that the serviceable limited truth may turn out to be an insidious half truth.

In spelling out the pitfalls of placing total reliance on the scientific method, Whitehead anticipated future shock. It would be brought about, he explained, through the reductionist technique of creating specialists in limited areas of thought, through the professionalization of knowledge. "Professionals are not new to the world. But in the past, professionals have formed unprogressive castes. The point is that professionalism has now been mated with progress. The world is now faced with a self-evolving system, which it cannot stop." Such is the rate of progress "that an individual human being, of ordinary length of life, will be called upon to face novel situations which find no parallel in the past. The fixed person for the fixed duties, who in older societies was such a godsend, in the future will be a public danger." The advantages of training experts are so obvious that our society has committed itself singlemindedly to this course. Whitehead pointed to the disadvantages. By the very nature of this exclusive concentration, this voluntary restriction of thought, this deliberate distortion of perspective, the expert becomes professionally incompetent outside his specialty. It is like the karate expert who toughens and hardens his hands until he has honed a pair of protoplasmic clubs. They are powerful instruments for what they are designed to do —break a spine. But those hands are of little use for other things, and certainly cannot produce music.

The uncalculated loss for society in the expert strategy, said Whitehead, is that the "leading intellects lack balance. They see this set of circumstances, or that set; but not both sets together. The task of coordination is left to those who lack either the force or the character to succeed in some definite career. In short, the specialized functions of the community are performed better and more progressively, but the generalized direction lacks vision. The progressiveness in detail only adds to the danger produced by the feebleness of coordination."

There are other shortcomings. As the scientist abstracts within his own field, there is a tendency to forget about banished factors even though they may require readmittance. "[T]he abstraction abstracts from something to which no further attention is paid. But there is no groove of abstraction which is adequate for the comprehension of human life. Thus in the modern world, the celibacy of the medieval learned class has been replaced by a celibacy of the intellect which is divorced from the concrete contemplation of the complete facts."

Moreover, because the human being has such a proclivity for symbolism there is a tendency for everyone—scientist and layman—to mistake the abstraction for the real thing, the dehydrated soup particles for the whole cup of broth, the formula for life. "It is very arguable that the science of political economy, as studied in its first period after the death of Adam Smith (1790), did more harm than good. It destroyed many economic fallacies, and taught how to think about the economic revolution then in progress. But it riveted on men a certain set of abstractions which were disastrous in their influence on modern mentality. It dehumanized industry." Since we interchange money and resources, we believe or at least behave as though they are equivalent; the disappearance of a resource (potable water, for instance) would quickly correct this misimpression.

Human beings are inclined to confuse abstractions in still another way. Whitehead called it the "Fallacy of Misplaced Concreteness," which can lead to inaccurate interpretations of reality. We have concretized time with hourglasses, clocks, and calendars. We know very well what time is in our own little corner of the universe. It is a function of the earth's rotation and revolution—our planet's relationship to the sun. But when we move out of the fixed Newtonian universe into the Einsteinian cosmos of relativity where there is no base relationship against which to measure everything else, our serviceable limited truth fails us and the concept of time becomes almost too elusive to grasp. Time is no more a thing than length or depth is a thing.

Bernard Strehler in *Time, Cells, and Aging* finally could tell "before" and "after" only by degrees of entropy. Entropy is a concept from thermodynamics (also used in information theory), a measurement of randomness or lack of organization. It is a consequence of the second law of thermodynamics which says that heat—energy—tends to be distributed uniformly. Thus our sun disperses its concentrated energy thinly into space in a one-way process. According to the second law, energy will become evenly distributed throughout the cosmos so that there will be complete randomness, no predictable relationships, no semblance of organization. That will be the end of time as a dimension.

While this disintegration is taking place on the total macrocosmic scale, it does not proceed linearly. As we know, matter still is coalescing to form stars, and the birth and development of a living creature is the creation of order out of randomness. However, these organizations are achieved without breaking the second law. The energy debt is paid with the result that despite the local packet of order the total amount of disorder is increased. And eventually, of course, the organizations dissolve. In the living organizations we call organisms this dissolution is death.

But what is death? We all know what it is. But, according to Robert Morison, professor of science and society at Cornell University, there is no such thing as death. Not only have we concretized this abstraction, he says, but we have even personified it. From "death (a thing) comes for the archbishop," we graduate to "a jostling woman in the marketplace of Baghdad or an old man, complete with beard, scythe, and hourglass, ready to mow down those whose time has come." Professor Morison says he has no wish to execute such poetic figures, but merely to point out that such modes of thinking interfere with our realizing that death is not an entity.

Death, we know, is the cessation of functions—breathing, heartbeat, brain control, metabolism. It is also the disappearance of more intangible characteristics—consciousness, a particular set of memories, a self. This is followed by structural disintegration. In a complex organism, such as a human being, the shutdown of functions proceeds unevenly—nerve cells die a few minutes after circulation stops, for example, whereas cartilage cells remain alive for several days. Everyone agrees, however, that a corpse cannot be considered alive merely because some of its cells still are living. Death is the irreversible disruption of the highest levels of a being's organization.

While we can readily distinguish between a dead person and a living one, we have great difficulty in determining the point of transition and usually arbitrarily assign it. It is still impossible for scientists to tell when a cell dies. They can only tell a dead cell from a living one after observing the telltale structural deterioration. Because inanimation is not an absolute sign of death, some people in the days of more primitive medicine wrote into their wills the provision that they were not to be buried until after their bodies began to putrefy—so great was their fear of being buried alive.

It becomes apparent that we know death only as a negative aspect of life. A dead body, in distinction from an inanimate body, is one that once was living but from which life has disappeared.

All right, then, what is life? "Life," Professor Morison reminds us, "is not a thing or a fluid anymore than heat is." What we observe are objects with a peculiar set of properties. "These objects we elect to call 'living things.' From here, it is but a short step to the invention of a hypothetical entity that is supposed to account for the difference between living and nonliving things. We might call this entity 'livingness,' following the usual rule for making abstract nouns out of participles and adjectives. This sounds rather awkward, so we use the world 'life' instead. This apparently tiny change in the shape of the noun helps us on our way to philosophical error." The noun seduces us into thinking of something "quite apart from the particular objects it characterizes. Men thus find themselves thinking more and more about life as a thing in itself, capable of entering inanimate aggregations of material and turning them into living things."

Philip Morrison, a physicist at the Massachusetts Institute of Technology, predicts that we will create two new kinds of life in the foreseeable future—life forms fashioned in test tubes by biologists using off-the-shelf chemicals and a form of machine life that will be an outgrowth of today's computer science. *New York Times* science writer Boyce Rensberger commented in his report of this prediction: "To think of a highly complex machine as a form of life is not so unthinkable as it once was for the traditional definitions of life are now quite shaky. . . . The essentials are functions and not forms. If wires and magnets and transistors can be made to function in ways analogous to the function of nerve fibers and protoplasm, are they not just as much alive?"

This question introduces still another inadequacy and signifies the ultimate ineffectuality of the analytical technique by itself to comprehend reality. We know what life is. We know it by what we feel, by what we observe, and from our instinctual heritage. We know life in the most immediate way possible, by experiencing it. We have buttressed this knowledge with the observations, insights, judgments of wise people who have gone before us; these guides are accumulated in such documents as the Bible, the Talmud, the Koran, the plays of Shakespeare, the writings of Thoreau and Emerson, and so on. Even biology at one time could give us a sure idea of what life is. The entry from the College Outline Series still includes such standard characteristics as organization, metabolism, growth, reproduction, irritability, adaptation. But accretion of knowledge has eroded the certainty.

"One would think that the nature of life would be easy to define since we are all experiencing it," Nobel biochemist Wendell Stanley wrote as early as 1957. "However, just as life means different things to different people, we find that in reality it is extremely difficult to define just what we mean by life or by a living agent in its most simple form. There is no difficulty in recognizing an agent as living or nonliving as long as we contemplate structures such as man, cats, dogs or even small organisms such as bacteria or at the other extreme, structures such as a piece of iron or glass, an atom of hydrogen, or even a molecule of water, sugar or of our blood pigment, hemoglobin."

The difficulty arises when one reaches the edge of life, where Dr. Stanley had been exploring—with the viruses. A virus is a relatively simple (by life standards) organization of nucleic acid and protein that is both alive and not-alive, depending on the time and circumstances. Dried out viruses will join in a symmetrical pattern to form a crystal. But, unlike a crystal of salt, when placed in solution in the presence of living cells, these molecules spring to life, inject the virus DNA or RNA into cells, and commandeer the cellular materials to reproduce more viruses.

"Viruses were discovered by virtue of their ability to replicate, and in the last analysis this ability to reproduce remains today as the only definitive way in which they can be recognized." Stanley concluded: "The essence of life is the ability to reproduce. This is accomplished by the utilization of energy to create order out of disorder, to bring together into a specific predetermined pattern from semi-order or even chaos all the component parts of that pattern with the perpetuation of that pattern with time. This is life."

Dr. Stanley added that there is another basic property to life, although he did not believe it is absolutely necessary, and that is the ability to mutate and preserve the changes through reproduction. While perhaps not essential, Dr. Stanley said, "it certainly lends grandeur to life, for not only is it responsible for the whole evolutionary process and thus for the myriad kinds of life we have on earth but. most important for mankind, it permits one to dare to aspire. It is presumably responsible for man, his conscience and his faith."

The first of several definitions of life in *Biology and the Future of Man*, published in 1970 and whose various sections were contributed by leaders in their field, says: "A living organism is an entity that can utilize chemicals and energy from the environment to reproduce itself, can undergo a permanent change (a mutation) which is transmitted to succeeding generations, and by accumulation of numbers of such mutations can evolve into a distinctly new living form (a new species)."

Most of these qualities are not exclusive, however. A flame uses chemicals and energy from its surrounding environment in order to grow and can reproduce itself through sparks. It cannot mutate, however, and perhaps we should be grateful for that. Even though we speak of the spark of life, we can readily distinguish between a flame and life. Crystals, though, also can grow and reproduce themselves. And when those crystals are viruses, the physical dividing line between living and non-living things disappears; it is only a temporal frontier.

What *does* distinguish the nonliving molecular structure from the same organization of molecules alive? What *is* the essence of life? It turns out that the essential quality of life is the one Dr. Stanley believed desirable but not absolutely necessary. Like fire, crystals are unable to mutate and preserve the change through reproduction. Nonliving things are immutable. And so another definition of life in *Biology and the Future of Man* reads: "the unique attribute of living matter, from which all of its other remarkable features derive, is its capacity for self-duplication with mutation. . . . nonliving systems, being immutable, are incapable of evolution. Living things, on the other hand, are endowed with a seemingly infinite capacity to adapt themselves to the exigencies of existence. The endless variety and complexity of living organisms, the apparent purposefulness of their structure and behavior, are consequences of their mutability."

Talk of purposefulness begins to sound like God, and Aristotle's teleology that life is developing toward some predestined goal. Jacques Monod in his 1971 book *Chance and Necessity* set out to explain that purposefulness and at the same time to give the molecular biologist's answer to the question, What is life? The reductionist technique is pushed to the ultimate. Life is analyzed at its foundations upon inanimate chemicals.

Living things are strange objects in the universe of things, Dr. Monod begins. We know they are different, but how can we tell them apart from nonliving things? He decides to compare living objects with machines, since both are purposive entities. We see that it is extremely difficult to separate living things from sophisticated machines we can build today. But there are ways. For one, machines cannot build themselves; living things are self-constructing machines. However, crystals (another order of nonliving things) also can grow, so there is only a difference of degree in this characteristic. Second, machines cannot make other machines in their own image; living things are self-reproducing machines. Again, crystals also can reproduce.

But the third difference is shared by neither machines nor any other order of nonliving things. Machines are made by living things for particular purposes. Living things make themselves but their purpose (or the purposes of their organs and parts) is not superimposed from some predestined plan; rather, it is a product of the development. The human organism was not created, it is the revelation of evolution. That is Dr. Monod's answer to theists and Aristotelians.

An eye and a camera are similar in the ways they function and what they are meant to do, but they got that way by two extremely different routes. In a luminous exposition of the molecular realm, the Nobel laureate shows how function can grow out of structure. Each new kind of molecule, formed by pure chance, takes a particular configuration which is ordained by its particular atomic arrangement. These specific configurations influence—determine—the chemical activities and the structures of life. If some new arrangement is harmful, it is discarded. But when the change is beneficial, it is preserved and passed along. "A *totally* blind process," writes Dr. Monod, "can by definition lead to anything; it can even lead to vision itself."

Life might "appear to transcend the laws of chemistry if not to ignore them altogether," Dr. Monod says, but "it is in the structure of these molecules that one must see the ultimate source of the autonomy, or more precisely, the self-determination that characterizes living beings in their behavior." Biophysicist Robert Sinsheimer presented this view more concisely when he said, "Life is but a property of matter in a certain state of organization." And so the third definition of life in *Biology and the Future of Man,* the one supplied by molecular biologists, is: "life is the expression of the surface properties of the biopolymers."

This is the empty prize brought back by the reductionist expedition to the center of life. If one takes an electron microscope to search for ultimate reality at the core of matter, one finally comes to—nothing, the spaces between atoms. Prosecution of this strategy will lead to the state on the other side of the looking glass where the life scientists will be able to tell us everything we care to know about life, but no longer will know what it is they are talking about.

When it comes to understanding life, science no longer is sovereign. It must take its place along with more traditional methods to explore the texture which shields us from life's nothingness.

"Life," said another Nobel laureate, the Russian poet and novelist Boris Pasternak in *Dr. Zhivago,* "is not a material, but the principle of self-renewal. It is constantly renewing and remaking and changing and transfiguring itself." Here, from an entirely different perspective, is a restatement of biological mutability. Nineteenth-century evolutionist

August Weismann pondered the immortality of one-celled organisms. While there was no death, the individuals continually were changing. A part of each individual lives on, he observed, "but is it one and the same substance which continues to live? Does not life, here and everywhere else, depend on assimilation, that is on a constant change of material? What then is immortal? Apparently not a substance at all, but a certain form of motion." Alfred North Whitehead, from the route of philosophy, arrives at the same place. Life is not the atoms of Democritus, but the flux of Heraclitus. Life is process. Life *is* evolution.

If one accepts this view that life is a process of renewing and transfiguring, then to extend the life of an individual, indefinitely if possible, becomes at some point an act of antilife. That will be the dilemma for the looking-glass world of immortals: no matter what policy they adopt, it will be at the same time both for and against life.

To return to the dilemma of our own times, Whitehead targeted still another, crucial way that science abstracts in order to reach verifiable objective truth. Science omits value judgments—the priorities of society, ethics of philosophy, morality of religion. Such factors are not amenable to quantitative objectivity; they are qualities and subjective. How can one objectify good and evil when one man's good may be another man's evil? Scientists, therefore, said: "Ethics and such value judgments are outside our jurisdiction. We will be content to describe all of objective reality and leave ethics, morality, and social priorities to other spheres of human activity." Of course, what scientists told us about reality could color or change the values that guide our behavior.

The statements that "Life is the expression of the surface properties of the biopolymers" or "Life is but a property of matter in a certain state of organization" are perhaps as close as scientists can come to objectifying its quality. Those statements are sterilized of value judgments. Examine them as we will, we can get no hint if life is good, bad, or indifferent. Strain as we might, there is no clue to what life is all about. Total silence as to what life means. It is right here that we can appreciate the enormity of the sacrifice scientists have made in order to reach objective truth, the dimensions of their vows of poverty. Those statements about life are emptied of meaning for us. They tell us almost nothing about life, and what they do tell us God said first in Genesis: ". . . for dust thou art . . . ."

Although those statements are devoid of values, they are not neutral. Men and women, who inescapably live by and act according to values, can clearly infer from those statements that life has no meaning. Values may be sanitized from scientific knowledge, but as soon as knowledge approaches human affairs the contamination appears. The interplay of the two realms was illustrated as clergymen and scientists discussed the import of biomedical engineering in a CBS News Special, "Science and Religion: Who Will Play God?" broadcast in January 1968.

Dr. C. Walton Lillehei, a cardiovascular surgeon at Cornell Medical Center in New York City, was asked if he welcomed recent heart transplant operations. He replied: "Yes, I think this is another dramatic but definite advance in surgical management of human disease."

Dr. Harvey Cox of Harvard Divinity School agreed that donating an organ was a new way for humans to share valuable things with one another, but went on to say that what does trouble him "is why we have these more or less sensational advances in certain things like advanced surgery whereas the infant mortality rate, for example, in the United States remains so embarrassingly high. That is, why can't we have our technological imagination more directed toward the distribution of the medical services that we have rather than these spectacular things that may work for three or four people."

John, now Cardinal, Wright of Pittsburgh observed: "I think the explanation is very natural and probably altogether too natural. The generation that's doing the experimenting is the generation that managed to get itself born, and naturally it wants to preserve itself in existence."

Biologist James Bonner of the California Institute of Technology discussed genetic intervention, then said, "I would think that in the future and long before we artificially rearrange DNA molecules of the genes and chromosomes, programs of deliberate selection of human beings for desired qualities will be instituted. There are some characteristics of human beings that I think all of us could agree are desirable, like longevity, which has distinct hereditary components, and freedom from hereditary diseases, intelligence of certain kinds and perhaps non-aggressiveness." Anyway, he assured his listeners, some nation would try it soon and that would force other countries to upgrade their people or disappear into a backwash.

Said the then Bishop Wright: "Might breed out blind Homer, too, and that worries me very much indeed. And that's why I would hope that the genetics' norm and ideal patent would never be isolated from the cultural, political, moral and other values which protect us against that most ancient of fallacies: whatever is true is lawful, whatever can be done should be experimented with."

Dr. Cox added: "That's why I think it's wrong to say that anything is inevitable. I think to say anything is inevitable is really to say there's a kind of fate or Kismet which is moving us along and that we're not free human beings who can decide whether to do something and how to do it."

Drs. Bonner and Lillehei tried to reassure the theologians that diversity would be provided and by definition a race of supermen could solve all the problems troubling the present panel.

"What disturbs me about the whole prospect," said Dr. Franklin Clark Fry, president of the Lutheran Church in America, "is that the first evidences of this kind of change of personality have been in the wrong direction, haven't they? I mean the brainwashing techniques that have been developed that seem to change personality rather radically and so far for the worst. I just don't have the confidence in the integrity of the human being. I know something about what we in religion call sin. I'm keenly under the awareness of the ambiguity of human character and of human life. And when anyone gets right into the person and attempts to manipulate a man's personhood, he is taking upon himself a responsibility that I don't—that I know I'm not fit to undertake and that I gravely suspect the other man is not fit to do either."

The dream of biomedical engineering was expressed by biophysicist Robert Sinsheimer in a talk to a group of medical doctors. "For physicians it has been the better part of wisdom since Hippocrates to acknowledge that each cell in the body is far better informed as to its function than we are in any conscious sphere—and that the genius of innate homeostasis, accumulated in the long course of evolution, far exceeds our capacities to intervene. And thus derived the well-founded belief in the healing power of nature, if not tried too sorely, and the wisdom of the physician's restraint—his bent to facilitate the natural recovery."

But today's biochemical knowledge, Dr. Sinsheimer said, "is now providing us an insight into the substance and nature of life, into the genesis and pattern of functions—and malfunction—that can begin to bear comparison with the silent wisdom of the body. In this conscious knowledge, infused with intelligence, are the seeds of a newer medicine, a medicine impelled to a more active philosophy that will—soberly and thoughtfully, but deliberately—seek to improve upon nature's design."

And Dr. Comfort on a biological breakthrough in extending longevity: "It would represent the first instance in which science can be said to produce an artificial betterment of biological function, as against the best observed natural performance."

It remains for another biological scientist, Leon Kass of the National Academy of Sciences, to draw up the balance sheet and present the moral implications of presuming to meddle with intrinsic human biology. "Modern biology, and modern science in general, is fundamentally materialist and value-free. It rejects the idea that man has an inherent purpose or that science has anything to say about the good for man. These scientific notions are held to be vindicated and validated by the technological triumphs which they make possible. Here perhaps is the most pernicious result of advances in biomedical technology—more dehumanizing than any actual manipulation or technique, present or future. We are witnessing the erosion, perhaps the final erosion, of the idea of man as something splendid or divine, and its replacement with a view that sees man, no less than nature, simply as more raw material for manipulation and homogenization. Hence, our peculiar moral crisis."

"It is perfectly true that science outrages values," Jacques Monod writes. "Not directly, since science is no judge of them and *must* ignore them; but it subverts every one of the mythical or philosophical ontogenies upon which the animist tradition, from the Australian aborigines to the dialectical materialists, has made all ethics rest: values, duties, right, prohibitions." Science has the "terrible capacity to destroy not only bodies but the soul itself."

So the effects of science go beyond its proper sphere to influence those values which science says it is not qualified to deal with in the first place. The scrupulous refusal or impotent inability of scientists to find values in reality has conspired with the irresistible success of science to produce today's soul-shattering nihilism.

Our dilemma is that science is the best single method we have discovered for dealing with reality, but the intellectual order is purchased at increasing entropy of values. For scientific knowledge, we must trade our integrity. At the end of the process lies knowing everything, believing nothing. At the end: demoralization and dehumanization. Dr. Monod has lucidly presented the nature of our Faustian bargain:

"Modern societies are built upon science. They owe it their wealth, their power, and the certitude that tomorrow far greater wealth and power still will be ours if we so wish. But there is this too: just as an initial 'choice' in the biological evolution of a species can be binding upon its entire future, so the choice of scientific *practice*, an unconscious choice in the beginning, has launched the evolution of culture on a one-way path; onto a track which nineteenth-century scientism saw leading infallibly upward to an empyrean noon hour for mankind, whereas what we see opening before us today is an abyss of darkness."

Our problem is: How can we continue to procure the knowledge we will need to save ourselves without destroying ourselves?

Dilemmas cannot be solved with knowledge alone. What is required is wisdom. "Wisdom," said Whitehead, "is the fruit of a balanced development." The fruit of traditional science, which is deliberately unbalanced, is only knowledge. We cannot look to traditional science alone to solve our dilemmas.

It might be well at this point to review our long journey of thought, so that we may get a better fix on our direction. Sir James Frazer, at the end of his anthropological study of primitive thought and practice, *The Golden Bough,* summarized a similar excursion. This was in 1922, shortly before the Whitehead lectures:

> If then we consider, on the one hand, the essential similarity of man's chief wants everywhere and at all times, and on the other hand, the wide differences between the means he has adopted to satisfy them in different ages, we shall perhaps be disposed to conclude that the movement of the higher thought, so far as we can trace it, has on the whole been from magic through religion to science. In magic man depends on his own strength to meet the difficulties and dangers that beset him on every side. He believes in a certain established order of nature on which he can surely count, and which he can manipulate for his own ends. When he discovers his mistake, when he recognizes sadly that both the order of nature which he had assumed and the control which he had believed himself to exercise over it were purely imaginary, he ceases to rely on his own intelligence and his own unaided efforts, and throws himself humbly on the mercy of certain great invisible beings behind the veil of nature, to whom he now ascribes all those far-reaching powers which he once arrogated to himself. Thus in the acuter minds magic is gradually superseded by religion, which explains the succession of natural phenomena as regulated by the will, the passion, or the caprice of spiritual beings like man in kind, though vastly superior to him in power.
>
> But as time goes on this explanation in its turn proves to be unsatisfactory. For it assumes that the succession of natural events is not determined by immutable laws, but is to some extent variable and irregular, and this assumption is not borne out by closer observation. . . . Thus the keener minds, still pressing forward to a deeper solution of the mysteries of the universe, come to reject the religious theory of nature as inadequate, and to revert in a measure to the older standpoint of magic by postulating explicitly, what in magic had only been implicitly assumed, to wit, an inflexible regularity in the order of natural events, which, if carefully observed, enables us to foresee their course with certainty and to act accordingly. In short, religion, regarded as an explanation of nature, is displaced by science.
>
> But while science has this much in common with magic that both rest on a faith in order as the underlying principle of all things . . . the order on which magic reckons is merely an extension, by false analogy, of the order in which ideas present themselves to our minds, the order laid down by science is derived from patient and exact observation of the phenomena themselves. The abundance, the solidity, and the splendour of the results already achieved by science are well fitted to inspire us with a cheerful confidence in the soundness of the method. . . .

Yet the history of thought should warn us against concluding that because the scientific theory of the world is the best that has yet been formulated, it is necessarily complete and final. We must remember that at bottom the generalisations of science or, in common parlance, the laws of nature are merely hypotheses devised to explain that ever-shifting phantasmagoria of thought which we dignify with the high-sounding names of the world and the universe. In the last analysis magic, religion, and science are nothing but theories of thought; and as science has supplanted its predecessors, so it may hereafter be itself superseded by some more perfect hypothesis, perhaps by some totally different way of looking at the phenomena—of registering the shadows on the screen.

Among the persons most deeply concerned by the conflict between scientific knowledge and values have been scientists themselves. This soul searching began with work on the atomic bomb and realization of the implications of putting such tremendous physical power into shaky human hands. The issue gained impetus with the discovery of radioactive fallout from nuclear testing. It never occurred to nuclear physicists to worry about such an eventuality. They are not geared or qualified to consider the pervasive effect of bombs on biological systems. So who could blame them? That is one of the beauties of specialization for the practitioner and, as Whitehead cautioned, one of the penalties for society. A few scientists began to speak out on the ethics of continued testing of nuclear weapons.

But the breakthrough was Rachel Carson's *Silent Spring*. Here was a scientist using science for, committing it to, a value—the integrity of nature, the diversity upon which that integrity depends, and the human welfare which the integrity supports. As if by some magic, some mental prestidigitation, the scientific pursuit of knowledge had been merged with values, and ethics. Although no one quite realized it at the time, the revolutionary import of the book was that it crumbled the proud tradition that segregated knowledge and ethics, a tradition which bestowed upon scientists the luxurious estate of moral irresponsibility for their professional work. For the first time, the public could judge who is right and who is wrong—not in the scientific sense of correct and incorrect, for that issue could be obfuscated with scientese—but who is right and wrong morally. That is why there was enacted the National Environmental Policy Act. The law is a political and legal embodiment of the new ethical code that we must respect the integrity of nature, and if we intend to interfere, then we must carefully examine the consequences of what we propose to do. Eventually, even scientific curiosity lost its immunity to moral judgment, as witness the public reaction to experiments with germ warfare.

By observing the devastating impact of DDT and other chlorinated hydrocarbons upon wildlife—the disenfranchised of our land—Miss Carson was putting back into the model factors that had been subtracted and forgotten by chemists, entomologists, and their employers. Miss Carson was a sapper who undermined the tight little paradigm of never-ending improvements and always-escalating profits of the agrochemical industry. She also helped the American people to read a little better the camouflage of their economic predators. The scientific establishment never forgave Rachel Carson for *Silent Spring*, which was accused of being emotional and unscientific (as human beings will, people in entrenched authority resisted the challenges every step of the way); but the ecological viewpoint which she championed has been a liberating force for scientists and everyone else. It encouraged people to consider consequences outside their field of expertise. It encouraged scientists to move toward that more balanced development which Whitehead said is the prerequisite for wisdom.

Ecology has shown us all how science can break out of the reductionist trap. In their particular pursuits of knowledge, ecologists have been forced to think big rather than small—to think in terms of populations, ecosystems; wholes rather than parts; systems rather than individuals or events. Ecologists use the analytical method where it is useful, appreciate it where it is helpful, abide by its rigorous discipline. But it is not the only tool in their cabinet. They do not don blinders in order to concentrate better on their own subject. They range over the biological sciences, chemistry, physics, paleontology, history, political affairs. All of nature is their laboratory. This approach requires ecologists to be both multidisciplinary and interdisciplinary. It invites not exclusion, but cooperation; breadth as well as depth—balance.

We are seeing today in science and in higher education a movement toward this multidisciplinary-interdisciplinary approach toward knowledge and the problems which beset us. In the area of biomedicine, whose problems are just dawning upon us, new groups are being formed such as the Institute of Society, Ethics, and the Life Sciences at Hastings on Hudson, New York. Scientists, physicians, clergymen, philosophers engage in a dialogue of equals. Out of this new intellectual ecumenism hopefully will emerge the wisdom we need to cope with the reality toward which we are rushing.

The fork in the evolutionary road before us is the question of our relationship with nature. The ecological and biomedical debates are twin aspects of the same question: Are we going to continue to evolve away from nature or are we going to decide it is time now for accommodation? This question severs genetic from social gerontology and reveals them to be pointed toward different paths even though their goals are parallel.

In the ecological realm, we already have come upon warnings that we are approaching dead ends in some regions. In the biomedical area, we perhaps have not advanced so far, but Jacques Monod sees plainly where the road leads. If man accepts the message of human science as the supreme value, Dr. Monod says, "accepts all it contains—then man must at last awake out of his millenary dream; and in doing so, wake to his total solitude, his fundamental isolation. Now does he at last realize that, like a gypsy, he lives on the boundary of an alien world."

That is the vision of a man who has studied life through a microscope. Ecologists who have taken a macroscopic view of life see man as an integral part of nature. They believe that if human beings act upon this ecological perspective, they have a chance to achieve harmony with their world and with themselves.

The magic word of traditional science and technology has been "more." More is the Siren's song that wins every one of us. For we are covetous . . . of power, wealth, knowledge, life, ease, conveniences. *Todos queremos mas.* We have pledged our troth to science and technology and in return they always must give us more.

But in the world on the other side of the looking glass, beyond more is less. More knowledge without the necessary selection, organization, synthesis, judgment—without wisdom—is mind-blowing confusion. Intellectual elevation by itself leads to spiritual debasement. We have won our independence from nature. Beyond independence lies not more independence, but alienation. We already see unmistakable signs that we are arriving at this state. More life means . . .

Well, we don't know the answer to that one yet. The answers keep changing, depending on how much more. The full answer will be revealed to us, no doubt, at the proper time. In the meantime, we could try pronouncing the magic word of the Golden Mean and Buddha's Middle Way. Force ourselves to mouth it and then listen to it. It might come in handy.

Enough.

NOTES

Notes

Introduction

Page xv-xvii

The introductory remarks about science are based on *The Structure of Scientific Revolutions* by Thomas Kuhn, University of Chicago Press, Chicago, 1962, 1970; *Issues In Science and Religion* by Ian Barbour, Harper Torchbook, N.Y., 1966; and distilled from a great number of sources, many of them given in detail in the notes on Chapter X. A basic theme was stated by Nobel biologist James Watson in the *New York Times* March 22, 1973: "We must never forget that for the most part we have little insight about the truly unknown—the world we live in is immensely complicated and on the whole its natural phenomena are remarkably unpredictable." President Nixon compared the medical campaign against cancer to the Manhattan Project to build the atomic bomb and the Apollo program to go to the Moon, but several scientists have pointed out that the cancer campaign is not comparable to the two other achievements because they were carried out after the requisite basic scientific knowledge already was known. In the case of cancer, we do not know if we possess all the necessary basic knowledge. In the same article quoted above, Dr. Watson said: "It would be nice to believe that we now possess all the basic scientific facts needed for the conquest of cancer. . . . The truth, however, does not fit this fantasy and despite the stunning achievements of the modern biological revolution that have revealed the nature of the gene as well as the operation of the genetic code, huge gaps still exist in our knowledge of the fundamental biology and genetics of normal human cells, much less of the cancerous counterparts."

Chapter I. A Loss of Paradise

Page 3-7

The evolution story is based on: *Red Giants and White Dwarfs: The Evolution of Stars, Planets and Life*, by Robert Jastrow (New York: Harper & Row, 1967); the articles on Paleontology and Evolution in *Encyclopedia Americana* (1965); "The First Three Billion Years of Community Evolution," by George Gaylord Simpson, in *Diversity and Stability in Ecological Systems*, Biology Symposium Number 22, Brookhaven National Laboratory, May 26-28, 1969; "Man's Ecosystem," by LaMont Cole, in *Environments of Man*, edited by Jack Bresler (Reading, Mass.: Addison-Wesley); article originally in *BioScience*, April 1968; *Early Man*, by F. Clark Howell and the Editors of Time-Life Books (New York: Time-Life, 1970); "Tools and Human Evolution," by Sherwood Washburn, in *Scientific American*, Sept. 1960; "The Brain," Part I, by Adrian Hope, in *Life*, Oct. 1, 1971; "The Brain," Part III, "The Mind in Action," by Rick Gore, in *Life*, Oct. 22, 1971.

Page 3
"And God said, Let there be light" is from Genesis 1:3.

Page 3
Egyptian mythology for the creation presciently emphasized the concept of evolution. It is thought-provoking to compare the account given by E. A. Wallis Budge in *The Egyptian Book of the Dead* (New York: Dover, 1895, 1967), and Jastrow's scientific explanation in *Red Giants and White Dwarfs* (cited above).

Budge, p. xcix: "In a late copy of a work entitled the 'Book of knowing the evolution of Ra,' the god Neb-er-tcher, the 'lord of the company of the gods,' records the story of the creation and of the birth of gods:—'I am he who evolved himself under the form of the god Khepera, I, the evolver of the evolutions evolved myself, the evolver of all evolutions, after many evolutions and developments which came forth from my mouth.' (The variant version says, 'I developed myself from the primeval matter which I had made' and adds, 'My name is Osiris, the substance of primeval matter.') 'No heaven existed, and no earth, and no terrestrial animals or reptiles had come into being. I formed them out of the inert mass of watery matter, I found no place whereon to stand. . . .' "

Red Giants and White Dwarfs, p. 117: "Out of what materials were the planets formed? The bulk of the parent cloud must have been composed of the light gases, hydrogen and helium, because they are the most abundant elements in the universe. Other elements relatively abundant in the universe, although less so than hydrogen and helium, are carbon, nitrogen and oxygen, metals such as iron, magnesium and aluminum, and silicon. These substances must also have been present in relatively great abundance in the parent cloud of the planets. No doubt the remaining eight-odd elements were also represented, but in smaller amounts.

"All the familiar chemical compounds of these substances would have formed in the cloud in a relatively short period of time. Hydrogen combines readily with oxygen to form molecules of water vapor; hydrogen also combines with nitrogen to form molecules of ammonia gas, and it combines with carbon to form methane, also called marsh gas, which is used extensively today for cooking. Carbon and oxygen combine to form carbon dioxide. Considerable amounts of each of these compounds must have formed in the parent cloud. However, they were probably not present in the form of gases, because of the low temperature—about 100 degrees Fahrenheit below zero—prevailing in the region of the cloud out of which the earth was formed. At this temperature they congealed into a slushy mixture of water, ammonia and methane ice in liquid and solid form, plus carbon dioxide—dry ice. The other elements that were present in abundance—silicon, aluminum, magnesium and iron—combined with oxygen to form grains of rocklike materials and metallic oxides.

"These, then, are the substances out of which the planets condensed: a Neopolitan sherbet of frozen water, ammonia and methane, plus various kinds of rocky substances—all immersed in a gaseous cloud of hydrogen and helium."

Page 3
"And God said, Let the waters . . ." is from Genesis 1:20.

Page 4
Biochemists Robert Macnab and Daniel Koshland of the University of California, Berkeley, reported to the American Chemical Society in Sept. 1972 that bacteria, the elementary single-celled organisms probably closest to the most ancient life forms (specifically the intestinal bacterium *Salmonella typhimurium*), have shown a rudimentary form of memory. (*Time,* Sept. 18, 1972, p. 63.)

Page 4
"And God said, Let the earth . . ." is from Genesis 1:24.

Page 5
Life Before Man (New York: Time-Life, 1972) says that new studies indicate that a supernova close to the earth caused gamma ray radiation and a brief lowering of earth temperature which killed the dinosaurs but not the less-evolved mammals.

Page 5
"And God said, Let us make man . . ." is from Genesis 1:26.

Page 5
On the basis of immunological distance, three scientists recently have estimated an early divergence of the human line from the anthropoid apes 12 to 14 million years ago; from monkeys 37 million years ago; and from lemur and loris forms about 65 million years ago. In "Primate Phylogeny and Immunological Distance," by C. Owen Lovejoy, Albert Burstein, Kingsbury Heiple, in *Science,* May 19, 1972.

Page 6
The new find, a skull with a cranial capacity of 800 cubic centimeters, was made by Richard Leakey in Kenya, and was reported in the *New York Times,* Nov. 10, 1972.

Leopold and Ardrey place the first tool-using man at 2.6 million years ago and say the first evidence of use of fire goes back only 300,000-350,000 years although earlier anthropological sources had assumed an earlier date, specifically fire associated with Peking man 500,000 years ago—but the date for this example of *Homo erectus* now has been pushed back to 1 million years. Leopold and Ardrey say that the consistent use of fire—a fire culture in which men could make fire at will—dates back only some 40,000 years in Near East caves that housed successive layers of human cultures. See "Toxic Substances in Plants and the Food Habits of Early Man," by A. Carl Leopold and Robert Ardrey, in *Science,* May 5, 1972. Also letters to the editor about the article by C. B. Goodhart and Leopold and Ardrey in *Science,* Sept. 8, 1972.

Page 6
The discovery of the 200,000-year-old skull was reported by Walter Sullivan in the *New York Times,* Oct. 13, 1971.

Page 6-7
The discovery of the ancient calendar is based on work by researcher Alexander

Marshak and was reported by Walter Sullivan in the *New York Times,* Jan. 24, 1971. Marshak has elaborated on his findings in *The Roots of Civilization* (New York: McGraw-Hill, 1972).

Page 7
The figure 10 million species is from "The Origins of Taxonomy," by Peter Raven, Brent Berlin, and Dennis Breedlove, in *Science,* Dec. 17, 1971.

Page 7
This passage is not meant to contend that some other mammals do not have some comprehension of the meaning of death. Jane Goodall's observations of chimpanzees indicate not only that they do but that one youngster died from grief shortly after his mother's death. However, the uniquely human signs— the burial ceremony and the grave laden with artifacts and food—signify that the survivors grasp what death means for them as well as a belief that something lives on despite the inevitable corporeal conclusion.

Page 7
The Toynbee quotation "The oldest, most numerous . . ." is from *Man's Concern with Death,* by Arnold Toynbee and others (New York: McGraw-Hill, 1968), pp. 59-60.

Page 7
The Lewis Mumford quotation "Soon after one picks up . . ." is from *The City in History* (New York: Harcourt, Brace and World, 1961), pp. 6, 7.

Page 7-8
The Loren Eiseley quotation "And down the untold centuries . . ." is from *The Firmament of Time* (New York: Atheneum, 1960, 1969), p. 113.

Page 8
Information on the Neanderthal graves is from *Early Man* (cited above), pp. 128-130.

Page 8-9
The Malinowski quotation "Nowhere is the duality . . ." is from *Magic, Science and Religion* (Garden City: Doubleday Anchor, 1954; originally written in 1925), pp. 31-32.

Page 9
The Frazer quotation "The general attitude . . ." is from *The Fear of the Dead in Primitive Religion* (London: Macmillan, 1933), p. 10.

Page 9
The Henderson quotation "[S]ince as far as . . ." is from *The Wisdom of the Serpent,* by Joseph Henderson and Maud Oakes (New York: Braziller, 1963), p. 5.

Page 9
The Origin of Death: Studies in African Mythology, by Hans Abrahamson

(Uppsala, Sweden: Almqvist & Wiksell, 1951), lists the myths under the following categories: The Message that Failed, Sleep and Death, Death in Bundle, The Divine Test, Discord in the First Family, Begetting and Death, Man Desires Death, Man Buys Death, Death as Personification, The Forbidden Fruit, The Premature Burial, Death Makes Men Glad, Death Came with Disease, Death as the Punishment for Different Sins.

Probably the most popular modern fable of Death as Personality is the W. Somerset Maugham passage quoted by John O'Hara to preface his 1934 novel, *Appointment in Samarra*. A merchant's servant is jostled by Death in the market place in Baghdad. The frightened servant begs his master for a horse so that he can flee to Samarra. Later that day, the merchant meets Death and asks why he had threatened the servant. "That was not a threatening gesture," Death says, "it was only a start of surprise. I was astonished to see him in Baghdad, for I had an appointment with him tonight in Samarra."

Page 9
The Four Sons myth is from *The Origin of Death* (cited above), p. 4.

Page 10
Sir James Frazer in *The Belief in Immortality* (London, 1913), p. 59, labels "the tales of two messengers" as the most common African myth.

Page 10
The Ngoni reaction to the two messengers myth is from *The Origin of Death* (cited above), p. 20.

Page 11
The Galla and Gudji myths are from *The Origin of Death* (cited above), p. 16.

Page 11
The Zambezi myth relating to overpopulation is from *The Origin of Death* (cited above), pp. 22-23.

Page 11
The Woman and Serpent Must Choose myth is from *The Origin of Death* (cited above), p. 44.

Page 11
The Tsetse Fly myth is from *The Origin of Death* (cited above), p. 45.

Page 11
The Kumbi myth is from *The Origin of Death* (cited above), p. 44.

Page 11
The Fire myth is from *The Origin of Death* (cited above), p. 113.

Page 11-12
The Prometheus myth is amalgamated from *A History of Ideas about the Prolongation of Life*, by Gerald Gruman, Transactions of the American Philosophical Society, Vol. 56, Part 9 (Philadelphia: American Philosophical Society,

1966), p. 11. Gruman for his version refers to Hesiod in *Hesiod, the Homeric Hymns and Homerica* (London: Loeb Classical Library,) p. xxvi, and *The World of Hesiod*, by Andrew Burn, in *The History of Civilization* (London, 1936), p. 31. Also: *Bulfinch's Mythology*, Modern Library edition (New York: Random House), pp. 16-17; the Prometheus article in *Encyclopedia Americana* (1965); *Prometheus Bound* by Aeschylus.

Page 12
The Ewe myth about the old couple and the receding sky is from *The Origin of Death* (cited above), p. 109.

Page 12-13
The Pangwe myth of the gorilla, chimpanzee, serpent, and Mode is from *The Origin of Death* (cited above), pp. 70 and 94.

Page 13
The Cameroons myth of a life-tree is from *The Origin of Death* (cited above), p. 137.

Page 13
The Efik myth about Abassi and Atai is from *The Origin of Death* (cited above), p. 69.

Page 14-15
The account of the sect of Assassins is from *The Travels of Marco Polo,* Modern Library edition (New York: Random House), pp. 52-55.

Page 15
The Garden of Eden quotation "And the Lord God said, Behold . . ." is from Genesis 3:22-23.

Gerald Gruman in *A History of Ideas about the Prolongation of Life* (cited above), p. 13, says: "Frazer, the great investigator of comparative mythology, wrote that, 'the gist of the whole story of the fall appears to be an attempt to explain man's mortality, to set forth how death came into the world.' On the basis of his studies of primitive folklore, Frazer deduced that in its original form the Eden myth revolved entirely about the question of immortality; the tree of the knowledge of good and evil, he felt, was a later addition. The two trees in the earlier version, according to Frazer, were simply the tree of life and the tree of death. God told Adam and Eve to eat of the tree of life and to avoid the tree of death, but the serpent deceived them into choosing the wrong tree and gained for himself, as in the Gilgamesh legend, the power of rejuvenation by the periodic shedding of skin." Gruman cites as the source *Folk-Lore in the Old Testament,* by James Frazer (London, 1918), Vol. 1, pp. 47-77.

As a possible basis for a physical Eden, René Dubos has written in the chapter "Gardens of Eden" in *Mirage of Health* (New York: Harper, 1959), p. 25: "As suggested by Lewis Mumford, the interglacial periods may have provided a relatively idyllic environment of ease and abundance, breathing spells in the midst of tropical luxuriance that contrasted with the recurrent hardships of the glacial periods contemporary with man's early development."

Page 15-17
The Gilgamesh Epic story is taken from *The Gilgamesh Epic and Old Testament Parallels,* by Alexander Heidel (Chicago: University of Chicago Press, 1946). Professor Heidel, in pp. 1-16, discusses the discovery of the Gilgamesh tablets, summarizes the epic, discusses the central theme—"a meditation on death, in the form of a tragedy"—and goes into the epic's sources and age.

Page 16
The Babylonians had a tradition of a great flood similar to that of the Hebrews.

Page 17
The Heidel quotation "But since there is . . ." is from *The Gilgamesh Epic and Old Testament Parallels* (cited above), p. 10.

Page 17
The Gilgamesh quotation "Gilgamesh, whither runnest . . ." is from Table X, column iii in *The Gilgamesh Epic and Old Testament Parallels* (cited above), p. 70.

Page 17-18
The quotation "Go thy way . . ." is from Ecclesiastes 9:7-10.

Page 18
The Sophocles quotation "Never to have been born . . ." is from the translation by Sir George Young, quoted in *Bartlett's Familiar Quotations* (Boston: Little Brown, 1951), p. 1081.

Page 18
The Byron quotation "Whom the gods love . . ." is from *Don Juan,* Canto IV, Stanza 12.

Page 18
The Housman quotation "Smart lad . . ." is from *The Collected Poems of A. E. Housman* (New York: Holt, 1945), p. 32.

Page 18-19
The Roman Kalanta story was reported in *Time,* July 31, 1972, pp. 27-28.

Page 19
The Nathan Hale quotation "I only regret . . ." is from *Bartlett's Familiar Quotations* (cited above), p. 195.

Page 19
The quotation from Christ "Greater love hath no man . . ." is from John 15:13.

Page 19-22
The discussion of Hedonism, Epicureanism, Cynicism, and Stoicism is based on the following articles in *Encyclopedia Americana* (1965): Philosophy, History of Philosophy, Ethics, Hedonism, Epicureanism, Epicurus, Lucretius,

Cynics, Stoicism, Epictetus, Marcus Aurelius; *The Story of Philosophy,* by Will Durant (New York: Simon and Schuster, 1926), pp. 105-117; "Thanatology: A Historical Sketch," by Morris Saffron, in *Loss and Grief: Psychological Management in Medical Practice,* edited by Bernard Schoenberg *et al.* (New York: Columbia University Press, 1970); *Death and Modern Man,* by Jacques Choron (New York: Collier-Macmillan, 1964); *The History of the Decline and Fall of the Roman Empire,* by Edward Gibbon, Vol. I, Modern Library edition (New York: Random House), pp. 1-85; *Man's Concern with Death* (cited above).

Page 19-20
The Lucretius quotation "Therefore, O man . . ." is from *Of the Nature of Things,* translated by William Leonard (New York: Dutton, 1950), pp. 131-132.

Page 20
The Greek word *logos* begins the Gospel of John and is translated as "the word," one of the indications of Stoicism's influence on Christianity.

Page 20
The Epictetus quotation "You will break it" is from *Great Political Thinkers: Plato to the Present,* by William Ebenstein (New York: Holt, Rinehart and Winston, 1951, 1960), p. 138; also from *The Story of Philosophy* (cited above), p. 114.

Page 20-21
The Marcus Aurelius quotations are from *The Meditations of the Emperor Marcus Aurelius Antoninus,* translated by George Long (New York: A. L. Burt): "Of human life the time . . . ," p. 150; this famous quotation was written in Carnuntum, a town on the south side of the Danube River about 30 miles east of the present site of Vienna. "Though thou shouldest be . . . ," p. 148; a similar thought is expressed in the fourth verse of Psalm 90. "Alexander the Macedonian . . . ," p. 197; "Nature which governs the whole . . . ," p. 212; "He who fears death . . . ," p. 239; "If then, whatever the time . . . ," p. 287.

Page 21
The Gibbon quotation "He was severe . . ." is from *Decline and Fall* (cited above), pp. 69-70.

Page 22
The Gallup report on belief in life after death is from American Institute of Public Opinion, Inc., Princeton, N.J.: for release Dec. 26, 1968.

Page 22-23
The survey results "You & Death," by Edwin Shneidman, were published in *Psychology Today,* June 1971.

Page 22-23
The three fears of death listed by philosopher Jacques Choron in *Death and*

Modern Man (cited above), are fear of what happens after death, fear of the event of dying, and fear of ceasing to be. Dale Gordon in *Overcoming the Fear of Death* (New York: Macmillan, 1970), p. 111, says: "The fear of death is really a conglomerate composed of the fears of time, decay, the unknown, irreversibility, the loss of pleasurable sensations, the loss of thought, and the loss of self." Thomas Powers in "Learning to Die" in *Harper's,* June, 1971, says, "In general, the fear of death has been broken down into the specific fears of pain, loneliness, abandonment, mutilation, and, somewhat more difficult to define, fear of the loss of self."

Page 23
The Sheila Cole quotation "All of these stories . . ." is from the *New York Times Book Review,* Sept. 26, 1971, p. 12.

Page 23
The American Way of Death, by Jessica Mitford (Greenwich, Conn.: Fawcett Crest, 1963).

Page 24
The Loved One, by Evelyn Waugh (New York: Dell, 1948).

Page 24-28
The discussion of the predicament of the dying person is based on "Learning How to Die," by David Dempsey, in the *New York Times Magazine,* Nov. 14, 1971; "Learning To Die" (cited above); "The Psychology of Death," in *Newsweek,* Sept. 14, 1970; "Neglect of Dying Patients' Emotional Needs Is Linked by Doctors to Cultural Inability to Face Death," by Nancy Hicks, in the *New York Times,* Aug. 26, 1970; "Toward a Better Death" in *Time,* June 5, 1972; *On Death and Dying,* by Elisabeth Kubler-Ross (New York: Macmillan paperback, 1969); *Loss and Grief: Psychological Management in Medical Practice,* by Schoenberg, Carr, Peretz and Kutscher (cited above); *The Dying Patient,* by Brim, Freeman, Levine, and Scotch (New York: Russell Sage Foundation, 1970); *Awareness of Dying,* by Barney Glaser and Anselm Strauss (Chicago: Aldine, 1965); *The Meaning of Death,* edited by Herman Feifel (New York: McGraw-Hill, 1959); "On the Dying of Death," by Robert Fulton, in *Explaining Death to Children,* edited by Earl Grollman (Boston: Beacon, 1967); *Death and Dying: Current Issues in the Treatment of the Dying Person,* edited by Leonard Pearson (Cleveland: Case Western Reserve University Press, 1969).

Page 24
The Feifel quotation "Significantly stronger death fears . . ." is from "Learning How to Die" (cited above).

Page 24
The Kutscher quotation "There is no justification . . ." is from "The Psychology of Death," in *Newsweek* (cited above).

Page 25
The paragraph on the right to die is based on "The Right to Die," by Paul Wilkes, in *Life,* Jan. 14, 1971; "Dignity in Dying Is Goal of New Studies," by

Jane Brody, in the *New York Times,* May 3, 1971; "There's a Time, They Say, to Let People Die," by Judy Klemsrud, in the *New York Times,* March 1, 1971; "A Person's Right to Die," by Louis Lasagna, M.D., in *The Johns Hopkins Magazine,* Spring 1968; "The Right to Choose Death," by O. Ruth Russell, in the *New York Times,* Feb. 14, 1972; "Adult Honesty to a Dying Child Urged," by Jane Brody in the *New York Times,* Jan. 23, 1972; "Court Overrules Wife on Surgery, Lets Pacemaker Operation on Husband Proceed," by Walter Waggoner, in the *New York Times,* Jan. 28, 1972.

Elizabeth Halsey, executive director of the Euthanasia Educational Fund, says: "I think it's a great question of whether you consider longevity as something absolutely desired above everything else. We don't—we think there is a quality of life and a quantity of life and "quantity is not the important part." "When you are ready, when a person has wished that they could die and said so right along and the family agrees they don't want to see the person have any more pain or that they have nothing further to live for, then they should be allowed to die. They should not be given a lethal dose necessarily, but they should be allowed to die with dignity and in peace and not be kept alive just this many months or this many years for no purpose in particular."

The New York Sate Medical Society statement "The use of euthanasia . . ." is from an Associated Press story published Jan. 12, 1973. The American Hospital Association's "Bill of Rights for Patients" was reported by Lawrence Altman in the *New York Times,* Jan. 9, 1973.

Page 26-27
The story of Miss T. is from "The Dying Patient's Point of View," by Elisabeth Kubler-Ross, in *The Dying Patient* (cited above), pp. 161-165.

Page 27
The Ross quotation "Among the over . . ." is from *On Death and Dying* (cited above), p. 38.

Page 27-28
The Ross quotation "If a patient has had enough . . ." is from *On Death and Dying* (cited above), pp. 112-113.

Page 28
The La Rochefoucauld quotation "One can no more . . ." is from "Learning to Die" (cited above).

Page 28
The criminal homicides statistic is from "Psychology of Murder," an essay in *Time,* April 24, 1972.

Page 28
The quotation "Every second you expect . . ." about the wolf fight is from *King Solomon's Ring,* by Konrad Lorenz (New York: Crowell, 1952), p. 188.

Page 29
The footnote on the U.S. Supreme Court death penalty decision is based on "The Death Penalty and a Free Society," by Anthony Amsterdam, in the

New York Times, Nov. 4, 1972, and "Death Penalty: Conflicting Trends," in the
New York Times, Nov. 26, 1972.

Page 29
Saturnalia quotation "Thirty days before . . ." is from *The Golden Bough,*
by Sir James Frazer (New York: Macmillan, 1922, 1947), pp. 584-585.

Page 30
For Mongol practices, see *Genghis Khan, Emperor of All Men,* by Harold
Lamb (New York: Bantam, 1953; original copyright, 1927).

Page 30
For disappearance of Zoroastrianism, see article on Zoroastrianism in *Encyclopedia Americana* (1965).

Page 30
Re Christian dissidents, the History of Medicine in *Encyclopedia Americana*
(1965) says that by 1782 more than 300,000 "witches" were burned to death
in Europe.

Page 30-31
The Schopenhauer segment is based on the Schopenhauer chapter in *The Story
of Philosophy* (cited above).

Page 30
The Hegel paragraph is based on *The Story of Philosophy* (cited above), pp.
317-325.

Page 30
The Hegel quotation "To him who looks . . ." is from his *Philosophy of History,* cited in *Bartlett's Familiar Quotations* (cited above), p. 1177.

Page 30
Hegel's reference to history as the slaughter bench of progress is from "The
Ideology of Death," by Herbert Marcuse, in *The Meaning of Death* (cited
above), p. 75.

Page 31
The Schopenhauer quotation "Consciousness is the mere surface . . ." is from
The World as Will and Idea, given in *The Story of Philosophy* (cited above),
p. 339.

Page 31
The Schopenhauer quotation "Unconsciousness is the original . . ." is from
The World as Will and Idea, given in *The Story of Philosophy* (cited above),
p. 343.

Page 32
The Durant quotation about philosophy "is the front trench . . ." is from his
introduction to *The Story of Philosophy,* p. 2.

Page 32

The Nietzsche section is based on the Nietzsche chapter in *The Story of Philosophy* (cited above). I have also read and taken into consideration "Existentialism and Death," by Walter Kaufmann, in *The Meaning of Death* (cited above); "Existentialism," by John K. Ryan of The Catholic University of America, in *Encyclopedia Americana* (1965); George Alfred Schrader, Jr.'s preface to his *Existential Philosophers: Kierkegaard to Merleau-Ponty* (New York: McGraw-Hill, 1967), in which he chooses between Kierkegaard and Nietzsche as the most important existentialist precurser; the obvious importance of Nietzsche to Freud as indicated by the recurring citations in Chapter I of *Life Against Death* (Nietzsche 17 references to 2 for Schopenhauer); the references to Nietzsche in *Death and Modern Man* (cited above); and particularly to Walter Kaufmann's defense of Nietzsche and his exposition to "distinguish his actual views from those imputed to him by popular misconception" in his article "Nietzsche" in *Encyclopedia Americana* (1965). However, I chose to abide by the interpretation presented by Durant in *The Story of Philosophy*. This was published in 1926 before Hitler came to power and before Existentialism became an influential school of philosophy. In other words, Durant had no ulterior motive to "explain what Nietzsche really meant." Durant simply took the philosopher's words at face value, and the events of the succeeding decades validated the judgment of both Durant and Nietzsche. This interpretation of Nietzsche, then, is not pejorative, but vindicates his terrifying vision of human nature. Finally, it seems to me, Schopenhauer is the one who made the great leap, focusing attention on the importance of the irrational. Nietzsche and then Freud followed along the path opened by Schopenhauer.

Page 32

The Nietzsche quotation "I felt for the first time . . ." is from *The Story of Philosophy* (cited above), p. 441, where the original source is given as Forster-Nietzsche, *The Young Nietzsche* (London, 1912), p. 235.

Page 32

"I teach you the Superman" quotation is from Prologue, Chapter 3, *Thus Spake Zarathustra,* translated by Thomas Common, in *Bartlett's Familiar Quotations* (cited above), p. 1194.

Page 32

"Man is the cruellest animal . . ." quotation is from *The Story of Philosophy* (cited above), pp. 459-460; original sources: *The Genealogy of Morals and Beyond Good and Evil.*

Page 32

The quotation "Too long has the world been a madhouse . . ." is given by Norman O. Brown in *Life Against Death* (cited above), p. 15.

Page 32

The "born posthumously" phrase is from "Existentialism and Death," by Walter Kaufmann, in *The Meaning of Death* (cited above), p. 60.

Page 32-33
During World War II, in 1943, psychoanalyst Walter Langer wrote a study of
Hitler for the Office of Strategic Services which finally was published as *The
Mind of Adolf Hitler* (New York: Basic Books, 1972). In it Langer describes
Hitler as "probably a neurotic psychopath bordering on schizophrenia"—not
insane but emotionally sick and lacking normal inhibitions against antisocial
behavior. Dr. Langer predicted Hitler would grow worse with German defeats
(and so he did manufacture ruthless "victories" over the Jews as the Nazis lost
on the battlefields) and finally end in suicide.

Page 33-37
The section on Freud is based primarily on *An Outline of Psychoanalysis*, by
Sigmund Freud (New York: Norton, 1949), and Ernest Jones' article "Freud,"
in *Encyclopedia Americana*. But the segment also reflects extensive reading of
Freud over many years, including *The Basic Writings of Sigmund Freud*
(*Psychopathology of Everyday Life, The Interpretation of Dreams, Three Contributions to the Theory of Sex, Wit and Its Relation to the Unconscious, Totem
and Taboo*), Modern Library edition, (New York: Random House); *Civilization
and Its Discontents* (London: Hogarth Press and the Institute of Psycho-
Analysis, 1949); *The Ego and the Id* (London: Hogarth Press and the Institute
of Psycho-Analysis, 1949); *Group Psychology and the Analysis of the Ego*
(New York: Liveright, 1949); *Moses and Monotheism* (New York: Vintage,
1955).

Page 33
The quotation "The power of the id . . ." is from *An Outline of Psychoanalysis*
(cited above), p. 19.

Page 33
The quotation "dreams bring to light . . ." is from *An Outline of Psychoanalysis* (cited above), pp. 49-50.

Page 34
Walter Kaufmann in "Existentialism and Death," in *The Meaning of Death*
(cited above), translated Freud's *Gesammelte Schriften* (Leipzig: Interna-
tionaler Psychoanalytischer Verlag, 1924), and quotes Freud: "After all, one's
own death is beyond imagining, and whenever we try to imagine it we can
see that we really survive as spectators. Thus the dictum could be dared in
the psychoanalytic school: At bottom, nobody believes in his own death. Or,
and this is the same: In his unconscious, every one of us is convinced of his
immortality."

Freud himself was unusually concerned with death, perhaps in part because
of heart attacks he suffered in his thirties. His last 16 years before his death
in 1939 were a stubborn, stoical bout with a discomforting cancer of the jaw,
described by his personal physician Max Schur in *Freud: Living and Dying*
(New York: International Universities Press, 1972).

Page 35
The quotation "We may suppose . . ." is from *An Outline of Psychoanalysis*
(cited above), p. 20.

Page 35
The quotation "This interaction . . ." is from *An Outline of Psychoanalysis* (cited above), p. 21.

Page 36
The quotation "If we suppose that living . . ." is from *An Outline of Psychoanalysis* (cited above), pp. 20-21.

Page 36
The quotation "to the pair of opposing forces . . ." is from *An Outline of Psychoanalysis* (cited above), p. 21.

Page 36
Karl Menninger's psychiatric work is expounded in *Man Against Himself* (New York: Harcourt, Brace, 1938).

Page 36-37
The quotation "The fateful question . . ." is from *Civilization and Its Discontents* (cited above), pp. 143, 144.

Page 37-38
Quotations from *Life Against Death,* by Norman O. Brown (Middletown, Conn.: Wesleyan University Press, 1959): "[I]t begins to be apparent . . . ," p. x; "Stated in more general terms . . . ," p. 4; "The existence of a repressed . . . ," p. 6; "Neurosis is not . . . ," p. 6; "The doctrine of the . . . ," p. 6; "The necessity of the psychoanalytical approach . . . ," pp. 15-16; "Archaic man conquers . . . ," p. 285; "Man, the discontented animal . . . ," p. 93; "Hegel was able to develop . . . ," p. 102; "The death instinct is the core . . . ," p. 284; "The incapacity to accept death . . . ," p. 284.

Page 39
"Take therefore no thought for the morrow. . ." is from the Sermon on the Mount, Matthew 6:34.

Page 39
"This is an evil among things . . ." is from Ecclesiastes 9:3.

Chapter II. Regaining Paradise

Page 40
The Frazer quotation "belief in immortality . . ." is from *The Fear of the Dead in Primitive Religion* (London: Macmillan, 1933), pp. 6-7. Frazer begins this book by stating: "Men commonly believe that their conscious being will not end at death, but that it will be continued for an indefinite time or for ever, long after the frail corporeal envelope which lodged it for a time has mouldered in the dust. This belief in the immortality of the soul, as we call it, is by no means confined to the adherents of those great historical religions which are now professed by the most civilized nations of the world; it is held with at

least equal confidence by most, if not all, of those peoples of lower culture whom we call savages or barbarians, and there is every reason to think that among them the belief is native; in other words, that it originated among them in a stage of savagery at least as low as that which they now occupy, and that it has been handed down among them from generation to generation without being materially modified by contact with races at higher levels of culture. It is therefore a mistake to suppose that the hope of immortality after death was first revealed to mankind by the founders of the great historical religions, Buddhism, Christianity and Islam; to all appearances, it was cherished by men all over the world thousands of years before Buddha, Jesus Christ, and Mohammed were born. Indeed, it is safe to conjecture that these great religious revolutionaries were not in this respect innovators, but that they owed in some measure the rapid success which attended their teaching to the circumstances that they accepted the current and popular belief in immortality and built on it, as on a sure foundation, their towering structures of theology which would topple over and crash to the ground if the belief in immortality were to be proved baseless."

Page 40
The Frazer quotation "[T]he eminent Finnish . . ." is from *The Fear of the Dead in Primitive Religion* (cited above), pp. 9-10 .

Page 40-41
On persistence of spirit and its material needs, *The Fear of the Dead in Primitive Religion* (cited above), pp. 12-13 .

Page 41
On the change for the worse after death, *The Fear of the Dead in Primitive Religion* (cited above), pp. 10-11.

Page 41
The discussion of animism, mana, and magic is based on *The World's Living Religions,* by Archie Bahm (New York: Dell, 1964), pp. 36–44. The basic work for myth and magic is *The Golden Bough,* by Sir James Frazer (cited in Chapter I).

Page 41
The Malinowski quotation "Early man seeks . . ." is from *Magic, Science and Religion* (cited in Chapter I), p. 19.

Page 41-42
The Frazer quotation "Wherever sympathetic . . ." is from *The Golden Bough* (cited in Chapter I), pp. 48-50.

Page 42
The discussion of shamanism is from *Encyclopedia Americana* (1965).

Page 42
The Krujit quotation "They naturally think . . ." and the Frazer quotation

"because he feels . . ." are from *The Fear of the Dead in Primitive Religion* (cited above), p. 40.

Page 42
Variations in the belief in immortality are from *The Fear of the Dead in Primitive Religion* (cited above), pp. 7-8.

Page 43
The Henderson quotation "Whenever we find . . ." is from *The Wisdom of the Serpent* (cited in Chapter I), p. 4.

Page 43
The Inanna and Ishtar legends are from *The Wisdom of the Serpent* (cited above), pp. 15-16.

Page 43
The Persephone legend is from *The Wisdom of the Serpent* (cited above), pp. 119-121.

Page 44
The Cybele and Attis, Isis and Osiris legends are from *The Wisdom of the Serpent* (cited above), p. 17. A more detailed story of Osiris and Isis is in *The Egyptian Book of the Dead* (cited in Chapter I), pp. xlviii-lii. Adonis is another god with vegetative origins. Sir James Frazer in *The Golden Bough* (cited above), p. 385, notes that both Herodotus and Plutarch remarked at the extreme similarity in rites to the Egyptian Osiris and the Greek Dionysus; Herodotus believing, therefore, that the Greeks must have borrowed from the more ancient Egyptians. But Frazer believes that Dionysus originated as a god of agriculture in Thrace where they were very fond of drinking. Frazer goes on: "In the preceding chapters we saw that in antiquity the civilized nations of Western Asia and Egypt pictured to themselves the changes of the seasons and particularly the annual growth and decay of vegetation, as episodes in the life of gods, whose mournful death and happy resurrection they celebrated with dramatic rites of alternate lamentation and rejoicing. But if the celebration was in form dramatic, it was in substance magical; that is to say, it was intended, on the principles of sympathetic magic, to ensure the vernal regeneration of plants and the multiplication of animals, which had seemed to be menaced by the inroads of winter."

Page 44
The Phoenix myth is from *Encyclopedia Americana.*

Page 44
Dr. Henderson's quotation "The wisdom of the serpent . . ." is from *The Wisdom of the Serpent* (cited above), p. 36.

Page 44-48
The discussion of Hinduism, Buddhism, Jainism, and Zen Buddhism is based on *The World's Living Religions* (cited above), the chapters on Hinduism and Buddhism; the following articles in *Encyclopedia Americana:* India—Religion

and Philosophy, Hinduism, Buddhism, Jainism, Immortality; *The Wisdom of the Serpent* (cited above); "Zen, Universal Style," by Nancy Wilson Ross, in the *New York Times,* June 24, 1972.

Page 45
The Dylan Thomas quotation "Do not go gently . . ." is from *The Collected Poems of Dylan Thomas* (New York: New Directions, 1957), p. 128, copyright by Dylan Thomas, 1952.

Page 45
Henderson in *The Wisdom of the Serpent* (cited above), p. 11, says that Schopenhauer was influenced by reading the *Upanishads.*

Page 47
It is true that Buddha "would never say that on the dissolution of the body the saint who has lost all depravity is annihilated, perishes, and does not exist after death" and uses such synonyms for nirvana as not-death and immortality. Nevertheless, he achieved a release and cessation from existence. "In showing men how to die" is also meant in the sense of Plato's and Socrates' saying that the man who has pursued philosophy in the right way—"practiced death"—can meet death easily. In this sense, it is overcoming the dread of death.

Arnold Toynbee writes in *Man's Concern with Death* (cited in Chapter I), p. 71: "In this spiritual struggle to attain nirvana, death (i.e. the death of the current life in the series) is an unimportant incident. Nirvana may be attained at death, but it may also be attained while the former sufferer is still living what will now have been the last of his successive lives."

Page 47-48
The death of Buddha, quoted in *The Wisdom of the Serpent* (cited above), pp. 216-217, is taken from *The Bible of the World,* edited by Robert Ballou (New York: Viking, 1939), p. 240.

Page 48-51
The discussion of Socrates-Plato is based on *The Story of Philosophy* (cited in Chapter I), the first chapter on Plato; the article on "Socrates," by André Michalopoulous, in *Encyclopedia Americana; Death: Meaning and Mortality in Christian Thought and Contemporary Culture,* by Milton Gatch (New York: Seabury, 1969), the second chapter, on "The Greek Traditions"; the Introduction to *Phaedo* in *Plato,* Classics Club edition, published by Walter Black, Roslyn, N.Y.; and a reading of Plato's *The Republic,* The Modern Student's Library edition (New York: Scribner, 1928).

Page 50
The Pericles quotation "And then when the moment . . ." is from Thucydides' *History,* Vol. II, Loeb Classical Library (Cambridge, Mass.: Harvard University Press), pp. 331-335.

Page 50-51
The quotations from *Phaedo* are from *The Collected Dialogues of Plato, Including the Letters* (New York: Bollingen Series, LXXI, 1961).

Page 51-52
The section on the crucifixion is based on the four Gospels, the Holy Bible, King James version.

Page 52
The Sermon on the Mount quotation "Love your enemies . . ." is from Matthew 5:44.

Page 52
"No man can serve two masters . . ." is from Matthew 6:24.

Page 52
"If therefore thine eye be single . . ." is from Matthew 6:22.

Page 52
"Which of you by taking thought . . ." is from Matthew 6:27.

Page 52
The reference to the lilies of the field is from Matthew 6:28.

Page 52
The parable of the Sower is from Matthew 13:3-12.

Page 52
In Luke 17:20-21 Christ is specific in saying, ". . . for, behold, the kingdom of God is within you."

Page 52
"Neither cast ye your pearls . . ." is from Matthew 7:6.

Page 52
"Father, forgive them . . ." is from Luke 23:34.

Page 52
"Verily, I say unto thee . . ." is from Luke 23:43.

Page 52
"Father, into thy hands . . ." is from Luke 23:46.

Page 52
"It is finished" is from John 19:30.

Page 52
"My God, my God, why hast thou forsaken me?" is from Matthew 27:46 and Mark 15:34.

Page 52
"I am the resurrection . . ." is from the Order for the Burial of the Dead in *The Book of Common Prayer* of the Episcopal Church.

Page 52-55
The discussion of Judaism and Zoroastrianism is based on reading the Bible and the following articles in *Encyclopedia Americana:* Jewish History and Society, Bible, Immortality, Civilization, Zoroaster, Zoroastrianism; *Death: Meaning and Mortality in Christian Thought and Contemporary Culture* (cited above); *Ten Great Religions,* by James Freeman Clark (Boston: Osgood, 1871).

Page 53
"I will make you a great nation" quotation is from Genesis 12:2 for Abraham, and also references at Genesis 17:20 and 18:18; for Jacob-Israel, Genesis 35:11 and 46:03.

Page 53
Babylonian and Old Testament parallels are discussed at length in Heidel's *The Gilgamesh Epic and Old Testament Parallels* (cited in Chapter I).

Page 54
The Clark quotation "In the mouth of two witnesses . . ." is from *Ten Great Religions* (cited above), p. 205.

Page 54-55
Re the apocalyptic message after the Persian captivity, Toynbee writes in *Man's Concern with Death* (cited above), p. 88: "The Christian and Muslim conceptions of the judgment of souls after death and of heaven and hell to which the souls are consigned respectively, in accordance with the verdict, are evidently derived, in the main, not from pre-Christian religion of Egypt, but from Zoroastrianism—presumably via Pharisaic Judaism, which—unlike the Sadducean Judaism of the post-exilic Jewish 'establishment' in Judea—laid itself open to Zoroastrian influences that played upon Judaism after the incorporation of Babylonia, Syria, Palestine, and Egypt in the Persian Empire in the sixth century B.C."

Page 55
Marco Polo tells of traveling to the city in Persia from which the three wise men set out and the Castle of the Fire-Worshippers where the story of the three Magi was known. Polo says the rationale for the offering of gold, frankincense, and myrrh was to determine the prophet's nature: if he accepted the gold he was an earthly king, if he accepted the incense a God, if the myrrh a physician. From *The Travels of Marco Polo* (cited in Chapter I), pp. 37-38. The word "magician" is derived from the Persian *magus,* or plural *magi,* for sorcerer.

Page 55-57
The discussion of resurrection and the apostle Paul are based on the following articles in *Encyclopedia Americana:* Christianity, Bible, Jewish History and Society, Paul, Immortality, Resurrection; the Bible; *Death: Meaning and Mortality in Christian Thought and Contemporary Culture* (cited above); *The Wisdom of the Serpent* (cited above).

Page 56
The footnote on Zoroastrian origins is from the article on Zoroastrianism in *Encyclopedia Americana.*

Page 56
"Now if Christ be preached . . ." is from I Corinthians 15:12-14.

Page 56
"For since by man . . ." is from I Corinthians 15:21-22.

Page 56
"For when ye were . . ." is from Romans 6:20-23.

Page 57
For a detailed discussion of the exegetical competition between the concepts of Pauline resurrection and Platonic soul, see *Death: Meaning and Mortality in Christian Thought and Contemporary Culture* (cited above).

Page 57
"Christ the first fruits . . ." is from I Corinthians 15:23-26.

Page 57-60
The section on Tutankhamen is based primarily on "Tutankhamun's Golden Trove," by Christiane Desroches Noblecourt with photographs by F. L. Kenett, in *National Geographic,* Oct. 1963; also on articles on Tutankhamen, Akhenaten, Pyramids in *Encyclopedia Americana;* references by Corliss Lamont in *The Illusion of Immortality* (New York: Frederick Ungar, 1935, 1965); the information on Egyptian embalming is from "X-Raying the Pharaohs," by James Harris and Kent Weeks, in *Natural History,* Aug.-Sept. 1972.

Page 58
In the introduction to *The Egyptian Book of the Dead* (cited above), E. A. Wallis Budge says, "We are in any case justified in estimating the earliest form of the work to be contemporaneous with the foundation of the civilization which we call Egyptian in the valley of the Nile." And in a footnote, Budge writes, "The date of Mena, the first king of Egypt, is variously given B.C. 5867 (Champollion), B.C. 5004 (Mariette), B.C. 5892 (Lepsius), B.C. 4455 (Brugsch)." He says the papyrus is known to have been used by Egyptians from about 3500 B.C.

Page 60
The Horace quotation is from his *Odes,* Book III, xxx.

Page 61
"Intimations of Immortality," by Frederik Pohl, in *Playboy,* June, 1964.

Page 61-64
The discussion of science-philosophy-religion is based on *The Story of Philosophy* (cited above); the following articles in *Encyclopedia Americana:* Copernican System, Copernicus, Cartesianism, Descartes, Galileo, Newton,

Mechanics, Mechanism, Materialism, Pascal, Fouché; *Issues in Science and Religion* (cited in Introduction), *The Crime of Galileo* by Giorgio DeSantillana (Chicago: University of Chicago Press, 1955); *The Illusion of Immortality* (cited above); *Death and Modern Man* (cited in Chapter I); "Thanatology: A Historical Sketch," by Morris Saffron, in *Loss and Grief* (cited in Chapter I).

Page 63
The Joseph Fouché proclamation "Death is an eternal sleep" is from *Bartlett's Familiar Quotations* (cited above), p. 1175.

Page 63-64
The discussion of Tolstoy is from *Death and Modern Man* (cited above), pp. 179-180.

Page 64
The Rilke reference is from *Life Against Death* (cited in Chapter I), p. 108.

Page 64
Malraux's attitude is from *Death and Modern Man* (cited above), pp. 182-185.

Page 64
The Existentialist attitude, from the article on Existentialism in *Encyclopedia Americana* and Kaufmann's "Existentialism and Death," in *The Meaning of Death* (cited in Chapter I).

Page 64
On science picking its shots and solving the easy ones—from interviews and discussions with René Dubos: the unsolved and often untackled ecological, urban, and societal problems. See also "The Welfare of Science in an Era of Change," by William Bevan, in *Science*, June 2, 1972.

Page 64-65
The discussion of parapsychology is based on an interview with Karlis Osis, research director, at American Society for Psychical Research in New York City, Oct. 15, 1972; also "Three Papers on the Survival Problem," by Gardner Murphy, published by the ASPR, the three articles appearing in the *Journal* of the ASPR in Jan., July, Oct. 1945; "Discussion," by Gardner Murphy in the conclusion of *The Meaning of Death* (cited above); *Immortality: Parapsychology, the Scientific Evidence*, by Alson Smith (New York: Signet, 1954).

Page 64
In *Death: Its Causes and Phenomena with Special Reference to Immortality*, by Hereward Carrington and John Meader (London: Rider, 1913), the authors report on attempts to photograph the soul immediately after death, weighing the body just before and after death to account for a missing soul and other psychic phenomena that began to arouse curiosity toward the end of the nineteenth century and led to formations of both the British and the American Psychical Societies. This coincided with a diminution of faith in the universe and the person as a machine.

Page 64-65
The estimate of ESP's primary importance to parapsychology is from Dr. Osis.

Page 65-66
The discussion of Unamuno is based primarily on *Death and Modern Man* (cited above), p. 181. Dr. Choron gives the Barea quotation which is from *Lorca: The Poet and His People*, by Arturo Barea, translated by Ilsa Barea (New York: Harcourt, Brace, 1949), pp. 93-94.

Chapter III. Is It in an Elixir, a Fountain, a Testicle?

Page 67-74
The section on alchemy is based upon *The Origins of Alchemy in Graeco-Roman Egypt*, by Jack Lindsay (New York: Barnes & Noble, 1970); *The Royal Art of Alchemy*, by Reinhard Federmann (Philadelphia: Chilton, 1964); *The Forge and the Crucible*, by Mircea Eliade (New York: Harper, 1956); *A Short History of Chemistry*, by Isaac Asimov (Garden City: Doubleday, Anchor, 1965); *Alchemy*, by E. J. Holmyard (Baltimore: Penguin, 1957); *A History of Ideas about the Prolongation of Life* (cited in Chapter I); "The Origins of Greek Alchemy," by F. Sherwood Taylor, in *Toward Modern Science*, edited by Robert Palter (New York: Dutton, 1969); *The Origins of Chemistry*, by R. P. Multhauf (New York: Watts, 1966); the articles on Alchemy, Arabian Nights, Harun al-Rashid, and Paracelsus in *Encyclopedia Americana* (1965).

Page 70
The fable of the Sicilian plowman is from Bacon's *Opus Majus*, Robert Belle Burke translation, p. 622.

Page 72-73
The section on atomic structure, nuclear transmutation is from *Red Giants and White Dwarfs* (cited in Chapter I), pp. 34-36, and the article on Alchemy in *Encyclopedia Americana* (1965).

Page 73
The idea of businessmen as modern alchemists is from *Life Against Death* (cited in Chapter I), pp. 258, 299.

Page 73-77
The section on Chinese alchemy and Taoism is based on *A History of Ideas about the Prolongation of Life* (cited above); *The Forge and the Crucible* (cited above); "The Origins of Greek Alchemy" (cited above); and the article on Taoism in *Encyclopedia Americana* (1965).

Page 74
The Chinese historian is Ssu-ma Ch'ien who lived in the first century B.C.; he is quoting the alchemist Li Shao Chun, who advised Emperor Wu Ti. The quotation is from *Alchemy and Other Chemical Achievements of the Ancient Orient*, by Obed Johnson (Tokyo, 1936), pp. 76-77.

Page 75
The Gruman quotation "Modern experiments show . . ." is from *A History of Ideas about the Prolongation of Life* (cited above), p. 41.

Page 76
The Gruman quotation "It is not surprising . . ." is from *A History of Ideas about the Prolongation of Life* (cited above), p. 43.

Page 76
The Maspero quotation "He who is able . . ." is from "Tao Tsang," by Henri Maspero, in the *Journal Asiatique*, Vol. 229 (1937), pp. 384-385.

Page 77
The blocked *ching* quotation "is about to be discharged . . ." is from "Tao Tsang" (cited above), p. 385. This is a form of contraception reportedly practiced in Turkey, Armenia, and the Marquesa Islands.

Page 77
The Gruman quotation "the Taoist religion . . ." is from *A History of Ideas about the Prolongation of Life* (cited above), p. 35.

Page 77
The Australian aborigines' use of semen is from *Rejuvenation*, by Eric Trimmer (New York: Award Books, 1970), p. 45.

Page 77
Studies in the Psychology of Sex, by Havelock Ellis (New York: Random House, 1936).

Page 77-78
The subject of gerocomy is from *The Process of Ageing*, by Alex Comfort (New York: Signet/NAL, 1964), p. 11.

Page 78
The King David story is from I Kings 1:1-4.

Page 78
Roger Bacon on gerocomy is from *A History of Ideas about the Prolongation of Life* (cited above), p. 65.

Page 78
The experiment with aging male rats was conducted by Otto Muhlbock in the Netherlands and reported in "Factors Influencing the Life Span of Inbred Mice" in *Gerontologia*, Vol. 3 (1959), pp. 177-183.

Page 78-79
The section on Ponce de Leon and the Spanish explorers is based on *A History of Ideas about the Prolongation of Life* (cited above), pp. 24-25; articles on Ponce de Leon and Mexico—Spanish Conquest and Colony in *Encyclopedia Americana* (1965); *A Political and Cultural History of Modern Europe*, by

Carlton Hayes, Vol. I (New York: Macmillan, 1916, 1932), pp. 66-82; *A Basic History of the United States,* by Charles and Mary Beard (New York: Doubleday, Doran, 1944).

Page 79-80
The section on Cornaro is based on *A History of Ideas about the Prolongation of Life* (cited above), pp. 68-71; *The Civilization of the Renaissance in Italy,* by Jacob Burckhardt (London; Phaidon, 1955), pp. 204-206.

Page 79-80
The quotation "In the spring and autumn . . ." is from *The Civilization of the Renaissance in Italy* (cited above), pp. 205-206.

Page 80
The quotation "the marshes and foul air . . ." is from *The Civilization of the Renaissance in Italy* (cited above), p. 205.

Page 80
"And these enjoyments . . ." is from *The Civilization of the Renaissance in Italy* (cited above), p. 206.

Page 80
The quotation "no better doctor" is from *Discourses on the Temperate Life,* by Luigi Cornaro, in *The Art of Living Long,* edited by William Butler (Milwaukee, 1903), p. 58. The quotation "I feel, when I leave . . ." is from p. 107.

Page 80
The quotation "then died an easy Death" is from *History of His Own Time,* by Jacques Auguste de Thou (London, 1734).

Page 80-81
The lifespans of Parr and Jenkins and the lifespan estimate are from *A History of Ideas about the Prolongation of Life* (cited above), p. 75.

Page 81
The section on Descartes is based on *A History of Ideas about the Prolongation of Life* (cited above), pp. 77-80 .

Page 81
The Descartes quotation "we could free ourselves . . ." is from *A History of Ideas about the Prolongation of Life* (cited above), p. 78.

Page 81
The Descartes quotation "I have found another . . ." is from *A History of Ideas about the Prolongation of Life* (cited above), p. 79.

Page 81-82
The segment on Bacon is based on *A History of Ideas about the Prolongation of Life* (cited above), pp. 80-83; *The Story of Philosophy* (cited above), pp.

117-160; *The English Philosophers from Bacon to Mill,* edited by Edwin Burtt, Modern Library edition (New York: Random House), pp. 5-123.

Page 82
The Bacon quotation "Our physicians . . ." is from *The Story of Philosophy* (cited above), p. 134.

Page 82
The Bacon quotation "This is a new part . . ." is from *The Story of Philosophy* (cited above), p. 134.

Page 82
The Franklin quotation "all diseases may be . . ." is from *Man Adapting* by René Dubos (New Haven: Yale University Press, 1965), p. 344.

Page 82
The Condorcet quotation "Would it be absurd . . ." is from *A History of Ideas about the Prolongation of Life* (cited above), p. 87. Gruman's source is *Progress* by Condorcet, p. 200 .

Page 83
The Godwin quotation "In a word . . ." is from his *Enquiry Concerning Political Justice, and its Influence on Morals and Happiness,* Vol. III, p. 224, cited in *A History of Ideas about the Prolongation of Life* (cited above), p. 85.

Page 83
The Malthus paragraph is based on "Malthus Starts the Argument" by Garrett Hardin, "An Essay on the Principle of Population" by Thomas Malthus, "Doubling Times and Population Growth" by Hardin, "Malthus Under Attack" by Hardin—all in *Population, Evolution and Birth Control,* by Garrett Hardin (San Francisco: Freeman, 1964, 1969); "The Human Ecosystem," by Marston Bates, in *Resources and Man,* by National Academy of Sciences/National Research Council (San Francisco: Freeman, 1969); *A History of Ideas about the Prolongation of Life* (cited above), p. 86.

Page 83-89
The section on rejuvenation is based upon *Rejuvenation* (cited above); *The Youth Doctors,* by Patrick McGrady, Jr. (New York: Coward-McCann, 1968); *Extended Youth,* by Robert Prehoda (New York: Putnam, 1968); *The Process of Ageing* (cited above); the articles on Claude Bernard and Charles Brown-Séquard in *Encyclopedia Americana* (1965).

Page 84
The Brown-Séquard quotation "Today I was able . . ." is from *Extended Youth* (cited above), p. 64.

Page 85
The description of Brown-Séquard's Rube Goldberg-like device is from *MD Magazine,* Vol. 5, Sept. 1961, quoted in *Rejuvenation* (cited above), p. 145.

Page 85
The newspaper quotations are from *The Youth Doctors* (cited above), p. 41.

Page 85
The Comfort quotation "This was a strictly . . ." is from *The Process of Ageing* (cited above), p. 17.

Page 85
The Comfort quotation "We can give . . ." is from *The Process of Ageing* (cited above), p. 16.

Page 86
P. S. Timiras in *Developmental Physiology and Aging*, p. 536, says: "Eunuchs and castrated men are known to age prematurely and frequently to simulate senile women in appearance. . . . The earlier the castration, the more pronounced the changes. Generally, these symptoms are ascribed to androgen deficiency and consequent hormonal imbalance." He adds, however, "it cannot be asserted that androgen depletion is the cause of the aging process or that its exogenous administration can rejuvenate, in the strict sense of the word."

Page 86
The quotation "the gland transplantation . . ." is from *Rejuvenation* (cited above), p. 164. Trimmer cites *Medical Journal and Record*, 187:28.

Page 87
The Voronoff quotation is from the book jacket of *The Sources of Life* (Boston: Bruce Humphries, 1943).

Page 87
The Metchnikoff quotation "One day . . ." is from *Rejuvenation* (cited above), p. 98.

Page 88
The Sir Henry Gray allusion to "abdominal spring cleaning" is from *Rejuvenation* (cited above), p. 105.

Page 88
The Comfort quotations "It ill becomes us . . ." and "the methods advocated . . ." are from *The Process of Ageing* (cited above), p. 17.

Page 89
Dr. Strehler's position is from his paper "Myth and Fact: Consequences of the Understanding of Aging," by Bernard Strehler, delivered at the Extension of the Human Life-span Conference sponsored by the Center for the Study of Democratic Institutions, Santa Barbara, California, April 13, 1970.

Page 89-90
The section on cryonics is based on "Immortality and the Freezing of Human Bodies: The Case For . . . ," by John Wiley, Jr., ". . . and the Case Against," by J. K. Sherman, *Natural History*, Dec. 1971; *The Prospect of Immortality,*

by Robert Ettinger (New York: Macfadden-Bartell, 1964, 1969); "Physics and Life Prolongation," by Gerald Feinberg, in *Physics Today*, Nov. 1966; *Immortality*, Spring 1971, a quarterly magazine issued by the Cryonics Society of New York (CSNY); *Manrise Technical Review*, Vol. I, No. 1, Aug.-Sept. 1971; Table of Contents for "Instructions for the Induction of Solid State Hypothermia in Humans"; several brochures from CSNY; two private letters from CSNY secretary Saul Kent; a letter from Joseph Cannon of Cry O Era Corporation, makers of cryogenic equipment at Appleton, Wis.

Page 89
The quotation "An invitation to help . . ." is from a form letter sent by CSNY with a membership application.

Page 89
The quotation "The Cryonics Society . . ." is from the CSNY brochure "Life Extension through Cryonics."

Page 89
The quotation "At present, it is necessary . . ." is from the CSNY brochure "Life Extension through Cryonics."

Page 89
On Dec. 15, 1971 Saul Kent of CSNY wrote me: "Fourteen people have been frozen to date, four in New York, and most of the rest in California." On Jan. 28 and 29, 1972 the *New York Post* and the *New York Times* reported the freezing of an eight-year-old girl in California.

Page 89
The thought of dying or of some form of suspended animation and then coming back to life to see the earth at some later age occurred to Benjamin Franklin, who told of some flies which had apparently drowned in wine and then revived. Gruman in *A History of Ideas about the Prolongation of Life* (cited above), p. 84, quotes a Franklin letter: "I wish it were possible from this instance, to invent a method of embalming drowned persons, in such a manner that they may be recalled to life at any period, however distant; for having a very ardent desire to see and observe the state of America a hundred years hence, I should prefer to any ordinary death, the being immersed in a cask of Madeira wine, with a few friends, till that time, to be recalled to life by the solar warmth of my dear country." But, Franklin wistfully concluded, "in all probability we live in an age too early and too near the infancy of science, to hope to see an art brought in our time to its perfection. . . ."

Page 90
The Sherman quotation "These heterogenous . . ." is from "Immortality and the Freezing of Human Bodies . . . and the Case Against" (cited above).

Page 90
In addition to maintenance costs, estimates of interment range from $8,500 to $20,000.

Page 90
The footnote on the Hope Knoll Cemetery Association is based on its booklet
"For Your Consideration."

Chapter IV. The Long Diagnosis

In general this chapter is based on the following: *History of Medicine,* fourth
edition, by Fielding Garrison (Philadelphia: W. B. Saunders, 1929); *Great
Adventures in Medicine,* edited by Samuel Rapport and Helen Wright (New
York: Dial, 1961); *Mirage of Health,* by René Dubos (New York: Harper,
1965); "History of Medicine," by Felix Marti-Ibanez, in *Encyclopedia Ameri-
cana* (1965); *Health and Disease,* by René Dubos, Maya Pines, and the Editors
of Time-Life Books (New York: Time-Life, 1965); *The Physician,* by Russel
V. Lee, Sarel Eimerl and the Editors of *Life* (New York: Time-Life, 1967);
A History of Pathology, by Esmond Long (New York: Dover, 1928, 1965);
Medical Advance, Public Health and Social Evolution, by Charles Wilcocks
(New York: Oxford, Pergamon, 1965); *Microbe Hunters,* by Paul De Kruif
(New York: Harcourt, Brace, 1926, 1953); *A History of Medicine,* Vols. I and
II, by Henry Sigerist (New York: Oxford University Press, 1951, 1961); *Vic-
tory over Pain: Morton's Discovery of Anaesthesia,* by Betty MacQuitty (New
York: Taplinger, 1969); *The Dreams of Reason,* by René Dubos (New York:
Columbia University Press, 1961); *Man, Medicine and Environment,* by René
Dubos (New York: Mentor/NAL, 1968); "The Natural History of Disease,"
in *The Forest and the Sea,* by Marston Bates (New York: Random House,
Vintage, 1960); "The Ecology of Human Disease," by Jacques May in *Environments of Man,* edited by Jack Bresler (Reading, Mass.: Addison-Wesley,
1968); and *Annals of the New York Academy of Science,* Vol. 84 (1960), pp.
789-794; "Disease," by Jacques May in *Encyclopedia Americana* (1965);
Human Ecology and Public Health, fourth edition, edited by Edwin Kilbourne
and Wilson Smillie (New York: Macmillan, 1969); articles on Hippocrates,
Hygiene, Public Health, Heart, Galen, Aesculapius, and Hygeia in *Encyclopedia Americana* (1965).

Page 91
The hominid lifespan figure was cited in a lecture "Modern Environments and
Their Influence on Human Health," given April 8, 1970, by Lawrence Hinkle,
Jr., director of the Human Ecology Division, Cornell Medical College. Dr.
Hinkle put hominid life expectancy at 18 years.

Page 91
The Sarton quotation "this history of man's . . ." is from *Great Adventures in
Medicine* (cited above), p. 8. Original source is "The History of Medicine
Versus the History of Art," by George Sarton, delivered as the Fielding Gar-
rison Lecture at the 17th Annual Meeting of the American Association of the
History of Medicine, May 1941.

Page 91
The Hippocratic quotation "To know is one thing . . ." is from *The Physician*
(cited above), p. 12.

Page 91-92
The Garrison quotation "In his attempts . . ." is from *History of Medicine* (cited above), p. 21.

Page 92
The Garrison quotation "A further association of ideas . . ." is from *History of Medicine* (cited above), p. 21.

Page 92
The Garrison quotation "Prehistoric and primitive man . . ." is from *History of Medicine* (cited above), p. 31.

Page 92
The two examples of Iroquois Indian herb medicine are from Garrison's *History of Medicine* (cited above), p. 26.

Page 93
The third and second of Dr. Lee's reasons are from *The Physician* (cited above), p. 10, and the quotation "The phrase . . ." is from pp. 9-10.

Page 94
The Dubos quotation "The Jewish tribes . . ." is from *Mirage of Health* (cited above), p. 114.

Page 94
The study referred to is "A Study of Health Practices and Opinions" released Oct. 6, 1972. The study was conducted for the Food and Drug Administration by National Analysts, Inc. of Philadelphia. A number of other agencies co operated in the study, including Administration on Aging, National Institute of Child Health and Human Development, National Institute of Mental Health, and Veterans Administration.

Page 94
The Garrison quotation on Hippocrates' clinical descriptions is from *History of Medicine* (cited above), pp. 94-95.

Page 95
The Hippocrates quotation "are chiefly responsible for . . ." is from "Casualties of Our Times," by Amasa Ford, in *Science*, Jan. 16, 1970.

Page 95-96
Footnote on Dr. Holmes' change impact scale is based on "Doctors Study Treatment of Ills Brought on by Stress" by Jane Brody in the *New York Times*, June 10, 1973. And from "The Social Readjustment Rating Scale" in *Journal of Psychosomatic Research*, Vol. II, Pergamon Press, 1967.

Page 96
The quotation "his treatment . . ." from Hippocrates is quoted in *Encyclopedia Americana* (1965), p. 452.

Page 96
The quotations from the Hippocratic Oath are taken from *Great Adventures in Medicine* (cited above), p. 7.

Page 97
Quotation from the Maimonides Oath is taken from *Great Adventures in Medicine* (cited above), p. 7.

Page 97
The information about Aesculapius' existence about the twelfth century B.C. is from *Mirage of Health* (cited above), p. 110 .

Page 97
The Dubos quotation "For the worshipers of Hygeia . . ." is from *Mirage of Health* (cited above), pp. 110-111.

Page 97
The Dubos quotation "[T]he followers of Aesculapius . . ." is from *Mirage of Health* (cited above), p. 111. The quotation "To ward off disease . . ." is from p. 110.

Page 97
On Hippocrates' tombstone are carved the words: "Here lies Hippocrates who won innumerable victories over disease with the weapons of Hygeia."

Page 97
The quotation "health depends upon . . ." is from *Mirage of Health* (cited above), pp. 114-115.

Page 98
The Second Conference on Psychophysiological Aspects of Cancer is reported in *Annals of the New York Academy of Sciences,* Vol. 164, Part 2, pp. 307-634. Dr. LeShan's quotation "an individual . . ." is from pp. 628-629. Dr. Schmale's quotation "Cancer appears . . ." is from p. 630.

Page 98-99
Aristotle's teaching on the heart is from *History of Medicine* (cited above), p. 247.

Page 99
The Esmond Long quotation "Today we know . . ." is from *A History of Pathology* (cited above), p. 21, as is the quotation "[H]e emphasized . . ."

Page 100
Garrison has an exposition of Galen's "numbers' game" in *History of Medicine* (cited above), p. 113.

Page 100
The Garrison quotation "Galen, as Neuburger puts it . . ." is from *History of Medicine* (cited above), p. 116.

Page 100
The Galen quotation "I have done . . ." is from *On Various Medical Subjects,* by Clarissimus Galen, in *Great Adventures in Medicine* (cited above), p. 53.

Page 101
The Garrison quotation "While written in Latin . . ." is from *History of Medicine* (cited above), p. 219.

Page 101
The Vesalius quotation "once more [to] be able to . . ." is from *History of Medicine* (cited above), p. 219.

Page 101
The Garrison quotation "In the drawings . . ." is from *History of Medicine* (cited above), p. 246.

Page 101-102
The Vesalius quotation "We are driven . . ." is from *History of Medicine* (cited above), p. 220 .

Page 102
The quotation "motions and uses of the heart . . ." is from "Vesalius and Harvey; The Founding of Modern Anatomy and Physiology," by Michael Foster, in *Great Adventures in Medicine* (cited above), pp. 120-121.

Page 102
The Harvey quotation "unless the blood should somehow find its way from . . ." is from Foster, in *Great Adventures in Medicine* (cited in preceding item), p. 122; the quotation "not only feared . . ." is from p. 122.

Page 102-103
The Aubrey quotation "I have heard . . ." is from "The Only Contemporary Character Sketch of William Harvey," by John Aubrey, in *Great Adventures in Medicine* (cited above), p. 120.

Page 103
The reference to Harvey reading under a hedge during the battle of Edgehill is from Foster, in *Great Adventures in Medicine* (cited above), p. 120.

Page 103
The quotation "In the year 1675 . . ." is from "Very Small Living Creatures . . . ," by Anton van Leeuwenhoek, in *Great Adventures in Medicine* (cited above), p. 210.

Page 103
The footnote that Leeuwenhoek took the secret of his microscope lenses to the grave with him is from *Health and Disease* (cited above), p. 57.

Page 103
Figures on Greek deaths after surgery are from "History of Medicine," in *Encyclopedia Americana* (cited above). Figure given: as high as 78 percent.

Page 104
Paré quotation "I expected to find them all dead . . ." is from *The Physician* (cited above), p. 33.

Page 104
References to the fast surgeons are from *History of Medicine* (cited above): Langenbeck on p. 494, Fergusson on p. 484, Cheselden on p. 343.

Page 104-105
The Nathan Rice quotation "A pulley is attached . . " is from *Victory over Pain* (cited above), p. 68.

Page 105
The use of nicotine is mentioned in *Victory over Pain* (cited above), p. 67.

Page 105
The source for "bite the bullet" is Richard Cappelletti, a surgeon, of Kinderhook, N.Y.

Page 105
The "brutal remark" reference is from *History of Medicine* (cited above), p. 505: "Hypnotism was also employed, and even suggestion, as where Dupuytren induced a convenient fainting spell by a brutal remark."

Page 105
The Davy quotation "it may probably be used . . ." is from *History of Medicine* (cited above), p. 505.

Page 105-108
The section on anesthesia is based on *Victory over Pain* (cited above); "The Death of Pain," by James Flexner, in *Great Adventures in Medicine* (cited above), pp. 401-426, and originally published in Flexner's *Doctors on Horseback* (New York: Viking, 1937); *History of Medicine* (cited above), pp. 505-506; *The Physician* (cited above), p. 37.

Page 107
The Wells letter is from *Victory over Pain* (cited above), p. 144.

Page 108-110
The Ignaz Semmelweis story is based on "The Cry and the Covenant," by Morton Thompson, in *Great Adventures in Medicine* (cited above), pp. 220-247 and originally from *The Cry and the Covenant*, by Thompson (Garden

City: Doubleday, 1949); *History of Medicine* (cited above), pp. 435-437; *The Physician* (cited above), p. 31.

Page 108
The footnote on opposition to use of anesthesia to ease pain of childbirth is from *Sir James Y. Simpson,* Famous Scots Series (Edinburgh, 1896), pp. 63-65.

Page 109
Rokitansky's 30,000-plus necropsies is from A *History of Pathology* (cited above), p. 105.

Page 110
The footnote on the Oliver Wendell Holmes note is from *History of Medicine* (cited above), p. 435.

Page 110
The Virchow section is based on A *History of Pathology* (cited above), pp. 114-124; *History of Medicine* (cited above), pp. 569-572, 451-453, 455-456; History of Medicine in *Encyclopedia Americana* (1965); *The Physician* (cited above), pp. 34, 35.

Page 110
The Virchow quotation "A new growth . . ." is from *History of Medicine* (cited above), p. 570.

Page 110
The phrase "republic of cells" is from History of Medicine, in *Encyclopedia Americana* (1965), p. 572.

Page 110
The Virchow quotations "a cell state . . ." and "a conflict of citizens . . ." are from *The Physician* (cited above), p. 35, and *History of Medicine* (cited above), p. 570.

Page 110-113
The section on Pasteur, Koch, Lister, and von Behring is based on *Health and Disease* (cited above), pp. 57-59, 38; *The Physician* (cited above), pp. 35-37; A *History of Pathology* (cited above), pp. 142-155; *History of Medicine* (cited above), pp. 575-585, 588-592, 372-375; History of Medicine, in *Encyclopedia Americana* (1965), p. 573; *Great Adventures in Medicine* (cited above), pp. 204-208.

Page 111
Source of footnote on milk companies balking at pasteurization: René Dubos, during an interview in Feb. 1969.

Page 112
Pasteur quotation "Don't you see . . ." is from *Health and Disease* (cited above), p. 58.

Page 112
Esmond Long writes about Virchow on tuberculosis and his reaction to Koch
in *A History of Pathology* (cited above), pp. 123-124: "There was never anything half-hearted about Virchow's pronouncements, so that it is not surprising
that he made mistakes, and bad ones. As a matter of fact he lived to see re-
vision or reversal of his views on inflammation, thrombophlebitis, tumors, and
tuberculosis, while the event of bacteriology ushered in a whole series of
changes he could not possibly foresee. Although he wrote voluminously on
tuberculosis he never made himself clear on the subject. . . . The final unification brought about in after-years through recognition of the infectious cause
was a hard pill to swallow, and it is not altogether astonishing that the old
fighter could never quite bring himself to cordial terms with the great bacteriologist Robert Koch."

Page 112
The Ehrlich quotation "That evening . . ." is from *Great Adventures in
Medicine* (cited above), p. 206.

Page 113
The Esmond Long quotation "For a few . . ." is from *A History of Pathology*
(cited above), p. 151.

Page 113
Garrison has a reprise of the rush of discoveries and developments in the late
nineteenth century in *History of Medicine* (cited above), pp. 582-584.

Page 113-114
The limitation of antitoxins is cited in *History of Medicine* (cited above), p.
584, and *A History of Pathology* (cited above), pp. 151-152.

Page 113-114
"Approaches to the Control of Human Infections," by Edwin Kilbourne, in
Human Ecology and Public Health (cited above), pp. 209-283, discusses diseases and control approaches. Table on p. 272 lists vaccines in common use,
table on p. 270 lists antitoxic antibodies.

Page 114
Reference for 100 different strains of pneumococcus and streptococcus: *Health
and Disease* (cited above), p. 61.

Page 114
Reference for more than 300 viruses known to produce disease: *Human Ecology
and Public Health* (cited above), p. 72.

Page 114-115
The Paul Ehrlich story is based on *Microbe Hunters* (cited above), pp. 308-
330; *History of Medicine* (cited above), pp. 708-710; *A History of Pathology*
(cited above), pp. 153-154; Ehrlich, in *Encyclopedia Americana* (1965). For

a feeling of the pre-penicillin treatment of syphilis, the article on Syphilis in *Encyclopedia Americana* (1965), is curiously antiquated, based on literature circa 1937, but enlightening for the period attitude and attendant insecurity regarding the disease. That and Garrison serve as the antidote to De Kruif's raves.

Page 115
Source for 30 million deaths in 1918 influenza pandemic: Influenza, *Encyclopedia Americana* (1965).

Page 115
Moynihan quotation "The craft of surgery . . ." is from "Surgery," by John Thwaites, in *Great Adventures in Medicine* (cited above), p. 778.

Page 115-116
The sulfanilamide-antibiotics section is based on "Chemotherapy," by Alexander Fleming, in *Great Adventures in Medicine* (cited above), pp. 767-776, and originally from *Chemotherapy: Yesterday, Today, Tomorrow,* by Fleming (London: Cambridge University Press, 1946); also the articles on Antibiotics, Sulfonamides, and History of Medicine, in *Encyclopedia Americana* (1965).

Page 116
The discussion on surgery is based on "Surgery," by John Thwaites, in *Great Adventures in Medicine* (cited above), pp. 776-807, and originally from *Modern Medical Discoveries,* by Thwaites (New York: Dutton, 1958); private discussions with Richard Cappelletti, M.D., surgeon.

Page 116
Life expectancy figures: *Human Ecology and Public Health* (cited above), p. 13, for 1900 figure; *Statistical Abstract of the United States, 1971,* for current figures.

Page 117
Source for halving of TB deaths in last half of nineteenth century: *Health and Disease* (cited above), p. 59: from four deaths per 1,000 in 1850 to just under two deaths per 1,000 in 1900.

Page 117
Source for mortality of English children: *Health and Disease* (cited above), p. 54.

Page 117
Source for hundreds of thousands of U.S. child laborers and high death rates in New York, Philadelphia, and Boston: *Health and Disease* (cited above), p. 59.

Page 117-118
1850, 1860, 1870 infant death rates in New York City are from *The City in History* (cited in Chapter I), p. 467.

Page 118-119
The discussion of the pneumonia-diarrhea complex is based on "Demography, Culture, and Economics and Evolutionary Stages of Medicine," by Walsh Mc-Dermott, in *Human Ecology and Public Health* (cited above), pp. 7-28; the 14 in 100 infant deaths is from p. 11.

Page 118
Human Ecology and Public Health (cited above), p. 12: infant mortality from the pneumonia-diarrhea complex fell from 7.5 per 100 in 1898 to 1.7 per 100 in 1930 and "it dwindled away to negligible proportions in the years thereafter."

Page 118
Quotation "we have today no decisive . . ." is from *Human Ecology and Public Health* (cited above), p. 13.

Page 118
The source for the statement about more than half the deaths in the under-developed world in the first five years of life is *Human Ecology and Public Health* (cited above), p. 17.

Page 118
The quotation "the truly great killer . . ." is from *Human Ecology and Public Health* (cited above), p. 20.

Page 118
The quotation "We do know . . ." is from *Human Ecology and Public Health* (cited above), p. 13.

Page 119
The quotation "It may be recalled . . ." is from *Human Ecology and Public Health* (cited above), p. 20.

Page 119
In 1900 tuberculosis was just behind pneumonia-influenza as the leading cause of death in the United States, with just under two deaths per 1,000. In 1930 TB was the fifth leading cause of death, its rate nearly halved to just over one death per 1,000. By 1952 three anti-TB drugs were in use. In 1954 the death rate dropped to .34 per 1,000. Source: *Aging and Society*, Vol. I, by Matilda Riley, Anne Foner, and associates (New York: Russell Sage Foundation, 1968), pp. 168, 199.

Page 119
The footnote on von Pettenkofer is from History of Medicine, in *Encyclopedia Americana* (cited above), p. 573.

Page 120
The Bernard quotation "The constancy . . ." is from *Man, Medicine, and Environment* (cited above), p. 83.

Page 121-123
The section on the plague is based on *Health and Disease* (cited above), pp. 31-34; "Plague" by George Rosen, professor of Health Education, Columbia University in *Encyclopedia Americana* (1965); *Mirage of Health* (cited above), pp. 156-159; *History of Medicine* (cited above), pp. 187-189; "The Plague," by Giovanni Boccaccio (1358), in *Great Adventures in Medicine* (cited above), pp. 70-75.

Page 123
Re ecological view of disease, Jacques May says in "The Ecology of Human Disease" in *Environments of Man* (cited above), p. 80: "The ancient formula of one ill, one pill, which seems to have been the credo of physicians for many generations, should be abandoned. Disease is a biological expression of maladjustment. This is what should be taught to our students in medical school, and this phenomenon against which they are going to fight all their lives cannot be understood without an ecological study in depth that should give equal importance to the three approaches: the environment, the host, and the culture."

Page 123-124
The Dubos quotation "Thousands of people . . ." is from *Health and Disease* (cited above), p. 13 .

Page 123
The footnote on altitudinal malaria in Vietnam is from "The Ecology of Human Disease" in *Environments of Man* (cited above).

Page 123
The reference to Cortez in the footnote is from *The Forest and the Sea* (cited above), p. 172.

Page 124
The Cartesian influence on medical practice is elaborated by Dubos in *Man, Medicine, and Environment* (cited above), pp. 76-79.

Page 124
For conquest of ecological disease, see "The Natural History of Disease" in *The Forest and the Sea* (cited above), p. 173: "In the parts of the world with a highly developed economy, the dangerous infections have come to be very largely under control: ecological hazards to the life of the individual have been drastically reduced." Edwin Kilbourne, in "Genetic Interaction of Man and Microbes—Implications of a Changing Ecology," in *Human Ecology and Public Health* (cited above), pp. 47-77: "The great plagues of mankind have all but disappeared from industrialized society" and most of the lesser epidemics, too, although Dr. Kilbourne cautions that we still do not know enough about genetic

evolution to be complacent. Dr. Dubos, in *Health and Disease* and *Mirage of Health,* goes further, seeing the civilized disease syndrome as replacing the defeated diseases of less organized society.

Page 124
Figures for 1968 influenza pandemic are from *Time,* Aug. 21, 1972. Medical scientists now are trying to perfect, or believe they have perfected, a vaccine for the next flu epidemics so that they will not be caught "fighting the last war." In Feb. 1973 researchers at Pasteur Institut in Paris announced that they had produced such a vaccine to counter the organism that the flu virus will evolve into.

Page 124
The Dubos quotation "the ability to function . . ." is from *Health and Disease* (cited above), p. 10.

Page 124
The Jacques May quotation "Disease . . ." is from "The Ecology of Human Disease," in *Environments of Man* (cited above), p. 80.

Page 124-125
In 1900 infectious diseases, external causes, and childbirth caused about two-thirds of the deaths in the United States. In 1969 infectious diseases caused about 10 percent or less of the deaths in the United States. Figures for 1900 from *Aging and Society* (cited above), p. 198; 1969 figures from *U.S. Statistical Abstract, 1971.* For a discussion of the changing causes of death, see "Casualties of Our Time," by Amas Ford, in *Science* Jan. 16, 1970 (cited above). Among the many points Dr. Ford makes is that deaths from arteriosclerotic heart disease rose in epidemic proportions during the decade 1957–1966; also, with obesity a national problem: "Citizens of the United States have an average of over 3000 calories of food energy available daily, which is twice the minimum required to sustain life."

A revelatory if unintentional documenting of the association of microbial and behavioral diseases (malfunctioning) can be seen in a story in the *New York Times,* Dec. 7, 1972, headlined "TB Rate Is High In Singles Hotel—City Acts to Stem Disease at Uptown Residence Called a Center for Crime," by Max Seigel. The lead sentence reads: "The City's Department of Health yesterday disclosed it had found a high concentration of tuberculosis cases in the Harvard Club, 304 West 99th Street, a single-room-occupancy facility described by the police as a major crime center."

Page 125
The statistics on American deaths from privately owned guns is from "Americans Can—and Should—Live Longer," by Marshall Loeb, an essay in *Time,* July 10, 1972.

Page 125
The source for child-abuse estimate is Vincent Fontana, M.D., St. Vincent's

Hospital in New York City; he is one of the nation's foremost authorities on the subject.

Page 125-126
The cancer death statistics and summary of gains against cancer given in the footnote are based on " '72 Cancer Facts & Figures," published by the American Cancer Society; *Hearings, National Cancer Attack Act of 1971,* U.S. Government Printing Office, Washington, D.C.; "Cancer Census" in *Time,* Nov. 15, 1971.

Page 125
The Burnet quotation "There is virtually . . . ." is from *Immunological Surveillance* by Macfarlane Burnet, Pergamon, Oxford, 1970, p. 134.

Page 126
The statistic on cancer-causing chemicals is from testimony before Congress by Carl Baker, then director of the National Cancer Institute, in Sept., 1971, in *Hearings, National Cancer Attack Act of 1971,* (cited above), p. 164.

Page 126
Lung cancer statistics are from " '72 Cancer Facts & Figures," (cited above).

Page 126
The ACS booklet "The Key Factors on the Dangers of Smoking" estimates 300,000 cigarette-related deaths in a year in the United States.

Page 126
The asbestos statistic is based on findings by two pathologists, Milton Kannerstein of Barnert Memorial Hospital in Paterson, N.J. and Jacob Churg of Mount Sinai School of Medicine in New York City and reported in the ACS journal *Cancer,* Vol. 30, No. 1, p. 14, 1972.

Page 126
The ACS statement "Most lung cancers . . ." is from " '72 Cancer Facts & Figures," (cited above).

Page 126
The federal government tobacco revenue figure cited by Robert Sherrill, Washington correspondent of *The Nation,* in a review of the book *Cigarette Country* in the *New York Times Book Review,* Oct. 17, 1971.

Page 127
Life expectancy projections based on cures of heart disease and cancer are from a World Health Organization study of life expectancies in 34 countries in the decade 1958–1968 and reported in "Study Finds Increases in Life Expectancy at Birth," by Walter Sullivan, in the *New York Times,* July 6, 1972.

Page 127
The Bierman estimate of benefits of solving cancer and arteriosclerosis is from

"Background and Issues—Research and Demonstration, White House Conference on Aging" (1971), p. 31.

Page 127
The footnote on survival rates is from *Developmental Physiology and Aging* (cited above), pp. 590, 600.

Chapter V. What Is Aging?

In general, this chapter is based on the following: *Developmental Physiology and Aging*, by P. S. Timiras (New York: Macmillan, 1972); *Aging and Society*, Vol. I, by Matilda Riley, Anne Foner, and associates (New York: Russell Sage Foundation, 1968); lectures "Biological Processes of Aging," by Anita Zorzoli, and "Psychological Processes of Aging," by Darrell Slover, given at the Seminar on Gerontology and Higher Education, sponsored by the Syracuse University School of Social Work in New York City, Dec. 9-11, 1971; *Time, Cells, and Aging*, by Bernard Strehler (New York: Academic Paperbacks, 1962); *The Ages of Life*, by Lorus and Margery Milne (New York: Harcourt, Brace, 1968); *The Process of Ageing*, by Alex Comfort (New York: Signet/NAL, 1961, 1964); *Aging and Levels of Biological Organization*, edited by Austin Brues and George Sacher (Chicago: University of Chicago Press, 1965); *Aging Life Processes*, edited by Seymour Bakerman (Springfield, Ill.: C. C. Thomas, 1969); *Ageing: The Biology of Senescence*, by Alexander Comfort (New York: Holt, Rinehart and Winston, 1956, 1964); *Red Giants and White Dwarfs*, by Robert Jastrow (New York: Harper & Row, 1967); *Childhood and Society*, by Erik Erikson (New York: Norton, 1950, 1963); *The Coming of Age*, by Simone de Beauvoir (New York: Putnam, 1972).

"Research and Demonstration—Background and Issues, White House Conference on Aging" (1971), by George Maddox and Edwin Bierman; "Can We Live to Be 100?" by Nathan Shock, second draft of manuscript for *Science Yearbook, Encyclopedia Brittanica*, March 1970; "The Physiology of Aging," by Nathan Shock, in *Scientific American*, Jan. 1962; "Age with a Future," by Nathan Shock in *The Gerontologist*, Vol. 8, No. 3 (Autumn 1968); "Physiologic Aspects of Aging," by Nathan Shock, in *Journal of the American Dietetic Association*, Vol. 56, No. 6 (June 1970); "The Physiology of Aging," by Nathan Shock, in *Surgery of the Aged and Debilitated Patient*, edited by J. H. Powers (Philadelphia: W. B. Saunders, 1968); "A Long Look at Aging," by Nathan Shock, in *The Johns Hopkins Magazine*, Spring 1968; *The Johns Hopkins Magazine*, Spring 1968, the entire issue; "Biologic Concepts of Aging," by Nathan Shock, *Psychiatric Research Report*, American Psychiatric Association, Feb. 1968; "Biological Aspects of the Aging Process," by Anita Zorzoli, *Public Health News*, New Jersey State Department of Health, Vol. 49, No. 7 (July 1968); "The Life Span of Animals," by Alex Comfort, in *Scientific American*, Aug. 1961; "Biochemistry of Aging," by F. Marrot Sinex, in *Science*, Nov. 3, 1961; "Animal Ages," by David Willoughby, in *Natural History*, Dec. 1969; "Energy in the Universe," by Freeman Dyson, in *Scientific American*, Sept. 1971; "Child Health and Human Development: Progress 1963-1970," a report of the National Institute of Child Health and Human Development; "The Effect of the Prolongation of Life on Health," by Leroy Duncan Jr., and "What Is the Aim of Gerontology," by Fritz Verzár—both papers presented at the Extension of Human Life-span Conference, sponsored by the Center for the Study of Democratic Institutions at Santa Barbara, Calif., April 1970.

Page 128
The T. S. Eliot quotation "I grow old . . ." is from "The Love Song of J. Alfred Prufrock," in *Collected Poems* (New York: Harcourt, Brace, 1936).

Page 128
Sir George Pickering, Regius professor of medicine at Oxford University, told Associated Press science writer Alton Blakeslee, May 26, 1966, that aging is "a preparation for death."

Page 128
The Galen reference is from *A History of Ideas about the Prolongation of Life* (cited in Chapter III), p. 16. Galen believed that in the embryo the heat contributed by the male semen dried the amorphous material supplied by the female. This drying process led to the formation of organs and tissues, and also to the hot-dry humoral condition of youth. However, when the drying continued into early adulthood, it ceased being beneficial and instead dried up the body's fuel or innate moisture, leading to the cold-dry state of adulthood.

Page 128
The quotation "is like living on an island . . ." is from *The Johns Hopkins Magazine* (cited above), p. 1.

Page 128
The Maurice Chevalier quotation is from *Time*, Aug. 3, 1970.

Page 129
Shakespeare's "ages of man" is from *As You Like It*, Act II, Scene 7.

Page 131
The Timiras quotation "embryonal and fetal . . ." is from *Developmental Physiology and Aging* (cited above), p. 375.

Page 131
On prenatal environmental influences, *Developmental Physiolgy and Aging* (cited above), p. 377: "The respective roles of genetic and environmental factors during prenatal life have been calculated by Penrose (1961) from a relatively large population of newborns. According to his figures, which used variations in birth weight as an arbitrary index of comparative growth and development, 38 percent of the total variations observed could be ascribed to hereditary factors (20 percent to maternal inheritance, 16 percent to fetal inheritance, 2 percent to sex) and 62 percent of the total were due to environmental factors (24 percent to maternal health, 7 percent to parity, 1 percent to maternal age, 30 percent to unidentified intrauterine influences). Although the physiologic significance of these mathematically derived data must be interpreted with some reservations, these calculations suggest that environmental factors play an important role even during uterine development."

Page 131
The footnote on spontaneous abortions is based on "Child Health and Human Development: Progress 1963–1970" (cited above), p. 8; the quotation "Evidence currently . . ." is from p. 9.

Page 132
On nutrition and prenatal development, *Developmental Physiology and Aging* (cited above), p. 385: "[T]he first studies of the effects of nutrition on fetal development were not initiated until the mid-twentieth century. Hale (1937) conclusively established that vitamin A-deficient sows produced malformed young. It is now known that nutritional disturbances may influence all stages of prenatal growth and development from implantation to birth."

Page 132
Examples of agents that can disturb the embryo-fetus are taken from p. 378, "Table 19-1, A Partial List of Known Malformation-Producing Agents (Teratogens)," and p. 382, "Table 19-2, A Partial List of Drugs Influencing Growth and Development of Human Fetus or Newborn," in *Developmental Physiology and Aging* (cited above).

Page 132
The Public Health Service report on smoking is from "Women Smokers Warned of Fetal and Infant Risks," by Harold Schmeck, Jr. in the *New York Times,* Jan. 18, 1973. *Developmental Physiology and Aging* (cited above). p. 383, states: "Numerous clinical reports have correlated a high incidence of premature birth, spontaneous abortion, and low birth weight with heavy smoking during pregnancy (Yerushalmy, 1964), and animal studies have also shown that when nicotine is administered chronically to gestating rats, the growth and development of the fetus are impaired (Becker *et al.,* 1968)."

Page 132
The information on possible chromosomal damage by LSD is from *Developmental Physiology and Aging* (cited above), p. 380. The most recent study, published in Dec. 1972, by Cecil Jacobson, of George Washington University, and Cheston Berlin, now at the Milton Hershey Medical Center, Hershey, Penn., reported on 148 pregnancies in which the parents used LSD prior to delivery. There were 83 live births, with eight of these infants suffering major congenital defects: approximately 10 percent compared to the normal 1 percent. Two infants died after birth. Approximately half of the infants had chromosome breakage, but most of the damage mended naturally in the first three to six months. Reported in *Science,* March 23, 1973.

Page 133
Information on maternal age and the offspring's welfare is from *Developmental Physiology and Aging* (cited above), pp. 532, 529, 379.

Page 133
The 76 types of embryonic cell degeneration are cited in *Biology and the Future of Man,* edited by Philip Handler (New York: Oxford, 1970), p. 703.

Page 134
The statistics on 17,000 accidental deaths among children are from *Developmental Physiology and Aging* (cited above); in "Exhibit 9-1, Mortality from leading causes, by age, United States, 1962," in *Aging and Society* (cited above), p. 196, there is a five to three ratio of deaths from accidents in the one-to-four age group compared to the five-to-fourteen age group.

Page 134
The Comfort quotation "If we could stay . . ." is from *The Process of Ageing* (cited above), p. 8.

Page 134
The footnote on salmon is from "The Puzzle of Aging," in *Time*, Nov. 1, 1968, p. 59.

Page 135
For longevous shift in Gompertz curve in the United States, see Figure 24-2, p. 464, in *Developmental Physiology and Aging* (cited above).

Page 135
The Cureton chart on physical ability is in *The Physiological Effects of Exercise Programs on Adults,* by Thomas Cureton (Springfield, Ill.: C. C. Thomas, 1969), p. 25.

Page 135
The figures for speed, skill, and endurance peaks are from "Man's Potential—And His Performance," by Joseph Still, in the *New York Times Magazine,* Nov. 24, 1957.

Page 136
The Shock quotation "Fifty percent overweight . . ." is from "Age with a Future" (cited above).

Page 136
Smokers' lungs ten years old physiologically, cited by Daniel Rogers, Public Information Officer, Gerontology Research Center, referring to Center's longitudinal study.

Page 136
The NIMH study is reported in *Human Aging II: An 11-Year Followup Biomedical and Behavioral Study,* edited by Samuel Granick and Robert Patterson, National Institute of Mental Health (1971).

Page 136
The Cureton Information is from *Physiological Effects of Exercise Programs on Adults* (cited above).

Page 136
The medically supervised exercise program is from "New Spas Fill the Prescription," by Grace Lichtenstein in the *New York Times,* Jan. 15, 1973.

Page 137
The University of California, Davis, program and the story of Noel Johnson
are from an Associated Press story in Oct. 1971, and a personal letter from
Jack Wilmore, Nov. 17, 1971. Wilmore's quotations are from the letter, Johnson's quotation is from the wire story.

Page 137
Dr. Cureton's quotation "We have the beginnings . . ." is from *The Physiological Effects of Exercise Programs on Adults* (cited above), p. 16.

Page 137
Developmental Physiology and Aging (cited above), p. 411: "In contrast to
other periods of the life cycle in which the onset is clearly marked by specific
physiologic events, aging has so far defied all attempts to establish objective
landmarks that would precisely characterize its earlier stages."

Page 138
Data on volume of blood per body size, blood-sugar levels, and the rise of
cholesterol are from "Biological Processes of Aging," by Anita Zorzoli (cited
above).

Page 138
Nathan Shock, in "The Physiology of Aging," in *Surgery of the Aged and Debilitated Patient* (cited above), says fat accumulates throughout adult life
and then diminishes after ages sixty to sixty-five, and body weight increases
slowly until about age sixty and then declines. P. S. Timiras, in *Developmental
Physiology and Aging* (cited above), puts the peaks at age fifty.

Page 138-140
The various statistics on physiological decline are from "Physiologic Aspects of
Aging" (cited above); "The Physiology of Aging," in *Scientific American* (cited
above); "Perspectives of the Aging Process" (cited above); "Can We Live to
Be 100?" (cited above); *Developmental Physiology and Aging* (cited above);
"Biological Processes of Aging" (cited above).

Page 139
Shock quotation "Most of the debilities . . ." is from "The Physiology of
Aging," in *Scientific American* (cited above).

Page 139
Bernard Strehler cited the 1 percent per year physiological decline in "A New
Age for Aging," in *Natural History*, Feb. 1973, and so did F. Marrot Sinex in
an interview, Oct. 1971, with Crixpo, Inc.

Page 140
The news-wire story of the couple that died from heat prostration in the desert
is from memory, when I was working at WCBS-TV News in the late 1960s.

Page 140
The section on the eye and sensory capacity is based on Shock, Timiras, Zorzoli, and "Critical Sensory Changes Affecting Environmental Adjustment of Older Persons," a communication Aug. 10, 1971 from Leon Pastalan of the University of Michigan's Institute of Gerontology to Millhaven, Inc., Tacoma, Wash., detailing essential data for designing environments for the elderly.

Page 141
For typical menopausal age, *Developmental Physiology and Aging* (cited above), p. 531: "Figures from highly industrialized nations give an average of 48, whereas recent data from a population of New Zealand women reports a mean age of 50 to 51 for the onset of menopause (Burch and Gunz, 1967)." *Biology and the Future of Man* (cited above), p. 706, cites a 1960–1962 survey of American women as showing the average age for menopause as 49.7.

Page 141
Bernard Strehler in "Genetic and Cellular Aspects of Life Span Prediction," in *Prediction of Life Span,* edited by Erdman Palmore and Frances Jeffers (Lexington, Mass.: D. C. Heath, 1971), p. 35: "There is absolute certainty that maximum life span possible for the member of a given species is determined by the nature of the DNA that species contains. The validity of this generalization is attested to by the fact that a given life span is a characteristic of each species."

Page 141-142
For a discussion of genetic control of lifespan, see "The Biology of Aging" by William Reichel in *Journal of the American Geriatrics Society,* Vol. 14, No. 5, 1966.

Page 142
Life expectancy statistics are from "United States Life Tables: 1959–61" by the U.S. Public Health Service, and *U.S. Statistical Abstract, 1971.* The life expectancy of white males, age sixty, since 1789, is from "Vital Statistics of the United States, 1963," Vol. II, Section 5, Life Table 5-5.

Page 142
The 13,000 figure is from the booklet "Every 10th American" by the Administration on Aging. The Social Security Administration, HEW, Baltimore, listed 6,995 centenarians on its rolls as of Jan. 1972.

Page 142
The Soviet centenarian figures were published in a survey by the World Health Organization, submitted by the director of the Soviet Institute for Gerontology at Kiev, Dmitri Chebotarev, and reported in the *Baltimore Evening Sun,* Dec. 16, 1971.

Page 142
The Chebotarev estimate of percentage of centenarians is from "Longevity and the Role of Its Investigation in the Elucidation of Aging Processes," at the 8th International Congress of Gerontology, Washington, D.C., published Aug. 1969.

Page 142
The NICHHD quotation "often takes far less . . ." is from "Child Health and Human Development: Progress 1963–1970" (cited above), p. 46.

Page 142
The Comfort quotation "Birth certificates were introduced . . ." is from "The Life Span of Animals," in *Scientific American* (cited above).

Page 142
The Comfort quotation ". . . Pierre Jourbet . . ." is from *The Process of Ageing* (cited above), pp. 40-41.

Page 142
The Duncan quotation "The maximum lifespan . . ." is from "The Effect of the Prolongation of Life on Health" (cited above).

Page 142
The Comfort lifespan estimate of 115 years plus is from both "The Life Span of Animals" (cited above), and *The Process of Ageing* (cited above). The Strehler estimate of 118 years plus is from *Time, Cells, and Aging* (cited above), p. 47.

Page 142-143
The discussion of the aged people in the Andes, Hunza land, and the Caucasus is based on "Andes Evidence Indicts Cholesterol," by David Andelman, in the *New York Times*, April 22, 1971; "Every Day Is a Gift When You Are Over 100," by Alexander Leaf, in *National Geographic*, Jan. 1973; "Why They Live to Be 100, or Even Older, in Abkhasia," by Sula Benet, in the *New York Times Magazine*, Dec. 26, 1971; "Scientists Seek Key to Longevity," by Walter Sullivan in the *New York Times*, Feb. 11, 1973.

Page 143-144
The footnote on oldest Americans is based on private communications from Herman Brotman, April 12, 1973, and the Social Security Administration in Baltimore.

Page 144-148
Comparative ages of organisms from "The Life Span of Animals" (cited above); *The Process of Ageing* (cited above); "Some Fairly Authentic Lifespans," pp. 311-314, in *The Ages of Life* (cited above); *Aging and Levels of Biological Organizations* (cited above); *Time, Cells, and Aging* (cited above); for Galapagos tortoise, *The Ages of Life*, pp. 202-203.

Page 144-145
The Sacher findings are based on *Aging and Levels of Biological Organization* (cited above), pp. 266-294, and *The Ages of Man* (cited above), pp. 181-182, 308.

Page 144
Greater relative brain size, more neural control, is cited in *Developmental Physiology and Aging* (cited above), p. 567.

Page 145
The lifespans and deaths of our sun and other stars is based on "Energy in the Universe," by Freeman Dynson, in *Scientific American* (cited above), and from *Red Giants and White Dwarfs* (cited above), pp. 40-43.

Page 145-146
The Strehler quotation "Time breeds disorder . . ." is from *Time, Cells, and Aging* (cited above), p. 16.

Page 147
The quotation "By current taxonomic . . ." is from "The Origins of Taxonomy," cited in Chapter I.

Page 147
The story of the sea anemone is from *Time, Cells, and Aging* (cited above), pp. 39-40.

Page 148
The Strehler quotation "that there is no inherent . . ." is from *Time, Cells, and Aging* (cited above), p. 40.

Page 148
The study and longevity of the sponge are reported in "Marine Lab at Aquarium Studies Sea and Sea Life," by John Devlin, in the *New York Times*, Jan. 8, 1973.

Page 148
The paragraph on how individuals can cease to exist and the three categories of organisms are from *Time, Cells, and Aging* (cited above), pp. 38-39.

Page 149
The Timiras quotation "[O]ne of the main characteristics . . ." is from *Developmental Physiology and Aging* (cited above), p. 170.

Page 149
That Roger Bacon equated aging and disease is from *The Coming of Age* (cited above), p. 19. Mlle de Beauvoir, on p. 18, says Galen regarded aging as something between illness and health. Gruman in *A History of Ideas about the Prolongation of Life* (cited above), pp. 16-17, emphasizes that Galen considered aging a natural event and not a disease.

Page 149
Selye's attributing stress as cause of both aging and disease is from *Extended Youth* (cited above), pp. 159-164.

Page 149-151
The discussion of diseases of the aged and atherosclerosis is based on chapters 24 and 25 in *Developmental Physiology and Aging* (cited above), and "The Cardiovascular System," in *Aging and Society* (cited above), pp. 225-229.

Page 150
The source for the 2 percent of the U.S. population being eighty years or older

is "Resources of People 65 or Over," published by the Office of Research and Statistics of the Social Security Administration and based on a Social Security survey of aged persons in 1968: chart 2, on p. 7.

Page 150
The figure of one person in 250 being eighty-five years or older is from "Longevity and the Role of Its Investigation in the Elucidation of Aging Process" (cited above). Chebotarev says that the eighty-five plus population ranges between 1.2 and 6.8 per 1,000. I arbitrarily took the mean between those extremes.

Page 150
The Timiras quotation "Atherosclerosis dwarfs . . ." is from *Developmental Physiology and Aging* (cited above), p. 477.

Page 151
Footnote is based on "Atherosclerosis and the Arterial Smooth Muscle Cell" by Russell Ross and John Glomset in *Science*, June 29, 1973.

Page 151
Footnote on coronary heart disease factors is taken from *Developmental Physiology and Aging* (cited above), p. 496.

Page 151-152
The information on the aged Andes people and Dr. Leaf's quotation "there were only a couple . . ." are from "Andes Evidence Indicts Cholesterol" (cited above). Most of the diet information is from Leaf's "Every Day Is a Gift When You Are Over 100" (cited above). Dr. Leaf cites a U.S. Department of Agriculture study for the American daily intake of 3,300 calories.

Page 152
The Strehler quotation "that a species . . ." is from "Environmental Factors in Aging and Mortality," in *Environmental Research*, June 1967.

Page 152
The information on the Mabaans in the Sudan is from *The Ages of Man* (cited above), pp. 220-222.

Page 153
The Timiras quotation "[O]ld age cannot be regarded . . ." is from *Developmental Physiology and Aging* (cited above), p. 6.

Page 153
The NICHHD quotation "The aging process . . ." is from "Child Health and Human Development: Progress 1963–1970" (cited above), p. 46.

Page 153
The Ana Aslan estimate and de Beauvoir quotation "I cannot agree . . ." are from *The Coming of Age* (cited above), p. 28.

Page 154
The Eisdorfer statement "There is no necessary . . ." was made at the White
House Conference on Aging, Nov. 29, 1971.

Page 154
The discussion of progeria and Werner's syndrome is based on: "Progeria and
Werner's Syndrome as Models for the Study of Normal Human Aging," by
William Reichel, Rafael Garcia-Bunel, and Joseph Dilallo, in the *Journal of
the American Geriatrics Society,* May 1971; an interview with Dr. Reichel in
Baltimore, Dec. 16, 1971; and "Aging: The Eternal Quest for Eternal Youth"
by Walter Sullivan, in the *New York Times,* Oct. 24, 1971.

Page 155
The references to Buber and Goethe are from "Looking Forward to What? The
Life Review, Legacy, and Excessive Identity Versus Change," by Robert
Butler, in *American Behavioral Scientist,* Sept./Oct. 1970.

Page 155
The Rubinstein quotation "Sometimes I feel bad . . ." is from an interview in
the *New York Times,* Jan. 28, 1972, with Donal Henahan, "Rubinstein at 85:
Still a Fresh Outlook," on the occasion of his eighty-fifth birthday.

Page 155
The Picasso quotation "We don't get older . . ." is from a book review of
Janet Flanner's *Paris Was Yesterday,* by Robert Phelps, in *Life,* July 28, 1972.

Page 155
The Still estimates on intellectual growth and the quotation "Memorizing
ability . . ." are from "Man's Potential—And His Performance" (cited above).

Page 155-156
The Freudian ages of sexual development are from "Erik Erikson's Eight Ages
of Man," by David Elkind, in the *New York Times Magazine,* April 5, 1970.

Page 156-157
Darrell Slover's sociological events in old age are from "Psychological
Processes of Aging" (cited above).

Page 157-161
The discussion of Erik Erikson's ages of human development is based on
Chapter 8, "Eight Ages of Man," in *Childhood and Society* (cited above), and
"Erik Erikson's Eight Ages of Man" (cited above). The following quotations
are from *Childhood and Society:*

Page 157
"to balance . . ." and "The first demonstration . . . ," p. 247.

Page 158
"There is in every child . . . ," p. 255.

Page 159
"is by no means entirely. . . ," p. 262.

Page 159
"The strength acquired . . . ," p. 263

Page 160
"It has taken psychoanalysis . . . ," pp. 266, 267.

Page 160
"Only in him who in some way . . . ," p. 268.

Page 160-161
"The lack or loss . . ." and "[H]ealthy children will not . . . ," pp. 268-269.

Page 160-161
Developmental Physiology and Aging (cited above), p. 412; "[I]t is not surprising, particularly in view of its highly phenomenal nature, that aging still eludes conclusive definition."

Chapter VI. The Science of Senescence

In general, the chapter is based on the following:

BOOKS: *Aging and Society,* Vol I: An Inventory of Research Findings, by Matilda Riley, Anne Foner, and associates (New York: Russell Sage Foundation, 1968); *Middle Age and Aging,* edited by Bernice Neugarten (Chicago: University of Chicago Press, 1968); *Prediction of Life Span,* edited by Erdman Palmore and Frances Jeffers (Lexington, Mass.: D. C. Heath, 1971); *Normal Aging, Reports from the Duke Longitudinal Study, 1955–1969* (Durham, N.C.: Duke University Press. 1970); *Human Aging, a Biological and Behavioral Study,* edited by James Birren, Robert Butler, Samuel Greenhouse, Louis Sokoloff, Marian Yarrow, HEW, Public Health Service Publication No. 986, U.S. Government Printing Office, Washington, D.C.; *Human Age II, An Eleven-Year Followup,* edited by Samuel Granick and Robert Patterson, National Institute of Mental Health, HEW Publication No. HSM 71-9037 (1971); *Foundations of Practical Gerontology,* edited by Rosamonde Boyd and Charles Oakes (Columbia, S.C.: University of South Carolina Press, 1969); *8th International Congress of Gerontology, Proceedings,* Vol. I, International Association of Gerontology, Washington, D.C. (1969); *The Process of Ageing,* by Alex Comfort (New York: Signet/NAL, 1961, 1964); *The Future of Aging and the Aged,* edited by George Maddox, Foundation Seminar Books, Southern Newspaper Publishers Association, Atlanta, Ga., (1971); *Later Life: Geriatrics Today and Tomorrow,* by Ivor Feldstein (Baltimore: Penguin, 1969); *Perspectives in Experimental Gerontology,* edited by Nathan Shock (Springfield, Ill.: C. C. Thomas, 1966); *Extended Youth,* by Robert Prehoda (New York: Putnam, 1968); *Old Age: The Last Segregation,* Ralph Nader's Study Group Report on Nursing Homes, Claire Townsend, Project Director, Grossman, N.Y. (1971); *Sexual Life after Sixty* by Isadore Rubin, (New York: Basic Books, 1965); *A History of Ideas about the Prolongation of Life* by Gerald Gruman (Philadelphia: American Philosophical Society, 1966).

PAPERS: "Review of Government Supported Research on Aging," Vols. I-III, prepared by the National Institute of Child Health and Human Development (1971); "Research and Training in Gerontology," a working paper prepared for the U.S. Senate Special Committee on Aging (1971); "A Pre-White House Conference on Aging Summary of Developments and Data," a report of the Senate Special Committee on Aging, Nov. 19, 1971; "Facts & Figures on Older Americans, No. 4: Federal Outlays in Aging," HEW, Administration on Aging (1971); "Facts & Figures, No. 5: An Overview for the Delegates," HEW, AoA (1971); "White House Conference on Aging: A Report to the Delegates from the Conference Sections and Special Concerns Sessions, Nov. 28–Dec. 2, 1971"; *Aging*, bimonthly magazine of the AoA, Jan.-Feb. 1972, March-April 1972, Nov.-Dec. 1972; *Aging*: "Facts on Aging," May 1970; "Background and Issues: Research and Demonstration, White House Conference on Aging" (1971); "Predicting Longevity: A Follow-up Controlling for Age," by Erdman Palmore, in *The Gerontologist*, Winter 1969; "Are We Dying Too Soon?" by Robert Musel, United Press International, Feb. 10, 1963; "Leading Components of Upturn in Mortality for Men, United States, 1952–1967," Vital Health Statistics, Series 20, No. 11; "The Security of Social Security: The Young Pay for the Old," by Edwin Dale, Jr., in the *New York Times Magazine*, Jan. 14, 1973; "Taxes: Painful New Year's Bite," in *Time*, Jan. 15, 1973; "Every Day Is a Gift When You Are Over 100," by Alexander Leaf, in *National Geographic*, Jan. 1973; "Why They Live to Be 100 or Even Older, in Abkhasia," by Sula Benet, in the *New York Times Magazine*, Dec. 26, 1971; "Andes Evidence Indicts Cholesterol," by David Andelman, in the *New York Times*, April 22, 1971; "The Good Life and the Aging Brain," by Henry Mark, in *The Johns Hopkins Magazine*, Spring 1968; "Intelligence and Blood Pressure in the Aged," by Francis Wilkie and Carl Eisdorfer, in *Science*, May 28, 1971; "The Effects of Ageing on Intelligence," by Dennis Bromley, in *Impact of Science on Society*, Vol. XXI, No. 4 (1971); "Age: The Life Review," by Robert Butler, in *Psychology Today*, Dec. 1971; "The Effect of Medical and Health Progress on the Social and Economic Aspect of the Life Cycle," by Robert Butler, in *Industrial Gerontology*, June 1969; "Grow Old Along with Me! The Best Is Yet to Be," by Bernice Neugarten, in *Psychology Today*, Dec. 1971; "Growing Old in America: The Unwanted Generation," by Ruth Brine, in *Time*, Aug. 3, 1970; "The Misunderstood Generation," in *The Johns Hopkins Magazine*, Spring 1968; "The Foreshortened Life Perspective," by Robert Kastenbaum in *Geriatrics*, Aug. 1969; "Age: Getting There Ahead of Time," by Robert Kastenbaum, in *Psychology Today*, Dec. 1971; "Assumptions about Aging and the Aged," from "Training Manual for Human Service Technicians Working with Older Persons," Part I, by Louis Lowy (1968); "Resources of People 65 or Over," Social Security Administration (1970); "Social Context—A Neglected Variable in Research on Aging" by Ruth Bennett, in *Aging and Human Development*, Vol. I, No. 2; "Distinguishing Characteristics of the Aging from a Sociological Viewpoint," by Ruth Bennett, in *Journal of the American Geriatric Society*, Vol. 10, No. 2 (1968); "Concepts, Knowledge and Commitment: The Education of a Practicing Gerontologist," by Walter Beattie, Jr. Also the following papers presented at the Extension of the Human Life-span Conference, sponsored by the Center for the Study of Democratic Institutions at Santa Barbara in April 1970: "Healthy, Longer Lives," by William Ewald, Jr.; "What Is the Aim of Gerontology," by Fritz Verzár; "The Effect of the Prolongation of Life on Health," by Leroy Duncan, Jr.; "A Few Questions Concerning the Implications for Public Policy of

Longevity and Aging Research," by Byron Gold; "Patterns in Senior Activities, 1970," by A. M. G. Russell.

MEETINGS: White House Conference on Aging in Washington, D.C., Nov.–Dec., 1971, particularly the Research and Demonstration section, interviews with Carl Eisdorfer and a number of other gerontologists; Syracuse University's Seminar on Gerontology and Higher Education, held in New York City, Dec. 9-11, 1971; visits to the Gerontology Research Center in Baltimore in Dec. 1971, and the University of Southern California Gerontology Center in July 1971; interview with William Reichel at Franklin Square Hospital in Baltimore, Dec. 16, 1971; interview with Lissy Jarvik at Columbia Presbyterian Hospital in New York City, Dec. 6, 1971; interview with Ruth Bennett at Columbia University, Dec. 7, 1971.

Page 163
Gruman says the word "gerontology" apparently was introduced by Metchnikoff in *The Nature of Man: Studies in Optimistic Philosophy* (New York: 1903), p. 298.

Page 163-164
The Felstein quotation "When I set foot . . ." is from *Later Life: Geriatrics Today and Tomorrow* (cited above), pp. 13-14.

Page 164
The Carl Eisdorfer quotation "I'm interested in the first week . . ." was made as he led a subsection on Research and Demonstration at the White House Conference on Aging, Nov. 29, 1971.

Page 165
The Kiev Gerontology Institute has a staff of 600 including 170 qualified scientists.

Page 165
The figures on schools giving gerontology courses are from Dean Walter Beattie's discussion at the Seminar on Gerontology and Higher Education (cited above).

Page 165-166
Information on the Gerontology Research Center is based on "Bio-Medical Research on Aging," by F. Marrot Sinex, in *Research and Training in Gerontology* (cited above); "The Gerontology Research Center," a booklet prepared by NICHHD; "A Long Look At Aging," in *The Johns Hopkins Magazine* (cited above).

Page 166-167
Agencies that disburse funds for aging based on "Facts & Figures on Older Americans, Number 4" (cited above), and a supplemental "Estimated Federal Outlays in Aging, Fiscal Years 1971–1973."

Page 167
Information on funding AoA is from "A Pre-White House Conference on Aging Summary of Developments and Data" (cited above), pp. 40-41.

Page 167
President Nixon's quotation "We want to begin by . . ." is from *Aging*, Jan.–Feb. 1972 (cited above).

Page 167-168
The Frank Church quotation "Among the complaints . . ." is from "A Pre-White House Conference on Aging Summary of Developments and Data" (cited above), p. iv.

Page 168
Funding for gerontology in NICHHD is from "Facts & Figures, No. 4" (cited above).

Page 168
The quotations "In fiscal year 1968 . . ." and "Thus aging research . . ." are from "Review of Government Supported Research on Aging" (cited above), Vol. I, p. 57.

Page 168
Statistics on health-care spending are from "Facts & Figures on Older Americans, No. 5" (cited above).

Page 168
The Gerald Hirsch quotation "Cancer and heart disease . . ." is from a statement made to me at the University of Southern California, July 22, 1971.

Page 169
Maddox quotation "the wisdom of funding . . ." is from "Background and Issues: Research and Demonstration, White House Conference on Aging" (cited above), p. 5.

Page 169
The Robert Finch quotation "I agree that the amount of research . . ." is from "Healthy, Longer Lives" (cited above); the quotation is from a letter by Secretary Finch to Ewald June 7, 1969.

Page 169-170
Some of the information on the difficulty of attracting scientists to gerontology is based on remarks by Dean Walter Beattie to the Seminar on Gerontology and Higher Education (cited above).

Page 170-171
Social Security funding statements are based on "Estimated Federal Outlays in Aging, Fiscal Years 1971–1973," supplied by AoA and cited above.

Page 171
Source for statistics on expansion of U.S. populations: "Facts & Figures on Older Americans, No. 5" (cited above), p. 2.

Page 171
Source of statistics for year 2000: "Census Estimate at Century's End Cut
by 20 Million," by Jack Rosenthal, in the *New York Times,* Dec. 18, 1972.

Page 171
The Carl Eisdorfer estimate of 40 million older Americans in the year 2000
was made in an interview at the White House Conference on Aging, Nov. 30,
1971.

Page 171-172
The estimate of an equilibrium aged population is from "The Effect of the
Prolongation of Life on Health" (cited above).

Page 172
Statistics of aged turnover are from "Facts & Figures, No. 5" (cited above).

Page 172
The various national life-expectancy statistics are from "Health of Nation Lags
Behind Scientific Gains," by Harold Schmeck, Jr., in the *New York Times,*
July 16, 1971, which uses a chart copyrighted by *Scientific American.*

Page 172
The Butler quotation "It is extraordinary . . ." is from "The Effect of Medical
and Health Progress on the Social and Economic Aspects of the Life Cycle"
(cited above).

Page 172
The statistics on minority aged are from "Facts & Figures, No. 5" (cited
above).

Page 172-173
Black-white, male-female life expectancy statistics are from *U.S. Statistical
Abstract* (1971).

Page 172
The statistic 100 older men to 98 older women in the year 1900 is cited by
Herman Brotman, Assistant to the Commissioner, Statistic and Analysis, Administration on Aging. In 1900, there were 1,555,418 men and 1,525,080
women aged 65 or older in the United States.

Page 172-173
The composition of older population statistics, from "Facts & Figures, No. 5"
(cited above), and from "New Profile of Elderly Americans" by the Central
Bureau in the *New York Post,* June 11, 1973.

Page 173
The Beattie quotation "We are doing poorly . . ." is from the Seminar on
Gerontology and Higher Education (cited above) and from "New Profile of
Elderly Americans" by the Census Bureau in the *New York Post* June 11, 1973.

Page 173-174
The Lissy Jarvik information is based on interview (cited above).

Page 174
The Ruth Bennett quotations are from interview (cited above).

Page 174
Alex Comfort discusses sex longevity differences in *Ageing: The Biology of Senescence* (New York: Holt, Rinehart and Winston, 1956, 1964), pp. 177-181.

Page 174
Dr. Zorzoli's comments are from the Seminar on Gerontology and Higher Education (cited above).

Page 174
Male-female brain ratios are from *The Ages of Life*, by Lorus and Margery Milne (New York: Harcourt, Brace, 1968), p. 309.

Page 174-175
Information on the quantitative equality of X and Y spermatozoa and superiority of male-bearing sperm cells to fertilize is from discussion in *Developmental Physiology and Aging*, by P. S. Timiras (New York: Macmillan, 1972), pp. 16-32.

Page 175
Statistics on stillbirths are from *Aging and Society* (cited above), p. 200.

Page 175
Statistics that by age eighteen females outnumber males is from Walter Beattie, Jr. at the Seminar on Gerontology and Higher Education (cited above).

Page 175
The Bruno Bettelheim quotation "he must come to the conclusion . . ." was reported in the *New York Times*, Jan. 17, 1973.

Page 175
The statement that women take better care of themselves than men is from a study by Blackwell cited by Anita Zorzoli at the Seminar on Gerontology and Higher Education (cited above).

Page 175-176
The source for male deaths: "Leading Components of Upturn in Mortality for Men, United States—1952–1967," HEW Publication No. 72-1008 (cited above).

Page 176
Statistics on marital status are from "Facts & Figures, No. 5" (cited above).

Page 176
Geographical statistics on the aged are from *Aging*, Oct. 1971, and "Facts on Aging" from *Aging*, May 1970 (cited above).

Page 176-177
The Martin quotation "You have the best chance . . ." is from an interview at
the Gerontology Research Center, Dec. 15, 1971.

Page 177
The Kastenbaum survey is cited in "Age: Getting There Ahead of Time"
(cited above).

Page 177
The Neugarten quotation "from social workers who serve the poor . . ." is
from "Grow Old Along with Me!" (cited above).

Page 178
Three major problem areas were cited by Darrell Slover in the Seminar on
Gerontology and Higher Education (cited above).

Page 178
Elderly per capita health costs are cited from "A Pre-White House Conference
on Aging Summary of Developments and Data" (cited above), and "Facts &
Figures, No. 5" (cited above).

Page 178
That about four in five suffer from some chronic condition is cited in *Aging
and Society* (cited above), p. 205.

Page 178
That nine of ten older people get around without help is from *Aging:* "Facts on
Aging" (cited above).

Page 178
That one in 20 aged is in an institution is from "Facts & Figures, No. 5" (cited
above).

Page 178
The rise in age of old people in institutions was cited by Walter Beattie, Jr.
in the Seminar on Gerontology and Higher Education (cited above).

Page 178
The Neugarten quotation "Old persons are not dumped . . ." is from "Grow
Old Along with Me!" (cited above).

Page 178
The 8 percent mental impairment of elderly figure is from "The Misunderstood
Generation," in *The Johns Hopkins Magazine* (cited above).

Page 178
The Medicare figure is from "Facts & Figures, No. 5" (cited above).

Page 178
That one-half of the retired would not be able to work because of health impairment is from "Background and Issues, Research and Demonstration, White House Conference on Aging" (cited above), p. 11.

Page 178
Income figures are from "Facts & Figures, No. 5" (cited above).

Page 178
That one in four old people is impoverished is cited in "A Pre-White House Conference on Aging Summary of Developments and Data (cited above), p. 7.

Page 179
The numbers of elderly poor increasing since 1968 was cited by Walter Beattie, Jr., in the Seminar on Gerontology and Higher Education (cited above).

Page 179
The quotation "Inadequate incomes . . ." is from "A Pre-White House Conference on Aging Summary of Developments and Data" (cited above), p. 5.

Page 179
President Nixon's quotation "In addressing the challenges . . ." is from *Aging*, Jan.-Feb. 1972 (cited above).

Page 179
Social Security information is based on "The Security of Social Security: The Young Pay for the Old" (cited above), and "Taxes: Painful New Year's Bite" (cited above).

Page 179
The figures on percentages of income supplied by Social Security are from "Wiser Social Security," an editorial in the *New York Times*, July 17, 1972.

Page 179
That nearly 70 percent of older Americans own their own homes is from President Nixon's address to the White House Conference on Aging, cited in *Aging*, Jan.-Feb. 1972.

Page 179
That virtually all aged couples maintain their own homes is from "Resources of People 65 or Over" (cited above), p. 8.

Page 179
Figures on assets of the aged are from Walter Beattie, Jr., in the Seminar on Gerontology and Higher Education (cited above).

Page 179-180
The question of the middle-age group supporting the young and old was cited by Walter Beattie, Jr., in the Seminar cited above.

Page 180
Figures for young entering the job market later and old leaving earlier are
cited in "The Changing Age-Status System," by Bernice Neugarten and Joan
Moore, in *Middle Age and Aging* (cited above), p. 10.

Page 180
That more than half of workers choose to retire at age sixty-two was cited by
Walter Beattie, Jr., in the Seminar, cited above; this was also the source for
his prediction on earlier retirement age.

Page 180
French and Italian retirement ages are from *Epoca,* April 18, 1971.

Page 180
The Maddox quotation "In our cultural tradition . . ." is from "Growing Old:
Getting Beyond the Stereotypes" by George Maddox in *Foundations of Prac-
tical Gerontology* (cited above), p. 8.

Page 180
The Robert Butler quotation "we leave immune . . ." is from "The Effect of
Medical and Health Progress on the Social and Economic Aspects of the Life
Cycle" (cited above).

Page 181
The Maddox quotation "Research findings . . ." is from "Growing Old: Getting
Beyond the Stereotypes" (cited above); also "We are prone . . ." and
"[T]here is evidence . . . ."

Page 181
The Neugarten quotation "They (old people) are not . . ." is from "Grow Old
Along with Me!" (cited above); also "[O]ld persons do not become . . . ."

Page 181
The study showing four of ten aged couples desisted from sex is from *Aging
and Society* (cited above), p. 259, from a Newman and Nichols study with
150 volunteers (1960).

Page 181
Kinsey studies are in *Aging and Society* (cited above), p. 260, from Kinsey
et al. interviews (1953) with several thousand men and women.

Page 182
The Masters and Johnson quotation "may be corrected easily . . ." is from
"Human Sexual Response: The Aging Female and the Aging Male," by
William Masters and Virginia Johnson, in *Middle Age and Aging* (cited above),
p. 269.

Page 182
Masters and Johnson, in the foregoing paper, refer to Kinsey findings on
women's postmenopausal sex drives.

Page 182
The Masters and Johnson quotation "suggests that a woman who . . ." is from "Human Sexual Response: The Aging Female and the Aging Male" (cited above), pp. 271 and 273, in *Middle Age and Aging* (cited above).

Page 182
Footnote: *Biology and the Future of Man* is cited in Chapter V, p. 708.

Page 183
The Masters and Johnson quotation "[I]f elevated levels . . ." is from *Middle Age and Aging* (cited above), p. 275.

Page 183
The Masters and Johnson quotation "Once impotent under . . ." is from *Middle Age and Aging* (cited above), p. 278.

Page 183-186
The section on intelligence is based on "The Effects of Ageing on Intelligence" (cited above); "The Good Life and the Aging Brain" (cited above); *Aging and Society* (cited above), pp. 255-258; "Behavioral and Social Research," by George Maddox, in "Research and Demonstration, White House Conference on Aging" (cited above); "Rate of Change on Selective Tests of Intelligence: A Twenty-Year Longitudinal Study of Aging," by June Blum, Lissy Jarvik, and Edward Clark, in *Journal of Gerontology*, Vol. 25, No. 3 (1970); "Growing Old in America," in *Time* (cited above); "Background and Theories of Aging," by Carl Eisdorfer, in *The Future of Aging and the Aged* (cited above).

Page 184
The Bromley quotations "Fluid abilities are . . ." and "Crystallized abilities . . ." are from Bromley's "The Effects of Ageing on Intelligence," in *Impact* (cited above), pp. 292, 293. Studies by psychologist on Jon Kangask at University of Santa Clara Counseling Center showed that the IQ's of 48 men and women in the San Francisco Bay area rose 20 points between childhood and middle age. Men with stimulating jobs showed highest increases. (*Time*, Feb. 26, 1973, p. 58.)

Page 185
The drop in intelligence/high blood pressure correlation is from "Intelligence and Blood Pressure in the Aged" (cited above).

Page 185
Sharp intelligence test declines related to early death are cited by Palmore in *Prediction of Life Span* (cited above), p. 286; *Aging and Society* (cited above), p. 257; and by Lissy Jarvik in an interview, Dec. 6, 1971.

Page 185
The Blum, Jarvik, Clark quotation "These results lead to . . ." is from "Rate of Change on Selective Tests of Intelligence: A Twenty-Year Longitudinal Study of Aging" (cited above).

Page 185-186
Duke University research on memory and learning is discussed by Maddox in "Behavioral and Social Research" (cited above); also in *Aging and Society* (cited above), p. 258; "Growing Old in America" (cited above); and by Carl Eisdorfer in *The Future of Aging and the Aged* (cited above), from which comes the quotation "we demonstrated . . . ," p. 6.

Page 186
The source of statements on the aged not regarding themselves as poorly as young people and having a clearer sense of self-identity is from *Aging and Society* (cited above), p. 289.

Page 186
Admission of shortcomings is from *Aging and Society* (cited above), p. 290, from Gurin *et al.* (1960), U.S. samples of 2,500 adults.

Page 186
Negative perception from *Aging and Society* (cited above), p. 291, from Gurin *et al.* (1960).

Page 186
Health ratings are from *Aging and Society* (cited above), p. 293, from Sheatsley (unpublished, 1955) and Suchman *et al.* (1958).

Page 186
Information on lack of education is from *Aging and Society* (cited above), p. 298, from Gurin *et al.* (1960).

Page 186
Data on feelings of inadequacy are from *Aging and Society* (cited above), pp. 300, 301, from Gurin *et al.* (1960).

Page 186
On feeling older is from *Aging and Society* (cited above), pp. 303, 304, from Batten, Barton, Durstine, and Osborn (1966), and Phillips (1957).

Page 186
Lack of mastery and emphasis of individual responsibility is from *Aging and Society* (cited above), p. 315.

Page 186
Attitudes toward doctors and hospitals is from *Aging and Society* (cited above), p. 319, from Sheatsley (unpublished).

Page 186
On pessimism, p. 329, from Back and Gergen (1966).

Page 186
General life satisfaction goes down, from *Aging and Society*, p. 341.

Page 186
Happiness study, p. 342, from Gurin *et al.* (1960).

Page 186
Worry study, p. 344, from Back and Gergen (1966).

Page 186
Morale study, p. 343, from Kutner *et al.* (1956).

Page 186-187
Work-socioeconomic status-health study, p. 351, from Streib (1956).

Page 187
That Erikson's study is virtually the only one on aging but is not widely tested is attributed to Darrell Slover in the Seminar on Gerontology and Higher Education (cited above).

Page 187
The disengagement theory was first presented in *Growing Old* by Elaine Cumming and William Henry (New York: Basic Books, 1961).

Page 187-189
Discussion of the disengagement theory is based on "Disengagement and Patterns of Aging," by Robert Havighurst, Bernice Neugarten, and Sheldon Tobin, in *Middle Age and Aging* (cited above); "Personality and Patterns of Aging," by Bernice Neugarten, Robert Havighurst, and Sheldon Tobin, in *Middle Age and Aging* (cited above); "Grow Old Along with Me!" (cited above); lecture by Darrell Slover, "Psychological Processes of Aging," at Seminar on Gerontology and Higher Education (cited above).

Page 187-188
The quotation "In other words, those older . . ." is from "Personality and Patterns of Aging," in *Middle Age and Aging* (cited above), p. 173.

Page 189
Discussion of foreshortened life perspective is from "The Foreshortened Life Perspective," by Robert Kastenbaum, and "Age: Getting There Ahead of Time" (both cited above).

Page 189
The quotation "foresaw fewer good years ahead . . ." is from "Age: Getting There Ahead of Time" (cited above).

Page 189
The discussion of life review theory is from "Age: The Life Review" (cited above).

Page 189-190
Anita Zorzoli's recommendations on living better, longer are from her lecture at the Seminar on Gerontology and Higher Education (cited above).

Page 190
Ruth Bennett's recommendations on living better, longer are from an interview (cited above).

Page 190
The Robert Kastenbaum classroom experiments on preexperiencing old age are from "Age: Getting There Ahead of Time" (cited above).

Page 190
Columbia University's discrimination against older people was cited by Ruth Bennett in an interview (cited above).

Page 190-191
The Isaac Presler story is from *Time*, May 8, 1972, p. 61.

Page 191
The absence of Soviet mandatory retirement age was cited by Ruth Bennett in an interview (cited above).

Page 191-193
Discussion of the two longitudinal studies is based on *Human Aging II* (cited above); *Prediction of Life Span* (cited above); *Normal Aging* (cited above).

Page 191
The government report quotation "and where findings are similar . . ." is from *Human Aging II* (cited above), p. 4.

Page 192
The Palmore quotation "These findings suggest that . . ." is from *Prediction of Life Span* (cited above), p. 246.

Page 193
The Palmore quotation "It is significant . . ." is from *Prediction of Life Span* (cited above), p. 241. A second Duke study conducted at Chapel Hill with a larger panel of 864 aged persons showed the chief predictor of longevity to be physical mobility; but the next three predictors were socioeconomic—education (the more the better the chance of survival), occupation (professors lived longest, white collar workers next, farmers least), and employment (better chance of surviving if still working).

Page 193
The McHarg attitude was expressed in "What Would You Do With, Say, Staten Island?" in *Natural History*, April 1969.

Page 194
Manley Fleischmann, chairman of the New York State Commission on the Quality, Cost and Financing of Elementary and Secondary Education, commented on Commission findings in the *New York Times*, Jan. 8, 1973: "Further, many of us learned for the first time that an incredible situation had developed involving excessive pension arrangements for teachers, and that this

situation threatened the future financial integrity of the state particularly New York City. Some of our recommendations dealt with these questions." Another study commissioned by Citizens Union Research Foundation shows that police, firemen, and sanitation men stand to get even higher pension payments. This study report was published in the *New York Times,* Jan. 15, 1973.

Page 194
The Bevan editorial was in *Science,* Sept. 8, 1972.

Page 194
The Nathan Shock quotation "If I had my way . . ." is from the *Los Angeles Times,* July 31, 1966.

Page 195
The quotation "Changes in cultural practices . . ." is from *Human Aging II* (cited above), p. 137.

Page 195
The Eisdorfer quotations "by 1990, the American lifespan . . ." and "for a whole new creative approach . . ." are from an interview at the White House Conference on Aging, Nov. 30, 1971.

Page 195
Forty-eight states have Administration on Aging programs and some cities have departments on aging which can provide all sorts of useful information about ways elderly people can conserve money. take advantage of existing benefits, and so forth. The Administration on Aging in the Department of Health, Education and Welfare can be similarly helpful. The U.S. Department of Agriculture puts out a booklet "A Guide to Budgeting for the Retired Couple," A1.77:194/2, S/N0100-01518, which may be purchased for 10¢ from the Superintendent of Documents, U.S. Government Printing Office, Washington, D.C.

Page 195-196
Mrs. A. M. Russell's discussion is from "Patterns in Senior Activities" (cited above).

Page 196
Walter Beattie, Jr.'s discussion is from the Seminar on Gerontology and Higher Education (cited above).

Page 197
William Reichel's plan for geriatric home service and his quotations are from a private communication, Dec. 20, 1971.

Page 197
The new, expanded role for nurses in New York State was signed into law in March 1972, and the State Education Department now is constructing a new educational training program to implement the law.

Page 198
Figures on nursing-home construction are from Bevan's editorial in *Science* (cited above).

Page 198
The story on the Gray Panthers and Margaret Kuhn's quotations are from "Gray Panthers Out to Liberate Aged," in the *New York Times,* May 19, 1972; additional information is from an Associated Press dispatch from Philadelphia, published June 19, 1972.

Page 198
The idea of today's aged as pioneers is suggested by William Ewald in "Healthy, Longer Lives" (cited above).

Page 198-201
The continued discussion of the long-lived people is based on "Every Day Is a Gift When You Are Over 100" and "Why They Live to Be 100, or Even Older, in Abkhasia" (cited in Chapter V).

Page 199
Pearl studies in "Experiment Studies on the Duration of Life," by Raymond Pearl, S. L. Parker, B. M. Gonzalez, in *American Naturalist,* Vol. 57, pp. 153-192 (1923).

Page 199
Animal studies correlating longevity to parents are cited in "The Promise and Problems of Longevity Studies," by Erdman Palmore, in *Prediction of Life Span* (cited above), p. 4.

Page 199
The survey showing low correlation between longevity and parental longevity is from "Longevity and the Role of Its Investigation in the Elucidation of Aging Processes" (cited in Chapter V).

Page 199
The Palmore quotation "My interpretation . . ." is from a private communication, Jan. 14, 1972.

Page 201
The Sula Benet quotations "My own view . . ." and "Since what they are taught . . ." are from "Why They Live to Be 100, or Even Older, in Abkhasia" (cited above).

Page 201
The quotation "Live joyfully with thy wife . . ." is from Ecclesiastes 9:9.

Page 202
The Gabriel Chapnian quotation "Hmm . . . too literate," is from "Every Day Is a Gift When You Are Over 100" (cited above).

Chapter VII. Biological Gerontology

Page 203
The Sinex quotation "is one of the major things . . ." is from an interview
with Crixpo, Inc., Oct. 1971.

Page 203
The Sinsheimer quotation "Even the timeless patterns . . ." is from his address, "The End of the Beginning" (1966).

Page 203
The Ruth Bennett quotation "it is just as difficult . . ." is from an interview
(cited in Chapter VI).

Page 204-205
Facts about Weismann's life are from *Encyclopedia Americana* and his ideas
on death and immortality are based on extensive quotations in *Time, Cells
and Aging* (cited in Chapter V): "Let us now consider . . ." from p. 35;
"Normal death . . ." from p. 36; "because the unlimited . . ." from p. 220;
"worn-out individuals . . ." from pp. 219-220; "Death itself . . ." from p. 34.

Page 205-206
The Saturnid moth study by A. D. Blest is cited by Sacher in *Aging and
Levels of Biological Organization* (cited in Chapter VI), and by Comfort in
The Process of Ageing (cited in Chapter V), but a more complete account is
given in *The Ages of Life* (cited in Chapter V), p. 202. The original source
cited in that book is "Longevity, palatability, and natural selection in five
species of New World saturid moths," in *Nature*, March 23, 1963.

Page 206
The account of the Galapagos tortoise is from *The Ages of Life* (cited above),
pp. 202-203.

Page 206-207
There is a long, interesting, discursive discussion of aging and evolution in
Aging and Levels of Biological Organization (cited above), pp. 266-312.

Page 206
The Sacher quotation "From the standpoint of evolution . . ." is from *Aging
and Levels of Biological Organization* (cited above), p. 267.

Page 206-207
For a further discussion comparing Weismann and the Medawar-Comfort
views, see "Abnutzungstheorie," by George Sacher, in *Perspectives in Experimental Gerontology,* (cited in Chapter VI).

Page 207
The Comfort quotation "[W]e probably age because . . ." is from *The Process of Ageing* (cited above), p. 93.

Page 207
The Strehler quotations "is essentially a result . . ." and "their organization into . . ." are from *Time, Cells, and Aging* (cited above), pp. 224-225.

Page 207-208
The Rubner and rate of living figures are from *Extended Youth*, by Robert Prehoda (New York: Putnam, 1968), pp. 185-187, and *The Ages of Life* (cited above), p. 181.

Page 208
Long life of the bat and desert mouse cited by Bernard Strehler in "Myth and Fact: Consequences of the Understanding of Aging," a paper presented at the Extension of the Human Life-span Conference sponsored by the Center for the Study of Democratic Institutions at Santa Barbara, Calif., April 13, 1970, p. 22.

Page 208
The Raymond Pearl experiment is cited in "Is Biological Aging Inevitable?" by Donald Carpenter and John Wrobel, Jr., in *Analog*, Dec. 1969.

Page 208
The Loeb and Northrop experiment is cited in *Extended Youth* (cited above), p. 185.

Page 208
McCay's rat experiments are reported in *Extended Youth* (cited above), pp. 35-36.

Page 209
Barrows' rotifer experiment material is based on "Ecology of Aging and of the Aging Process—Biological Parameters," by Charles Barrows, Jr., in *The Gerontologist*, Summer 1968; "Programmed Biological Obsolescence," in *The Johns Hopkins Magazine* (cited in Chapter V); "Research on Aging: Is An Organism's Life Programmed?" by Nathan Shock, in *American Professional Pharmacist*, Jan. 1969; an interview with Dr. Barrows at the Gerontology Research Center, Dec. 15, 1971.

Page 209
The Barrows quotation "there is a program . . ." is from "Ecology of Aging and of the Aging Process—Biological Parameters" (cited above).

Page 210
The Walford experiment with the fish *Cynolebias* is reported in "Aging," in *Medical World News*, Oct. 22, 1971.

Page 210
The Strehler data and quotation "it follows, therefore . . ." are from "Myth and Fact: Consequences of the Understanding of Aging" (cited above).

Page 210
The Eisdorfer quotation "It's just a technical problem . . ." is from "Aging," in *Medical World News* (cited above).

Page 210
The Footnote on the Robert Good findings reported in "Aging: The Eternal Quest for Eternal Youth," by Walter Sullivan, in the *New York Times* Oct. 24, 1971. The Morris Ross quotations are from a private letter to the author, Jan. 24, 1972.

Page 211
The Barrows quotation "Reduced temperature in homeotherms . . ." is from an interview (cited above).

Page 211
The Lissy Jarvik statement on genetic clock is from an interview (cited in Chapter VI).

Page 211-212
The Bjorksten section is based on "The Crosslinkage Theory of Aging," by Johan Bjorksten, in *Finska Kemists. Medd.*, 80 N:O 2 (1971); "The Cross-linkage Theory of Aging," by Johan Bjorksten, in *Journal of the American Geriatrics Society*, April 1968; "Gerogenic Fractions in the Tritiated Rat," by Johan Bjorksten *et al.*, in *Journal of the American Geriatrics Society*, July 1971; "Could We Live Longer?" by Johan Bjorksten, in *New Scientist*, Vol. 15, pp. 552-554; "Interview with Johan Bjorksten at Press Conference, Madison, Wisconsin, April 19, 1955"; author's interview with Dr. Bjorksten at his home in Madison, April 18, 1972; "The Youth Pill," by Patrick McGrady, Jr., in the *Ladies' Home Journal*, July 1971; *Extended Youth* (cited above); discussions of collagen and the cross-linkage theory in *Developmental Physiology and Aging* (cited in Chapter V); a reference to the theory in *Aging and Levels of Biological Organization*, p. 312; "Is Biological Aging Inevitable?" (cited above).

Page 211
The Bjorksten quotations "a strange resemblance . . ." and "The aging of living . . . is from *Extended Youth* (cited above), pp. 92, 93; original sources *Chemical Industries*, June 1941, and Jan. 1942.

Page 212
The Bjorksten quotation "The effect is like . . ." is from "Could We Live Longer?" (cited above).

Page 212-215
The Denham Harman section is based on an interview in New York City,

Jan. 21, 1972; "The Biological Clock: The Mitochondria?" by Denham Harman; "Free Radical Theory of Aging: Effect of the Amount and Degree of Unsaturation of Dietary Fat on Mortality Rate," by Denham Harman, in *Journal of Gerontology*, Vol. 26, No. 4 (1971); "Chemical Protection Against Aging," by Denham Harman, in *Agents and Actions*, Vol. 1, No. 1 (1969); "Aging," in *Medical World News* (cited above).

Page 212, 213
The Harman quotations "a natural consequence . . ." and "It's like tossing . . ." are from author's interview (cited above).

Page 213
The Bjorksten estimate that free radicals cause 10 percent of cross-linking is from author's interview (cited above).

Page 213
The Harman estimate of cross-linking is from the interview cited above.

Page 213
Robert Kohn of Case Western Reserve University also found that 2-MEA and BHT lengthened the average lifespans, but not maximum lifespans, of test animals. His findings are reported in "Effect of Antioxidants on Life-Span of C57BL Mice," in *Journal of Gerontology*, Vol. 26, No. 3 (1971).

Page 213-215
The Tappel section is based on: "Biological Antioxidant Protection against Lipid Peroxidation Damage," by A. L. Tappel, in *The American Journal of Clinical Nutrition*, Aug. 1970; "Will Antioxidant Nutrients Slow Aging Processes?" in *Geriatrics*, Oct. 1968; "Researchers Find Vitamin E Link to Aging," in the *Chicago Tribune*, Sept. 30, 1970; "Lipid Peroxidation and Fluorescent Molecular Damage to Membrane," by A. L. Tappel, a manuscript (April 1971) prepared for *Pathological Aspects of Cell Membranes*, Vol. 1, edited by B. F. Trump and A. Arstila (New York: Academic Press); *Developmental Physiology and Aging* (cited above).

Page 213-214
"Lipid Peroxidation: Its Measurement, Occurrence, and Significance in Animal Tissues," by Albert Barber and Frederick Bernheim, in *Advances in Gerontological Research*, Vol. 2, edited by Bernard Strehler (New York: Academic Press, 1967), is a definitive report on the peroxidation of unsaturated fats in the body.

Page 213-214
The Tappel quotation "To suppress atherosclerosis . . ." is from "Will Antioxidant Nutrients Slow Aging Processes?" (cited above).

Page 214-215
The Discussion of vitamin E is based on "Experts Assert Vitamin E Has No Value in Treating Common Ills," by Lawrence Altman, in the *New York Times*,

Nov. 26, 1971; "Sales of Vitamin E Way Up in Latest Nutrition Fad," by Boyce Rensberger, in the *New York Times*, March 13, 1972; *Vitamin E: Your Key to a Healthy Heart*, by Herbert Bailey (New York: ARC Books, 1964, 1970); "Factors Affecting Aging: Pharmacologic Agents," by Michael Granich, in *Developmental Physiology and Aging* (cited above); "Lipid Peroxidation: Its Measurement, Occurrence, and Significance in Animal Tissues" (cited above); "Accumulation of Lipofuscin-Like Pigment in the Rat Adrenal Gland as a Function of Vitamin E Deficiency," by William Weglicki, William Reichel, and Padmanabhan Nair, in *Journal of Gerontology*, Oct. 1968.

Page 214
Dr. Harman is the source for information on Dr. Tappel's vitamin E supplement.

Page 214
The Medical Letter quotation "no established value . . ." is from "Experts Assert Vitamin E Has No Value in Treating Common Ills" (cited above); also the quotation "little unequivocal evidence . . . ."

Page 215
The inquiry by the Beverly Hills physician was answered by Daniel Rogers, PIO of the Gerontology Research Center.

Page 215
The Comfort aging tests are reported in "Aging," in *Medical World News* (cited above).

Page 215
The Verzár reaction to Comfort's tests is from "What Is the Aim of Gerontology?" (cited in Chapter V).

Page 215-216
The Kohn-Hamlin experiment on collagen cited in "Evidence for Progressive Age-Related Structural Changes in Post-Mature Human Collagen," by C. R. Hamlin and R. R. Kohn, in *Biochimica et Biophysica Acta*, Amsterdam, p. 236 (1971); a report of the work in *The Extramural Program of Research on Aging* of the National Institute of Child Health and Human Development Fiscal Year 1970; and a private communication from Dr. Kohn, Jan. 25, 1972.

Page 216
The Sinex proposal for FDA testing of anti-aging drugs was made in "Research and Training in Gerontology (cited in Chapter VI), p. 7.

Page 216
Harman's comments on flavinoids and ginseng are from his interview (cited above). The report on ginseng's apparent beneficial effect on postmitotic cells is from "Experimental Modification of the Chemistry and Biology of the Aging Process," By Charles Kormendy and A. Douglas Bender, in the *Journal of Pharmaceutical Sciences*, Feb. 1971.

Page 216
Strehler on royal jelly and procaine is from "Myth and Fact: Consequences of the Understanding of Aging" (cited above).

Page 216
Procaine has not been licensed for use in the United States, but once again it is under study, at Rockland State Hospital in Orangeburg, N.Y., to alleviate mental depression sometimes associated with old age. Dr. Nathan Kline reported to the *New York Times,* March 18, 1973 that the first results of his study have been favorable enough to continue, but not strong enough to allow any conclusions to be drawn.

Page 216
There are extensive discussions of anti-aging drugs in "Factors Affecting Aging: Pharmacologic Agents," by Michael Granich, in *Developmental Physiology and Aging* (cited above); "Experimental Modifications of the Chemistry and Biology of the Aging Process" (cited above); and "Chemical Interference with Aging," by Charles Kormendy and A. Douglas Bender, in *Gerontologia,* Vol. 17, pp. 52-64 (1971).

Page 216
The report on immunosuppressants is from "Factors Affecting Aging: Pharmacologic Agents," in *Developmental Physiology and Aging* (cited above).

Page 216-218
The immune-theory section is based on *The Immunologic Theory of Aging,* by Roy Walford (Baltimore: Williams and Wilkins, 1969); "The General Immunology of Aging," by Roy Walford, in *Advances in Gerontological Research,* Vol. 2 (cited above); *Immunological Surveillance* cited in Chapter IV; "Aging," in *Medical World News* (cited above); *Developmental Physiology and Aging* (cited above), both for its discussion of how the immune system works and "Theories of Aging," by Paul Spiegel, on the immunologic theory; "Defending Against Disease," in "Toward Cancer Control" in *Time,* March 19, 1973; the articles on immunity and blood in *Encyclopedia Americana* (1965).

Page 218
Dr. Goldstein's quotations "This direct evidence . . ." and "We know that . . ." are from "Thymus Hormone Held Major Factor In Aging Process," an Associated Press dispatch from Atlantic City published in the *New York Times,* April 17, 1973. The news account was based on prepared remarks delivered by Dr. Goldstein at the Symposium on Immunopathology of Aging at the 57th annual meeting of the Federation of American Societies of Experimental Biology. For further information on thymosin research, see "Purification and Biological Activity of Thymosin, a Hormone of the Thymus Gland" by Allan Goldstein *et al.* in *Proceedings* of the National Academy of Sciences, July 1972, pp. 1800-1803; and "The Thymus Gland: Experimental and Clinical Studies of Its Role in the Development and Expression of Immune Functions" by Allan Goldstein and Abraham White in *Advances in Metabolic Disorders,* Vol. 5, Academic Press, N.Y., 1971.

Page 218
Dr. Walford's estimate of the immunologic theory of aging and first causes is discussed in *The Immunologic Theory of Aging* (cited above), p. 20.

Page 218-220
The Alexis Carrel section is based on *Encyclopedia Americana* (1965); Corliss Lamont's reference to the chicken heart in *Illusion of Immortality* (New York: Frederick Ungar), pp. 71-72; "Aging," in *Medical World News* (cited above); *Man the Unknown,* by Alexis Carrel (New York: Harper, 1935); "Human Cells and Aging," by Leonard Hayflick, in *Scientific American,* March, 1968.

Page 219
The Carrel quotations "Men of genius . . ." and "chiefly because . . ." are from *Man the Unknown* (cited above), pp. 62, 155.

Page 219-221
The Hayflick section is based on "Human Cells and Aging" (cited above); "Theories of Aging," in *Developmental Physiology and Aging* (cited above); "Scientists Seek Key to Longevity" by Walter Sullivan, in the *New York Times,* Oct. 24, 1971 (cited in Chapter V).

Page 220
The Hayflick quotation "It has been found . . ." is from "Human Cells and Aging" (cited above).

Page 221
The Martin experiments from "Replicative Life-Span of Cultivated Human Cells," by George Martin, Curtis Sprague, and Charles Epstein, in *Laboratory Investigation,* Vol. 23, No. 1 (1970); and from "Aging," in *Medical World News* (cited above).

Page 221
The Hayflick quotation "What does us in now . . ." is from "Aging," in *Medical World News* (cited above).

Page 221
Robert Hay's assessment was made in a private communication to author, Jan. 21, 1972.

Page 221
Footnote 5 on indecision on cell division in the body is from "A New Age for Aging," by Bernard Strehler, in *Natural History,* Feb. 1973.

Footnote 6 on James Danielli's work is based on "Inheritance of the 'Life-Spanning' Phenomenon in Amoeba Proteus," by Audrey Muggleton and James Danielli, in *Experimental Cell Research,* Vol. 49, pp. 116-120 (1968); "Some Alternative States of Amoeba, with Special References to Life-Span," by James Danielli and Audrey Muggleton, in *Gerontologia,* Vol. 3, No. 2 (1959); "Aging: The Eternal Quest for Eternal Youth" (cited above).

Page 222-224
The section on the cell is based on Chapters 2 and 3 of *Biology and the Future of Man,* edited by Philip Handler (New York: Oxford, 1970); Chapter 2 of *Developmental Physiology and Aging* (cited above); *Tools of Modern Biology,* by Melvin Berger (New York: Crowell, 1970); "New Clues on Makeup of the Gene and the Cell," by Walter Sullivan, in the *New York Times,* June 7, 1970; visit to laboratory of, and interview with, Dorothy Travis at the Gerontology Research Center, Dec. 16, 1971.

Page 222
The figure 60 trillion cells in the human body is from "Child Health and Human Development: Progress 1963–1970," p. 6.

Page 222
Four kinds of tissue are mentioned by Professor J. K. Sherman of the Department of Anatomy, University of Arkansas, in "Immortality and the Freezing of Human Bodies . . . the Case Against" (cited in Chapter III).

Page 222
Categorization of cells is from "Experimental Modification of the Chemistry and Biology of the Aging Process" (cited above), and "A New Age for Aging" (cited above).

Page 223-224
Harman's theory is from "The Biologic Clock: The Mitochondria?" (cited above).

Page 224-226
The account of Mendel is based on the chapter about Mendel in *Man, Time, and Fossils,* by Ruth Moore (New York: Knopf, 1953); also articles on Mendel and Genetics in *Encyclopedia Americana* (1965).

Page 227-229
Early genetics data are based on articles on Genetics, Genes, and Chromosomes in *Encyclopedia Americana* (1965), and the section on Lamarck in *Man, Time, and Fossils* (cited above).

Page 229
The section on Morgan and the Columbia University geneticists is based on a paper delivered at the meeting of the American Association for the Advancement of Science, Dec. 27, 1972, "The Transition from the Mendelian Unit to the Individual Gene," by Elof Carlson, Professor of Biology, SUNY, Stony Brook; the articles on Morgan and Genetics in *Encyclopedia Americana* (1965).

Page 229
H. Bentley Glass in "Genes" in *Encyclopedia Americana* (1965) says, "Genes are very stable yet do occasionally change to new stable or unstable forms, at frequencies ranging from approximately 1 per 1,000 to 1 per 1,000,000 gametes, depending on the kind of gene." *Biology and the Future of Man*

(cited above), p. 21, speaking of bacteria, states :"Under these circumstances, the chances are excellent for finding any particular type already present in the culture if it occurs by mutation of the parent strain with the usual mutational frequency of one in a hundred million." Jacques Monod, in *Chance and Necessity* (New York: Knopf, 1971), p. 121, writes: "Altogether, we may estimate in the present-day human population of approximately three billion there occur, with each new generation, some hundred billion to a thousand billion mutations."

Page 229-230
The information on centrifugation, electrophoresis, and chromatography is based on a visit to the molecular biology laboratory at the University of Southern California; *Biology and the Future of Man* (cited above), Chapter I; *Tools of Modern Biology* (cited above); *Developmental Physiology and Aging* (cited above), Chapter II.

Page 230
The estimate of 150,000 enzymes is from "Those Enterprising Enzymes," by Lee Edson, in *Empire* magazine, Jan. 9, 1972.

Page 230
The "one gene, one enzyme" experiments were conducted by Beadle and Tatum, as reported in *Developmental Physiology and Aging* (cited above), p. 47.

Page 230-231
Information on the electron microscope is based on a visit to the laboratory of Dorothy Travis (cited above); "The Scanning Electron Microscope," by Thomas Everhart and Thomas Hayes, in *Scientific American*, Jan. 1972; *Tools of Modern Biology* (cited above).

Page 231-237
The section on the development of molecular genetics is based on "The New Genetics: Man into Superman," in *Time*, April 1971; "Molecular Genetics—A Survey of Highlights," by Gordon Edlin, in *BioScience*, Feb. 1972; *Biology and the Future of Man* (cited above), Chapter II; *The Double Helix*, by James Watson (New York: Atheneum, 1968); *Tools of Modern Biology* (cited above).

Page 234
The 6 billion nucleotides in the human genome is cited in "Repeated Segments of DNA," by Roy Britten and David Kohne, in *Scientific American*, April 1970; also reported by Walter Sullivan in "New Clues on Makeup of the Gene and the Cell," in the *New York Times*, June 7, 1970.

The at least 1 million genes figure is from *Biology and the Future of Man*, cited above, p. 153. The Watson quotation "we still do not have . . ." is from the *New York Times*, March 22, 1973.

As for the number of proteins, Jacques Monod in *Chance and Necessity* (cited above), p. 48, writes: "Even the simplest organisms contain a very great number of different proteins. It may be put at 2500±500 for the bacterium

Escherichia coli (weighing 5×10^{-13} grams and 2 microns in length, approximately). For the higher mammals such as man, one may suggest a figure on the order of a million." That bacteria have about 6 million nucleotides is from "Repeated Segments of DNA" (cited above).

Page 234-235
The operon model of genetic control is based on *Chance and Necessity* (cited above); "Molecular Mechanisms for the Regulation of Cell Functions," by Lewis Kleinsmith, in *BioScience*, June 1972; "Molecular Genetics—A Survey of Highlights" (cited above); *Biology and the Future of Man* (cited above), Chapter I.

Page 235-237
The latest concept of the genetic system is based on an interview with William Reichel (cited in Chapter VI); *Chance and Necessity* (cited above); "Molecular Mechanisms for the Regulation of Cell Function" (cited above); "Gene Regulation for Higher Cells: A Theory," by Roy Britten and Eric Davidson, in *Science*, July 25, 1969; "Gene Regulation in Higher Cells," by C. H. Waddington, in *Science*, Oct. 31, 1969; "Control of Specific Gene Expression in Higher Organisms," by Gordon Tomkins *et al.*, in *Science*, Vol. 166, pp. 1474-1480 (Dec. 1969); "Repeated Segments of DNA" (cited above); "Oncogenes of RNA Tumor Viruses as Determinants of Cancer," by Robert Huebner and George Todaro, in *Proceedings of the National Academy of Sciences*, Vol. 64, pp. 1087-1094, communicated Sept. 16, 1969; "Prospects for Genetic Intervention in Man," by Bernard Davis, in *Science*, Dec. 18, 1970; "Molecular Genetics—A Survey of Highlights" (cited above).

Page 235
The four control points are from "Molecular Mechanisms for the Regulation of Cell Function" (cited above).

Page 236
The Huebner-Todaro quotation "Evidence from sero-epidemiological studies . . ." is from "Oncogenes of RNA Tumor Viruses as Determinants of Cancer" (cited above).

Page 236
The Britten-Davidson quotation "Cell differentiation is based . . ." is from "Gene Regulation for Higher Cells: A Theory" (cited above).

Page 237
The Orgel error theory is based on "The Maintenance of the Accuracy of Protein Synthesis and Its Relevance to Ageing," by Leslie Orgel, in *Proceedings of the National Academy of Sciences*, April 1963; *Developmental Physiology and Aging* (cited above), Chapter 29; "Scientists Seek Key to Longevity" (cited above).

Page 237
One erroneous amino acid every 3,000 times is cited in *Developmental Physiology and Aging* (cited above), p. 576, in an experiment by Loftfield in 1963.

Page 238
The Strehler and Johnson findings on aged dog brains are reported in "A New Age for Aging" (cited above).

Page 238
The Strehler paradigm is based on an interview with Dr. Strehler at the University of Southern California, July 22, 1971; "Genetics and Cellular Aspects of Life Span Prediction," by Bernard Strehler, in *Prediction of Life Span* (cited in Chapter VI); "A New Age for Aging" (cited above).

Page 238
The Strehler quotation "is that a highly deterministic . . ." is from "Genetic and Cellular Aspects of Life Span Prediction (cited above).

Page 239
Professor Gurdon's frog experiment is reported in "We Have the Awful Knowledge to Make Exact Copies of Human Beings," by Willard Gaylin, in the *New York Times Magazine*, March 5, 1972.

Page 240
The transformation of the aged cells cultured by Dr. Hayflick by the Simian Virus 40 is reported in "Scientists Seek Key to Longevity" (cited above).

Page 240
Walter Sullivan, science editor of the *New York Times,* in "Scientists Seek Key to Longevity" (cited above), states: "But increasingly, medical researchers are becoming hopeful that aging can be understood—and possibly controlled." Also: "Thus some researchers in the field believe that cancer, in destroying the mechanism for control of normal cell growth, may also cancel the aging factor. This would mean that it confers a form of immortality on the individual cells while at the same time, causing the ultimate death of the individual."

Bernard Strehler in "Genetic and Cellular Aspects of Life-Span Prediction" (cited above), writes: "The second direction lies in the reactivation of the controller genes that affect one's ability to make specific substances or cells needed for indefinite existence. Because the nature of these controller substances may be more simple than was previously supposed and might well be inserted into cells in a very precise manner, the chance for a chemical modification of the maximum life span is probably closer to realization than most persons anticipate."

In a private communication to the author, Feb. 7, 1972, Robert Sinsheimer, chairman of the Biology Division, California Institute of Technology, wrote: "I would guess in practical terms that extension of the life span will come gradually as we successively learn how to cope with the various degenerative processes which lead to heart failure, stroke, kidney failure, etc.—i.e. as we progressively take care of one, another will become limiting. However, again, I see no *intrinsic* limitations to the process."

Among a great many publications consulted in order to make some discrimination among an almost bewildering array of theories to explain aging biologically and to give me a better understanding of genetic concepts—but which have not been referred to specifically in the notes for this chapter—the following should be mentioned:

The Molecular Biology of Development, by James Bonner (New York: Oxford University Press, 1965).

Topics in the Biology of Aging, edited by Peter Krohn (New York: Interscience-John Wiley, 1966).

Biological Mechanisms of Aging, by Howard Curtis (Springfield, Ill.: C. C. Thomas, 1966).

Aging Life Processes, edited by Seymour Bakerman (Springfield, Ill.: C. C. Thomas, 1969).

Proceedings—Vol. I, 8th International Congress of Gerontology (Washington, D.C., 1969).

Perspectives in Experimental Gerontology, edited by Nathan Shock (Springfield, Ill.: C. C. Thomas, 1966).

Ageing: The Biology of Senescence, by Alex Comfort (New York: Holt, Rinehart and Winston, 1956, 1964).

"Environmental Factors in Aging and Mortality," by Bernard Strehler, in *Environmental Research,* Vol. 1, pp. 46-88 (1967).

"The Biology of Aging," by William Reichel, in *Resident Physician,* Jan. 1968.

"Aging Research—Coming of Age," by Joseph Hrachovec, in *Industrial Research,* Sept. 1969.

"Biological and Medical Research," by Edwin Bierman, in "Research and Demonstration—White House Conference on Aging 1971."

"The Immortal Carrot," by Arthur Galston, in *Natural History,* April 1972.

"The Naked Cell," by Arthur Galston, in *Natural History,* June-July 1972.

Chapter VIII. Prognosis

Page 241
The Clarke data is from his book *Profiles of the Future,* by Arthur C. Clarke (New York: Harper, 1962).

Page 241-242
The Gordon-Helmer Delphi study data are from *Report on a Long-Range Forecasting Study,* by T. J. Gordon and Olaf Helmer (Santa Monica, Calif.: Rand Corporation, Sept. 1964).

Page 242
The Bender Delphi study data are from *A Delphic Study of the Future of Medicine,* by A. Douglas Bender, Alvin Strack, George Ebright, and George von Haunalter, prepared for the Research and Development Division, Marketing Division, Smith, Kline and French Laboratories, Philadelphia, Penn., Jan. 1969.

Page 242
The Strehler quotation "that the abolition . . ." is from *Time, Cells and Aging* (cited in Chapter V), p. 225.

Page 242
Strehler's 1971 predictions were made to the author in an interview (cited in Chapter VII).

Page 242
Strehler's 1973 prediction and quotation "If the institute . . ." are from "A New Age for Aging" (cited in Chapter VII).

Page 242
The Reichel estimate is from an interview (cited in Chapter VI).

Page 243
The gene transplant experiment was reported in "Human Cells in Test Use Genetic Matter Native to Bacteria," by Harold Schmeck, Jr., in the *New York Times,* Oct. 14, 1971, and in *Time,* Oct. 25, 1971.

Page 243
The Hirsch quotation "I think that . . ." is from a private communication to the author, Jan. 21, 1972.

Page 243
The Bernard Davis quotation "My general view . . ." is from a private communication to the author, Oct. 6, 1971.

Page 244
The Nathan Shock quotation "As of today . . ." is from "Can We Live to Be 100?" (cited in Chapter V).

Page 244
Loss of brain cells is reported in "Organization of the Cerebral Cortex, III. A Study of Aging in the Human Cerebral Cortex," by Harold Brody, in *Journal of Comparative Neurology,* Vol. 102, pp. 511-556 (1955). Dr. Brody's estimate on brain loss was made during an interview at the White House Conference on Aging, Nov. 30, 1971.

Page 244
The Strehler quotation "What we want to preserve . . ." is from an interview (cited above).

Page 245
The Ruth Bennett quotation "it is just as difficult . . ." is from an interview (cited in Chapter VI).

Chapter IX. The Ecology of Immortality

Page 249-250
The LaMont Cole quotation "At this stage man could hardly . . ." is from "Man's Ecosystem," in *BioScience,* April, 1966, pp. 243-248.

Page 250
The Jacques Monod quotation "That is why Mendel's defining . . ." is from
Chance and Necessity (New York: Knopf, 1971), p. 104.

Page 250
The Garrett Hardin quotation "History will show . . ." is from "Not Peace,
but Ecology," in *Diversity and Stability in Ecological Systems,* a report of a
symposium at Brookhaven National Laboratory, May 26-28, 1969.

Page 250
Levels of the organization of life and the quotation "Since introductory biology
courses . . ." are from *Fundamentals of Ecology,* by Eugene Odum (Philadelphia: W. B. Saunders, 1959).

Page 251
The Jain's remark to Alexander "by doing what is . . ." is from *Twelve
Against the Gods* by William Bolitho, Viking, N.Y., 1957, p. 45.

Page 251
The Frank Fraser Darling quotation "a science of identifying causes . . ." is
from "The Unity of Ecology," a presidential address to the British Association,
Aug. 29, 1963.

Page 251
The Herbert York quotation "You know, it just isn't possible . . ." is from
California Science: A Reporters' View, edited by Kenneth Goldstein, a mono-
graph of the Institute for the Study of Science in Human Affairs, Columbia
University, N.Y. (1969), p. 53.

Page 251-252
The Peter Medawar quotation "No one could have foreseen . . ." is from
"Science and the Sanctity of Life," in *Encounter,* Dec. 1966.

Page 252
The René Dubos quotation "Any attempt to shape . . ." is from *Mirage of
Health* (New York: Harper, 1959), p. 223.

Page 252
The Garrett Hardin quotation "The practical implication . . ." is from "Not
Peace, but Ecology," in *Diversity and Stability in Ecological Systems,* a re-
port of a symposium held at Brookhaven National Laboratory, May 26-28, 1969.

Page 252
The Barry Commoner quotation "There is no such thing as a free lunch," is
from *The Closing Circle* (New York: Knopf, 1971).

Page 253
The Alex Comfort forecast of a 20 percent extension of lifespan by 1990 was
made in an article "Longer Life by 1990?" for a British magazine *New Scien-*

tist, Dec. 11, 1969. The prediction is hedged with ifs. If the level of aging research continued as it was, then "direct experiment on the delaying of ageing in Man is virtually certain to be in hand somewhere by 1975 . . . ." And if "by good luck one of the currently fancied rodent techniques proves directly applicable," then we'd know if the agent worked in 15 years—by 1990—and the increase in lifespan "could be as much as 20 per cent, possibly more . . . ." This is the central message of the article, also conveyed by the title (which is carefully protected with its own hook-remover, the question mark). This is the most widely circulated paper I came across in gerontology (although the useful statistics on physiological decline with age uncovered by Nathan Shock's group in Baltimore are used most frequently in other articles written about the subject). "Longer Life by 1990?" was used as a basic background paper to brief delegates in advance at both the Extension of the Human Life-span Conference held by the Center for the Study of Democratic Institutions in Santa Barbara, Calif., in April 1970, and at the Control of Human Aging Conference sponsored by the Gottlieb Duttweiler Institute for Economic and Social Studies at Zurich, Switzerland, in Sept. 1971. Along with a reprint of Dr. Comfort's article, the Institute's advance letter to delegates included this statement: *"Scientific studies now predict* [italics added] that it will be possible to control the human aging process in such a way that our period of vigorous life could be increased by 20% or more before the year 2000." Because of Dr. Comfort's position of authority in the field of biological gerontology (he well might be the top authority in his field for most social gerontologists), his hunch has created a climate of expectation. He has also cited the Smith, Kline and French Delphic study, reported in Chapter VIII, as coinciding with his own estimate.

Page 253
The Comfort quotations beginning "Bearing in mind the rate . . ." is from "To Be Continued," in *Playboy,* Nov. 1971.

Page 253
The Bernard Strehler quotation "lies in the reactivation . . ." is from "Genetic and Cellular Aspects of Life Span Prediction," in *Prediction of Life Span* (cited in Chapter VI).

Page 253
The Strehler quotation "If we did not age . . ." is from "A New Age for Aging," in *Natural History,* Feb. 1973.

Page 253
In I Corinthians 14:12, Paul says, "For now we see through a glass, darkly . . ." In I Corinthians 15:26, Paul says, "The last enemy that shall be destroyed is death."

Page 253
Dr.Orentreich's work with plasmapheresis is reported in *The Youth Doctors,* by Patrick McGrady, Jr. (cited in Chapter III), and in "Technological Forecasting, Longevity and Demography," by Robert Prehoda, a paper read at the

Extension of the Human Life-span Conference held by the Center for the
Study of Democratic Institutions at Santa Barbara, Calif., April 1970. The cost
for plasmapheresis and the kidney dialysis figure are taken from the Prehoda
paper.

Page 254
The Alex Comfort quotation "will not be luxury medicine" is taken from "To
Be Continued" (cited above).

Page 254
A reprint of Dr. Strehler's paper "Ten Myths About Aging" is among material
provided at the Syracuse University Seminar on Gerontology and Higher Education held in New York City, Dec. 9-11, 1971 (cited in Chapter VI). An
elaborated version "Myth and Fact: Consequences of the Understanding of
Aging" was presented at the Center Conference on Life-span Extension (cited
above). The quotation "Added years of comparative youthfulness . . ." is
identical in both papers.

Page 254
The Alex Comfort quotation "will catch us unprepared to iron out . . ." is
from "To Be Continued" (cited above).

Page 254-255
The Robert Prehoda quotation "The conquest of aging . . ." is from *Extended
Youth* (cited in Chapter VII), p. 237.

Page 255
The René Dubos quotation "certainly contributed to the modern world . . ."
is from *The Dreams of Reason: Science and Utopias* (New York: Columbia
University Press, 1961), p. 39.

Page 255
The Dubos quotation "the responses of the human mind . . ." is from *The
Dreams of Reason* (cited above), p. 49.

Page 255
The Alex Comfort quotation "Every gain in our ability . . ." is from "To Be
Continued" (cited above).

Page 256
The quotation "Greater love hath no man . . ." is from John 15:13.

Page 256
The quotation "Had we but world enough, and time" and the rest of the
poetry is from "To His Coy Mistress," by Andrew Marvell.

Page 257
The Albert Rosenfeld quotation "Presumably no one would be required . . ."
is from "The Longevity Seekers," in *Saturday Review of the Sciences*, March
1973.

Page 257
The Alexander-Jain exchange is from *Twelve Against the Gods* (cited above), p. 45.

Page 258
The Byron Gold quotation "While I am willing to accept . . ." is from "A Few Questions Concerning the Implications for Public Policy of Longevity and Aging Research," a paper presented at the Extension of Human Life-span Conference of the Center for the Study of Democratic Institutions (cited above).

Page 258
The Richard Kalish quotation "I suspect that a sudden . . ." is from "Added Years: Social Issues and Consequences," in *Prediction of Life Span* (cited in Chapter VI).

Page 259
The Kalish quotation "The prospect of adding a decade . . ." is from "Four Score and Ten," a paper presented at the Extension of Human Life-span Conference of the Center for the Study of Democratic Institutions (cited above).

Page 260
The Leon Kass quotation "Let us not fail to note a painful irony . . ." is from "Biomedical Research and Social Policy" presented at the Seminar on Science and Public Policy of the Council for the Advancement of Science Writing, Washington, D.C., Feb. 22, 1971.

Page 261
Dr. Strehler made his prediction of the manageable population impact of a 20-year increase in longevity during an interview with the author at the University of Southern California, July 22, 1971, and also in "Ten Myths About Aging" and "Myth and Fact: Consequences of the Understanding of Aging" (cited above). Dr. Comfort made his prediction in "To Be Continued" (cited above).

Page 262-263
Robert Sinsheimer, chairman of the Division of Biology, California Institute of Technology, and a herald of the potentialities of the new genetics, wrote in a personal letter, Feb. 7, 1972: "Obviously, were man to achieve essential immortality this would require the cessation of reproduction in order to stabilize the population at some level. I am inclined to agree that this would likely result in evolutionary stagnation—again both biological and social."

Page 262
Robert Prehoda's one-child family plan is from "Technological Forecasting, Longevity and Demography" (cited above).

Page 262
Gerald Feinberg's comments were made during an interview at Columbia University, June 2, 1971.

Page 262
The Erik Erikson quotation "The fashionable insistence on dramatizing . . ."
is from *Childhood and Society* (cited in Chapter V), pp. 266-267.

Page 263
The Johan Bjorksten quotation "The reason for this long time lag . . ." is
from "Could We Live Longer?" in *New Scientist*, Vol. 15, pp. 552-554.

Page 263
The Arthur Clarke quotation "Death (though not aging)is . . ." is from *Profiles of the Future* (cited in Chapter VIII), p. 208.

Chapter X. Dialectic

The following contributed to the thinking in this chapter:

BOOKS: *The Dreams of Reason: Science and Utopias*, by René Dubos (New
York: Columbia University Press, 1961); *Issues in Science and Religion*, by
Ian Barbour (New York: Harper, 1966, 1971); *Science and the Modern
World*, by Alfred North Whitehead (New York: New American Library,
1925); *California Science: A Reporter's View*, a, monograph of the Institute
for the Study of Science in Human Affairs, edited by Kenneth Goldstein (New
York: University Press, 1969); *Chance and Necessity*, by Jacques Monod
(New York: Knopf, 1971); *Silent Spring*, by Rachel Carson (Greenwich,
Conn.: Crest-Fawcett, 1962); *Come, Let Us Play God*, by Leroy Augenstein
(New York: Harper, 1969); *The Story of Philosophy*, by Will Durant (New
York: Simon and Schuster, 1926); *Science and Survival*, by Barry Commoner
(New York: Viking, 1963); *So Human an Animal*, by René Dubos (New York:
Scribner, 1968); *The Golden Bough*, by Sir James Frazer (New York: Mac-
millan, 1922, 1947); *Tongues of Conscience*, by Robert Reid (New York:
Walker, 1969); Innumerable ecological sources listed in *Where Have All the
Flowers Fishes Birds Bees Water and Air Gone?* by Osborn Segerberg, Jr.
(New York: McKay, 1971).

ARTICLES: "Biomedical Research and Social Policy," by Leon Kass, a speech
presented to the Council for the Advancement of Science Writing, Feb. 22,
1971, and a similar paper by Dr. Kass, "The New Biology: What Price Relieving Man's Estate," in *Science*, Nov. 19, 1971; "The New Genetics: Man into
Superman," in *Time*, April 19, 1971; "Ethics Debate Set Off by Life Science
Gains," by science writer Jane Brody and religion editor Edward Fiske, in the
New York Times, March 28, 1971; "The Welfare of Science in an Era of
Change," by William Bevan, in *Science*, June 2, 1972; Essays on "Compen-
sation" and "Moral Laws," by Ralph Waldo Emerson; "The Roots of Our Ecological Crisis," by Lynn White, Jr., in *Science*, Vol. 155, pp. 1203-1207 (1967);
"Ethical Perspectives in the Use of Genetic Knowledge," in *BioScience*, Nov.
15, 1971; "Futurism," by E. J. Mishan, in *Encounter*, March, 1971; "The
Real Responsibilities of the Scientist," by Jacob Bronowski, in *Bulletin of
the Atomic Scientists*, Jan. 1956; "Ethics for the Scientist," by John Haybittle,
in *Bulletin of the Atomic Scientists*, May 1964; "The End of the Beginning,"
a lecture delivered in 1966, "The Implications of Recent Advances in Biology
for the Future of Medicine," and "The Prospect of Genetic Change," all by
Robert Sinsheimer, the latter two articles published in *Engineering and Science*

magazine of the California Institute of Technology in Oct. 1970, and April 1969; "The Prolongation of Vigorous Life," by Alex Comfort, in *Impact of Science on Society*, Oct.-Dec. 1970; "Can Science Survive in the Modern Age?" by Harvey Brooks, in *Science*, Oct. 1, 1971; "Science: A Technocratic Trap," by Theodore Roszak, in *Atlantic Monthly*, July 1972; "The Scientist as Shaman," by Malachi Martin, in *Harper's*, March 1972; "Social Control of Science and Technology," by Michael Baram, in *Science*, May 7, 1971; "Public Interest Science," by Frank von Hippel and Joel Primack, in *Science*, Sept. 29, 1972; "We Have the Awful Knowledge to Make Exact Copies of Human Beings," by Willard Gaylin, in the *New York Times Magazine*, March 5, 1972; "The Dead Body and the Living Brain," by Oriana Fallaci, in *Look*, Nov. 28, 1967; "Man and Computer: Uneasy Allies of 25 Years," by Boyce Rensberger, in the *New York Times*, June 27, 1972; "A Conversation with John Lilly," by Sam Keen, in *Psychology Today*, Dec. 1971; "Energy in the Universe," by Freeman Dynson, in *Scientific American*, Sept. 1971; "Death: Process or Event?" by Robert Morison, in *Science*, Aug. 20, 1971; "Death as an Event: A Commentary on Robert Morison," by Leon Kass, in *Science*, Aug. 20, 1971; "The Tragedy of the Commons," by Garrett Hardin, in *Science*, Vol. 162, pp. 1243-1248 (1968).

TELEVISION BROADCAST: "Science and Religion: Who Will Play God?" a CBS News Special broadcast over the CBS Television Network, Jan. 21, 1968.

INTERVIEWS: with René Dubos at the Rockefeller University, Feb. 1969, and with Paul Ehrlich at Stanford University, July 1971.

Page 264
The Bernice Neugarten quotation "If we are indeed facing . . ." is from "Social Implications of a Prolonged Life-Span," presented at the 9th Congress of Gerontology, Kiev, USSR, July 3, 1972 and reprinted in *The Gerontologist*, Winter 1972.

Page 264
The Ewald Busse quotation "What worries me . . ." is from "Aging," in *Medical World News*, Oct. 22, 1971.

Page 264
The James Watson quotation "the possibility of our having . . ." is from "Ethics Debate Set Off by Life Science Gains," by Jane Brody and Edward Fiske (cited above).

Page 264
The Leon Kass quotation "Thus, engineering the engineer . . ." is from "Biomedical Research and Social Policy" and "The New Biology: What Price Relieving Man's Estate" (cited above).

Page 264
The Alex Comfort quotation "I am as worried . . ." is from "To Be Continued" (cited in Chapter IX).

Page 264-265
The Alex Comfort quotation "possibility of anguished and unproductive argument . . ." is from "The Prolongation of Vigorous Life" (cited above).

Page 265
On understanding as the purpose of science: Barbour in *Issues in Science and Religion* (cited above), discusses this question, pp. 137-187. In setting down what he intends to do on the subject "The Methods of Science" (p. 138), he writes: "The concluding section defends a critical realism which holds that the goal of science is to understand nature, not simply to control it or make predictions." The latter two goals, Barbour makes clear, often can be accomplished empirically without comprehending the natural principles which are being manipulated and are inferior to the loftier and true aim of understanding nature (which does not proscribe human action but which may indicate a wiser and less deleterious course). Robert Sinsheimer, chairman of the Division of Biology, California Institute of Technology, in a private communication, Feb. 7, 1972: "Control is certainly not a proper goal for science. The proper goal of science is understanding. Control may very well be a proper goal for technology. Control, of coures, must be exercised with wisdom." William Bevan, publisher of *Science* and executive officer of the A.A.A.S., in "The Welfare of Science in an Era of Change" (cited above), writes: "The goal of the scientist is to understand nature. . . . In contrast, the technologist's goal is to create socially useful things . . . ." See also note for p. 265, below, on control of nature as a goal of science.

Page 265
The Lynn White, Jr. quotation "[I]t was not until . . ." is from "The Historical Roots of Our Ecological Crisis" (cited above).

Page 265
On substituting control for understanding of nature as a perversion of science, Leon Kass writes in "The New Biology: What Price Relieving Man's Estate?" (cited above): "We have difficulty recognizing the problems of the exercise of power in the biomedical enterprise because of our delight with the wondrous fruits it has yielded. This is ironic because the notion of power is absolutely central to the modern conception of science. The ancients conceived of science as the *understanding* of nature, pursued for its own sake. We moderns view science as power, as *control* over nature; the conquest of nature 'for the relief of man's estate' was the charge issued by Francis Bacon, one of the leading architects of the modern scientific project." Also see note for p. 265, above, on understanding as the goal of nature.

Page 265
Aside from society's legal authority to regulate the actions of technology, William Bevan, in "The Welfare of Science in an Era of Change" (cited above), points out that public resentment at being excluded from scientific and technological developments which affect its welfare and scientific resistance to heed the priorities set by society are underlying causes for cuts in public funding for scientific research—that funding being an essential for today's science and a practical persuader for scientific accountability to the public. Eliminating the confusion in science's role—that is, science discovers, technology acts—shows how harmful changes can be governed without infringing upon freedom of inquiry.

Page 266
The Jonas Salk quotation "We have always quested for immortality . . ." is from a KEBS-TV, San Diego, interview for the Corporation for Public Broadcasting (1969).

Page 266
The James Carse quotation "Immortality must be avoided . . ." is from an interview with Dr. Carse at New York University, Sept. 23, 1971.

Page 267
The Whitehead quotation "made it impervious to criticism" is from *Science and the Modern World* (cited above), p. 67.

Page 268
The Whitehead quotation "Professionals are not new . . ." is from *Science and the Modern World* (cited above), p. 205.

Page 268
The Whitehead quotation "that an individual human being . . ." is from *Science and the Modern World* (cited above), p. 196.

Page 269
The Whitehead quotation "leading intellects lack balance . . ." is from *Science and the Modern World* (cited above), p. 197.

Page 269
The Whitehead quotation "[T]he abstraction abstracts from . . ." is from *Science and the Modern World* (cited above), pp. 196-197.

Page 269
The Whitehead quotation "It is very arguable that . . ." is from *Science and the Modern World* (cited above), p. 200.

Page 269
The Whitehead quotation "Fallacy of Misplaced Concreteness" is from *Science and the Modern World* (cited above), p. 52.

Page 269-270
Bernard Strehler's discussion of time is from *Time, Cells, and Aging* (New York: Academic, 1962), pp. 4-10.

Page 270
The Robert Morison quotations on death and life are from "Death: Process or Event?" (cited above).

Page 270
Differential deaths of cells, including nerve and cartilage cells, are cited in *Principles of Pathology*, by H. C. Hopps (New York: Appleton-Century-Crofts, 1959), p. 78.

Page 271
The fear of inadvertently being buried alive is cited in *Death,* by Hereward
Carrington and John Meader (cited in Chapter III).

Page 271
The Boyce Rensberger report on physicist Philip Morrison and the quotation
"To think of a highly complex machine . . ." is from "Man and Computer:
Uneasy Allies of 25 Years" (cited above).

Page 271-272
Biological characteristics are from *Biology,* Barnes & Noble College Outline
Series No. 4, by Gordon Alexander (New York: Barnes & Noble, 1935, 1966).

Page 272
The Wendell Stanley quotations are from "On the Nature of Viruses, Cancer,
Genes and Life—A Declaration of Independence," from the *Proceedings of the
American Philosophical Society,* Vol. 101, No. 4 (August 1957).

Page 272, 273
The quotations "A living organism is an entity . . ." and "the unique attribute
of living matter . . ." are from *Biology and the Future of Man* (cited in
Chapter VII), pp. 7, 165.

Page 274
The Jacques Monod quotations "A *totally* blind process . . ." and "appear
to transcend the laws . . ." are from *Chance and Necessity* (cited above), pp.
98, 78. On p. 95, Dr. Monod states: "In a sense, in a very real sense, it is at
this level of chemical organization that the secret of life lies, if indeed there
is any one such secret. And if one were able not only to describe these sequences but to pronounce the laws by which they assemble, one could declare
the secret penetrated, the *ultima ratio* discovered."

Page 274
The Robert Sinsheimer quotation "Life is but a property of matter . . ." is
from "The End of the Beginning" (cited above).

Page 274
The quotation "life is the expression . . ." is from *Biology and the Future of
Man* (cited above), p. 82.

Page 274
The Boris Pasternak quotation "Life is not a material . . ." is from *Dr.
Zhivago* (New York: Pantheon, 1958), p. 338.

Page 275
The August Weismann quotation "but is it one and the same substance . . ."
is from *Time, Cells, and Aging* (cited above), p. 41.

Page 275
In *Science and the Modern World* (cited above), p. 74, Whitehead writes: "Thus nature is a structure of evolving processes. The reality is the process."

Page 276-277
The CBS television broadcast on science and religion is cited above.

Page 277
The Robert Sinsheimer quotations "For physicians . . ." and "is now providing . . ." are from "The Implications of Recent Advances in Biology for the Future of Medicine" (cited above).

Page 277
The Alex Comfort quotation "It would represent . . ." is from "The Prolongation of Vigorous Life" (cited above).

Page 277-278
The Leon Kass quotation "Modern biology, and modern science in general . . ." is from "Biomedical Research and Social Policy" (cited above); a slightly different version of some parts of the passage appears in "The New Biology: What Price Relieving Man's Estate?" (cited above).

Page 278
The Jacques Monod quotation "It is perfectly true . . ." is from *Chance and Necessity* (cited above), p. 172; the quotation "the terrible capacity to destroy . . ." is from p. 173.

Page 278
René Dubos in *The Dreams of Reason* (cited above), pp. 60-61, has written on the issue of knowledge and values: "Science itself, in its pure form, is concerned with phenomena and laws on which all qualified and thoughtful persons eventually agree irrespective of their individual beliefs, opinions, and tastes. But, unlike pure knowledge, the applications of science are concerned with the desires of mankind, its whims and fancies, as much as with its biological needs. As stated by J. M. Clark, 'There are two worlds, the world of impersonal investigation of cause and effect, and the world of desires, ideals and value judgments. The natural sciences deal with the first, ethics with the second.' The physicist who works on the industrial applications of any form of energy cannot help becoming involved in the problems of ethics; and this is true also of physicians and the biologists working on medical problems . . . ." Social gerontologist Ruth Bennett said during an interview at Columbia University, Dec. 7, 1971: "Science is not value-free. The value is set by who buys it." And this quotation from *In the Name of Profit* (Garden City: Doubleday, 1972), p. 138: "Dr. Turner Alfrey, Jr., a senior Dow chemist in the field of polymers, said: 'When we complete a process, it is taken from us by the production people, the finance people, the marketing people, and the sales people. We have nothing more to do with it."

Page 278
The Monod quotation "Modern societies are built . . ." is from *Chance and Necessity* (cited above), p. 170.

Page 278
The Whitehead quotation "Wisdom is the fruit . . ." is from *Science and the Modern World* (cited above), p. 197.

Page 279-280
The Sir James Frazer quotation "If then we consider . . ." is from *The Golden Bough* (cited above), pp. 711-712.

Page 280
In "SIPI Takes Over as Publisher of *Environment* Magazine," by John Walsh, in *Science,* March 9, 1973, the growth of scientific awareness of "side" effects is traced. Biologist Barry Commoner and some colleagues at the University of Washington in 1958 first put out a mimeographed bulletin called *Nuclear Information.* They also created the St. Louis-based Committee for Environmental Information. Initial concern about the misuse of nuclear weapons—the *Bulletin of Atomic Scientists* was an earlier outgrowth of scientists' concerns in this area—turned to concern over radioactive fallout. One article in 1961 traced the effects of fallout through the food chain from lichens to caribou to people. "The Alaska thing got us into ecology," says Commoner. "We realized we were dealing with an ecosystem." In 1963 several of these local scientists' information groups got together to form the Scientists' Institute for Public Information (SIPI) and changed the name of the publication to *Scientist and Citizen.* During most of the 1960s its circulation ranged only between 2,000 and 4,000. In 1969 the name of the magazine was changed to *Environment* and in four years its circulation grew to 26,000; the influence and activities of SIPI increased concomitantly.

Page 281
Other groups formed recently to consider the impact of biomedicine and other scientific impacts upon society include: The Committee on the Life Sciences and Social Policy of the National Academy of Sciences, which is headed by biochemist Leon Kass; the Institute of Religion and Human Development at the Texas Medical Center in Houston; the Institute for Theological Encounter with Science and Technology at St. Louis University; an interdisciplinary Program on Science, Technology, and Society at Cornell University; the Joseph and Rose Kennedy Institute of Bioethics at Georgetown University. Columbia University's College of Physicians and Surgeons offers a four-year interdisciplinary course on ethics; and the University's Graduate School of Journalism provides a course on advanced science writing to produce a new breed of science reporters: not merely uncritical translators of scientific jargon for laymen, but critical envoys of society who grasp the social implications of scientific work. SIPI (mentioned in preceding note) and its many local affiliates have played a pioneering and leading role in acquainting the public with the many implications of scientific activities, and in the process have helped to establish and normalize procedures where scientists and citizens collaborate in

matters of mutual concern. Scientists began playing active roles with lawyers and interested citizens in lawsuits through the Environmental Defense Fund, a great number of ad hoc groups, and Natural Resources Defense Council.

Page 282
The Jacques Monod quotation "accepts all it contains . . ." is from *Chance and Necessity*, (cited above) pp. 172-173.

INDEX

Index

About the Author

OSBORN SEGERBERG, JR. was a John Hay scholar at Brown University and was graduated with honors in English. He has worked for United Press, United Press Movietone newsfilm syndication service, CBS News and WCBS-TV News, United Nations Television and other news or broadcast organizations. He has written for *Esquire*, *New York* and other magazines; one previous book on ecology, *Where Have All the Flowers Fishes Birds Trees Water And Air Gone?* and an environmental study guide for the New York State Department of Education. Mr. Segerberg lives with his wife, Nancy, and three children in Kinderhook, New York.